CHESTER A. ARTHUR

A Quarter-Century of
Machine Politics

AMERICAN CLASSICS

CHESTER A. ARTHUR

A Quarter-Century of
Machine Politics

By
GEORGE FREDERICK HOWE

Illustrated

FREDERICK UNGAR PUBLISHING CO.

NEW YORK

GEORGE FREDERICK HOWE was born
in Vermont, received his doctorate in
history from Harvard University.
He has taught at the University of
Cincinnati and has lectured at many
colleges here and in Latin America.
Dr. Howe was chief of the Mediter-
ranean division of the History Division, U.S. War Department, during
World War II, and has been Historian for the U.S. Department of
Defense since 1954. Among his other
books are *A General History of the
U.S.A. since 1865* and *A Battle History of the First Armored Division.*

Printed in the United States of America

Library of Congress Catalog Card Number 57-12324

PREFACE

THE preparation of this biography began with the writing of a doctoral dissertation in history at Harvard University, in which I had the friendly guidance of Professor Arthur M. Schlesinger. That monograph has been thoroughly rewritten upon a foundation of added research, in which I have been aided by many persons and several institutions. I would acknowledge especially the assistance of Elihu Root, Arthur H. Masten, Miss Alice Arthur, Miss Susan Arthur, John Waterhouse Herndon, Arthur F. J. Crandall, Charles Moore, Willis R. Putney, Mrs. Matthew F. Maury, Jr., Mrs. Robert Alter, Mrs. William A. Cox, Miss Esther G. Ely, Victor H. Paltsits, Elmer E. Ellis, Robert Shafer, Harold M. Vinacke, James P. Baxter, III, Lester B. Shippee, Charles R. Lingley, and Allan Nevins, the editor. I have received unstinted help from my friend, H. William Taeusch, and from my wife, Esther Babbitt Howe.

Certain libraries have been particularly generous. I am pleased to express my appreciation here of aid from the Harvard University Library, Library of Congress, New York Public Library, the Public Record Office (London), University of Cincinnati Library, Public Library of Cincinnati, Hayes Memorial Library, Ohio Historical and Philosophical Society, State Historical Society of Iowa, and the New York Historical Society.

From the University of Cincinnati, assistance has taken various forms, including the encouragement of colleagues in the department of history and a generous grant-in-aid from the Charles Phelps Taft Memorial Fund, both of which the author gratefully acknowledges.

G. F. H.

v

18181

TABLE OF CONTENTS

TABLE OF CONTENTS

ix

ILLUSTRATIONS

ON a sultry September night in 1881 a nation waited in anxious suspense while the President of the United States lay with life ebbing away. On the streets of the cities the newsboys shouted "Garfield is dying— Garfield . . . dying!" Those who heard them sorrowfully tried not to believe, unwilling that one so heroic in affliction should be taken from them. But on the coast of New Jersey, at Elberon, President Garfield's family and dearest friends despairingly recognized that the end was near.

In New York City, another man walked nervously about his home, struggling to control a feverish anxiety, hoping that he might escape the responsibilities involved in Garfield's death. For two months, Vice President Arthur had remained a virtual prisoner in his own house, in readiness to do what duty required, shunning the importunities of self-appointed advisers, and refusing to take the slightest advantage of the President's manifest disability. That morning, September nineteenth, a telegram from Garfield's Cabinet had warned that death was approaching. Not until late that evening, when darkness would shelter him from the curious, did Arthur go out, and then, at the very time that Garfield was breathing his last, he took a brief walk near his Lexington Avenue house. Returning to find no word from Elberon, he joined a few friends who had called to divert his mind and to cheer him.

About midnight the doorbell rang. Silence fell on the group in Arthur's study. The Negro servant went to the door. Before he could return, the Vice President followed him into the hall, unable to bear the suspense.

"The President is dead," a newspaper reporter called to him.

"Oh, no, it cannot be true. It cannot be. I have heard nothing."

"The dispatch has just been received at the office," insisted the reporter.

"I hope—my God, I do hope it is a mistake," said General Arthur, his voice breaking as tears filled his eyes. He went back to his friends in the study.

"They say he is dead," he told them. "A dispatch has been received

1

at the *Sun* office." For several minutes, no one spoke. Then a telegram was brought. He broke open the envelope and, with shaking hands, read the message. Then Arthur bowed his face in his hands as the others read:

It becomes our painful duty to inform you of the death of President Garfield, and to advise you to take the oath of office as President of the United States without delay. If it concur with your judgement, we shall be very glad if you will come here on the earliest train tomorrow morning.

William Windom

W. H. Hunt

T. L. James

Wayne MacVeagh

S. J. Kirkwood

For a long time Arthur struggled to compose his mind and control his features. The months of confinement and worry had almost broken his health. Ordinarily he would have risen to the situation with adequate dignity and serenity of mind, but now the effort was heavy. His thoughts reverted to the bitter criticisms of the press in the last few months; the prospect of four years of such hateful assaults was enough to unnerve any man of sensibility. Then came the thought of his inexorable duty, and he rose to consult with the others upon the proper course of action.

The advice of the Cabinet was to take the oath of office "without delay." No arrangements had been made, but the recommendation could not be ignored. A member of the New York Supreme Court was needed. Elihu Root and Dr. Pierre C. Van Wyck drove off in one carriage; Stephen B. French and Daniel G. Rollins in another. Root and Van Wyck returned with Justice John R. Brady, and shortly afterward the others escorted Justice Charles Donohue to the Arthur home. General Arthur's son, Alan, a Columbia College freshman, drove up in time to be present at the ceremony. Someone wrote out the presidential oath on a scrap of paper and Judge Brady administered it. Then Arthur kissed his son, gravely shook hands with his friends, and the ceremony was over. He was President.

Next morning the press related the details of Garfield's death and of Arthur's accession. Comment was sharply divided. A serious lack of ability in President Arthur was inferred by some from his political associations and his behavior as Vice President; while others based their confidence in his capacity upon his breeding and experience and the fact that he was in the prime of life.

If in 1881 the American public was fairly well informed about Chester A. Arthur's earliest years, it was because of an interesting hoax. A New York attorney, Arthur P. Hinman, startled the voters of the country shortly after the election of 1880 by interviews in which he accused General Arthur of being a British subject. To support the claim, he presented an elaborate story of Arthur's birth, purporting to show that he had been born in Canada, of a British father and an American mother.[1] The enterprising New York *Sun* investigated Hinman's tale and published a complete refutation the day after Arthur took the oath as President. His origins were thus widely understood when he became the twenty-first President of the United States.

The blood of English and Scotch-Irish forebears mingled in Chester Alan Arthur. His mother, Malvina Stone, came of English settlers in New Hampshire. Her grandfather, Major Uriah Stone, was a veteran of the French and Indian wars when he arrived at Haverhill, New Hampshire, in 1763, soon after that river township had been set off. When his cabin was carried away by a freshet, he moved to Piermont, a few miles southward. By a combination of industry, pluck, thrift, and shrewdness he ran a ferry over the Connecticut River, built up a prosperous farm, and reared twelve children before his death in 1810. The seventh child was George Washington Stone, born January 22, 1777, when the Continental general was being praised in patriot homes for his glorious victories at Trenton and Princeton. This seventh son was the father of Malvina.

Five of Uriah Stone's sons moved to the Vermont township of Berkshire in, or near, the year 1800,[2] and among them was George, who had just been married. On his farm near the Canadian border, his daughter Malvina was born, April 24, 1802,[3] among frontier Yankees, frugal, God-fearing, and industrious. Her Uncle John, who frequently preached at Baptist meetings, became known to the people of Berkshire as "Elder Stone," and embodied Malvina's earliest ideals of greatness. Some years later, her father moved a few miles north into

[1] Hinman finally published his yarn in a pamphlet *How a British Subject Became President of the United States.*

[2] Lewis C. Aldrich, ed., *History of Franklin and Grande Isle Counties, Vermont*, p. 534.

[3] Her mother was Judith Stevens, of Newbury, Vt., daughter of Simeon and Sarah Hadley Stevens. She married George W. Stone on March 23, 1800.

Dunham, Quebec, where he lived until his death on January 12, 1854.

The Arthurs lived near Ballymena, County Antrim, in Ulster, where Chester Alan Arthur's father, William, was born in 1796. Family tradition credits him with a degree from the University of Belfast. Shortly after coming of age, William Arthur emigrated to Canada, settled for a time at Stanstead, Quebec, as a teacher, and then took a school in Dunham, where he met and married Malvina Stone in 1821.

The young husband, while making a living as a teacher, wished to become a lawyer, and to this end about three years later moved across the border to Burlington, Vermont, where teaching might be better paid and a county seat furnished opportunities to read law in some attorney's office. Family tradition is again authority for the most important step in William Arthur's life. While working to become a lawyer, he attended a Baptist revival, was convinced that he had been "called," and dropped his legal future and Anglican past to become a Baptist minister.

Ordination in 1827 opened a larger field for Elder Arthur's boundless energies. He was soon employed as part-time pastor by small churches in the neighboring Vermont villages of Richford, Berkshire, Fairfield, and probably Waterville, the region of his wife's girlhood. He attracted favorable notice from fellow clergymen and parishioners. In May, 1830, when the numbers of the Fairfield Baptist Church warranted its division into two separate bodies, he was retained by the more numerous North Fairfield congregation and went to live among them. Late in October, he was an active participant in the State convention of his denomination at Hinesburgh.[1]

In his new parish, Elder Arthur's eloquence attracted congregations which over-crowded the schoolhouse and forced a transfer to a large barn. While he occupied a log cabin outside the village, the church leaders undertook to build a parsonage. It is not certain whether his family were with him, or remained in Waterville until he should have a better home. In either case, they had to wait while the parsonage progressed very slowly with volunteer labor, performed in the spare time of hard working farmers. When the scaffolding was complete, the people gathered for the customary ceremony, enlivened by horseplay. One of the local youths is said to have outraged the feelings of many

[1] For Elder Arthur's career as a Vermont clergyman, consult Henry Crocker, *History of the Baptists in Vermont*, pp. 371, 388, 390, 409, 444; *Proceedings of the Fifth Annual Meeting of the Baptist Convention of the State of Vermont, passim.*

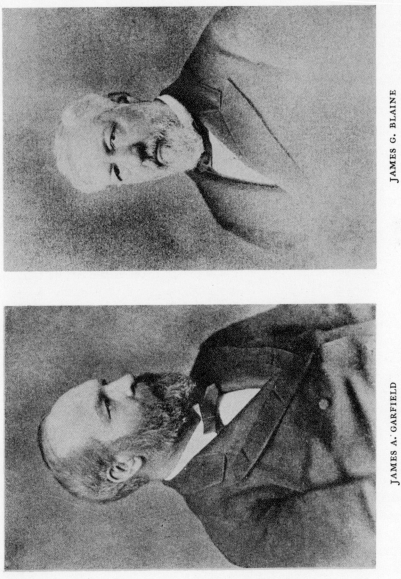

JAMES A. GARFIELD

JAMES G. BLAINE

by clambering up just before the ceremonies began and shouting from the rafters:

> This is a shell
> That looks like Hell
> Wrought out of crooked wood.
> But I'll bet a curse
> Were it ten times worse,
> Baptists would call it good.

Completion of the dwelling dragged through the summer and early autumn of 1830. The eagerness of the minister's family to move into it was accentuated by the imminence of a fifth child. Four girls, Regina, Jane, Almeda, and Ann Eliza, had been born to them already. It would be a source of gratification to Elder Arthur to signalize their entrance into this new home by the advent of a son.

On October 5, 1830, the Baptist minister of North Fairfield submitted for a moment to the wiles of the Old Serpent. He danced! He danced with joy when told that his fifth child *was* a boy. Out of friendship, relationship, and gratitude, the infant was given the name of the doctor who brought him into the world, Dr. Chester Abell, a cousin of Mrs. Arthur.

Elder Arthur's family always placed Chester's birth in the town of Fairfield, but a tradition in that part of Vermont still insists that he was born in Waterville. The descendants of a woman who worked for Mrs. Arthur at the time report her as saying throughout her life that the infant was brought a few days after birth to the new parsonage from the older residence in Waterville, fifteen miles away.

More interesting but entirely without foundation was the Hinman myth circulated in 1880 and 1881. This story asserted that Elder Arthur had three sons: William Chester Alan Arthur, born at the home of his mother's parents in Dunham, Province of Quebec; Chester Abell Arthur, born at Fairfield; and William Arthur, Jr., born at Hinesburgh, Vermont. When William Arthur, Jr., was born, the oldest son dropped the William and retained the names Chester Alan, as he could do because of the death in infancy of his brother, Chester Abell. He later, according to the Hinman story, appropriated the birth record of the second son in order to sustain his American citizenship. No death record existed to prove this substitution because the father had sold the infant's body to a medical school! On the basis of these allegations, the American public were assured that Arthur was a British subject and in consequence disqualified for the Vice Presidency or Presidency. It was a political maneuver, and, as such, ineffective.

North Fairfield was a tiny village, not the place to educate a family according to Elder Arthur's standards, and hardly able to yield sufficient income for so large a family as his. When an opportunity came in 1832 to move to Williston, near Burlington, he promptly grasped it. Williston was a flourishing town on a stage route between Burlington and Montpelier, with an agricultural population of about 1600. For three years it had maintained an academy, taught by the Baptist pastor, and to his dual rôle Elder Arthur succeeded.

William Arthur was an interesting person, and in some respects picturesque. His congregation looked upon a dark-haired man of medium height, who moved haltingly about his pulpit with a decided limp. His sermons, despite his strong Scotch-Irish accent, impressed them with the readiness and richness of his knowledge. They heard no hesitating, contemplative addresses, but earnest exhortations made the more impressive by the strong, intelligent face of the speaker. He was always vigorously partisan, never indifferent or neutral. His sharp tongue and conspicuous want of tact were constantly getting him into trouble and alienating his potential friends. Such misfortunes he no doubt set down as necessary evils for one who would preserve his independence. He was nothing if not independent!

His genius for sharply critical comments may be recognized in the story of an occurrence in a Baptist convention. A long-winded fellow minister who had recently returned from the West addressed the convention interminably on the subject of denominational conditions there. "I can tell the brethren," he shouted, "that if they think any sort of ministers will do for the West, they are mistaken." At this, Elder Arthur impetuously jumped to his feet and interrupted. "Mr. Moderator," he said, "I never knew before why the brother came back."

A combination of inharmonious associations with his churches and the restlessness which had first brought him to this country kept Elder Arthur on the move all through life. He was at Williston only a little more than a year before he moved to neighboring Hinesburgh. Two years later he joined the stream of migration from Vermont to western

New York, where he lived near the Erie Canal at Perry, in Genesee County, and at York, in Livingston County. In the autumn of 1839, he arrived at Union Village (Greenwich), not far from Saratoga, and settled down for a pastorate that lasted five years.

Chester was nine when the family reached Union Village. An academy had been organized there three years before by James I. Lowrie, a graduate of Union College, in whose school the boy at once entered. The principal was able, highly respected, and perhaps responsible for the later enrollment of Arthur and many other pupils among the students of his alma mater. In later years he remembered Arthur as a lad "frank and open in manners and genial in disposition." A boyhood companion wrote long after that Arthur at this time showed traits foreshadowing his future methods in politics. "When Chester was a boy, you might see him in the village street after a shower, watching boys building a mud dam across the rivulet in the roadway. Pretty soon he would be ordering this one to bring stones, another sticks, and others sods and mud to finish the dam; and they would all do his bidding without question. But he took good care not to get any of the dirt on his hands." [1]

Elder Arthur's new church at Union Village had been severely disturbed before his coming by the questions of slavery and temperance, political issues on which his predecessor had held too outspoken views. The slavery question came rapidly to the fore in those days of Garrisonian abolition and Texan independence. Elder Arthur cannot have been more successful than his predecessor in avoiding that subject unless he departed from a lifelong habit of speaking his mind. He was a radical antislavery man, and with his warm friend, Erastus D. Culver, gave support to Gerrit Smith, the wealthy abolitionist of Utica. Culver, a Union Village lawyer and State Assemblyman, was destined to become a Whig member of the House of Representatives from 1846 to 1847.

In the campaign of 1840, Chester was too young to know what was conveyed by the symbolic log cabins, but in 1844 he joined other lads in a typical tribute of the times to Henry Clay, the raising of an "ashpole." Possibly Andrew Jackson's identification with "Old Hickory" moved Clay's admirers to adopt the ash as his symbol and to advance its superior merits. In 1844, however, it was Polk, not Jackson, who claimed the favors of Clay's foes, and some of his most youthful ad-

[1] "C." in New York *Evening Post*, April 2, 1900.

herents in Union Village endeavored to push over the obnoxious "ash-pole." In the struggle which ensued, Chester's first political battle, the Whigs were triumphant—the future politician had his first taste of the sweets of victory.

However successfully Elder Arthur may have restrained himself in the pulpit, at home he must have expressed his abolitionist ideas again and again. His son Chester was early imbued with such views and never lost them; they prompted him to action in two of the most striking incidents of his later career. It is possible that the father's radicalism on the slavery issue was responsible for his retirement from the Union Village pastorate in 1844; whatever the reason, he left in August for Schenectady to be pastor of the First Baptist Church there.

At that time, Schenectady was in a stage of economic stagnation, but it possessed at least two educational institutions with claims to distinction—Union College and the Lyceum. For Arthur, the latter offered a preparation for the college. Throughout the winter of 1844–45 he went to the curious three-story octagonal building at Union and Yates Streets, then only ten years old and supposedly the last word in school construction.

On September 5, 1845, Arthur entered Union College as a sophomore in good standing. The institution, attended by about two hundred and fifty students, was one of the best known Eastern colleges and in the full tide of its effectiveness.[1] Its buildings stood on the present site, the main units being North and South College Halls. Then, as now, a college education was a complex compound derived from the curriculum, the personalities of teachers, the interests of fellow students, and the general spirit of the place and community. Union College was then under the domination of its greatest leader, Dr. Eliphalet Nott. As early as 1828, students entering his college might choose between the traditional "Classical Course" and an established course in natural science; and when Chester Arthur entered, engineering was offered as a third alternative. This early deviation from tradition exemplified the pioneering spirit of the old president. Arthur's choice of the classical curriculum may be regarded as an indication of his own conservatism, or of his father's wishes.

Most Union College students were drawn from the neighboring

[1] His father was voted an honorary degree of Master of Arts on July 23, 1845, by the trustees of Union College. (Union College Records.)

region, but there were notable exceptions. Dr. Nott was responsible for the admission of many boys who had been expelled from other institutions for trifling misdemeanors which he was inclined to over-look. Strict external control did not accord with his views of the train-ing in self-discipline appropriate for young men. His welcome to out-casts from other colleges brought down upon the institution at Schenectady the unfavorable name of "Botany Bay."

The college sport of those days was debating, and Union College, like other institutions, had two leading debating societies whose ac-tivities were both social and intellectual. Saturdays were turned over to the societies, and, from time to time, their champions contended over current questions, but no record exists to show that Chester Arthur was ever enrolled in either society. In later life he never relished speaking from the platform, and, unlike his father, seems to have had no readiness for contention.

Union College was also the institution at which the American college fraternity originated. Phi Beta Kappa had a chapter there, which had abandoned secrecy during the anti-Masonic movement of the preceding decade, and was a model for the organization of Greek-letter fraterni-ties with more distinctly social purposes. The liberality of Dr. Nott preventing any administrative veto, by the time that Arthur entered Union several such societies existed, and he became a member of Psi Upsilon.

College life was not all play for a student in the classical course. He read parts of Livy, Horace, Xenophon, Herodotus, Thucydides, Cicero, Demosthenes, Tacitus, Juvenal, Homer, Hesiod, and the Greek and Latin dramatists. He studied algebra, plane and solid geometry, trigonometry, rhetoric, chemistry, natural philosophy, political econ-omy, moral philosophy, astronomy, technology, botany, geology, min-eralogy, anatomy and physiology, Heeren's *Ancient Greece* and Butler's *Analogy*. At any rate, the catalogue warned him of this prospect.

A minister's son must usually earn a portion of the costs of his edu-cation. Twice in the long winter vacations, arranged to make teaching possible, Chester Arthur left Schenectady to conduct schools in neigh-boring towns. In 1848, he taught at district school No. 14 in Schaghti-coke and was paid $18 a month. Tuition cost him $28 during his three years, and board and room about $125 a year.

Arthur was not an unusual member of his class in college. Like the average boy, he cut his name here and there about the college. At that time his carvings were probably not appreciated, but now the institution treasures among its relics the boards on which his name appears. Apparently he made his mark in no other way. The grades kept for each student defy modern comprehension; of the seventy-nine who were listed in the class of 1848, ten had the perfect record of 500, seven, including Arthur, got 499. In his second year he received only 99 in attendance, but future Presidents should note that in conduct his grade was 100. He was elected to Phi Beta Kappa upon graduation, and that seems to have been his one college "honor." On the commencement program, his topic was one of forty-four listed items, not including prayers, the Greek and Latin salutatories, and music; it bore the engaging title, "The Destiny of Genius." [1]

[1] Union College Records.

UPON graduating from college in July, 1848, Arthur proposed to become a lawyer. With family encouragement, he went first to Ballston Spa for a few months in a law school, and then continued his preparations by private study at home and while teaching school. In 1851, he taught at North Pownal, Vermont, not far from his family in the New York village of Hoosick Corners. Curiously enough, three years later James A. Garfield kept a writing school in the same spot, a coincidence which was to be capitalized in the campaign biographies of 1880.

Garfield had been on a trip to Boston in 1878 when he wrote in his diary:

Caught a glimpse of Pownal, where I taught penmanship (Alas! now a lost art) and saw the spires of dear old Williams which seemed so grand and aweful in 1854.[1]

Arthur went from North Pownal to Cohoes in 1852 to become principal of the academy for a few months. There he completed the studies which qualified him for admission to a lawyer's office and made a record as principal which won him the esteem of the community. Upon taking over the school, he taught the "high department," in which a rowdy bunch of boys had triumphed over several of his predecessors. He was warned that discipline would be his greatest problem. His first act was to explain to the class that he knew its reputation and intended to deal fairly but firmly with every misdemeanor. With considerable resourcefulness, Arthur eventually gained complete mastery of the entire department.

In 1855, Elder Arthur went to Albany as pastor of the Calvary Baptist Church, living quietly in the neighboring village of Newtonville. When his pastorate ended in 1863, he took a few boys as boarding pupils and prepared them for college. In his younger days, he had possessed great mental and physical energy. In Schenectady his intellectual tastes had found expression in the publication of what was meant to be the first number of a periodical, *The Antiquarian and Gen-*

[1] Garfield Journal, August 30, 1878, Garfield Papers.

eral Review, an ambitious affair, "comprising whatever is useful and instructive in ecclesiastical or historical antiquities; serving as a book of useful reference on subjects of research and curiosity." For three years it appeared serially; then, in 1849, only the complete fourth volume, bound at Lansingburgh, was published; and, with that, it stopped. Again, as he grew older, he used part of his time in Albany in the compilation of his better known *Derivation of Family Names,* a book published in New York City in 1857. It was "an Etymological Dictionary of Family and Christian Names with an Essay on their derivation and import." One's first impulse is to turn to the name Arthur for enlightenment. There, on page 56, one reads:

Arthur (British) A strong man; from *Ar* (Lat. *vir*) a man, and *thor,* strong. In the Gaelic, *Air* is the same as *Fear,* a man; and the ancient Scythians called a man *Aior. Thor* was the Jupiter of the Teutonic races, their god of thunder. In Welsh, *Arth* is a bear, an emblem of strength and courage, and *ur* a noun termination, a man. Arthur, a bear-man, a hero, a man of strength; the name of a British prince.

When Chester Arthur's law studies had reached the stage at which practical application became desirable, he considered to whom he might apply for such an opportunity. Where should he practice? How could he get a start? His ambitions were high and his abilities promising; his father was eager to have him attain the heights of the profession; so, when it was agreed that he should try his fortunes in New York City, an application for aid was made to Elder Arthur's friend, Erastus D. Culver. In 1850, Mr. Culver had moved to Brooklyn, and entered into a partnership, under the name of Culver & Parker, with a New York office at 289 Broadway. He now undertook to receive Chester in the firm's office and to give him the final training essential for the New York bar. In March, 1853, the tall, handsome young man appeared to begin his work; on May 1, 1854, "Culver & Parker, Attorneys and Counsellors," certified to the Supreme Court of New York that he had studied in their offices "for more than a year last past" and was "of good moral character." Three days later, Arthur himself swore that he was a native born citizen of the United States and "of the age of twenty-one years," therewith completing the preliminaries. He was admitted to the bar and taken into the partnership. All that remained was to acquire a practice.

When he was accepted as a clerk in Culver & Parker's office, Mr. Culver had become interested in one of the famous antislavery suits, the Lemmon case. In November, 1852, Jonathan and Juliet Lemmon arrived in New York on the vessel *City of Richmond* with eight slaves, whom they were taking from Virginia to Texas. The slaves, a young man, two young women with infants, and three boys, were lodged at a rooming house on Carlisle Street until the next boat for Texas should be ready to start. A free Negro discovered them, and applied to Judge Elijah Paine of the Superior Court of New York City for a writ of *habeas corpus* freeing them from bondage. Judge Paine was prepared to grant the writ, but the Lemmons appeared with counsel to argue that, since the slaves were in transit only, they were not *residing* in a free State, and so were not emancipated by their presence there. On November 9, the court room at City Hall was crowded while the final arguments were made by Erastus Culver and John Jay in behalf of the slaves, and H. D. Lapaugh and a Mr. Clinton for the Lemmons. The newspapers, especially Greeley's *Tribune,* had taken up the litigation as a matter of great interest. While decision was reserved, the Lemmon case became a matter of increasing public concern, until, on November 15, Greeley felt justified in devoting two columns of editorial and three of news to Judge Paine's judgment that the slaves were freed.

The country was then in a state of sectional equilibrium resulting from the compromise agreements of 1850. The South was particularly concerned with the enforcement of the new fugitive slave law. There had been several notorious cases already in which it had been flouted by abolitionists, while the Underground Railway continued to function in efficient secrecy. The willingness of the North to return runaways was still a matter of doubt on which the fate of the two-year-old compromise depended. The Lemmon case seemed to indicate not merely reluctance to return fugitives, but unblushing theft of slaves who were in no sense escaping from their masters. If Judge Paine's decision should prevail, the port of New York could no longer expect the patronage of Southerners accompanied by their slaves. The entire State must expect retaliation from a South to which comity had been denied. What was more, the dormant sectional antagonism of the entire North and South might again be aroused; the Union would again be threatened.

Such considerations moved James Watson Webb in his *Courier and Enquirer* to warn Judge Paine, before his decision, "of the embarrassments and disturbances likely to result" from a refusal to return the slaves, and to insist, after the case had been decided, that the outcome "will do more to separate North and South than any other event which has happened since the birth of our Confederation." [1] Greeley in reply declared that the occupation of "Union-saving" was proving "fruitless." "Seriously," he wrote, "is it not clear that Union-saving has paid its best dividends? If a judge's enunciation of the law as it stands thus speedily undoes all that has been so laboriously gained, is not the further prosecution of the contest hopeless?" [2] When the New York *Journal of Commerce* raised a fund of $5240 to remunerate the Lemmons, Greeley raised a much smaller amount to maintain the slaves, pending the appeal which the Lemmons had promptly taken, and pointed out that the slaves were not worth more than $3200. Despite the profit to the Lemmons, editorial writers in Southern journals appeared to be utterly unplacated, some of them threatening reprisals. [3]

Virginia was indeed so thoroughly aroused that its legislature authorized the attorney general to appear before the New York Supreme Court and to retain other lawyers to aid him. Charles E. O'Conor, New York's outstanding Democratic member of the bar, was soon enlisted on the side of Virginia and the slave owners.

It was not until five years later that the case was again argued. In the meantime, Chester A. Arthur had been admitted to the bar and was looking for work. The common antislavery convictions which had drawn together his father and Mr. Culver, he had grown up to share. The Lemmon case was therefore attractive to him as a professional opportunity, and he busied himself in securing at Albany, in 1855, the appointment of his partner, Mr. Culver, as a special associate of the attorney general of New York in the next argument. When, in 1856, Attorney General Hoffman died, William M. Evarts was given his duties in this case, and in December, 1857, Judge Paine's decision of 1852 was sustained. Again, in 1860, it was argued, this time before the Court of Appeals, Evarts and Joseph Blunt opposing O'Conor. The decision, given in March, 1860, once more sustained Judge Paine.

[1] Quoted in the N. Y. *Tribune*, Nov. 15, 17, 1852.
[2] *Ibid.*, Nov. 17, 1852.
[3] N. Y. *Tribune*, Nov. 23, 29; Dec. 1, 4, 1852.

The slaves were at last free.[1]

Arthur's part as a young attorney in the Lemmon case was obscure. He never argued it but may have assisted in the preparation of the case for argument. It seems more likely that his connection consisted in urging that the State respond to the challenge of the Commonwealth of Virginia, thus elevating the controversy from private litigation to a celebrated case. It was unquestionably a subject of great national interest.[2]

At about the same time, the young abolitionist lawyer became interested in another case involving Negro rights. The office of Culver, Parker, & Arthur in 1855 was sought one day by a delegation of the leading colored men of the city, who had come to ask the firm to protect them. A colored woman named Lizzie Jennings had been ousted by force from one of the Brooklyn street cars, by the conductor and others, with injury to her person and clothing. Her ejection was prompted by the demands of a white passenger, and carried out despite her strongest objections. The position of Mr. Culver in the Lemmon case probably caused them to seek him, but the legal action against the street car company was put in the hands of the new young partner. It was a clear case of a corporation's obligation, under statute, for an injurious act by its agent. A judgment of $500 was won. More important, the street car company instructed its conductors to allow Negroes to ride unmolested.

In 1856, the firm of Culver, Parker, & Arthur was dissolved because Mr. Culver had been promoted to the bench in Brooklyn. Arthur and a young lawyer named Henry D. Gardiner then formed a partnership. There is a tradition that, before setting up in New York City to face its extreme competition, Arthur and his friend went west as far as Kansas,[3] that there they bought some land but became discouraged by the unsettled conditions of life, possibly by the resort to lynch law rather than to the lawyers' brand, and returned to the metropolis. At any rate, by the end of the year they were established in modest offices at 117 Nassau Street, and Arthur had moved in from Williams-

---

[1] Argument before Judge Paine, 5 Sandford 681; Argument before Supreme Court of New York in December, 1857, 26 Barbour 270; Argument before Court of Appeals, Jan. 24, 1860, 20 N. Y. Court of Appeals Reports 562. Evarts's argument in last trial, Sherman Evarts, ed., *Arguments and Speeches of William Maxwell Evarts*, Vol. I, pp. 5–90. See also, Brainerd Dyer, *The Public Career of William M. Evarts*, 34–39.

[2] 5 Sandford 681, note.

[3] Atchison, Kansas, *Champion*, Undated clipping. (In private possession.)

burg to reside at a "family hotel" at 904 Broadway, the Bancroft House. He was soon making himself useful in the nascent political organization of the Republican Party.

Arthur had come of age in 1851. Winfield Scott, Whig candidate for President the next year, had received his first vote, for he was of the Whig cast throughout his life and cherished a strong enthusiasm for Henry Clay. But he held firm antislavery convictions and attended the "Anti-Nebraska" convention at Saratoga on August 16, 1854, from which momentum was gained for the fusion of New York Whigs with other elements outraged by the Democrats' Kansas policy.[1] A year later, through the masterful arrangements of Thurlow Weed, the amalgamation was effected; in 1856, New York voters had an opportunity to elect Republican nominees.

Out in Buffalo, an industrious young law student named Grover Cleveland was not much attracted by the new party in his State. The candidacy of John C. Frémont for the Presidency had too much of "fuss and feathers" about it to satisfy his conservative soul. He gave his support to James Buchanan, though still too young to vote.[2] But Chester A. Arthur was heart and soul for Frémont, serving on the executive committee of a group which took the swelling title of Eighteenth Ward Young Men's Frémont Vigilance Committee. He took his place, also, as an inspector of elections at the polls. From the start, he was an organization man and a "worker."

*   *   *

One of Arthur's associates at the Bancroft House was a young medical student from Virginia, Dabney Herndon. For so young a man, he had had a varied experience, which stood in great contrast to Arthur's. A voyage around Cape Horn had taken him to California in the gold rush, from which he had returned with many an interesting tale. In 1852, he had entered the United States Military Academy at West Point, and, after two years, transferred to the University of Virginia. In 1857, he came North again to study medicine in New York University, preparing to practice the profession of his father, Doctor Brodie Herndon of Fredericksburg. He and Chester A. Arthur be-

---

[1] DeA. S. Alexander, *Political History of the State of New York*, Vol. II, pp. 194, 211–13.

[2] Robert McElroy, *Grover Cleveland, the Man and the Statesman*, Vol. I, p. 18; Allan Nevins, *Grover Cleveland*, p. 44.

came warm friends.

Dabney Herndon had an interesting family. Besides his distinguished father, two uncles were winning fame in the United States Navy. On his way home from California in 1851, he had stopped at Lima, Peru, and while walking about, chanced upon one of them, Lieutenant William Lewis Herndon, who was preparing for a famous exploring expedition down the Amazon. This journey, described in an extensive report [1] to the Secretary of the Navy, was to win him lasting honor. The second uncle was Lieutenant Matthew Fontaine Maury, head of the United States Naval Observatory at Washington, whose work as oceanographer made him deservedly famous. Maury and Lieutenant Herndon were drawn together both by marriage and professional interests, and their families were intimate. In the summer of 1853, when Maury went to Europe for a naval conference at Brussels, he took his two eldest daughters and their two cousins, Ellen Maury and Ellen Lewis Herndon, the latter the only daughter of the explorer, on a trip through England and northern Europe. For Ellen Lewis, then a vivacious sixteen year old girl, it was an unforgettable experience, arousing a taste for travel which never left her.

Tragedy had befallen the family of Lieutenant Herndon when his nephew was studying medicine in New York. In 1857, he was in command of the *Central America,* carrying mail and passengers between Aspinwall and New York City. On September 7, she left Havana, heavily loaded, and off Cape Hatteras ran into a furious gale. A leak which got ahead of both the pumps and the bailing crews extinguished the fires. About noon next day, while the wind abated somewhat, the brig *Marine* from Boston lay by and took aboard the women and children, brought to her in the lifeboats in two long trips. Heroically, an exhausted crew rowed back once more to the steamer. It was on the very verge of sinking; Herndon ordered them back, lest they be engulfed. Dressed in full uniform, standing on the bridge, with indomitable gallantry he went down to death with his ship. So supremely courageous was his conduct, that at Annapolis a shaft was erected to his memory, and in his honor a medal struck by order of Congress. To his widow, grateful citizens of New York City gave a house, to which she brought her daughter in 1858. [2]

[1] Published in 1853 by Congress as 32nd Cong., 2d sess., *Senate Executive Doc. No. 36.*
[2] The house was at 34 West 21st Street.

Dabney Herndon was always welcome at his aunt's. His sister was Ellen Lewis's dearest friend, as well as her cousin, and made long visits there, while he was often in the house. He once brought his friend, Chester Arthur. Five years of New York life had filled out Arthur's tall figure, and cultivation had given him more than usual presence for a man of less than thirty. Over six feet in height, black-eyed and brown-haired, with ruddy cheeks, regular features, and a fine broad forehead, he was unusually handsome. A certain dignity in his manner and conversation commanded respect as well as interest. Humor and a taste for literature, both family traits, with a cheery amiability, made him an entertaining talker and appreciative listener. He soon established a bond of interest with Ellen Lewis, seven years younger than he. This acquaintance passed through friendship to love, and in the autumn of the next year, on October 25, 1859, they were married at Calvary Church.[1] Two weeks later they were at home to their friends in the house from which the bride had been married. There they were to live until the outbreak of the Civil War.

It was difficult for a young lawyer of Arthur's type to develop a lucrative practice. His abilities lay not in court but in office work, which calls for caution, resourcefulness, and skill in personal consultation. To build up a clientele required an extensive acquaintance and Arthur was a recent arrival in the city without family connections to aid him. Moreover, a reputation for wise counsel had to be acquired, and he was young and unknown. It was an uphill fight, as he had no money, but there were ways by which he could advance his reputation. He could establish a connection with some famous litigation, as in the Lemmon and street-car cases; he could go into politics; he could join clubs, and be an active member. All these avenues of advancement were open to him and all were tried.

Politics, aside from its potential contributions to his law practice, was entirely in accord with his tastes and abilities. It brought him into association with men of prominence, and offered him a field in which to demonstrate judgment and capabilities analogous to those required by some branches of his profession. It did not yet absorb all his surplus energies; he continued his youthful habit of reading everything current in the English literature of his day. Politician he became, but by no means the sort of person indicated by the perennial expression,

[1] Fourth Avenue and 21st Street, near the Herndon home.

"one of the boys." His tastes were always far removed from the genial Philistinism suggested by that phrase. In his eyes, politics became a game for the promotion of a party to a position of control. He was not so much concerned with the use to which the control was put— so long as it was honest—as he was in getting and maintaining it.

Another way in which he enlarged his acquaintance was by joining the militia. In those days when he was comparatively free to indulge his interest in military matters, he combined his past training with his soldierly tastes by becoming Judge-Advocate-General of the Second Brigade of the New York militia. The staff used to meet almost weekly for a study of military tactics and regulations. As a result, he could later fill a uniform without a sense of novelty.

In 1860, as one of the lesser lieutenants of the Republican organization in New York City, he assisted in reëlecting Edwin D. Morgan as Governor. Morgan wished a military staff which should be an ornament for official ceremonies, and having probably known Arthur since the Saratoga anti-Nebraska convention of 1854, welcomed the younger man to a place as engineer-in-chief. The position was intended to be decorative rather than useful, and Arthur was fitted by his appearance to discharge the duties creditably. Had his expectations been realized, he would have served through Governor Morgan's term with no more onerous demands upon his time than to wear gold braid on a few public occasions. Suddenly, all was changed when Confederate shells burst about the United States flag at Fort Sumter. The Civil War was Arthur's opportunity.

WHEN the Civil War broke out in April, 1861, a governor's staff of handsome supernumeraries was obliged to undertake the serious work of a military establishment. Arthur's post as engineer-in-chief was comparatively easy, even in war, but his capacities for work were recognized and immediately tested by appointment as assistant quartermaster general under Cuyler Van Vechten, quartermaster general of New York. He was stationed in New York City, with an office on Elm Street, and given full responsibility for supplying barracks, food, and equipment to thousands of troops. The situation was unprecedented. He had to create his own business system without delay. Everything had to be done at once.

Within a short time, regiments of New York militia were arriving to wait in readiness for entrainment or embarcation to Washington. From New England came other regiments, who stopped temporarily to swell the New York reservoir. All required shelter and food; some needed uniforms, arms, blankets, tents, or other equipment. To shelter the first detachments, Arthur turned to certain public-spirited owners and obtained the right to use their buildings. But the prospects that the war might last more than one summer, the continued raising of troops, and the need for buildings better adapted to military uses enforced the construction of special quarters. Heroic exertions accomplished the erection on City Hall Park of the first set of barracks. Later, similar buildings were constructed on Long Island, Staten Island, and Riker's Island.

To feed the troops, Arthur did not organize army kitchens and operate them within his department, but advertised for bids and awarded a contract to the lowest responsible bidder, thus saving money and lessening the size of the establishment to be supervised. This plan of dealing through private contractors was consistently followed to save both money and time to the Quartermaster's Department. It offered him a rich field for favoritism or profitable graft without the likelihood of breaking any law and it also demanded careful inspection, both to avoid receiving shoddy uniforms and blankets, and to prevent other failures to meet specifications. Arthur kept clear of these

20

avenues of danger. A friend who knew him well at this time later quoted him as saying: "If I had misappropriated five cents, and on walking down town saw two men talking on the street together, I would imagine they were talking of my dishonesty, and the very thought would drive me mad."

From the outset, he insisted upon returning the presents of saddles, trappings, uniforms, and the like which were offered to him. For every transaction, he gave or demanded receipts. Formal requisitions were insisted upon for every issue from the quartermaster's stores. Accounts were rigidly kept. Contractors were forced to meet specifications or their contracts were canceled. The entire work, despite the extraordinary demands and sudden emergencies, he carried on with system and dispatch. It was Arthur's evident merit as the assistant quartermaster general at New York which brought him unstinted praise from his superior officer, in his annual report of April 18, 1862, which later caused Arthur's promotion to be Van Vechten's successor.

In addition to discretion and reliability, he possessed a remarkable resourcefulness upon which his war work made continual demands. In November, 1861, for example, the United States and Great Britain reached a crisis over the *Trent* affair. For a time, war was believed to be imminent, and New York's harbor had to be put in readiness. As engineer-in-chief, Arthur was responsible for the necessary defenses, which Governor Morgan summoned him to Albany to discuss. Arthur was no engineer; he therefore sought to be relieved by a trained man. Governor Morgan preferred and, in fact, insisted that he retain the office and procure adequate assistance. The harbor defenses were in a bad state; the forts had long since become antiquated. New naval guns could easily make them untenable. The situation was grave.

On the day after Christmas, 1861, he summoned a board of engineers to cope with the problem. Their decision was to prevent vessels from entering the harbor by stretching across the channel an obstacle consisting of cribs of stone held together by chain cables. Its construction required a large quantity of timber for which no State appropriation was available and, delay being out of the question, Arthur, on his own responsibility, bought up thousands of feet of timber in so quiet a manner as to avoid an advance in price. Before it could be got to the city, some was frozen in the Hudson River, so he bought more to replace it. And then, before the barrier could be built, the Southern commissioners were returned to Great Britain, the crisis passed; and a young State officer, lacking a private fortune and without public money at his disposal, found himself possessing great quantities of superfluous timber for which he could be called upon to pay. A quick trip to Albany, a consultation with Governor Morgan, and the predicament was evaded by securing an amendment to a measure then pending in the legislature, authorizing the sale of unused war materials. Then he sold the lumber, according to report, at a profit to the State.

As engineer-in-chief, Arthur was responsible for drawing plans of construction to protect not only New York City, but the entire State. With the aid of professional engineers, a program was devised and reported to Governor Morgan on January 18, 1862.[1] It was thorough and definite. The inability of any existing permanent defenses in New York harbor to resist the newly developed variety and strength of naval attack made more formidable construction imperative. In the meantime, the report advised, floating or sunken barriers should be used to drive invaders within the range of the forts. In case the State should resort to sunken barriers, means of providing for their eventual removal were described in the recommendations. The Federal government, Arthur believed, should assure New York that it would be reimbursed for such expenditures, but the State ought then to advance the money for buying and fortifying good sites and strengthening those already held. The activities should embrace also the construction of foundries for manufacturing "large guns" and their appurtenances; making ammunition and projectiles for existing and for new guns; launching ironclad steamboats for the Great Lakes; training State militia to manage and fire heavy guns; surveying and planning new defense sites, and their purchase; and, finally, the testing, as soon as possible, of various plans for floating obstructions in the Narrows of New York harbor.

General Arthur's ambitious program was not adopted. At that stage, the State expected the war to be concluded before his plans could be executed. In March, therefore, nothing had been done to protect New York harbor when the news of the *Merrimac's* success in her first encounters gave the city a day of excited alarm. The ironclad was reported to be getting ready an expedition to shell New York. The Mayor and his committee of leading citizens talked of sinking stone-laden ships in the Narrows. At that point, Arthur intervened. His

[1] Printed in full, N. Y. *Herald,* Jan. 24, 1862.

general report had called for floating obstructions in the Narrows; the scheme under discussion would have closed the port to all vessels, perhaps for years. Warning them of the folly of such action, Arthur, instead, had the forts properly manned and supplied with powder for such shells as the old guns were capable of firing, and thus averted the closing of the harbor. Night fell with the venerable city fathers still in consultation; but with darkness came relief. Word from the South explained that, in the *Monitor,* the *Merrimac* had met its match, that the Atlantic ports of the North again were safe.

In the midst of such important problems, Arthur found himself obliged, on occasion, to show his capacity for handling men, both individuals and groups, whose actions interfered with the reasonable preparation of troops for the armies in the field. Many were truculent characters who obtained from the War Department in Washington authorizations to raise regiments which they should eventually command. Of such a type was "Billy" Wilson, a famous leader among the aldermen of New York from the roughest part of the city, who in 1861 was raising a volunteer regiment of which he was to be the colonel. His recruits, chosen from his district, were unwilling to eat army rations, and commenced to plunder the restaurants near their barracks for food more to their taste. Arthur, as soon as he had learned of the outrages, summoned Wilson to his office and told him to put a stop to them. His quiet manner was mistaken for weakness, and Wilson, with boldness and impudence, replied:

"Neither you nor the Governor has nothing to do with me. I'm a colonel in the U. S. army, and you've got no right to order me."

"You are not a colonel," Arthur replied with indignation, "and you will not be until you have raised your regiment to its quota of men and received your commission."

"Well, I've got my shoulder straps anyway," said Wilson, "and as long as I wear 'em I don't want no orders from any of you fellers."

This was too much for Arthur, who sprang at him, saying: "We'll make short work of those shoulder straps," and ripped them off. Then he put the man, who was completely overcome by the suddenness and strength of his superior, under arrest.

The famous Ellsworth Fire Zouaves also gave Arthur much trouble. He had quartered them in a building on Canal Street, and there they waited for their equipment. Insubordination developed, the story goes, when the boxes of muskets arrived. They refused to unpack and clean them. Colonel Ellsworth applied for assistance to Arthur, who went among them with several policemen and put the ringleaders under arrest as rapidly as they were designated. The regiment was cowed. But that was not all. On the day of its departure, orders came from Washington that the Zouave regiment should not be mustered into service or allowed to leave New York until it had complied with army regulations in its organization. It had just received a stand of colors from Mrs. John Jacob Astor, and, with other flags flying also, was on its way to the steamer to go South when ordered by Governor Morgan to return. General Wool overruled the detaining order under persuasion of the Zouaves' officers, and permitted them to go aboard after a review.[1] Over a thousand men went down the harbor, delighted at the move, and not yet concerned about their next meal. About an hour later, an officer strolled into Arthur's Elm Street headquarters and casually remarked that the Ellsworth Zouaves had at last got off.

"Got off? Got off? That's impossible!" Arthur cried. "Orders came from Washington forbidding their departure. There isn't a pound of food of any sort on their ship, as I countermanded my earlier order."

But they had gone, they were beyond recall, and they had to be provided for at once. Arthur dashed off in a carriage to an army contractor and ordered the rations, paying him a premium for unreasonable haste. In an hour, he prepared five days' provisions for the entire regiment, while Arthur collected tugs to carry them down the harbor. In the Narrows, they found the steamer at anchor; the food was put on board, and the vessel sailed that night. If Arthur felt that the Ellsworth Zouaves were no longer to disturb him, he was wrong.

Again in trouble while quartered in the Capitol's south wing in Washington, indulging "in levities and acts of indecorum," after the first battle of Bull Run they were sent back to New York to repent. There they refused to obey their officers and roamed through the city taking food from whatever restaurant seemed promising. Arthur, who had been made inspector general, was instructed to disband them, but instead arrested all the soldiers he found wandering, imprisoned them on a transport, and finally sent four hundred of them South again. There they were consolidated with another regiment, kept under strict army discipline, and given an opportunity to redeem themselves.

[1] C. A. Ingraham, *Elmer E. Ellsworth and the Zouaves of '61*, pp. 130-3.

By the autumn of 1861, when New York had furnished all the regiments called for, it was clear that the Federal Administration would receive as many more as could be raised. For this, numerous adventurers volunteered at Washington and received authorization, much like "Billy" Wilson. At one time, parts of over one hundred regiments are said to have been forming in the State of New York alone. In New York City, some were organized simply to shield large-scale thievery by the authorized leader through the sale of commissions or the running up of bills against the regiment. With their authorizations from Washington, these scoundrels defied any State authority. Probably on Arthur's advice, Governor Morgan obtained from Washington a commission as major-general, with full supervision over all troops raised in New York. The State became a department of the army organization, and through Morgan's combination of State executive and Federal army powers, all disputes as to superior authority were avoided.[1] Other States followed New York's example.

Early in the war, while driven with his work as assistant quartermaster general, Arthur was elected by the Ninth Regiment of New York militia to be its colonel. Governor Morgan persuaded him to decline. A little later, the Metropolitan Brigade of four regiments, raised in and about the city, might have fallen under his command had not Governor Morgan again refused to release him.[2] Arthur was eager for the chance to serve at the front. His brother William, on January 29, 1862, succeeded in getting a commission and saw much active service; he would have liked to do the same.

Like countless families during the Civil War, Arthur's was divided in its loyalties. His wife was a Virginian, and though faithfully observing the requirements of her position in public as the wife of a Northern officer, cannot have failed to express at home her misgivings and distress. She was greatly concerned for the numerous Herndons and Maurys who served in the Confederate armies. General Arthur not only had a brother in the Northern armies; Henry J. Haynsworth, the husband of his younger sister, Malvina, was an official of the Confederate government stationed at Petersburg, Virginia. In the first part of the war, Malvina was with him.

Early in 1862, operations in Virginia threatened the Herndons at

[1] See *Official Records*, Series III, Vol. I, p. 597.
[2] N. Y. *Times*, Nov. 19, 1886.

Fredericksburg, causing great anxiety to both Ellen Lewis Arthur and her husband. Arthur was gratified, therefore, to receive on April 14, 1862, a commission from Governor Morgan as inspector-general of New York troops in the field. Five days later came the first battle of Fredericksburg, as a result of which General McDowell took the town. Early in May, General Arthur was on the scene, inspecting the New York troops in McDowell's corps. With great solicitude, he visited the Herndons' home and sought to relieve their misfortunes. Dabney Herndon, his friend in New York, had been captured at Island Number 10 on April 8, he discovered, and much anxiety was felt for his well-being. Arthur promised to do what he could to have Dabney exchanged, and on July 31, this was effected.

Arthur's duties called him also to the Army of the Potomac, on the Chickahominy under General McClellan. There his principal object was to discover the steps required to recruit the depleted New York regiments up to full strength. At that time, McClellan had forced the evacuation of Yorktown and was calling for reinforcements for his advance toward Richmond. Being on the spot, with a further advance about to begin, Arthur planned to remain. In this he was disappointed. An urgent message from Governor Morgan summoned him to New York. On June 30, he was with Secretary Seward, Governor Morgan, Governor Curtin of Pennsylvania, and others in a momentous conference held at the Astor House.

McClellan's advance had been stayed; great losses had been sustained; the Confederate armies remained stubborn and strong. It was at last clear to the Administration that more men must be recruited and the war continued for some years. As this intelligence spread among the protesting people, provoking distrust of the leadership at Washington, and complaints against commanders in the field, the Union cause looked dark. At this juncture, a political move was undertaken to emphasize Lincoln's widespread support. Seward arranged that the Governors of the loyal States should publicly request him to summon more troops, and he drew up the answer which Lincoln made.[1] On July 2, 1862, Lincoln issued the famous call for "three hundred thousand more."

The quota of troops to be organized in New York that summer num-

[1] *Official Records,* Series III, Vol. II, pp. 180–8.

bered nearly 120,000, all to be trained and sent to the front as rapidly as possible. Once more there was an enormous demand upon the State's resources, with the brunt of the administrative burden falling upon the quartermaster's department. Arthur was Morgan's man for this task. On July 27, he received a commission as quartermaster general. He had already moved into a headquarters' office at 51 Walker Street and begun the last of his war tasks.

Under normal circumstances, General Arthur could have made requisitions in bulk upon the regular army, for issue to the New York regiments as they were raised. But this second great call to the colors, like the first, found that organization unable to supply full equipment for even the first twenty-eight New York regiments. Recruiting activities in the State were rapidly filling up those detachments, from which demands for uniforms and accoutrements poured into Arthur's headquarters, so that he had to let large emergency contracts to obtain what he needed. To foster discipline he thought it desirable to put recruits into uniform as soon as possible. Quartermasters were accordingly appointed for each regiment, at the very beginning of its organization, and called to New York City to receive thorough instructions before entering on their tasks.

The problem of shelter during the training period was serious. Tents were entirely inadequate for winter. Arthur finally obtained authority from the United States quartermaster general to build temporary wooden barracks wherever needed. From 51 Walker Street, orders went to the regimental quartermasters to construct the barracks, using enlisted men as much as possible. Over two hundred were built, out of rough hemlock, with pine roofs, more healthful and cheaper than large tents. The total cost of construction and repair was only $30,000. As they ceased to be needed, they were turned over to caretakers, or dismantled, the materials being returned to the owners from whom they had been rented. There was no waste.

In addition to uniforms, equipment, and shelter, transportation had to be provided. The government made an allowance per mile and the States could send the troops forward as they saw fit. Arthur made contracts with the railroads for special trains, saving something over $43,000 from the allowance made by the Federal government, or more than the cost of his barracks.

Upon completion of his service as quartermaster general on January 1, 1863, with the advent of a Democratic Governor, Arthur made his report, summarizing his activities as follows:

Through the single office and clothing depot of this Department in the city of New York, from August 1 to December 1, the space of four months, there were completely clothed, uniformed, and equipped, supplied with camp and garrison equipage, and transported from the State to the seat of war, sixty-eight regiments of infantry, two battalions of cavalry, and four battalions and ten batteries of artillery.[1]

That this was done in creditable fashion was recognized by his successor, who reported to Governor Seymour:

I found, on entering upon the discharge of my duties, a well-organized system of labor and accountability, for which the State is chiefly indebted to my predecessor, Gen. C. A. Arthur, who, by his practical good sense and unremitting exertion, at a period when everything was in confusion, reduced the operation of the department to a matured plan, by which large amounts of money were saved to the Government, and great economy of time secured in carrying out the details of the same.[2]

Upon his retirement from the quartermaster generalship, Arthur was poorer than when he began it. He simply had to earn some money. From a war service which had engrossed him for nearly two years, he plunged with equal ardor into a law practice which swiftly expanded and brought large fees.[3] It involved frequent trips to Washington or Albany to press before the proper officials claims for reimbursements and damages growing out of the war. Twice, at least, he was in Albany without going even the few miles to see his parents at Newtonville, hurrying back to New York at the earliest opportunity. And he rarely wrote. In January, 1863, he escorted his sister, Malvina Haynsworth, from New York only to Albany, whence his youngest sister, Mary Arthur McElroy, went with her to Newtonville and arrived unexpectedly at their parents' home. His intercession had enabled her to come "direct from Petersburg" through the Union lines, to remain in the North for a year.[4]

Shortly after his return from this trip, news came to Arthur and his

[1] *Report*, Dec. 31, 1862, p. 26.
[2] Report of Q. M. G., Dec. 31, 1863, *N. Y. Assembly Docs.*, 1864, Vol. VI, No. 127.
[3] N. Y. *Times*, Feb. 20, 1872.
[4] Malvina Stone Arthur to William Arthur, Jr., Jan. 26, 1863, William Arthur Papers.

wife that her first cousin, John Maury, a lieutenant in the Confederate army on staff duty at Vicksburg, had disappeared while alone on a reconnaissance. No record of his death and no official certainty of his imprisonment could be obtained. His fate has remained an unsolved mystery to this day. At Gettysburg, Dabney Herndon, who had re-enlisted after his return to the South, was wounded and taken prisoner on July 5, 1863. After recuperating at David's Island, he was paroled in New York City. The Arthurs took care that he had what he needed, and Ellen Lewis Arthur went to see him, but they avoided unwarranted suspicions by not receiving him at their home. Later in the year, when he was again imprisoned, Arthur once more secured his release.

The Arthurs sustained a bitter affliction in this terrible year. On December 10, 1860, a son had been born to them and had been given the name of his famous grandfather, William Lewis Herndon. During the busy months of the war, nothing was overlooked which could pro-tect the child's health. It was their custom to retreat to the quieter suburbs in New Jersey during the summer, when they were not able to go further afield. On July 8, 1863, while the North was exulting over Gettysburg, Chester wrote to his brother William:

I have sad, sad news to tell you— We have lost our darling boy.—He died yesterday morning at Englewood, New Jersey, where we were staying for a few weeks—from convulsions, brought on by some affection of the brain. It came upon us so unexpectedly and suddenly. . . . Nell is broken hearted. I fear much for her health. You know how her heart was wrapped up in her dear boy. . . . Pa has just come from Newtonville and Mr. Masten and John McElroy. . . .[1]

Elder William Arthur could face such blows with a deep religious faith to sustain his courage. Two of his children had died, one a boy less than two years old [2] and the other a daughter who had reached eighteen.[3] His wife, Malvina Stone Arthur, shared his adversities with similar support for her fortitude. But their two sons were sceptics, in harmony with the rationalistic current of their century, growing apart from the religious stream to which the elder generation belonged. "Oh that God would answer my prayer, that before I am taken from life,

[1] July 9, 1863, William Arthur Papers.
[2] George Arthur, born May 24, 1836, at Perry, N. Y.; died March 8, 1838, at York, N. Y.
[3] Jane Arthur, born March 14, 1824, at Burlington, Vermont; died April 15, 1842, at Greenwich, N. Y.

you and Chester may come out publicly, confess Christ, and be willing to be fools for his sake. I know he will lead you to everlasting life and glory, if you are willing," Malvina Arthur had written to her son William, shortly before.[1] Elder Arthur was an infrequent letter writer, an example followed, unfortunately, by both his sons. One of his rare missives to William, however, is in the same strain.[2]

For Chester, such solace seemed impossible. While religious faith strengthened his parents in their battle with poverty, and fortified their standards of right and wrong, Chester and William were upheld by their conception of human excellence. The humane tradition, nourished in them by omnivorous reading of good literature,[3] supplied them with models for their conduct. Allied with the habits of honesty and kindliness inculcated in their boyhood, it guided them through life in a way which would have both gratified and distressed their anxious parents—delighted by the results, but pained by the absence of religious motive. In the loss of his boy, Chester Arthur found no comfort save the sympathy of his family and friends, and the passage of time.

As the war continued, Elder Arthur's large family of sons and daughters were obliged to support their mother and father. His income had become a zero, with "no scholars, no salary, and two servants to pay."[4] Chester, whose absorbing practice as a claims agent was yielding him increasingly plentiful returns, was expected to give more than his quota and finally did. In May and June, 1864, he was in Washington almost continuously, but upon his return to New York, he promptly sent a check for $100.

Some insight into Arthur's life as the war entered its last year may be derived from one of his rare letters: [5]

Washington, June 12, 1864.

Dear William:

Your letter of the 3rd of June reached me yesterday having been forwarded to me from New York. I have been in Washington off and on, for four or five weeks, having business before some of the Congressional Committees. Indeed

[1] Jan. 26, 1863, William Arthur Papers.
[2] Oct. 1, 1862, *Ibid.*
[3] Both brothers were great readers, although William was perhaps more active and less reflective than Chester. Their oldest sister, Regina, twelve years older than William, with a semi-maternal interest in his welfare, wrote him frequently during his war years. At times she urged him to send for books as he wished them. Chester, she said, "might find something you have not read." July 3, 1864, *Ibid.*
[4] Regina Caw to William Arthur, Jr., April 19, 1864, *Ibid.*
[5] William Arthur Papers.

I was right glad to hear from you and to know that you are safe and sound through all this terrific fighting. We have all thought of you all the time most anxiously and earnestly. It is a great relief to hear from you, so write as often as you have opportunity. I am going to return to New York in two days and as I cannot well get the things you want here, I will wait until I return and get them immediately and send them on, the first chance I have or by mail (such as I can). I will send you newspapers regularly and write to you often, but you must keep me posted where to direct to you.

I have carefully examined all the dispatches and letters from the army to learn when and where your regiment has been engaged. I knew that the batallion under your command was in the fight of the nineteenth of May, as the accounts of it published in the *Herald* gave your name as commanding the batt'n in Kitching's Brigade of the Fifth Corps. We know that there has been desperate fighting since your letter is dated, but I do not see by any of the lists that any harm has happened to you.

The family are all well. Mrs. Haynsworth has been in New York for some weeks, staying with Nell, while I have been here. She went back to Cohoes last week. Of course she was very anxious about our taking Petersburg. Pa was at the convention in Philadelphia two weeks ago and stopped to see us when in New York but I did not see him, being here. Nell and I intend to stay in the city this summer and have taken a furnished house in 26th St. until the first of November. I don't suppose there is much chance of your being with us during the summer, or at any time until this campaign is finally closed.

I presume by this time the army is all over the James River though today, we have a rumor that Hancock has crossed the Chickahominy at Bottom's Bridge. When you have time to write (which I know must be seldom) tell me about the battles you have been in and the part your regiment has had in them and yourself especially. I can't get much of an idea of it from the newspaper accounts. The constant fighting in this campaign must have been a pretty severe school for your heavy artillery regiments, who have not seen any before. It will make veterans of them very rapidly, but by all accounts they have behaved exceedingly well. I know you well enough to feel that you are doing your duty well—that you are as plucky as the best of them and that you will reflect credit upon us all at home. May God keep you safely through it all.

I have not seen Nell since your letter came. She speaks of you in almost every letter I get from her.

The law practice of Arthur & Gardiner flourished. The hundreds of persons with whom Arthur had come in contact during his war service included many who had been impressed by his integrity and energy, and by the evident respect in which he was held by the authorities. They went to him with countless war claims, business of the most lucrative character for him. In the remaining period of the war, something over a year, he acquired a modest fortune and a legal reputation which promised a sustained income in the days of peace. Living in their own household at last, the Arthurs began to feel greater security from want. On July 25, 1864, a son was born to them and given his father's name.

Arthur was impatient to have the war pushed to an end by decisive measures on Lincoln's part. In common with thousands of others, he was heartily disgusted with the Administration in the spring of 1864. In the bosom of the family, he talked as though he were "almost a copperhead" and declared that "he would not vote at all rather than vote for Lincoln for next President." [1]

His sister Malvina had her troubles, for during the summer of 1864 Grant was pushing toward Richmond, and her husband was in his path. "If Grant has got Petersburg *mined,* and the papers [so] report, I hope you will contrive to let Henry know. I don't want him blown up," she admonished her brother William. Again she wrote, "I don't care how soon you take Petersburg, but *don't hurt Henry.*" [2] It may be doubted that William Arthur had long to contemplate his sister's advice. He was in command of a battalion of artillery that summer, fighting under General Hancock in Grant's bloody drive through the wilderness to Petersburg. On August 25, the loss of his superior officer placed him, although but a major, in command of his regiment, the Fourth New York Artillery, and while in action at Ream's Station he was cruelly, though not fatally, wounded.

After the war ended, the Arthur family held a reunion during the summer at Newtonville. At one time, the Chester Arthurs formed part of a household of twenty-seven. Elder Arthur had eleven boys as boarding students and various children and grandchildren as guests. There were servants, and two carpenters building a barn. In some confusion, Chester and Nell Arthur withdrew, leaving their son Alan, then about one year old, in the care of his nurse. For two weeks they visited Lake George, Mount Mansfield, Burlington, and the Vermont region in which he had spent his earliest years.

The Dabney Herndons of Fredericksburg were their guests at New York in the following winter, and for a time, the Haynsworths, while

---

[1] Regina Caw to Maj. Arthur, May 19, 1864, William Arthur Papers.
[2] July 25, August 2, 1864, William Arthur Papers.

Henry Haynsworth looked for work.[1] When, in the next summer, Nell Arthur visited with her son at the Herndon home in Fredericksburg, the old pre-war ties had been completely resumed.

[1] William Arthur had remained in the army as a commissioner of the Freedman's Bureau, in Florida, but Henry Haynsworth's Confederate connections barred him from many opportunities.

THE Reconstruction period brought continued prosperity to Chester A. Arthur. At its outset he was a young man of considerable promise; before its conclusion he had become a gentleman of means and position. Fortune began to shine on him, especially, in 1867. That year he moved into a better house on Lexington Avenue. His wife's spirits revived with the growth of her second son, and she renewed the pleasant tasks of hospitality. Her music, too, gave her occupation, for she frequently sang to her guests, and occasionally appeared in concert with the newly organized Mendelssohn Glee Club. The Arthurs moved in good society, if not the most exclusive or wealthy.

In 1867, also, Arthur was elected to the Century Club, a group distinguished in intellectual and social life. Among its members at the time were William M. Evarts, John Jay, James C. Carter, and Joseph Choate, lawyers; George William Curtis and E. L. Godkin, editors; Andrew D. White, Cornell University's first president; E. C. Stedman and H. D. Sedgwick, authors; Edwin Booth, the actor; Albert Bierstadt, landscape painter; and J. Pierpont Morgan, a rising financier. Raphael Pumpelly, the traveler and explorer, entered in the same year with Arthur, and in the next, John Bigelow, Henry Holt, and William C. Whitney. It was not a company to welcome an ordinary political boss; its members were accomplished gentlemen with literary tastes.

Arthur was an avid reader, especially of Scott, Thackeray and Burns. He was said to have been able to correct even a Scotchman in his recitation of *Tam o' Shanter* and, being challenged, to have completed it himself in flawless form. For this prowess, he was elected to a Burns Society of otherwise unadulterated Scotchmen.

Like most New Yorkers, the Arthurs had a constant stream of relatives passing through the city and stopping for brief visits at the comfortable house on Gramercy Park. In June, 1867, Chester's brother, William, was married in a military ceremony, with considerable dash and style, to Alice Bridge Jackson, a daughter of the Boston discoverer of ether, Dr. Charles T. Jackson, and niece of Ralph Waldo

Emerson.[1] On the trip which followed, they came to New York for a visit. Soon afterward, as in other summers, the house was closed and the Arthurs went into the country. Before the days of affluence, they remained near the city, in some such place as Englewood. Later, they visited the parents at Newtonville, and traveled about the Lake George-Lake Champlain region. Both were fond of Cooperstown, where they sought a hotel as a respite from housekeeping, and Arthur missed few chances to fish. Frequently the end of the summer found them at Newport, where Major Arthur was stationed for some years.

Arthur was a skillful and inveterate angler. When the season opened in the spring, he could usually be found trying for trout in some Long Island stream. As summer progressed, he sought the Catskill or Adirondack waters. Eventually he became particularly fond of the Thousand Islands region and the salmon waters running into the Bay of Chaleurs. In the seventies, he went to the Cascapedia River with R. G. Dun, D. Archie Pell, and George Dawson, an Albany journalist who later described the expeditions. It was Dawson's introduction to Canadian salmon, and his respect for Arthur's experienced sportsmanship was unbounded. Arthur's enjoyment of the life was keen. When he arrived a fortnight after the others, local residents and guides joined to give him a welcoming party at the fishing lodge; and, while the great fire crackled, each contributed his part of the entertainment. Arthur recited *Tam o' Shanter* and *A Cotter's Saturday Night* "in a most admirable manner." [2] Arthur was also an early member of the Restigouche Club, and for years had its record catch for weight. Fishing was his one great outdoor recreation. It contended with politics as his liveliest interest. In 1867, he took a recognized place among the city's Republican Party leaders.

New York City had been adversely affected by the war, had been strongly Democratic, and had increasingly inclined to support the group who favored "peace at any price." The Republican Party in New York had been divided, even before the war, into pro- and anti-Weed factions, for Thurlow Weed had carried his systematic domination of the New York Whigs into the new political alliance. During the conflict the breach had widened. The followers of Weed were identified with the conservative wing of the national party, while Horace Gree-

[1] Boston *Transcript,* June 6, 1867.
[2] George Dawson, *Pleasures of Angling with Rod and Reel for Trout and Salmon* (N. Y., 1876), pp. 141-2.

ley's adherents were numbered among the radicals. The conservatives steadily lost ground in New York. Although they sent Edwin D. Morgan to the Senate in 1863, in the next year, a radical leader, Reuben E. Fenton, became the party's candidate for Governor by choice of a large majority in the State convention.

General Arthur's position in the factional alignment is not certain. Drawn to Morgan by bonds of gratitude and personal esteem, he was by no means pleased with Lincoln's Administration, believing that Lincoln did not exert the full force at his disposal to hasten the conclusion of the war whose turning point, in 1864, had long been past.[1] Yet at the national convention that year he seems to have been among the conservatives and to have helped select the man for Vice President whom Lincoln preferred. At any rate, we find him in later years claiming a part in the nomination of Andrew Johnson.[2]

With Lincoln's assassination, the country plunged into the morass of Reconstruction vindictiveness. New York's conservative leaders, Seward, Weed, Morgan, and Raymond, at the outset aligned themselves with Andrew Johnson. The results of the Congressional and State elections in 1866, the critical year in the "Age of Hate," swept the conservatives out of the way, forced Weed to retire, and delivered the power both at Washington and within the Republican Party to the radicals. In New York, Governor Fenton set out, with Greeley's aid, to manage the party organization in the fashion established by Weed. A few months later, something occurred which upset his plans altogether.

A three-cornered contest for the election of a United States Senator resulted in a victory for Roscoe Conkling. The election was not a fight between radical and conservative factions, but rather a struggle within radical ranks.[3] Conkling was chosen primarily because of his oratorical abilities, already demonstrated during several years of service in the House of Representatives. In this election, Greeley and Fenton were at best lukewarm toward Conkling; they had already planned that Fenton should go to Washington from Albany as successor to Senator Morgan when his term expired in 1869. They had well warranted fears of what Conkling might do in the meantime.

[1] Regina Caw to William Arthur, May 19, 1864, William Arthur Papers.
[2] Boston *Herald,* June 13, 1880, gives the source of its information as an interview with Arthur. It had appeared in N. Y. *Times,* Jan. 1, 1880.
[3] DeAlva S. Alexander, *A Political History of the State of New York,* Vol. III, pp. 166–171.

With the approach of a presidential campaign in 1868, and with a temperamental aversion to divided leadership, Conkling promptly undertook to become the only Republican "boss" of New York. Fenton might have the advantage of a two years' start, but Conkling intended to surpass him, and what was more, to weld the two factions. In the State convention of 1867, Conkling's friends secured his choice as presiding officer. Assuming the chair, he delivered a speech outlining his policy for the New York Republicans, a course both unprecedented and audacious, typical of what was to be expected of him in the future.

The New York City conservatives, penitent after their fall from orthodoxy in the previous year, sent a delegation to the convention of 1867 which Conkling was disposed to welcome with tolerance. Fenton and most of the radicals, after a day of altercation and bitterness, caused the repudiation of this group, insisting that the Republican organization which bore the radical stamp was alone entitled to the party name. Conkling's unification of the factions was thus delayed, but in the succeeding months many New York conservatives became his followers. Among them Arthur was becoming prominent.

New York politics, at least from the days of Aaron Burr's activities there, have been outstanding for complexity and for domination by the spoils system. In the period in which Arthur became politically active in New York City, the complexity was such as to baffle all but the professional participants, while the tone of political morality had the traditional sanction of generations of the spoilsman's code. The devices resorted to by the Republican leaders were for the most part time-honored, if not time-worn; from Tweed they no doubt learned a few tricks, but most of the technique of practical New York politics was the application of old methods to new situations.

Organization was the fundamental dogma. That of the New York City Republicans, however, went far beyond what one might normally expect. The exigencies of Reconstruction factionalism, the zealous efforts of Tammany Hall to keep control over the city government, and the fact that the population of the city was swiftly growing and constantly shifting, all contributed to foster organization within organization to an almost bewildering extent.

In the city of New York there were, in Arthur's day, twenty-one Assembly districts, from each of which a member of the State Assembly was chosen. Each district had a Republican association, with a full set of officers, which selected candidates for local public office and delegates to party councils. Their membership was not open, but became, on the contrary, increasingly select. Not over fifteen per cent. of the city's Republican voters were ever enrolled. Admission of new members involved a procedure resembling that in an exclusive men's club. Names of the candidates were posted, a membership committee had to report favorably on them, and the association had to elect new members by a clear majority. If it did not wish to add certain candidates for membership, it might easily defer elections indefinitely; but if a man were elected to membership, he had to qualify further by taking an extended series of oaths and vows. Chief among these was his pledge "that he is a Republican, a voter, and a resident of the District; that he intends to support the Republican Party organization of which the Association is a *recognized* portion; and to honorably sustain all nominations made by the Republican Party through its legally constituted conventions, *called or recognized* by the *Central Committee;* and that he is not, and will not become, a member of any committee or body which does not recognize the authority of the organization." [1] Once a man had by the necessary promises become something more than a Republican neophyte, his adherence was not left entirely to his conscience, for in most districts investigating committees watched for violations of the pledges and reported them. Offending members were dropped from the rolls.

From the twenty-one Assembly district associations, of which Arthur's was the eighteenth, varying numbers of elected delegates were sent to a Republican general city committee of 159 members, while other delegates (and alternates) were chosen for the successive city, county, and State caucuses. The general city committee, or central committee, supervised the activities of district associations and set the local standards of Republican orthodoxy. But it was a large and unwieldy body. Its own functions were more than guided, they were controlled, by an executive committee in whose hands was placed "the general management of affairs," whose sessions were secret, and from whom were reported all matters to be discussed in the general com-

---

[1] See F. W. Whitridge, *The Caucus System, passim;* Dorman B. Eaton ("Junius"), *The Independent Movement,* Chapter VI (Italics are mine).

mittee. If this small committee did not choose to lay a subject before the larger group for action, it could not be forced to do so. In consequence of such a structure, the nominating machinery of the Republican Party in New York City was controlled by a small group of relatively irresponsible men.[1]

At the head of the party was a State central committee, theoretically capable of supervising and directing the subordinate units, but in practice subject to counterclaims of local self-determination. The State committee contained representatives from the congressional districts, in turn made up of associated Assembly districts. The delegates to the State conventions from each congressional district met during the conventions to elect their representative on the State committee. The congressional districts in New York were numerous; the State committee, like the New York City committee, was far too large for efficient action save through subdivisions. One of these, the executive committee, was headed during the campaign of 1868 by General Arthur.

Arthur had attached himself to Conkling's organization. He was a firm believer in the necessity of such a structure. Unity was an absolute necessity if New York was to be kept in Republican hands; and such unity, he knew, could be maintained only by one dominant organization possessing leadership and discipline. Accordingly, in 1867 he went into the city executive committee as the representative of the eighteenth Assembly district. The next year he became an ardent worker for the election of Grant. As chairman of the Central Grant Club of New York,. and of the executive committee of the State committee, he adapted his powers of organization and administration from wartime uses to the election of a wartime hero. "As a politician, he was brainy, thorough, careful, and devoted to research and minutiae." [2]

Arthur's responsibilities in the campaign of 1868 required a man of exactly that sort. Horatio Seymour of New York was Grant's opponent. He was a difficult man for New York Republicans to defeat. As a matter of fact, he proved too difficult, for the State chose Democratic electors by a majority of ten thousand votes, all of which could have been accounted for by fraudulent naturalization and multiple

[1] The persistence of machine arrangements is shown by the description in William M. Ivins, *Machine Politics and Money in Elections in New York City* (1887).
[2] Interview of Stephen B. French in N. Y. *Times*, Nov. 19, 1886.

voting in the metropolitan districts.[1]

The first Grant campaign over, the anticipated contest for the Senatorship arose. Senator Morgan would have been glad to succeed himself. For a long time Governor Fenton had been hoping to win the place. His "machine" was just strong enough to elect the Speaker when the legislature organized, and thus to control the membership of the powerful committees in the lower house. By refusing to appoint any committee until after the party caucus should name Fenton for the Senatorship, the Speaker forced the election of his leader in the face of apparently hopeless odds.

Fenton's arrival in Washington precipitated a sharp struggle between himself and Conkling for the privileged position at Grant's patronage table. Conkling was no easy man to oppose. He was a seasoned politician, a famous orator of the old "spread-eagle" type, not yet forty, vigorous, and personally impressive. From his carefully groomed red curls and beard to his pointed shoes, he was always beautifully dressed. He carried himself with grace and strength, for he kept his tall figure lithe and strong by athletic exercises and temperate habits, having, as his critics admitted, "the finest 'torso' in public life." A rich voice enhanced his speeches, full of imagination and vigor, and at all times, on the floors of Congress and in his conversation, a sharp blade of sarcasm gleamed and struck at those he opposed. All his endowments were bent to a will and ambition which in 1869 knew no bounds. Fenton was to feel their full force.

Grant was exceedingly anxious to reëstablish Republican sway in New York. He gave his favor to Fenton at first, but Conkling's wit, sarcasm, and forceful speech advanced his standing in the President's eyes; Fenton gradually lost ground, and finally fell completely. The occasion was a contest over Grant's appointment of a new Collector of Customs for the Port of New York.

Grant had met Thomas Murphy at Long Branch, and liked him personally, possibly because of their common admiration for good horses. In 1870, he decided, on his own initiative and without consulting either Senator, to make Murphy Collector at New York in place of Moses H. Grinnell. Murphy was a "Tammany Republican" of New York City. Both on personal and political grounds, Fenton

[1] See DeAlva S. Alexander, *A Political History of the State of New York*, Vol. III, pp. 215–18.

opposed him, but Grant's influence and Conkling's personal claims upon Democratic Senators resulted in a vote of forty-eight to three for confirmation. Fenton was down; Conkling, up, and up to stay.

In 1870, Arthur was wanted by the Conkling organization to serve on the State committee and help retain control of that body. In the sharp contest with Fenton, Arthur's election became increasingly difficult, since at least one of the four New York City district associations choosing delegates to the State convention (delegates by whom Arthur would have to be elected) was distinctly a Greeley organization, while in two others Arthur had strong opponents. An effort was made by the new Collector and Colonel George C. Bliss, Jr., Conkling lieutenants, to defeat Greeley in his own district by purchasing the majority vote of the district association through which he would otherwise be selected.[1] It was explained to Bliss by the leading light of the association that about 300 of its 350 members were men who "voted Republican when he told them to" but otherwise voted Democratic. They were members of a neighboring Democratic association, but also controlled the Republican association of the eleventh Assembly district. Murphy supplied four hundred dollars "for suppers" for the valiant three hundred, but when the votes were counted in a side room by a small group the result was announced as a victory for Greeley. Thereupon, a contesting delegation was organized. It appeared at the State convention, was seated as "regular," and joined with other delegates similarly admitted to guarantee the choice of Chester A. Arthur for the State committee.

Ever since early November, 1869, Greeley had been attacking so-called "Tammany Republicans" in his *Tribune* editorials. Again and again he insisted that Tweed and his Tammany ring were able to overcome Republican opposition in New York City by virtue of the information furnished to him from Republicans high in Republican organization councils. Just before the Saratoga convention of 1870, at a meeting there of Republican leaders, he denounced one of the police commissioners of New York City as among these "Tammany Republicans." After the convention had nominated Stewart L. Woodford for Governor and the State committee had gone into Conkling's hands, the war which Greeley had opened was taken up in earnest, but turned to the advantage of the Conkling machine.

[1] 42nd Congress, 2nd sess., *Senate Report No. 227*, Vol. III, pp. 452 ff.

Arthur's political sagacity was evinced in this affair. The legislature had established for New York City a tax commission of four members, supposedly nonpartisan. In 1869, Arthur received the post of counsel to the commission, whose members were Republicans, with the large salary of ten thousand dollars, undoubtedly a political plum. Early in the next year, Tweed had control of the legislature, and added a fifth member to the tax commission, over which his ring intended to get control. At the same time, Editor Greeley was continually attacking Republicans who accepted city offices, and Arthur grew apprehensive that no distinction would be recognized between his post with a State-created commission and a strictly city office.[1]

When Arthur talked it over with his friend, George C. Bliss, who held a similar relation to the boards of health and excise, the latter dissuaded him from resignation for the time being, but in July or August, 1870, Arthur did retire. He had anticipated the impending contest, for in the autumn of 1870, after the State convention, the Republican city committee met and passed resolutions designed to eliminate Tweed-controlled Republicans.

Arthur had already resigned his office as counsel, which was not, apparently, at the time he took it, a Tammany affair. He was free to remain in the organization. He was both free and ready to take up the fight against Tammany. Tweed, however, had no intention of surrendering without resistance. He promptly brought the pressure of threat, promise, and patronage upon a sufficient number of the 159 members of the Republican central committee to secure a repeal of the committee's action. When the test came, the minority, which was just about half of the central committee, retired from the stormy gathering on the plea that it was midnight, and the advent of Sunday required an adjournment. They always subsequently insisted that they had been more than half and that the repeal was carried after the meeting was properly terminated.

Of course, in this situation, a petition was presented to the State committee requesting a reorganization of the New York City Republicans. The State committee was deliberate. Five of its number, three or four of them Conkling men, spent a few weeks "investigating" and then reported favorably, whereupon the committee designated William

[1] 42nd Congress, 2nd sess., *Senate Report No. 227*, Vol. III, pp. 424 ff.

Orton and Jackson Schultz to supervise the reorganization.[1] Alleged "Tammany Republicans" were weeded out and carefully replaced by Grant men likely to be amenable to Conkling's leadership.

In the circumstances such an interference in the Republican organization of New York City could be resented as exceeding the rightful authority of the State committee. To be sure, some of the city committee, headed by Alonzo B. Cornell (the Surveyor of the Port), had petitioned for such an action; but the others could object that it was a minority request. The result was a double set of general committees, of city and county conventions, and of delegates to the State convention at Syracuse in 1871.

The convention of 1871 was a lively affair. The owner of the hall in which it was held took out special insurance against damage. The State committee had an abundance of stalwart Syracuse police to maintain order. Before the gathering assembled, rumors of probable rough tactics were flying about in New York City—rumors which were confirmed when the seats on the stage were seized by a gang of undoubted New York City toughs, some of whom had criminal records. Their presence was held to be the result of Tweed's orders, executed by a Republican police commissioner. Their function was afterwards believed to have been that of clearing the stage at a proper time in the deliberations, and turning it over to the discredited New York City leaders. But Cornell, chairman of the State committee, finding them there when he came, had them escorted out of the building by the police, and their seats taken by State committeemen.

The convention was obliged to decide which group of city Republicans was regular, the old Greeley-led committee, or the new pro-Conkling group. The committee on credentials, to be appointed by the temporary chairman, was therefore of the greatest importance to Conkling's success. In electing that officer, it was agreed that all might vote, including both sets of contesting delegates. Andrew D. White, who was expected to act impartially, was named by a vote of 188 to 159; but to the consternation of Conkling's foes, White at once appointed a committee on credentials, pro-Conkling twelve to two.[2] The

[1] The radicals had similarly reorganized the city Republicans in 1866. N. Y. *Tribune*, Sept. 26, 1866. Schultz was named only after Greeley had declined.
[2] Andrew D. White, *Autobiography*, Vol. I, pp. 164–8, says he had accepted the invi-

report of this committee recommended that the new Conkling city committee be recognized as the only "regular" one. Discussion was heated, eliciting a speech from Conkling in which he repudiated all offers of compromise.

The party was to be welded into one single organization; it was to send a united delegation to the national convention of 1872; and it was to endorse Grant for another term. Greeley had long since expressed himself against Grant's renomination,[1] and his leadership in New York City must end. Such were Conkling's views, and he made them prevail, cleverly utilizing the Tammany question to win support from anti-Grant Republicans.

Various delegates retired from the convention, most of them the "Tammany Republicans." What remained was undiluted orthodox Republicanism. The "regular" organization was securely in the hands of Conkling, Thomas Murphy, Arthur, and other lieutenants, with whom it was to remain for ten more years, a means of great political power and equivalent responsibility. Murphy was an experienced politician, loyal to Grant, and able to utilize Custom House patronage in the service of Grant's political fortunes. With Conkling he was, therefore, on common ground; with Arthur he had for several years been on terms of personal friendship as well. To Conkling's machine he gave great assistance. In Murphy's comparatively simple mind, since Grant was much interested in having New York support his Administration, it was the duty of the postmaster of New York, the district attorney, the United States marshal, the commandant of the Brooklyn Navy Yard, the assistant treasurer at New York, and all the leading officers of the Custom House, to join in forcing upon the State organization a leadership favorable to Grant. All patronage, even of the State, was to be used to advance Grant's cause. Grant was first to pick the Republican candidates for State offices, and then his leading appointees in New York City were to see that delegates were selected to the State conventions in 1870 and 1871 who would vote for the slate previously approved in Washington.

Murphy's predecessors as Collector had used their position to foster

tation of the State committee to be put up for temporary chairman only when assured that they would give full and fair representation on all committees to all factions. He could not know the leanings of all the delegates, and, as usual, appointed the list of committees furnished him from the State committee.

[1] N. Y. *Tribune*, May 19, 20, 25, 1871.

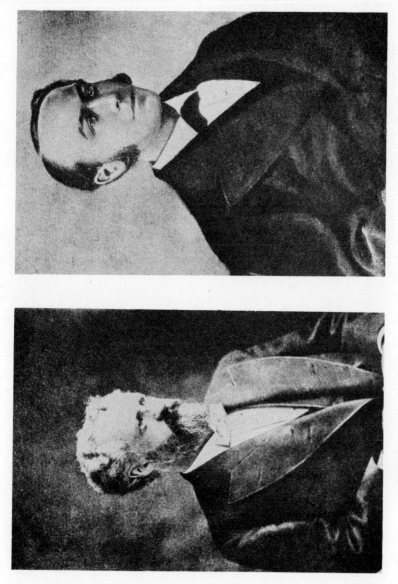

THOMAS C. PLATT

ROSCOE CONKLING

similar projects. Collector Smythe in 1866–69 removed 830 out of 903 officials in the Custom House, putting in their places Democrats and supporters of Andrew Johnson. Moses H. Grinnell, who succeeded him when Grant took office, held the place during the sixteen months of Fenton's ascendancy. He put out 510 out of 892 officials, replacing them with Fenton men so far as possible. Murphy's appointment was bitterly opposed by Fenton and as earnestly advocated by Conkling. It was not surprising that with ample precedent for the spoils system in the Custom House, Murphy promptly resorted to it. It was to be expected that Fenton men would go and Conkling men come in. They did. It was almost a procession.

Unfortunately, Murphy was entirely incompetent for the official responsibilities of a collector and depended upon Custom House subordinates for practically everything except the political manipulation for which he was responsible. Equally unfortunate was the extent of his admiration for President Grant. To please Grant, as he thought, he diverted to the firm of Leet & Stocking the business of storing imported freight between its arrival on a vessel and its being claimed by those to whom it had been sent; in the language of the Custom House, the "general-order business." Leet & Stocking then raised their charges, relying upon their monopoly as the officially designated storehouse and upon its continuance so long as Murphy was Collector. Of course there were complaints, led by certain large steamship lines. When protests to Murphy failed to produce results, the matter was taken up in Congress, where a Senate investigating committee was empowered to look into much more than this particular accusation.

The investigators included as a Democratic minority Thomas F. Bayard of Delaware and Eugene Casserly of California, men whose searching questions elicited testimony under oath which required Murphy's retirement. Not merely was his ignorance of the business of revenue collection made plain; in addition it was shown that he spent most of his time in political manipulation, like his predecessors, and that he was an old friend of Tweed, Sweeny, and Connolly, the arch-conspirators of the infamous Tweed ring. He had gone into real estate purchases with them; had accepted appointment on a commission for the widening of Broadway with two others, well-known associates of Tweed, whose duties were to appraise the damages to property which the city must pay. He had been one of the school commission authorized by the Tammany legislature and perverted to the filling of Tweed ring pockets with city money.[1]

It so happened that the exposures of the Tweed ring's incredible corruptions were at the time of this Custom House investigation the subject of general popular indignation. Any relationship to Tweed and his associates was contaminating. No degrees of guilt, no possibility of honest intent, no allowance for misplaced confidence, were recognized as possible. Murphy was a political liability to the Grant men of New York and the rest of the country from the moment that his long acquaintance with such a scoundrel as Tweed was made public. On November 18, 1871, having been in office only a little over a year, he resigned in a letter to Grant which evoked a most complimentary and cordial reply—and acceptance!

The Grant leaders of New York had already fixed upon a successor. The man they had chosen was Chester A. Arthur, then in his forty-second year, with an excellent reputation for honesty, a recognized capacity for executive work, and an unquestioned fidelity to the interests of Grant and the Conkling machine.

His political services had been quiet. He had not become a public figure. "For months before Arthur publicly received his appointment" it was known that he was to receive it, according to the New York *Times*.[2] "His name very seldom rises to the surface of metropolitan life, and yet, 'moving like a mighty undercurrent, this man during the last ten years has done more to mold the course of the Republican Party in this State than any other one man in the country." Murphy was "Arthur's tool." Arthur was "not a brilliant man nor a genius. . . . The secret of Arthur's success was his executive ability, and his knowledge of men." His appointment gave promise that the Custom House would be honestly run, for "when Arthur became quartermaster-general, he was poor. When his term of office expired he was poorer still." Although he had insisted on starting out with a new Deputy-Collector in place of Murphy's, he was attached to Conkling and could be expected to befriend all Grant men.

Horace Greeley's comments were not quite so enthusiastic. To the *Times*, Arthur stood "first in ability on the list of second-rate men," but to Greeley, it appeared that "the General will be in the Custom

[1] 42nd Congress, 2nd sess., *Senate Report No. 227*, Vol. III, pp. 422 ff.
[2] Feb. 20, 1872.

House a personal burlesque upon Civil Service Reform. He recently held a ten-thousand-dollar Tammany office from which he was only driven by the *Tribune's* exposure; and he is a devoted servant of the Murphy clique; but he is not personally an objectionable man." [1]

Arthur was reluctantly persuaded to take the position. Grant sent his private secretary, Horace Porter, to New York to overcome Arthur's objections.[2] He had always avoided public office, confining his positions to membership on party committees, and was at that time chairman of the executive committee of the Republican State committee, with another campaign coming on. He yielded in the expectation that Murphy's resignation would come somewhat later than it did. "I did not expect this office at this time," he told a reporter, and learned about it only from friends who saw notices in the papers.[3] No doubt it came as a surprise, for his thoughts were on other matters. That day, his only daughter was born!

[1] Issue of Nov. 21, 1871, cited in Bowers, *The Tragic Era,* p. 373.
[2] N. Y. *Times,* Nov. 21, 1886.
[3] N. Y. *World,* Nov. 21, 1871.

THE circumstances of General Arthur's appointment to the Collector-ship were exactly suited to his qualifications. He was honest. His prede-cessor had resigned during an investigation that turned up apparent proof that dishonesty in the Custom House was widespread. Improve-ment was expected by the public, and he could justify innovations to end dishonesty by pointing out to one type of objector that he was improving the service, while to another type, the politicians, he could explain that he was yielding to public opinion and so strengthening the party.

About a year after he took office, in December, 1872, the new civil service rules approved by General Grant were made operative at the Custom House. Candidates for appointment, no matter how strong their political "backing," had to run the gauntlet of the examinations; and if they failed, the Collector was not the object of reproach. If they succeeded, he had a surer guide to their abilities than a batch of fervid testimonial letters, and an argument to silence any reformers who objected to particular appointments. The examinations were un-questionably an aid to him, and perhaps to the very extent that they aided the Collector they enraged the old-style politicians. It was a courageous act, in view of his political associations, for Collector Arthur to write President Grant in April, 1874, words of measured praise for the merit system.[1]

Yet there were limits to which improvement of Custom House efficiency could go at the expense of Republican Party interests. Arthur was by no means a reformer; his approbation of civil service examinations was always subject to the proviso that they be not a sole criterion in making good appointments. He was a practical politician who believed firmly in the necessity of patronage to maintain an organ-ization, that absolute prerequisite to party success. The circumstances in which he took office enabled him, therefore, to take a mid-position, to appoint political friends if qualified for the work, and to refuse to remove good men merely to make room for others. In his entire term

[1] 46th Cong., 3rd sess., *House Exec. Doc. No. 94,* pp. 19 ff. The examinations ceased in December, 1874. See Arthur's testimony before the Jay Commission reported in N. Y. *Tribune,* May 26, 1877.

of five years and four months, he removed only 144 employees, notwithstanding a continual and enormous pressure for office, and there are reasons for believing that none of the removals was simply to punish political opposition.

Outside Washington, there was no Federal administrative unit so large and important as the New York Custom House. At that port, about two thirds of the tariff revenue was collected. The staff of officials when Arthur took the position totaled 923, and under his administration rose to 1011. Most of them were appointed by the Secretary of the Treasury at his request, and were not subject to Senate confirmation. The Collector, therefore, dispensed as much patronage as most Cabinet officers.

His post was of great political importance, probably unequaled outside of Washington. Moreover, it offered a heavy financial responsibility; while Arthur held it, over $860,000,000 was received and nearly $40,000,000 expended. With two exceptions, totaling $8,436.88, these huge sums were entirely accounted for. For any losses, the Collector was responsible, and to cover them he was under heavy bond. Only a special act by Congress could release him from paying whatever money disappeared through the dishonesty of subordinates.[1]

Naturally a position of such responsibility drew large rewards. In 1874, the Collector's salary was established at twelve thousand dollars per year, and the older system of compensation, based primarily on moieties of collected fines, abolished. For nearly three years, however, it had yielded Arthur an annual income of approximately forty thousand dollars. The drastic reduction left his salary above that of a Cabinet officer, and the political code then prevailing in New York continued to require of him an open-handed generosity. At State conventions, his suite of rooms was the caucus headquarters and his cigars and other refreshments were hospitably offered and cheerfully consumed. In addition, he was relied upon for contributions of money to meet unexpected political exigencies, especially among New York City's district leaders.

The change from moieties to salary followed the largest single fine which Arthur, and probably other collectors, ever collected. After he had been in office a year, a special agent of the Treasury Department came to him with evidence that the highly respectable and prosperous

[1] 49th Cong., 1st sess., *Sen. Rep. No. 1083.*

importing firm of Phelps, Dodge & Company had undervalued items in many of their importations for the past few months. William E. Dodge, one of the partners, was summoned to Arthur's office at the Custom House and confronted with the charges, and subsequently, in several conferences with Arthur and others, impressed with the extent of his liability. The law inflicted an enormous penalty intended to discourage any fraud. The entire value of each importation of which any part was undervalued was subject to forfeiture, making the company liable to a suit for $1,750,000, attended by long litigation and undoubted loss of prestige, or to the immediate payment of some smaller sum agreed upon as a compromise. It was finally determined that the total value of the undervalued goods should be paid, a sum of $271,-017.23, upon receipt of which it was divided between the special agent and the three leading officers of the Port. For legal services in construing the statute, according to report, large sums went to Roscoe Conkling, Ben Butler, and others.

The importers, after paying, discovered that the total amount of undervaluation was only $6,658.78, and that this was more than offset by their own overvaluations and excess payments to the government. When they further calculated that the duties of which their undervaluations had deprived the Custom House totaled $1,664.68, they concluded that they had been mulcted, and commenced prolonged and bitter protests which ultimately produced a congressional investigation. The committee recommended the abandonment of moieties, and Congress followed their advice. The much-discussed Phelps, Dodge collection proved to be a case of killing the goose that laid the golden egg.[1]

Arthur's part in it, while far from commendable, could be justified by what is ironically termed "business ethics." It was entirely within the law.

So large a staff as that of the Custom House was necessarily much subdivided. Associated with the Collector as principal officers were the Naval Officer, who was supervisor of a force of clerks for the computation of duties, and the Surveyor, whose direct subordinates were inspectors, weighers, gaugers, and keepers of storage places. At the Port there was also the Appraiser, whose office was administered entirely independently of the Collector. The appraiser's staff was charged with the responsibility of establishing the values of imports

[1] 43rd Cong., 1st sess., *House Misc. Doc. No. 264* (May 2, 1874).

subject to *ad valorem* duties, and consisted of persons supposedly expert in distinguishing and identifying the almost infinite variety of commodities brought into the country. Each of the four principal offices was organized into divisions performing similar tasks, under chiefs whose titles varied. The Collector also had special deputies to act in his place, officers whose functions were necessarily confidential. To those positions, Chester A. Arthur appointed John R. Lydecker and Thomas L. James.

The Custom House in Arthur's day was on Wall Street at the present site of the National City Bank. It was a building of dark granite with Ionic columns. Inside, under a large dome, in a vast rotunda, most of the business between the public and the clerks was transacted. It was a busy scene, clerks leaning over their desks, importers and "custom-house brokers," of whom there were some five hundred in the city, thronging about, and among them scores of official messengers carrying papers from one desk or one office to another. Visitors, too, came to see and be seen. Old Thurlow Weed, for example, once the actual ruler of New York, used occasionally to stroll through the rotunda leaning on his daughter's arm, and to enjoy the commotion created by his presence.

On the Wall Street side, secluded from the hubbub of the rotunda, the Collector had his suite of offices. He was not easily approachable. Arthur, like his predecessors, was not usually at the Custom House until it had been open for business an hour or more. Frequently it was noon before he arrived. Many callers were concerned with New York politics and not with other Custom House business. They were likely to find, upon entering the inmost office, a group of prominent politicians with whom the Collector was conferring between interviews with his other visitors. There was never any doubt which of the men was General Arthur. He was a dominating figure in any group—tall, portly, carefully dressed, his "Burnsides" well groomed, his frank, ruddy face noteworthy for the commanding dark eyes, his manner dignified and courteous. Visitors found the atmosphere of his office more like that of a city banker than of the usual political leader. The intelligence with which their business was undertaken was likewise impressive. Thomas L. James, a confidential deputy, found that "his knowledge of the revenue laws was perfect, and [that] he possessed a judicial mind, well balanced in every respect, which caused his decisions to be almost invariably right. His power of dispatching business was remarkable. Work did not wear on him as it does on many. He easily threw it off and he did it well." [1]

In Arthur's day, the Custom House, like all government offices, was well supplied with Civil War veterans. One of the most valuable members of the staff was Colonel William H. MacMahon, whose knowledge of tariff law later caused Arthur to appoint him to the Tariff Commission of 1882. A bullet through one of his eyes had carried away part of his head, yet he lived to become an invaluable Custom House officer. General N. M. Curtis, fiercely bearded, "the hero of Fort Fisher," was prominent, and for a time, "Corporal" Tanner, idol of the G. A. R., moved about the place on his two wooden legs, winning friends with his genial qualities. Among the messengers, mostly Civil War veterans, physical disabilities slowed up movement only less than the untamable persistence of many in stopping to chat with innumerable friends. These unfortunates contributed a general appearance of inefficiency to the Custom House staff, but their employment was an indirect form of pension then, and since then, widely tolerated.

Everyone in the Custom House was supposed to have a "backer," and the older clerks invariably sought to discover the influence which secured the appointment of any new addition. Many were there in response to the requests and recommendations of New York City leaders. While Collector, Arthur advanced his power as the Republican "boss" of the city, working through the Assembly districts in which he had loyal and active lieutenants. Especially prominent were some Republican Irishmen, with influence in their neighborhoods, whom the newspapers always hailed as "the boys" and favored with nicknames, such as "Johnny" O'Brien, "Barney" Biglin, and "Mike" Cregan. General Arthur himself was endowed by the reporters with the mythical sobriquet of "Chet," but no one in his family, and, so far as can be ascertained, no one among his political associates ever ventured to use such a name in his presence. To his family, he was always "Chester"; among the New York politicians, he was usually "General Arthur." The men whom he honored with his confidence in the machine were not all of the sort received in his home, but they were entitled to respect and maintained with him relations dignified as well as cordial.

It is interesting to realize that on the same days in which Arthur

[1] N. Y. *Times*, Nov. 19, 1886.

talked politics with men like these in a way which strengthened their comradeship, he talked well on other subjects, such as literature, in which he was well read, or fishing, in which he was an expert, with his friends in the Century Club, or at home. He was versatile, but with a versatility of interest and occupation rather than of manner. Like everyone else, he had a better self which did not always control his actions, but he did not lead the dual life of romance. His normal bearing was that of the gentleman.

His political foes realized it, when they knew him. He was not the ruthless partisan as Collector that his predecessors had been. On the Custom House roster were men whose "backers" included Blaine, Conkling's enemy, and George William Curtis, who went into the Liberal Republican movement in 1872 and worked with the Democrats for Horace Greeley in what Conkling called "that black, untamed, succotash coalition." Some, even, were Democrats. It may be doubted that Arthur appointed them, but it is certain that he did not remove them.

The conduct of political campaigns required funds. In the 1870's, these were for the most part derived from the candidates and the annual assessments of officeholders. In the 1880's, after laws prohibiting them began to be enforced,[1] assessments dwindled. At the same time, business men began to take an unusual interest in the outcome of campaigns, contributing extensively to the Republican chests in 1880 and 1884. Arthur was Collector during the period when assessments were under fire from the advocates of civil service reform, and upheld as "voluntary contributions" by the political leaders.

No doubt the new name, "voluntary contributions," was entirely a subterfuge in some offices, and to a large degree, in the New York Custom House. Under Collector Arthur, no employee was dismissed for failure to contribute, and compulsion to pay was felt principally by those who realized that other reasons might be discovered for removing them. Even if the official were of the Blaine faction, he could in safety decline to contribute. Arthur's only aid to the collection of these percentages must have been in permitting a list of the officials and their salaries to be taken for the party treasurers.

Conkling's machine was well established when Arthur became Collector. The struggle to rid the metropolis of Tweed redounded to the

[1] *Ex parte Curtis,* 106 U. S., 373.

advantage of Arthur's unit of the State organization. Alonzo B. Cornell of Ithaca and others in New York City were obliged to join forces with Conkling, while Richard S. Crowley of Buffalo, Thomas C. Platt of Owego, John H. Ramsey of Albany, George H. Sharpe of Kingston, and other subalterns flocked to his standard. Within the party, they were triumphant. The secession of the Liberal Republicans in the early months of 1872 was in part an acknowledgment of Conkling's supremacy, to which it contributed. At Philadelphia in June, Conkling led a New York delegation pledged to Grant. They returned to sweep the State in the November elections and claimed full credit for it. The party was in their hands, and the State belonged to the party. Governor John A. Dix was friendly to the machine, although not a member, while the legislature, on January 6, 1873, sent Conkling back to the Senate for six more years. The political sky was fair.

Clouds soon gathered for a storm. The crushing of Tweed not merely aided Arthur's New York machine; it produced a new Democratic leadership. "Honest John" Kelly returned from abroad to help drive Tweed out of Tammany Hall just as others were expelling him from the city government. Samuel J. Tilden, a leading Democratic participant in the attack on Tweed, devoted his political wizardry to restoring his party's strength throughout the State. By 1874, these two were ready to offer battle with the old-time Democratic strength.

A reaction against Republicanism followed very shortly after the reëlection of Grant. Scandals piled up about him. A financial panic broke, bringing business stagnation in its wake. The average voter was ready for a new cast on the governmental stage, and expected it to present a new play. In 1874, in New York, Tilden was borne into the Governor's chair on a tidal wave fifty thousand votes above General Dix. A few weeks later, Francis Kernan received the Senatorship that some Conklingite had expected in Fenton's place. Grant was going down, and Conkling's machine seemed bound to go down with him.

No sooner was Tilden installed at Albany than he commenced the exposure of a bipartisan "canal ring" begun in Fenton's palmy days. Before long, the disgusted New York public was filled with facts about plundering canal contractors flourishing in Republican atmosphere. Instead of joining in and claiming their share of the credit for cleansing the State, the injudicious Republicans sat back and poured invective on Tilden's motives. Engaged in this invidious task, their favor with State opinion was further reduced by the events in Washington. There the Administration which Conkling supported was staggering under the double load of czarism in Louisiana and of the whisky ring, with its trail of guilt from St. Louis up the Ohio Valley and across Pennsylvania to the very Executive Mansion itself. Grant, in letter-writing mood, proclaimed his faith in General Babcock's innocence, and announced in a separate communication the fact that he would not run again. Against these odds, Conkling might strive in vain; his machine was helpless. "The bright blade of his eloquence, with its keen satiric edge," might, as some admirer wrote,[1] flash defiantly; but the State went Democratic again in 1875 by fifteen thousand plurality.[2]

With the State Administration in Democratic hands, Conkling's machine made even greater demands on Federal patronage for its maintenance. The Custom House became more valuable than in the past. On December 17, Arthur was reappointed for a second term. Pressure for purely political appointments was immense. Under it, he increased the Custom House staff despite a pronounced decline in the volume of business during the economic depression. To weed out incompetents and attain the standards of honesty and efficiency which he desired became increasingly difficult.

As the presidential election of 1876 approached, Conkling prepared for his most ambitious project. Grant was, by his own declaration, out of the running. The field was open to his loyal subordinates, of whom Conkling sought to be foremost. It was, however, a bad year for "Grant men." The revelations of incompetent and corrupt service by some of the officials whom the President had honored with his confidence could not fail to undermine the popularity of all his associates. Those who had eagerly received him among their ranks and pushed him into the highest office had now to pay the price. In the face of such odds, and coming from a State no longer Republican, Roscoe Conkling sought in 1876 to gain for himself the Republican nomination for the Presidency.

In New York, the Conkling organization prepared to send an undivided delegation to the convention at Cincinnati, whose entire vote should be given to the leader. On March 22, the State convention met

[1] *The Nation*, Oct. 28, 1875, is incorrectly cited in Alexander, *op. cit.*, Vol. III, p. 330.
[2] Arthur left the campaign in October to go to his father, at Newtonville, in his last illness. Death came October 27 after a month of rapidly failing health.

at Syracuse and offered opposition to the plan. The anti-Grant sentiments of a large proportion of New York's Republican voters were voiced by a Reform Republican wing, led by George William Curtis. Restive under the machine's control of nominations, especially in New York City, and outspokenly opposed to a continuance of "Grantism" in their party, they concentrated their positive approval on the candidacy of Benjamin H. Bristow of Kentucky. Bristow, as Secretary of the Treasury under Grant, had drawn the veil from a corrupt "Whisky ring" in which close associates and friends of the President were numbered. His performance had been misrepresented to Grant, and he was about to be forced out of the Cabinet. An air of martyrdom, added to his sound claims as a reformer, made him the hope of the Republicans who had resolved to end the carnival of dishonesty at Washington.

New York City Republicans were chafing under the restraining control of the Arthur organization. On March 9, 1876, the Union League Club, home of the most orthodox and patriotic Republicanism, had been the scene of a protest meeting. A series of resolutions complained of the control of Republican affairs, particularly in New York City, "by an organized machinery of officeholders." The tide of opinion was strongly against Conkling and Arthur. It was felt that they made of the Republican organization a close corporation, rewarding their adherents with offices instead of nominating and electing the best men available.[1] Nevertheless, at the Syracuse convention it soon became apparent that the machine was undismayed. Though George William Curtis made a sturdy attempt to prevent the endorsing of Conkling's candidacy, New York's delegates were urged by the convention, 250 to 113, to strive for his nomination. Curtis could only proclaim the "moral victory" of the minority.[2]

At Cincinnati, Chester A. Arthur, custodian of Conkling's candidacy, arrived on the eighth of June and put up at the Grand Hotel. The New York delegation had its headquarters there, with spacious rooms and one of the best bands available. He had made the trip with DeWitt C. Wheeler and Stephen B. French, all three belonging to the "Conkling lobby."[3] They were not official delegates, but not exactly innocent bystanders, either. In fact, a busy week lay before them, with

[1] N. Y. *Tribune*, Mar. 10, May 24, 1876.
[2] *Harper's Weekly*, April 8, 1876, p. 282.
[3] Cincinnati *Daily Gazette*, June 9, 1876.

the convention opening its sessions on the fourteenth, and, in the interim, unlimited consultations. Conkling was not likely to command a large vote on the first ballot, and it was necessary to solicit Southern and Western delegations if he were to come forward after the initial bestowal of compliments to "favorite sons." In this sort of work, Arthur joined his colleagues.

The convention was dominated by two groups—the reformers, urging Bristow, and the adherents of Blaine, who probably was the choice of the largest proportion of the party's rank and file. Between these two groups, Conkling's supporters were ranked with those of Oliver P. Morton of Indiana and Rutherford B. Hayes of Ohio. All the efforts of Arthur, Cornell, and the other New York men made no headway against Grant's disrepute among the reformers, Blaine's notorious enmity for Conkling, and the skill of Ohio politicians in advancing the claims of Hayes. Even from their own State, a body of some fifty estimable Republicans came to sustain the lone delegate from New York who cast his ballot for Bristow. Before the full convention itself, this delegate, George William Curtis, emphasized the strong desire for Bristow in New York by reading a lengthy address approved by the New York City Reform Republican Club.

When the convention finally proceeded to ballot on the presidential nominees, Conkling had ninety-nine votes, a reasonable number for a beginning. But as subsequent ballots were taken, Conkling's column diminished from 99 to 93, then to 90, 84, 82, and on the sixth tally, only 81.[1] Then the delegation retired for consultation. Strategy required the transfer of New York votes to the victorious candidate, and if possible, to neither Blaine nor Bristow. When the New Yorkers returned to the hall, they had fixed upon Hayes as the man who would win. Before their turn came, Indiana withdrew Oliver P. Morton, and Kentucky, Benjamin H. Bristow; and both turned to Hayes with their votes. From New York came sixty-one more, virtually concluding the contest. Pennsylvania added a few, and the final count was 384 for Hayes to 351 for Blaine.

Once the presidential nominee had been selected from the Middle West, the vice presidential choice was to be taken from the populous East. In the discussions prior to Hayes's nomination the New Yorkers

[1] Edward Stanwood, *A History of the Presidency from 1788 to 1897* (Rev. ed., 1928), I, p. 373.

had been angling for the place. From the Conkling machine, Stewart L. Woodford's name was put forward. It was he who had nominated Conkling in an eloquent speech. But to the dismay of his friends, the convention preferred another New Yorker not a member of the dominant group—Congressman William A. Wheeler of Malone. He was considered more acceptable to the Blaine States, and when nominated by a delegate from Vermont was promptly selected. Rather sore at heart, but with the discipline of their calling, Arthur and his associates left Cincinnati to enter the impending campaign. The Republicans might yet regain their ascendancy in the State government, but within the party the machine was obviously losing its grip.

When the Republicans gathered at Saratoga on August 23 to choose a State ticket, the likelihood of success was seriously threatened by the fact that Samuel J. Tilden of New York had become the Democratic nominee for the Presidency. This choice could not fail to assist the Democratic candidates for State offices. It behooved the party to name candidates who would not weaken Hayes. With that idea in mind, the reform wing advanced on Saratoga with a substantial delegation organized in behalf of William M. Evarts for Governor. Evarts had been an able member of Andrew Johnson's counsel in the impeachment trial, and had served briefly as Attorney-General in Johnson's Cabinet. He had since participated in the Geneva arbitration, and was undoubtedly a man of great gifts. In 1873, Grant had considered him a suitable successor to Salmon P. Chase as Chief Justice, but was dissuaded by Conkling, and instead turned to Evarts's classmate at Yale, Morrison R. Waite. George William Curtis was Evarts's champion at Saratoga.

For the machine, Alonzo B. Cornell was the leading aspirant; but Edwin D. Morgan, New York's war Governor, likewise sought the place. Conkling was mysteriously absent, although expected; and management of the convention fell upon Arthur, who had gone as the active controller of a majority of the city's delegates, labeled by the newspapers as "Custom House men." [1] For the management of an entire convention, Arthur was not well fitted. A large and restless assortment of people confronted him, to be persuaded, cajoled, and swept by enthusiasm to ratify decisions reached in advance by the

[1] N. Y. *Tribune,* Aug. 23, 1876.

sages of Conkling's camp. Lacking oratorical accomplishments, he could not sway large bodies of men with the mastery of Conkling. He made hard work of what was at best a difficult task.

Ex-Governor Morgan was urged by many for whom Cornell would have been second choice. As Arthur's original patron, he had personal claims upon the leader which rivaled in some measure those which Cornell could advance from his long service in the machine. Arthur could not effect a withdrawal by either Morgan or Cornell until it was absolutely necessary to prevent the nomination of Evarts. Then Cornell retired, and Morgan swept to success on the first ballot by a vote of 242 to 126. This large minority vote was interpreted as a censure of the Conkling group, and declared by the *Tribune* to be a gentle, yet firm, rebuke to the leaders rather than a revolt against the existence of any organized machinery. The minority was said to represent party sentiment better than the "close corporation" of "machinists." [1]

Despite their defeat at Cincinnati and their partial defeat at Saratoga, the New York organization worked zealously in behalf of the party's nominees. Conkling made but one speech, and beyond that he did not participate in the canvass, sulking, said some; ill, according to his friends. The others struggled in vain against Tilden's skill and popularity. In the end, they failed. Tilden ran nearly thirty-three thousand votes ahead of Hayes, and Morgan lost by a margin somewhat smaller to Lucius Robinson. The centennial year, in the political circles where Arthur moved, was brightened by no rays of hope. Especially among the lower officers of the Custom House the election results spread utter consternation. If Tilden should become President, not merely would Arthur go, but so, they believed, would hundreds of clerks, war veterans and all. Arthur kept his thoughts to himself. But while the outcome was in doubt, and before the electoral commission had been established, he said to one of his deputies: "If we are defeated and accept the fact, I believe that the party will recover, but it will never recover if we should seat its candidate by unfair means." In some obscure way, he exerted himself in the disputed Southern States, probably raising funds for the needs of Republicans on the

[1] N. Y. *Tribune*, Aug. 26, 1876.

ground.[1]

Conkling, at Washington, labored for the Electoral Commission and then suddenly withdrew his support or seeming interest. It was even feared that he might endeavor to defeat its conclusions, when it had all but chosen Hayes. One can only surmise his reasons, but he may have had some foresight as to what would happen in New York if Hayes won. If Tilden came in, Federal patronage in New York was sure to go to the Democrats, on the recommendation of Senator Francis J. Kernan. If Hayes came in, and did not uphold the Conkling machine, it would be better to be free of the responsibility for seating him. In New York, especially, in view of the factional division of the Republicans, a leading question after Hayes's inaugural was, therefore, "What will he do about the offices?"

[1] William E. Chandler, in *The Presidents of the United States, 1789–1894*, edited by J. G. Wilson, Vol. III, p. 448. See also, John Bigelow, *Life of Samuel J. Tilden*, Vol. II, p. 21.

WHEN Hayes was inaugurated in 1877, Arthur had held the office of Collector for over five years. The place was a political prize eagerly sought by all who wished to take a leading part in New York State politics. Had the Conkling organization opposed Hayes's nomination, played a surly rôle in the campaign, or deserted him in the disputed election, according to the code prevailing among the politicians Arthur should have given way to some Republican more friendly to Hayes. But Conkling's machine, save for the leader, helped to nominate and elect President Hayes. Conkling's connection with the electoral count had been in some ways advantageous to Hayes; his part in the campaign had been limited only because of illness, his friends said, while his lieutenants, Arthur, Cornell, and Platt, had exerted themselves throughout the canvass. According to recognized standards of politics, therefore, Arthur need not expect to be removed.

Yet signs of trouble had manifested themselves by March 4, 1877, even before Hayes proclaimed in his inaugural address that a reform in the civil service should be "thorough, radical, and complete." [1] His New York adherents in the Reform Republican group found this announcement far more pleasing than did the Conkling machine. Having failed to nominate Evarts for Governor in 1876, the Reform Republicans were delighted to find him placed at the head of Hayes's Cabinet. Hayes had preferred him to Conkling for that position, and had refused the importunities of the New York machine to make Platt his Postmaster General.[2] Leaving aside all questions of personal fitness, Hayes's appointment of Evarts was a return for the latter's advocating his election before the Electoral Commission. To the Conklingites, it appeared that the new President thus denied the legitimate claims of the dominant group in New York, which had worked valiantly, if unsuccessfully, to carry the State for him, and deliberately favored the minority element from whom Evarts came. They could expect no friendliness from Evarts in questions of New York patronage, and found their consolation in the fact that the Custom House

[1] Richardson, *Messages*, Vol. VII, pp. 444–5.
[2] Memorial in Hayes Papers (Frémont, Ohio).

and most Federal offices lay in the Treasury Department, to be managed by John Sherman, a practical Ohio politician. But with Hayes's interest in civil service reform made clear through his inaugural, the New York machinists had cause for marked uneasiness.

Arthur had some reasons for fearing the political ax. His term had by 1877 outdistanced that of each of his predecessors for a generation past, all of whom had retired from the Collectorship to private life with the enmity of many and the calumny of most. He had striven to improve the service "without hindrance to the importers and additional expense to the government" [1] and had so far succeeded that his reappointment in December, 1875, had been ratified without even the formality of reference to a senatorial committee. "Considering how many reputations have been destroyed within the last few years, it is a thing for General Arthur to be proud of that he ends his first term of office with even a higher reputation than that which he enjoyed privately and in the legal profession when he entered upon it. If the question could be put to the vote, there would be a unanimous decision in favor of his reappointment," said the New York *Times*.[2]

A few months later, Secretary Bristow had sent special agents of the Treasury Department to investigate the New York Custom House. They had made their reports, containing, according to the newspapers, much of discredit to the office of the Appraiser and to Collector Arthur's chief deputy, John R. Lydecker.[3] On April 1, 1876, orders to dismiss ten inspectors and fifty night watchmen from the Surveyor's Department were carried out, and others later removed from office brought the total to eighty-four. From the Appraiser's office, three examiners were ousted and Stephen B. French, a friend of the Collector, was nominated to replace Appraiser William A. Darling.[4]

Each of these removals created antagonisms toward the Collector required to make them, but hardly a sense of injustice. Moreover, as was observed at the time, when a decapitation in the Custom House staff occurred, the decapitated, like medieval saints, took their heads under their arms, marched on the Collector's office with renewed testimonials, and joined the others seeking reappointment. Soon the number

[1] Letter to Sec. Wm. A. Richardson of Jan. 30, 1874; copy in Jay Commission Papers.
[2] N. Y. *Times*, Dec. 17, 1875. Next day it announced his reappointment, "literally without a complaint." See also, N. Y. *Evening Mail* of Dec. 17, 1875.
[3] N. Y. *Tribune*, Mar. 29, 1876.
[4] *Ibid.*, Apr. 1, 1876.

of officers returned to the original total. By the time Hayes took office, the Custom House was again overmanned.

Hayes was in close communication with reform influences. Of his Cabinet, Carl Schurz was an ardent advocate of new principles respecting appointments and removals. In New York, George William Curtis was another champion, who wrote on this subject, besides his editorials in *Harper's Weekly*, a series of private letters to Hayes.[1] The newspapers discussed the subject from time to time. The *Tribune* expressed a current idea when it asserted that the object of the reform movement was the operation of government "as if it were a factory." [2] Later on, the model was shifted from industry to commerce; for the New York Custom House the standards of a "prudent merchant" were declared appropriate.[3]

Arthur did not have long to wait before the Administration moved to effect changes in New York. While Secretary Sherman was reorganizing the Bureau of Engraving and Printing at Washington and reducing its pay roll by about six hundred persons,[4] and while Schurz was examining the Department of the Interior and applying a merit system,[5] several commissions investigated the personnel and operation of the principal custom houses. The investigation at New York attracted the most attention then and interests us the most now.

When on April 9, newspapers announced that the principal custom houses would be examined, they said that the Administration anticipated greater need of reform in New York and New Orleans than elsewhere. Preliminary investigations had shown "lax administration and general neglect on the part of many of the officers in the New York Custom House." Many were practicing lawyers, including Collector Arthur, who was represented as "able to do little more than sign a few papers which are presented to him in routine, and to give instructions to politicians." [6] Moreover, though a list had been presented to him bearing names of employees accused of receiving money from

---

[1] Hayes's Papers contain fifteen letters and two telegrams from Curtis regarding Hayes's messages and specific appointments.

[2] Issue of May 5, 1877.

[3] 45th Cong., 1st sess., *House Exec. Doc. No. 8,* pp. 15, 40 (Jay Commsn. reports).

[4] N. Y. *Tribune,* Apr. 14, May 1, 1877.

[5] Report of John B. Wolff to Schurz dated Wash., Aug. 6, 1877, Hayes Papers; Claude M. Fuess, *Carl Schurz, Reformer,* pp. 243–250.

[6] On January 1, 1872, Arthur had joined Benjamin K. Phelps and Sherman W. Knevals in a law partnership. Phelps was Republican, and District Attorney; Knevals was a Democrat.

importers or brokers "for what are called 'extra services' but which payments in point of fact are little better than bribes . . . [it] is not known to have received any consideration. There are no accusations against Collector Arthur's personal integrity . . . [and] if a change should be made in this office in the interest of reform, it will not be until after a searching investigation of all the accusations above enumerated; and then it will be in the interest of a thorough reorganization of the service there." [1]

Next day, it was explained that when Secretary Bristow had got the Whisky ring "off his hands," he had accumulated data on the custom houses, including many facts to the discredit of Deputy Collector Lydecker at New York. A number of instances in which Lydecker had permitted the passage of goods without duties were described as being in behalf of "a prominent United States Senator," "a celebrated English actress," "a prominent milliner and dressmaker in New York who had among her customers many influential politicians," and so on. [2]

General Arthur was naturally indignant. He habitually ignored newspaper innuendoes, but in the present circumstances more than misinformation about himself was involved. Without permitting a direct interview, he allowed the publication of denials by "officials" at the Custom House of the charges made on the previous day, and asserted that his normal day in his office was seven hours, shortened only because of public business or to escape place hunters. Lydecker, in the service for twenty-three years, denied directly the charges against him. [3] The investigation, according to the press, was to be undertaken at once, but no changes among the officers were contemplated in Washington "until about the time of the meeting of Congress in extra session." [4]

At the beginning it was not intended to replace Arthur. Secretary Sherman was urged to remove him, but when the Jay Commission had ended its sittings, he wrote to Hayes that "after full conversation with Collector Arthur and others, I think it would be well to let him know, in any way you think advisable, that he will not be disturbed during the continuance of his present office." Years later, in his published

[1] N. Y. *Tribune,* April 9, 1877.
[2] *Ibid.,* Apr. 10, 1877.
[3] *Ibid.,* April 13, 1877.
[4] *Ibid.,* Apr. 12, 1877.

memoirs, he declared that at the outset, "there was no purpose or desire on the part of the President or anyone to make a change in the officers of the New York Custom House." [1]

A friendly attitude was manifested when Arthur was allowed to help select the members of the special investigating commission. It was intended that the three men should represent the merchants, the officers of the Port, and the Treasury Department. As the choice of the officers, John A. Dix was first agreed upon; he would have been an excellent member, with the prestige of his splendid career.[2] Arthur called on him on the morning of April 16 only to receive his refusal, which Dix explained to Secretary Sherman was prompted by family reasons.[3] After a second nominee also declined, Arthur turned to Edwin D. Morgan for advice. On Morgan's recommendation, the merchants' representative was Lawrence Turnure of Moses Taylor & Company, "a Democrat, a comparatively young and vigorous man." For the Treasury Department, Secretary Sherman named its assistant solicitor, J. H. Robinson, who then exerted himself in the choice of the third member, the chairman of the commission. As it turned out, the man named, John Jay, was not a representative of the officers of the Port.

At Sherman's request, Arthur called upon John Jay with a draft of the instructions which Sherman had drawn for the investigators, in order to emphasize Sherman's declaration that the system of business, not the personnel, was to be examined. Jay had felt a reasonable hesitancy about going on a commission to scrutinize appointees of President Grant, with whose Administration he had definitely broken; and after reading the instructions, he went to Washington for a direct explanation from Sherman. Apparently he was satisfied, for on April 25, he was named chairman.[4] The public soon knew the group as "the Jay Commission," and, from its chairman's reputation as a reformer, a former abolitionist, and an advocate of "prohibition," had confidence that it would give no "whitewashing" report.

On the day of its final organization, the commission agreed upon its

[1] John C. Hopper to Sherman, Apr. 19, 1877, Jay Commsn. Papers (Washington); John Cochrane to Sherman, Apr. 4, 1877, Sherman Papers; Sherman to Hayes, July 5, 1877, Hayes Papers; John Sherman, *Recollections of Forty Years*, Vol. II, pp. 677-9.
[2] Morgan Dix, *Memoirs of John Adams Dix*, Vol. II, pp. 213 ff.
[3] Four days later, his son, John W. Dix, died. Morgan Dix, *op. cit.*, Vol. II, p. 275.
[4] Telegrams and letters between Jay and Sherman and Robinson and Sherman, and other letters bearing on the selection of the commission are in Jay Commission Papers (Washington) and Sherman Papers.

procedure. Sherman's instructions requested them to conduct "a thorough examination into the conduct of the business of the New York Custom House." They were to observe particularly whether the force were larger than necessary; "deficient in proper attention to business, or in business qualifications, or in integrity of character"; employed for an adequate number of hours each day, or engaged in other businesses; and especially, whether appointments had been made because of political influence without due regard to efficiency. The system in the appraiser's office was marked out as another field of particular concern. To deal with these matters, the commission resolved upon secret inquiries, from which the evidence should be sent daily to Secretary Sherman for release to the press as he saw fit.[1]

After four days of closed sessions, Sherman ordered that the hearings be opened to the public. Meanwhile, Arthur had been examined, and Silas W. Burt, Comptroller and Deputy Naval Officer, had partially completed his initial appearance. The reporters were particularly interested in what Surveyor George H. Sharpe had to say. His term was nearly out, and it was not certain that he would be a candidate to succeed himself. His remarks were candid. He admitted that his department, spread out over twenty-four miles of water front for weighing, gauging, and storing importations near the piers where the vessels arrived, contained many men who were not needed. He likewise agreed that there were some evils in appointments, instancing a man who was three times dropped from the service and who admitted having defrauded the revenue, but who was urged (in vain) for reappointment by a "prominent official" who knew of his guilt. Sharpe did not know of any dismissals of men who refused to pay "political assessments." He complained, moreover, that the Custom House had to administer seventeen different laws.[2]

The commission and the press showed great concern over a letter received in evidence and included in the reports. It was dated December 30, 1873, and read as follows:

Gentlemen: Please give bearer one gallon of brandy and one gallon of gin for me. I am sorry to trouble you; but this is New Year, and I hope you will honor my order. I will reciprocate on some other occasion.

Yours respectfully,
Gauger.

[1] N. Y. *Tribune*, Apr. 26, 1877.
[2] *Ibid.*, May 1–2, 1877.

As subordinate officers in the Custom House were questioned, they agreed that the staff was larger than necessary and that some of the appointees were incompetent, one man declaring that one third of the Appraiser's force were unable to perform their duties adequately.[1] Several admitted the possibility among lesser employees of dishonesty without apprehension. Only one officer reported cases requiring discipline which to his knowledge had not been promptly acted upon. Isaac D. Balch, Chief of a division with fifty clerks, said that he knew of six or seven instances in which goods had been sent direct to a milliner before being entered for payment of duties, instead of to the official stores according to law. He had discovered this by accident, and regarded this as a very dangerous practice, but, so far as he knew, nothing had since been done to stop it. He reported also that "he had complained of two clerks for misconduct in his department. A long time afterward they were transferred to another division, and their pay was increased." Balch also believed that the tipping of clerks could be eliminated if the superior officers insisted.[2]

Arthur was perfectly aware that his opponents in the city, and all enemies of the Conkling organization, would not hesitate to turn the investigation to their advantage if possible. His fears were well justified. A front page dispatch from Washington in the *Tribune* of May 14, 1877, misrepresented him as obstructing the investigation, and reported, as facts discreditable to him which the commission had discovered, things which were utterly untrue. On the next day, the same newspaper printed a letter from Arthur to the commission, denying the truth of the dispatch, and asking if they had any evidence on which such an attack could be based. Their reply, likewise published in full, completely exonerated him.

One of the very real evils in the Custom House, undervaluation, was not within the Collector's control. For years there had been complaints against the appraiser's office. Secretary Sherman had no sooner announced the investigation than he received a letter from a former appraiser at Philadelphia and the first of several letters from another former official [3] describing in great detail how undervaluations were

---

[1] John A. Bausch, First Assistant Appraiser, N. Y. *Tribune*, May 2, 1877.

[2] N. Y. *Tribune*, May 10, 1877.

[3] Louis Blodgett to Sherman, Apr. 11, 1877, Sherman Papers; H. A. Brown, Saxonville, Mass., Apr. 11, 1877, and several others, partly in Sherman Papers, and partly in Jay Commission Papers.

accomplished. The *Fifth Annual Report* of the Silk Association of America (May 9, 1877), sent to the Jay Commission, complained of the undervaluation of silks sold on consignment by dishonest foreign manufacturers with branches in the United States. Hayes's friend, William Henry Smith, whom he had made Collector at Chicago, wrote him that "by the use of money through the brokers," importers through New York got damage allowances which reduced their duties from five to twenty per cent., and that competitors were forced to become parties to the frauds or allow themselves to be undersold. Hayes replied that, although undoubtedly true, if these old charges were to be renewed, proofs must first be at hand.[1] An employee with whom Surveyor Sharpe had had a personal conflict, insisted that he was discharged for revealing that Sharpe had connived at the use of fraudulent scales for weighing sugar imported by a certain firm.[2] But against Arthur's staff, charges of wrongdoing boiled down to accepting tips and to the imputations against Deputy-Collector Lydecker.

The evidence having indicated an excessive pay roll, the commission asked in May for reports on suitable reductions. Naval Officer Cornell thought that by adding an hour to the working day, and assuming no more business, he could do with three less clerks of one type, but that he would have too few of another. Collector Arthur received reports from the chiefs of each division, and on May 21, reported that by a uniform extension of business hours in each, the work could be accomplished with forty-three fewer clerks and storekeepers. Three days later he stated that "after careful consideration of the subject, I am led to the conclusion that by putting the force upon a basis of the closest economy, a reduction of sixty-six employees can at this time be made. . . ."[3] This would be a twelve per cent. reduction, outside the Surveyor's department. Surveyor Sharpe wrote the commission that he understood they would advocate in their report a twenty per cent. reduction in the pay roll. "Whatever reduction is made at once should be much less than the amount named, as we are now in the busiest season of the year. A large proportion . . . could be made soon, and with gradual steps to effect the remainder, I think the whole may be

[1] Hayes to Smith, Dec. 16, 1877, in C. R. Williams, ed., *Diary and Letters of R. B. Hayes,* Vol. III, pp. 454–5.
[2] Treasury Department, Exec. Files, letters of William H. Grace; pamphlet published in N. Y., 1879, *Grace's Exposure, or Unsweetened Sugars.*
[3] Jay Commission Papers.

accomplished without prejudice to the service, or to the mercantile community." [1]

The commission made its report in several sections, the first on May 24.[2] It was concerned primarily with the proportion of surplus employees and the prevailing method of appointment. Reserving the Appraiser's department for a later report, the commission recommended the elimination of approximately twenty per cent. of the 1,038 employees in other branches. This reduction was to be contingent upon the lengthening of business hours by two. Admitting certain exceptions, the commission agreed that appointments "have been made in great part under political pressure, from party considerations, and with insufficient regard to the fitness of the appointees. . . . A part of the force now employed in the service is deficient in proper attention to business, as well as in business qualifications and integrity of character. A few of them are employed more or less in private business, to the possible detriment, in some cases, of the interests of the service. . . . Some fraudulently accept moneys for services rendered in their official capacity. . . . Under the existing system, the incumbents of offices . . . however high, responsible, or difficult may be the duties, . . . are appointed generally at the request of politicians and political associations in this and other States, with little or no examination into the fitness of the appointees beyond the recommendations of their friends." What were in practice political assessments were levied on the employees, some of whom took fees, in violation of law, to reimburse themselves. "These party assessments seem to have been quietly permitted, if not openly sanctioned." [3]

There were items in this report to which General Arthur could take exception. Chiefly, the errors were traceable to the common mistake of generalizing from the particular, and took the form of describing as a general practice what was restricted to a few instances. His own statement to the commission had been ignored in their general conclusions, although they had printed it as an appendix. It had been given during the closed sessions, and so the press had not made any use of it. Not until May 26, the day on which Sherman responded to the first report with a letter to John Jay covering one from the President, did Arthur's explanations become public. He declared:

[1] Jay Commission Papers.
[2] Printed in 45th Cong., 1st sess., *House Exec. Doc. No. 8.*
[3] 45th Cong., 1st sess., *House Exec. Doc. No. 8,* pp. 14–16; N. Y. *Tribune,* May 29, 1877.

There are not so many changes made in the Custom House as is generally supposed. . . . There are not so many new appointments made as is generally supposed. . . . 286 . . . outside of the civil service rules in the whole five and one-half years. Politics have more or less to do with a large proportion of the appointments made. This is no more so here in the Custom House than throughout the whole country. . . . The man who receives this appointment may have nothing to do with politics at all, and the Collector asks no questions on that point. Recommendations . . . are always carefully examined and no appointment is made unless the man has apparently sufficient capacity for the position. The new appointments are almost always made to the lowest grade in the several divisions. . . . The applicant's qualifications are the subject of inquiry to learn whether he has clerical ability, whether he will make a competent inspector, or whether he is fit only to become a night watchman or messenger. . . . In effect, new clerks are first taken on probation and if the chiefs of divisions and the Surveyor of the Port do their duty and report cases of incapacity and want of integrity, the best only remain and the others are gradually dropped. This is the real check upon the system of appointments.[1]

Sherman transmitted the report of May 24 to President Hayes, who at the same time was informed that Arthur's Republican central committee in New York City was openly hostile to his Administration.[2] The President grasped this occasion to compose a letter expressing his aspirations for the conduct of the Custom House.

I have read the partial report of the commission appointed to examine the New York custom house. I concur with the commission in their recommendations. It is my wish that the collection of the revenues should be free from partisan control, and organized on a strictly business basis with the same guaranties for efficiency and fidelity in the selection of the chief and subordinate officers that would be required by a prudent merchant. Party leaders should have no more influence in appointments than other equally respectable citizens. No assessments for political purposes, on officers or subordinates, should be allowed. No useless officer or employee should be retained. No officer should be required or permitted to take part in the management of political organizations, caucuses, conventions, or election campaigns. Their right to vote and to express their views on public questions, either orally or through the press, is not denied, provided it does not interfere with the discharge of their official duties.[3]

One month later, the ideas of this letter were embodied in a famous

[1] N. Y. *Tribune*, May 26, 1877.
[2] James H. Welsh to Hayes, May 24, 1877, Hayes Papers.
[3] Printed in C. R. Williams, ed., *Diary & Letters of R. B. Hayes*, Vol. III, pp. 435-6; and Richardson, *Messages*, Vol. VII, p. 450.

executive order to all government employees.[1] To this standard, suddenly proclaimed, Arthur and Cornell were to be held. In the meantime, Secretary Sherman gave his approval of the twenty per cent. reduction, and ordered the Collector to execute it prior to June 30, being guided by the President's letter and certain principles laid down by the Secretary himself.[2]

The removal of over two hundred employees was truly, as Sherman designated it, "a delicate and onerous duty." Arthur, after two weeks, requested the commission to submit any testimony respecting the unfitness of any person then employed which could assist him in this task, but the request was ignored.[3] To make the preliminary recommendations, he appointed a committee of three subordinates to draw up a list of those who were to be dismissed.[4] At the same time, he instructed Surveyor Sharpe to proceed in similar fashion to reduce the roster of his department.[5] He carefully checked the lists, made suggestions, not orders, in a few cases, and then accepted responsibility for the decapitation which ensued.[6] Within the twenty per cent. reduction, the Jay Commission had recommended that the offices of four deputy collectors be abolished; but Arthur, declaring that it would increase the difficulties of importers and the liability to fraud, refused.

The commission proceeded, meanwhile, with its hearings. On June 4, it heard the views of the Committee on Revenue Reform of the New York Chamber of Commerce. The scope of its work was enlarged by Sherman's instructions that it report on the salaries of Custom House officials with a view to the reduction and classification of those not fixed by law.[7] For this purpose, it called upon the Collector for needed information, but did not prolong the hearings. Next day it heard Arthur and others in private session for a while; then the reporters were admitted and Arthur made a statement in rebuttal against testimony received by the commission.[8]

[1] June 22, 1877; Richardson, *Messages*, Vol. VII, p. 450.
[2] 45th Cong., 1st sess., *House Exec. Doc. No. 8*, pp. 17–18. Sherman to Arthur, May 28, 1877; Sherman, *Recollections*, Vol. II, pp. 675–7.
[3] Arthur to Jay Commission, June 12, 1877, Jay Commission Papers.
[4] N. Y. *Tribune*, June 7, 1877, names the committee and prints Arthur's letter of instructions to it.
[5] Sharpe's committee is named. *Ibid.*, June 9, 1877.
[6] The work of his own committee was described by one of its members, Richard Grant White, in *North American Review*, CXXXV (Oct., 1882), pp. 46–7, in an article on "The Business of Office-Seeking."
[7] N. Y. *Tribune*, June 5, 1877.
[8] *Ibid.*, June 6, 1877.

On June 8, the commission adjourned to draw up their remaining reports, letting it be known that they would not feel bound to consult Collector Arthur in respect to any of their recommendations. They continued to receive documents from him, including one of special importance dated June 13,[1] listing the ninety employees of the Collector's department holding responsible positions with salaries of two thousand dollars or more. Seventy-nine were said to have reached those positions by promotion, fifty-nine of them by his orders, after many years of subordinate service. Eight were appointed by Arthur's predecessors. Three were appointed by Arthur after similar experience elsewhere had demonstrated their competence. It had become apparent to Arthur, that if the strictures of the first report could be derived from the scanty basis in fact made known to the Jay Commission, subsequent reports were almost certain to reflect more seriously upon his administration. He hastened to anticipate accusations by such exonerations, denials, and mitigating circumstances as he could get into the commission's records.

That his apprehensions were warranted was demonstrated by the second report, sent to Secretary Sherman on July 4.[2] Acknowledging that changes in the laws and regulations were required before the Custom House could be well run, the commission insisted that improvements in the personnel must first be effected. To support this conclusion they offered a description of prevailing conditions. The wholesale language in which they described the shortcomings in the staff was of dubious truth in the light of the evidence. A most damaging effect was created by their reporting, as current events, delinquencies actually occurring in several different years. In response to Sherman's request that they consider salaries paid in the Custom House, they gave a series of classifications; for the most part paying salaries as great as or greater than those that prevailed. Sherman, on July 24, approved the recommendations and requested Arthur and Cornell to recommend appropriate numbers of officials to fall within each classification.[3]

The third and fourth reports were submitted on July 21 and August 31.[4] They had reference to the department of weighers and gaugers

[1] Jay Commission Papers.
[2] 45th Cong., 1st sess., *House Exec. Doc. No. 8*, pp. 36–49.
[3] *Ibid.*, pp. 42–3.
[4] *Ibid.*, pp. 50 ff.

under the Surveyor of the Port, and to the Appraiser's department. In each they recommended great reductions in pay roll and improvement in the qualifications of the men. In the Appraiser's department, a rather extensive reorganization was urged to promote efficiency, to overcome frauds in valuations, and to check dishonest damage allowances. The sweeping changes in law and regulations requested by the New York Chamber of Commerce they thought should await a restoration of public confidence in the efficiency and integrity of the personnel.

At this point, not before, according to Secretary Sherman, the intention of replacing Arthur, Cornell, and Sharpe was broached by President Hayes. He had been persuaded that "the public service would be best promoted by a general change, that new officers would be more likely to make the radical reforms required than those then in the custom house." [1] A most untimely discovery that six inspectors of passengers' baggage at New York were guilty of receiving bribes for passing baggage without inspection was announced on September 1, and on that day, Arthur read in his *Tribune* a Washington dispatch as follows:

The reorganization of the New York Custom House and the appointment of new men to the most important positions in it—such as those of Collector, Surveyor, and Naval Officer—was incidentally mentioned in the Cabinet meeting today; but its formal consideration was postponed until next week, in order that it may be discussed in the presence of Secretary Evarts, who is expected to return on Monday or Tuesday. It is at least certain that no conclusion has yet been reached by the President and his Cabinet on this subject; but there is now every indication that it will be disposed of before the President starts on his Western and Southern tour, either by a request . . . to tender their resignations, or a decision to allow all of them except Surveyor Sharpe, whose term of office has expired, to remain until after the meeting of Congress.

Evarts may have had less legislative experience than others in Hayes's Cabinet,[2] notably John Sherman, but he appears to have dominated it. With his sharply aquiline face lighted by brilliant gray eyes, he sat at the President's right hand, stating his opinions with a flashing wit and terseness of expression quite the reverse of his custom

[1] Sherman, *Recollections*, Vol. II, p. 679.
[2] See my article, "President Hayes's Notes of Four Cabinet Meetings" in *American Historical Review*, Jan., 1932, pp. 286-9.

in court. He was a Yankee, with Yankee traits, among them the thrifty use of paper by running his lines to the very edge of the page and resorting to many hyphens. He was not a civil service reformer of the Schurz-Curtis school, nor was he an organization man of Conkling's type. He did not believe in either entirely disregarding or entirely considering politics in appointments to office. At the same time, he was quite disgusted with such restraint on nominations to elective office as the New York machine exerted. To demolish that organization, he believed, would be a service to the party, and to wrest the Custom House from their grasp would go far to end their sway. Sherman considered Evarts responsible for the decision to remove Arthur and Cornell.[1] Evarts may have suggested it to the President, or he may have sustained the President's initiative against Sherman and others, but he seems to have been responsible.

On September 4, the "long-looked-for changes in the administration of the New York Custom House" were again postponed; the decision of Hayes's Cabinet was declared to depend on the action of Naval Officer Cornell. If he resigned his chairmanship of the State Committee promptly, "the President and Cabinet will undoubtedly postpone taking any action in his case for the present,.since it is their desire to avoid even the appearance of doing injustice to any Government official. . . . It is not at all certain but that a clean sweep of all three of the highest officers . . . will be made . . . should Cornell neglect to resign before Thursday. . . . On this point, the Administration has evidently made up its mind." Hayes was told that Cornell's friends desired a delay, and would be much exasperated by an abrupt suspension.[2]

Arthur's fate, it thus appears, was intertwined with that of an associate whose particular blameworthiness lay in publicly flouting the executive order of June 22, 1877, forbidding government officials to participate in political management. As head of the State's organization, Cornell openly defied the order's injunctions. He was unwilling to resign, making instead a proposition which "virtually complied with the President's order," [3] and later defending himself by saying that he had been ready to retire from the State Committee when his term

[1] Sherman to Garfield, Jan. 23, 1881, Garfield Papers. Evarts to Hayes, Mar. 29, 1881, in Hayes Papers.
[2] N. Y. *Tribune,* Sept. 5, 1877; R. C. McCormick to Sherman (telegram), Sept. 4, 1877, Sherman Papers.
[3] McCormick to Sherman, Sept. 6, 1877, Sherman Papers.

ended, that all that remained of his duties was to summon two conventions, and that Hayes had agreed that this was unobjectionable.[1]

As Collector, Arthur was engaged in political management quite as publicly as Cornell. He was the recognized Republican "boss" of New York City. So long as either man remained in the Custom House, there could be no faithful compliance with Hayes's more extreme demands. For that reason, with a view to smashing the machine, and with a hardihood that quite overshadowed their discretion, Hayes and his advisers determined that Arthur, Cornell, and even Sharpe, the Surveyor whose term was so nearly out, should retire in favor of a new dispensation.

[1] *The Nation,* July 18, 1878.

THE newspapers of September 7, 1877, announced the Administration's decision to replace Arthur and Cornell and sought to explain it. The Washington dispatches presented the Administration's view, that Arthur, Cornell, and Sharpe were identified with the old régime, that they would undoubtedly obey instructions, "but they certainly could not have that interest which new officers not identified with the old order of things might feel in the success of reforms." [1] It might have been observed then, as it was later, that Arthur had made many of the same recommendations as the Jay Commission, and much earlier; and that their other suggestions, he showed to be undesirable. Instead, the *Tribune,* for example, described him as "a good natured and popular man" upon whom the public had mistakenly counted to reform the Custom House as Thomas L. James had cleaned up the Post Office. The Jay Commission's report indicated "that abuses still prevailed . . . which no political exigencies could ever have excused, and that the Collector who tolerated or failed to discover them would have to go." [2]

Evarts, as some suspected, may have wished to foster new leadership in the Republican organization in New York by introducing a fresh management into the Custom House. [3] Hayes, however, was not concerned with making an opportunity for another and different machine, but with taking the Custom House out of politics altogether. Sherman "preferred to try to execute the proposed reforms with . . . [Arthur] in office," [4] according to his own private statement; and, being denied that opportunity, tried to soften the asperities of the removal as best he could. Thus he wrote to John Jay that the changes had been "determined," but to Arthur described them as "probable," and at the same time conceded that more evidence was needed before he could act on the Jay Commission's report respecting the weighers' department. [5] He invited Arthur to Washington for a consultation, and,

[1] N. Y. *Tribune,* Sept. 7, 1877.
[2] *Ibid.*
[3] N. Y. *Sun,* July 12, 1878.
[4] Sherman to Justin S. Morrill, Dec. 14, 1878, Sherman Papers.
[5] Sherman to Jay; Sherman to Arthur, Sept. 7, 1877, Jay Commission Papers.

through a common friend, Governor R. C. McCormick, who had been secretary of the Republican national committee in the campaign of 1876, conveyed his desire that the changes be understood as prefacing a new system in the Custom House rather than as reflecting in any way upon the characters of the men removed. Governor McCormick reported to Sherman that Cornell's removal would not cause so much feeling as that of Arthur, "who is really very popular. I have just seen him and his only regret is that he was not permitted to resign before there was any announcement of a determination to remove him." [1]

On September 17, Arthur spent several hours in consultation with Sherman, insisting that he had anticipated most of the recommendations of the Jay Commission in his correspondence with Sherman's predecessors, and that the commission had shown willingness to hear unfavorable but not favorable testimony.[2] There was still time for the Administration to reverse itself, but not much likelihood of it. Arthur did not wish to resign during the investigation, but was expected by Sherman to retire at its conclusion. Before the end of October it was clear that he and Cornell must be forced out if others were to be appointed, and that the Conkling machine was unalterably antagonized by the Administration's course.

The Republicans of New York assembled on September 26 at Rochester in a convention thoroughly controlled by the Conkling organization. Hayes's inaugural address had declared that an "officer should be secure in his tenure as long as his personal character remained untarnished and the performance of his duty satisfactory," and that legislation might be desirable providing for a fixed tenure during which officers might be removed only by some species of impeachment.[3] These views received special praise in the New York platform, with the obvious implication that they had not been followed in the Custom House controversy.

George William Curtis understood the absence of an endorsement of Hayes's Administration to constitute a censure. He therefore offered a resolution declaring Hayes's title to the Presidency to be as "clear and perfect as that of George Washington," supporting his proposal with a brilliant speech not free from uncomplimentary allusions to

[1] Sherman, *Recollections*, Vol. II, pp. 680–1; McCormick to Sherman, Sept. 7, 1877, Sherman Papers.
[2] N. Y. *Tribune*, Sept. 18, 1877; Sherman, *Recollections*, Vol. II, p. 681.
[3] Richardson, *Messages*, Vol. VII, pp. 444–5.

Conkling and Platt. Conkling at once took the floor. In a speech of considerable length, he gave deliberate expression to a long-matured hatred of Curtis and all he stood for.

"Who are these men, who, in newspapers or elsewhere, are cracking their whips over Republicans and playing schoolmaster to the Republican Party? . . . They are of various sorts and conditions. Some of them are the man-milliners [shouted Conkling, shaking a long finger at Curtis], the dilettante and carpet knights of politics, men whose efforts have been expended in denouncing and ridiculing and accusing honest men. . . . Some of them are men who, when they could work themselves into conventions, have attempted to belittle and befoul Republican Administrations and to parade their own thin veneering of superior purity. Some of them are men who, by insisting that it is corrupt and bad for men in office to take part in politics, are striving now to prove that the Republican Party has been unclean and vicious all its life. . . . Some of these worthies masquerade as reformers. Their vocation and ministry is to lament the sins of other people. Their stock in trade is rancid, canting self-righteousness. They are wolves in sheep's clothing. Their real object is office and plunder. When Dr. Johnson defined patriotism as the last refuge of a scoundrel, he was unconscious of the then undeveloped capabilities and uses of the word reform. . . . They forget that parties are not built up by deportment, or by ladies' magazines, or gush. . . . For extreme license in criticism of administrations and of everybody connected with them, broad arguments can no doubt be found. Many might be found in the files of the journal made famous by the pencil of Nast. But a convention may not deem itself a chartered libertine of oracular and pedantic conceits." Closing with a denunciation of Curtis which he declared was restrained by the "proprieties" of the occasion, he suggested as a fitting model the judgment of a dispute between two Crusaders: "Let the future decide between you, and let it declare for him who carries furthest into the ranks of the enemy the sword of the cross." [1]

By a vote of 295 to 105, Curtis's resolution was rejected; Hayes's Administration remained unendorsed. This spectacular encounter between the two factional leaders was the fruit of a long personal antagonism, immeasurably fostered by Curtis's part in defeating Conkling's presidential ambitions. But the fury of Conkling's "defense" may also

[1] See A. R. Conkling, *Life of Roscoe Conkling*, pp. 538–49.

indicate the leader's realization that his machine was being not simply hindered and injured, but threatened with complete destruction. If the Custom House were to be used by some new leader as it had been in the past, Conkling's organization was doomed. If it were to be taken out of politics and if, in addition, the Democrats could be driven from Albany, success might reward the energies lavished by Conkling, Arthur, and the others to maintain control of the party. But since the Democrats might persist in victory, whether the Custom House became anti-Conkling or not, the prospect for Conkling's associates was gloomy and forbidding. He was naturally resolved to hold firmly every advantage then possessed, to fight Hayes, Evarts, and if need be Sherman, and, within New York, to fight the reform wing also.

If there had been the slightest irresolution as to the Custom House changes, when Hayes returned from his Western trip for the special session of Congress on October 15 he had fully determined to force the retirement of Arthur and Cornell. Sherman assured an applicant for the place, who had written on October 11, that it was too late for him to enter the lists.[1] On October 24, the President nominated Theodore Roosevelt for Collector, Edwin A. Merritt for Surveyor, and L. Bradford Prince for Naval Officer, to replace the incumbents.[2]

Roosevelt was one of the best-esteemed citizens of New York City, distinctly not an active politician. Prince, Sherman had been told, was "neither a Conkling man nor a Curtis man," [3] but further information had come, just too late to prevent his nomination from going in, that he had been open to the suspicion of complicity with Tweed when a member of the legislature.[4] Edwin A. Merritt, as Naval Officer in 1869 and 1870, had been a member of Fenton's organization. He was in 1872 a Liberal Republican, but had returned to "regular" Republicanism in 1874. The three nominees were not confirmed at the special session.

When Hayes had given his first annual message to Congress on December 6, 1877, and had again sent in the nominations of Roosevelt, Prince, and Merritt, he received a delegation from New York led by Postmaster James, which submitted a letter, signed by fifteen of the seventeen Republican New York Congressmen, asking the retention of

---

[1] Opdycke to Sherman, Oct. 11, 1877; Sherman to Opdycke, Oct. 12, 1877, Sherman Papers.
[2] See *Exec. Journal of the Senate*, Vol. XXI, pp. 98–9.
[3] C. C. Norwell to Sherman, Oct. 20, 1877, Sherman Papers.
[4] Geo. Wm. Curtis to Sherman, telegram and letter, Oct. 25, 1877, Hayes Papers.

Arthur, Cornell, and Sharpe. In the message just conveyed to Congress
was a passage which directly opposed the appearance of such a delegation in his office. Now, confronted by this group, he turned to a copy
of the Republican platform adopted in Cincinnati the preceding year,
and read to them as follows:

Under the Constitution, the President and heads of departments are to
make nominations for office; the Senate is to advise and consent to appointments, and the House of Representatives is to accuse and prosecute faithless
officers. The best interest of the public service demands that these distinctions
be respected; that Senators and Representatives, who may be judges and
accusers, should not dictate appointments to office.[1]

The New York group is said to have retired at once, in silence.[2]

On December 11, Merritt's nomination to succeed Sharpe (whose
term had expired) was reported favorably; the others', unfavorably.
Next day, "Senatorial courtesy" was upheld by Conkling's colleagues
when a vote of thirty-one to twenty-five sustained the objections to
Roosevelt. Prince, also, was rejected, but Merritt was confirmed.[3]
Arthur felt relieved. He continued in office, trying to meet the criticisms
of the Jay Commission and to use the evidence of dishonesty and fraud
unearthed by them to purify the staff. Certainly he had no reason to
think that Secretary Sherman expected the Custom House to be
operated with no regard for politics in the appointment of its employees. During the investigation, Sherman requested the appointment
of a man to please ex-President Grant; the day before the replacement
of Arthur, Cornell, and Sharpe was determined, he made other requests
of a similar sort; and in October, when it was decided to remove
Arthur and Cornell, since they would not resign, more appointments
or promotions were urged on grounds not approved by the reformers.[4]
Sherman knew that "parties are not built up by deportment, or by
ladies' magazines, or gush," and under different circumstances he
would probably have been gratified to coöperate with Arthur in improving the Custom House without resorting to extreme measures.
He had received from the Collector a long letter of defense against

[1] Edward Stanwood, *A History of Presidential Elections*, pp. 316–17.
[2] *Harper's Weekly*, Jan. 5, 1878, p. 2.
[3] *Exec. Journal of the Senate*, Vol. XXI, pp. 171–2.
[4] Sherman Papers, *passim;* Hayes to Sherman, Oct. 18, 1877, respecting appointment of
Corporal James Tanner as Auditor in the New York Custom House, Treasury Dept., Exec.
Files, 1877.

the findings of the Jay Commission,[1] which may well have impressed him.

General Arthur's letter was a complete review of the Jay Commission's methods and conclusions, its contents partly indicated by his remarks before that body. He complained that upon the commission, once John A. Dix had declined, the officers of the Port had no representative, all three members being picked by the Treasury Department. Their reception of some testimony not under oath, and of all without cross-examination and little rebuttal, led, he insisted, to one-sided reports which ignored the fact that no complaints had been made by "prominent and honorable merchants of this port," nor in regard to events of the past five years. The commission had hunted for evils and made no reference to improvements effected under Arthur, changes which promised still further betterment in the future. But even though they confined themselves to the shortcomings instead of giving a balanced description, the evidence did not support their "sweeping and general allegations." For example, in the first of their reports, dealing with the methods of appointments and promotions, they noted what the Collector and Surveyor had to say about complaints against employees, "but remembered to forget to add my further statement that all such complaints were investigated and acted upon." Allowing for the fact that evidence of bribery seemed impossible to get, General Arthur insisted that in following civil service principles respecting removals only for cause, promotions for merit, and prompt investigation of complaints and punishment of misconduct, he had surpassed any other branch of the government, present or past.

The Collector then turned to the recommendations made by the commission and declared: "Those which are not repetitions of recommendations long since made by me are chiefly unwise or impracticable, while one of them is in direct violation of the law." One after another, he took them up and maintained this characterization. The reduction of the force was too great and had been so demonstrated. He had arranged for a smaller (12%) reduction with Sherman's predecessor. The lengthening of hours from nine to four o'clock instead of from ten to three, had given many clerks nothing to do in the first hour and the "pressure which formerly existed between two o'clock and

---

[1] Dated November 23, 1877, and printed in 45th Cong., 2nd sess., *House Exec. Doc. No. 25*, pp. 7–16, and appendices.

three [had] . . . been transferred to the hour between three and four." For several years, clerks, brokers, and others "who violate [d] the law as to paying fees" had been excluded from the Custom House as had all those guilty of "any improper or irregular conduct whatsoever." The broad charges of misconduct against weighers and gaugers were based either on no evidence, or on testimony not transmitted to the Collector, as he requested, to help him to clear out the incompetent and dishonest. Unequivocally, and with forceful candor, Arthur met the indictments in the Jay Commission reports. It was, of course, a special plea [1] by a man defending himself, and had nothing to say about that relation of custom-house patronage to politics in New York and the rest of the country which Hayes wished to abolish. The letter, however, was written to a practical politician! [2]

Once the Senate had refused to confirm Roosevelt and Prince, Hayes might have nominated others had there been prospect of any advantage. The Administration, however, bided its time without any intention of dropping the matter. Hayes wrote in his diary:

In the language of the press, "Senator Conkling has won a great victory over the Administration." My New York nominations were rejected, thirty-one to twenty-five. But the end is not yet. I am right and shall not give up the contest.[3]

Secretary Sherman made more suggestions to Arthur for appointments on political or personal grounds, and took a very "practical" attitude.[4] When Theodore Roosevelt died in February, Sherman began

---

[1] A student of this controversy, Venila L. Shores ("The Hayes-Conkling Controversy," *Smith College Studies in History,* Vol. IV, No. 4, p. 237), concludes that this letter was somewhat irrelevant. Arthur "seemed to forget that the commission was not expected to decide whether the services were good or bad; its duty was merely to report to its superior, . . . in regard to complaints made, and to describe any conditions then existing which its members did not consider for the best interests of the service." One must observe that in this letter, Arthur criticizes the commission for reporting unfounded "complaints" and for describing "conditions" of which the testimony submitted to it did not conclusively prove the existence. In the second place, he was insisting to "its superior" that the valid findings did not warrant the removal of the Collector, whose record indicated that he would have been gratified to carry them out had his own recommendations been acted upon, in earlier years.

[2] John Jay, in an article on "Civil Service Reform" in the *North American Review,* Vol. CXXVII (1878), pp. 273–87, replied to Arthur's contentions. He pointed out that of some ninety witnesses, seventy were Custom House officials; suggested that many importers were intimidated and so did not testify adversely to the existing system; and fell back upon the instructions from Sherman as justification for not meeting Arthur's ideas of fairness in the methods employed.

[3] Williams, ed., *Diary & Letters,* Vol. III, p. 454.

[4] Sherman to Arthur, Jan. 7, 23, 1878, Sherman Papers.

to think of another substitute for Arthur. Whitelaw Reid, editor of the *Tribune,* urged that any nominee "be a man equal to all the practical duties of the place, which are necessarily and essentially political as well as mercantile." Sherman "fully concurred in" Reid's "general view of the considerations that should control the proposed appointment in New York." [1] Had Arthur known of this correspondence, it would have confirmed his suspicions that his removal would be used to strengthen some other Republican faction.

At the Custom House, matters went on in the first months of 1878 much as usual. Arthur left in June for his annual brief fishing trip to Canada, having spent the winter and spring executing some of the Jay Commission's recommendations which Sherman had approved. Hayes, on the basis of subsequent investigations, was easily convinced that Arthur had followed these orders "reluctantly" and that while he continued in office, there could be no hope of "systematic reforms or changes." [2]

In July, a special Treasury commission was again inspecting the management of the Custom House, looking for evils, and finding, according to rumor, much more serious derelictions than the Jay Commission had reported.[3] As before, all serious criticisms tended to implicate Deputy Collector Lydecker, who complained that he had been charged unjustly with nearly everything "except stealing Charley Ross." [4] With public opinion again stirred up, Secretary Sherman paid a visit to New York, and, on July 10, after calling at the Sub-Treasury, walked to the Custom House for an interview with Collector Arthur. Reporters, asking Arthur what the visit implied, were told, characteristically: "His visit at this time has a bearing upon several things which may become interesting to the public." [5]

Two days later, the public learned that upon the adjournment of Congress, Arthur and Cornell had been suspended from their offices and that temporary commissions, requiring Senate confirmation to become definitive, had been issued to Surveyor Merritt and Silas W. Burt to become Collector and Naval Officer, respectively.[6] Silas W. Burt,

---

[1] Reid to Sherman, Mar. 29, 1878, Sherman, *Recollections,* Vol. II, p. 683; Sherman to Reid, Apr. 2, 1878, Sherman Papers.
[2] Williams, *Life of Rutherford B. Hayes,* Vol. II, p. 91; N. Y. *Tribune,* July 12, 1878.
[3] N. Y. *Tribune,* July 12, 1878.
[4] *Ibid.,* July 13, 1878.
[5] *Ibid.,* July 12, 1878.
[6] L. Bradford Prince was not renominated, but in January, 1879, became chief justice

thus brought into the public eye, was an able man, with whom Arthur was well acquainted. At Union College, Burt was in the class just below Arthur's. During the Civil War, he had been Auditor of New York, and had received Arthur's commendation. Burt had been for some time the Deputy Naval Officer and was something of a civil service reformer. His appointment met with no protest, but Merritt's was not pleasing to some of the Administration's New York advisers.[1]

From his summer home in Windsor, Vt., Evarts wrote Hayes: "It seems to me so clear that these changes are both useful to the public service and to the unity of the party that I cannot anticipate any long discontent." To divert "spleen and criticism of the irrevocable," he recommended leaving the Surveyorship open for "some little time" to absorb the energies of the politicians.[2]

There was plenty of "discontent" and some "spleen." The New York *Sun* described the suspensions as "a blow aimed at Mr. Conkling by Hayes, Sherman and Evarts . . . bent on his defeat." The *Tribune* praising Arthur's letters to Sherman, asserted that "the course of the Administration . . . has been inconsistent, injudicious, and unmanly. The whacking which General Arthur has given the Administration has not been undeserved." *The Nation* could see no transformation to a new system of appointments and promotions in view, but simply a reorganization of the New York Republicans in a way which would ensure Conkling's defeat at the senatorial election to be held in January next.[3] Hayes himself felt that there should have been a statement of reform motives at the time of the suspensions, and confessed that the affair had been inefficiently managed.[4]

While Merritt perfected arrangements for his bond, Arthur spent his last week as Collector. "Local politicians and personal friends" thronged his offices to express their condolences, but he was ready for a rest and, after it, for the vigorous political activity he anticipated. At four o'clock on July 19, 1878, at the close of business, Merritt presented a letter from Secretary Sherman requesting General Arthur

of the supreme court of New Mexico Territory, *Exec. Journal of Senate,* Vol. XXI, pp. 431, 454.
    [1] J. M. Bundy to Sherman, July 13, 1878, Sherman Papers. See also James H. Welsh to Hayes, Dec. n.d., 1877, Hayes Papers.
    [2] Evarts to Hayes, July 13, 1878, Hayes Papers.
    [3] Curtis protested against appointing any "Fenton politicians," to Hayes, Aug. 20, 1878, Hayes Papers.
    [4] Hayes to William Henry Smith, Aug. 8, 1878, in Williams, ed., *Diary & Letters,* Vol. III, p. 496.

to relinquish the office to his successor. Arthur and Merritt exchanged a few "cordial" remarks and, as a last official act, the former promoted a former weigher to a clerkship. As an unofficial closing, he "drank a parting glass of wine" with Merritt and bade farewell to his deputies.[1] Thus he left the scene of over six years of active life and power.

During the summer, the Custom House controversy was temporarily calm. Merritt revamped the personnel and set about establishing a better record than his predecessor's for economy in collection. Neither he nor Sherman was unaware of the struggle which probably lay before them. Conkling was quietly observing the growth of the Greenback-Labor movement in his State, the menace it offered to Republican success serving to unite the hitherto quarreling factions. On September 26, the New York Republicans met at Saratoga for the State convention. A week before, Sherman had advised John Jay that "any expression of opinion by your State convention or by your people that will strengthen me in this effort [to make the suspensions permanent] will be gratefully received." [2] To Senator Samuel J. Kirkwood of Iowa he wrote, a month before the opening of Congress, "The truth is, the Custom House in New York needs a bold overhauling in Congress and I wish you would take it up and master the subject. I will cheerfully give you the facts upon which you could act." [3] Meanwhile, he prepared a bill of complaints to submit to the Senate when the time should come and, in his annual report, took pleasure in the statement that there had been great savings in collecting the revenue.[4]

Arthur's mastery of New York City politics did not cease when he retired from the Custom House. With the freedom obtained by his temporary release, he undertook the election of a mayor and managed the campaign of Edward Cooper. Since the City Republicans were a minority, they needed to fuse with the anti-Tammany Democrats under the leadership of Irving Hall. It was nothing new. The City Republicans had always had to coöperate with one faction of the Democrats to secure anything. In the course of the campaign, Arthur was attacked as a sovereign, who "dictated the nomination of Edward Cooper to the Anti-Tammany Democrats when they preferred another man. Chester A. Arthur will be Mayor of New York if Edward Cooper is elected."

[1] N. Y. *Tribune*, July 20, 1878.
[2] Sherman to Jay, Sept. 18, 1877, Sherman Papers.
[3] Sherman to Kirkwood, Nov. 7, 1878, Sherman Papers.
[4] Sec. of Treas., *Annual Report*, 1878, p. vii.

Arthur's success in this election prefaced a canvass for his own nomination for Governor in 1879.[1]

In compliance with the Tenure-of-Office Act, President Hayes sent the recess nominations of Merritt and Burt to the Senate for action at its first executive session in December, 1878. The nominations were referred to the committee on commerce, whose chairman for some years had been Roscoe Conkling. It was hoped that he would not resist confirmation, in view of the fact that he was then seeking reëlection by the New York legislature. Merritt, however, soon reported that **Conkling** was "belligerent" and could be expected to fight vigorously, aided perhaps by nine Democratic Senators. He urged a canvass of the Senate.[2] After sending supplementary communications, he wrote to Sherman, one month later:

In reply to your personal letter of the 8th [January, 1879] inst. . . . I can only say that I cannot add anything to the evidence already in your possession which seems to me to be of value for the purpose you suggest. Whatever relates to neglect of duty, or intrusting Govt. interests to unworthy hands, whereby, through negligence or corruption, much loss was occasioned to the revenue, are matters which, I suppose, if sustained at all, must be by evidence already furnished you from various sources. . . .

While in Albany, I ascertained that it was the deliberate purpose of Mr. Conkling and his friends to insure rejections of the nominations, if possible, and that they felt confident of their ability to accomplish it. Mr. Cornell for some time past, I understand, was disposed to withdraw from the contest, but that purpose has been changed—at least until after a rejection has been effected. . . .

It is reported, upon what I regard as pretty good authority, that Mr. Tilden is now advising his Democratic friends to support Mr. Conkling in this movement. . . .[3]

When action was delayed, on January 15 Sherman sent off a letter to the Senate advancing reasons for removing Arthur and Cornell. The next day's New York *World* summarized its contents. The reasons were no longer general; specific accusations designed to influence practical politicians were at last being made.

Arthur, the Senate was told, did not devote his attention to his official duties, but came late to the office and allowed Deputy Collector

[1] N. Y. *World*, Nov. 26, 1878.
[2] Merritt to Sherman, Dec. 4, 1878, Sherman Papers; Merritt to Hayes, Dec. 6, 1878, Hayes Papers.
[3] Merritt to Sherman, Jan. 11, 1879, Sherman Papers.

Lydecker to do the work. His office was carelessly, inefficiently, and recklessly managed. Since Merritt's advent in July, the costs of collection had been materially reduced from the excessive rates prevailing before. Lydecker had let in large quantities of goods duty-free and in other ways violated the law. Cornell did nothing as Naval Officer, but, leaving the work to Deputy Naval Officer Burt, occupied himself with political management. The Custom House had been so operated as to discriminate in favor of New York merchants and those who imported goods through New York instead of other ports.[1]

Sherman's letter was evidence that the Administration had entirely changed its tactics. The suspensions could be made permanent only by obtaining Senate support. Hayes might wish to base the removals on the need for an entirely new system of civil service appointments, but Sherman had been a Senator and knew the temper of that body. He intended to convince them (and the people who sent them to Congress) that the Custom House had been so badly managed that to keep the suspended men in office would be an encouragement of dishonesty, inefficiency, and local favoritism. He had to win. His own prestige was at stake. If he lost, he intended to resign. He had broken irretrievably with Arthur, Cornell, and Conkling; his only hope of New York support for his presidential candidacy in 1880 lay in the rising group who had long opposed the Conkling machine. The successful resumption of specie payments in January, 1879, was redounding to his credit with business men. It was now time to win favor with the reformers.

Collector Merritt was urged by Sherman to be "active" in the contest. "Only just for you and Burt and General Graham to be active in your defense," he wrote. "Any evidence of discontent at Albany with the position taken by Mr. Conkling, although it may not be successful, will be a check upon him. . . . Local influences should be brought to bear on Mr. Kernan." [2]

Conkling was seeking reëlection at Albany at this time. With Arthur and Cornell in the lobby to help him, he received the support of the Republican caucus without opposition. The Republicans held a substantial majority of the legislature, and on January 21 he was chosen

---

[1] N. Y. *World,* Jan. 16, 1879.
[2] Democratic Senator from N. Y. Sherman tried to see Kernan on January 28, but he was "called to N. Y." Sherman to Merritt, Jan. 18, 1879, Sherman Papers. See also Merritt to Sherman, Jan. 20, 22, 1879, Sherman Papers.

for another six years at Washington. Up to that time he had kept quiet in the Custom House appointments then before his committee of the Senate. Sherman's letter of January 15 had provoked no immediate reply. While Arthur and Cornell prepared their answers, Conkling made no move, even ignoring Sherman's request that copies of the answers be sent to him.[1]

Becoming alarmed, Sherman telegraphed for all the Jay Commission's papers. At the same time, the files of his department were ransacked for stray ammunition. During the period after his first letter, the intentions of Senators of both parties were carefully canvassed. Sherman had made some headway among the Republicans by a letter sent to Senator Justin S. Morrill of Vermont.[2] He was told on January 23 that "the Democrats will stand *solid* with perhaps one and possibly two exceptions, and if therefore even eight Republicans vote right, the result will be as we wish." [3] By the new line of argument which he was advancing, he expected to induce more than eight Republicans to "vote right."

On January 27, the Senate again took up the New York Custom House nominations. Secrecy was removed, Sherman's letter and replies from Arthur and Cornell were ordered to be printed and sent to the President, and next day's newspapers were full of the controversy.

General Arthur's answer to Sherman's complaints to the Senate was a long and carefully composed document sent to "Hon. Roscoe Conkling, Chairman," on January 21. Much of it was a restatement of his letter to Sherman of November 23, 1877.[4] In addition, he claimed to have introduced before his removal every reform authorized by the Treasury Department and attributed by Sherman to Collector Merritt, thus setting at rest the charge that he was unwilling to coöperate with the Hayes Administration in improving Custom House practice. Of the fifteen recommendations for changes made by the Jay Commission, two, he wrote, referred to procedure already followed, eight were repetitions of Arthur's own previous recommendations, one was unwise, one both unwise and illegal, and two referred to matters not under control of the Collector, but directly under the Treasury Department.

The alleged loss of income at New York due to his administration of

[1] N. Y. *World,* Jan. 27, 1879.
[2] Dec. 14, 1878, Sherman Papers.
[3] Beverly Tucker to Sherman, Jan. 23, 1879, Sherman Papers.
[4] 45th Cong., 2nd sess., *House Exec. Doc. No. 25,* pp. 7–16.

the Custom House, he protested, should be attributed to the business depression after 1873 and to changes in tariff duties. The figures offered by Sherman to show the increased expenses were made up by charging against the cost of collection many improper items. In the matter of free passage of goods, of which Deputy Collector Lydecker was accused, Arthur explained that the practice had prevailed for eighty years and that blanks used in such cases were furnished by the Treasury Department. Since Merritt's advent, at least thirteen hundred such permits had been issued. An instance of which Sherman had made much, when goods worth $53,000 were so admitted, Arthur described as entirely legal, upheld by a special investigation, and in no sense corrupt. The importation was, in fact, some jewelry belonging to the mother of James Gordon Bennett, which she had taken abroad before her death, and which had been sent back to become part of her estate. Finally, Arthur stated that while he often got to his office at noon, he did some work at home where he was free from callers, remained at the task late at night, if necessary, to complete it promptly, and exercised practically all the discretionary authority of the Collector in person.

It was a strong letter and did much to neutralize Sherman's charges. The Secretary, working over the Jay Commission papers and other documents, got off a rejoinder which, accompanied by a letter from President Hayes, was read to the Senate on January 31. The President, after dwelling particularly on his desire to take the Custom House out of politics, concluded:

> I regard it as my plain duty to suspend the officers in question and to make the nominations now before the Senate, in order that this important office may be honestly and efficiently administered.[1]

Sherman's second letter was a reiteration of his earlier attacks, on a level rather different from most of the President's message. It was offset by another of Arthur's letters to Conkling, elaborating on parts of his first. But among the Senators Sherman's extensive acquaintance, and possibly the patronage of his department, was used advantageously. To Allison of Iowa he sent a letter in which he pointed out that "if the restoration of Arthur is insisted upon, the whole liberal element will be against us and it will lose us tens of thousands of votes without

[1] Richardson, *Messages,* Vol. VII, pp. 511–12.

doing a particle of good. . . . It will be a personal reproach to me, and merely to gratify the insane hate of Conkling. . . ." [1] Allison was asked to show the letter to Senator Windom. When Conkling wished the question voted upon, a motion to postpone until Monday, February 3, was carried despite his objections, 35 to 26, ten Republicans voting against him. The question was not exactly a test vote, but Sherman was told that "the indications certainly are very encouraging." [2]

Conkling had reason to fear what the result would be on Monday. His control in New York was supreme.[3] But though New York Republicans might accept his domination, at Washington his chief resource was "Senatorial courtesy," the custom among Senators of the same party of sustaining each other in questions of patronage against the Chief Executive. While Conkling was mulling over the evil possibilities, President Hayes wrote in his diary what he would do if Conkling should be defeated:

In that case, I will lay down the law to my New York officers according to the doctrines of the strictest sect of civil service reformers. . . .

I shall say to General Merritt: Disregard all influence, all solicitation, all pressure—even if it come from me, or his immediate chief, the Secretary of the Treasury.[4]

The Senate met at one o'clock on February 3, 1879. Conkling was early on hand, apprehensive of failure, moving from knot to knot anxiously seeking to retain votes and to learn what support he might expect. Suppressed excitement was manifest among many of those present. When the Senate was called to order he offered a third letter from General Arthur, which it ordered printed. Realizing that failure awaited him if a final vote was taken, he welcomed a motion to recommit the nominations to his committee on commerce, with all the documentary evidence, and with power and instructions to investigate the conduct of the Custom House under Merritt.[5] But speaking on this motion, Conkling launched into a prolonged invective against the Ad-

---

[1] Sherman, *Recollections,* Vol. II, p. 684, Jan. 31, 1879.

[2] Tucker to Sherman, Jan. 31, 9 P. M., Sherman Papers.

[3] His opponents had acquired a petition from many Republican members of the New York legislature that the Senate confirm Merritt and Burt, but when it was presented, twenty telegrams from twenty signers declared their recantation. N. Y. *World,* Feb. 1, 1879.

[4] *Diary & Letters,* Vol. III, p. 519, Feb. 2, 1879.

[5] Motion by Senator Cockrell of Missouri, *Exec. Jour. of the Senate,* XXXI, p. 502.

ministration, so bitter and personal that he really defeated himself. The description by E. L. Godkin is delightful: [1]

The shock of battle in the Senate was postponed from last week, and in the interval the excitement among the henchmen was painful to witness. On the one side was their "gifted leader," well-combed and neatly attired, his brain full of the facts of the case, his coat-pockets crammed with damning letters, surrounded by piles of law books, a curl of scorn on his lips, and his torso bursting with "sarcasm." On the other was the shrewd and wily Secretary of the Treasury, working as he had never worked before, pursuing the Senators to their lodgings and constraining them to support the Administration for this once. . . .

On Monday, the opposing forces closed in deadly conflict, and the reports which have crept out represent the Conkling onslaught as one of the most shocking scenes of "sarcasm" and "scorn" ever witnessed in a legislative body. The real havoc he wrought in the Administration ranks, however, was effected with private letters, which showed that the President and members of the Cabinet had insisted on appointments in the Custom House for political reasons; that Judge Bradley had to have a son provided for in this way—for "manifest reasons"; and that Mr. J. Q. Howard, the author of a "Campaign Life," had to be furnished with a deputy-collectorship in consideration thereof.

The reading of these letters, which he must have obtained from Arthur, was most offensive to some Senators who were really indisposed to overthrow the custom of the Senate. An apparent approval, before Conkling's speech, by a *viva voce* vote, became, upon a call of yeas and nays at the end of his tirade, a refusal to recommit the nominations by thirty-two to twenty-five. On the question of confirmation, most Democrats followed the lead of Bayard of Delaware, who had been a member of the committee on retrenchment investigating the Custom House in New York in 1871–72, and had then become convinced that it was a corrupt place, badly run. In December, 1877, and again on February 3, 1879, he opposed Arthur and Cornell as unfit officers because of their devotion to practical politics. He had been of the minority on the first occasion, but now he led twenty-five Democrats, of the anti-Tilden wing, to support the Hayes Administration. Only fifteen Republicans voted to confirm Merritt. Among those who stood by Conkling, twenty-three were Republicans and seven Democrats. Prominent among them was James G. Blaine.[2]

[1] *The Nation*, Feb. 6, 1879.
[2] N. Y. *Tribune*, Dec. 13, 1877; N. Y. *World*, Feb. 4, 1879. I have included pairs. The votes cast were 33 to 24 for Merritt; 31 to 19 for Burt.

Hayes and Sherman were jubilant. A newspaper reporter surmised that "buttermilk flowed at the White House like water." Sherman was inundated with congratulatory letters and telegrams, many of them from New York. He was regarded as having won his spurs as a civil service reformer no less than as a financier. But in a large part of the country, his "victory" was recognized as involving no principle, simply success in a political contest between different groups struggling to control the Republican Party in New York.[1] By the *Tribune,* well disposed toward both Arthur and Sherman, the vote was described as no reflection upon the ex-Collector. It represented, instead, the conviction that some final step was necessary, and the preference of the majority for men agreeable to the Secretary of the Treasury. Within a week, Sherman was receiving an emissary of those New York Republicans who were eagerly striving to "break up the anti-Administration ring" which ruled Albany.[2] He was expected to utilize his victory in the time-honored way.

[1] See Rochester *Union,* Utica *Observer,* Buffalo *Commercial,* Lancaster *Intelligencer,* Boston *Herald,* Boston *Globe,* Baltimore *Gazette,* Baltimore *American,* Philadelphia *Times,* all issues of Feb. 4, 1879.
[2] Bradford Wood to Sherman, Feb. 10, 1879, Sherman Papers. See for this entire episode in Arthur's career, my article on "The New York Custom-House Controversy, 1877–1879," in *Mississippi Valley Historical Review,* XVIII (Dec., 1931), pp. 350–63.

THE Conkling-Arthur machine had lost the Custom House but not its organization or its hopes. In the city, Arthur remained a political power; the Republican Party was thoroughly organized and at its head sat the ex-Collector. Unless General Merritt should erect a new machine out of Custom House patronage, Arthur could look forward to continued domination through the district associations and the city's central committee.

As soon as Merritt, Burt, and Graham had been confirmed by the Senate, Hayes sat down to write to each of them. The letters grew successively shorter, but to each man he gave instructions that his office should be conducted "on business principles," and to Merritt, that, in making appointments and removals, he should "be perfectly independent of mere influence." [1] When the letters were received, Merritt's was believed to furnish the occasion for some desirable publicity. George William Curtis was consulted on February 13, and publication next morning agreed upon.[2] Should the acts of the new Custom House administration be in accord with its professions, it would cease to be an active factor in Republican Party politics. It became possible for *The Nation* [3] to proclaim that John Sherman was a civil service reformer, in addition to being a great financier, because both the Custom House and the Sub-Treasury in New York had been put under civil service rules. Other presidential aspirants were advised to watch him closely.

Arthur's machine in New York City seemed, therefore, to be fairly secure. But the Statewide organization required success in the autumn if it were to maintain its place at the party's helm. In September, 1879, for the first time in its history [4] all New York's chief officers were to be nominated for the elections in November. Not merely this novelty, but the relation of New York to national politics, gave more than usual interest to the choice of nominees. "As New York goes, the country goes," all politicians then believed. With the choice of a President to be made the next year, and Samuel J. Tilden preparing to win again,

[1] Williams, ed., *Diary & Letters of Hayes*, Vol. III, pp. 520–2.
[2] Telegram and Letter, Curtis to Hayes, Feb. 13, 1879, Hayes Papers.
[3] Mar. 13, 1879.
[4] *Harper's Weekly*, Aug. 16, 1879.

it seemed to Republicans everywhere that New York Republicans must put their most appealing members forward and convert their State to "the party of Union."

A note of special interest was sounded again and again in this situation—the latest aspect of "the Southern question." In 1876, when the amnesty bill for Southern leaders had been up in the House, James G. Blaine, by moving to except Jefferson Davis from its provisions drew the Southern Congressmen to their feet to protest, in a spirit which rapidly became passionate. In the ensuing election, the unconquered air of the Southerners became a basis for playing on Northern prejudices. In 1879, however, the Southerners did not need to be drawn out—their aggressive moves in Congress to keep control at home by eliminating Federal protection of the Negro vote were patent. It remained for Roscoe Conkling to emphasize that this was the fruit of amnesty. Ex-Confederates in House and Senate were conspiring, he said, for a Democratic "usurpation" of the Federal government, Executive and all. To attain this end they were defying the Fifteenth. Amendment, and by "riders" on all appropriation bills, overthrowing the qualified veto given to the President in the original Constitution. The refusal to permit the use of government money for carrying on the government unless they had their way he denounced as nothing less than revolution.

Conkling's outcry became the keynote of Republican speeches and writings in New York in the summer of 1879. The ranks, divided by Hayes's civil service reform endeavor, closed up again in the face of the common foe. They were bound to maintain Republicanism on the Southern issue; the reform movement against boss rule was temporarily overshadowed.

These factors—the coming presidential election, Southern suppression of the Negro vote, and the exigencies of Conkling's machine,— promoted an extraordinary interest in the New York nominations of September. The Administration was closely observant.[1] The "better element," led by George William Curtis of *Harper's Weekly*, was eager for a candidate of superlative merit, a Seward.[2] Conkling's organization was exceptionally energetic in preparing for the State nominating convention at Saratoga in September. In New York City, Arthur's

[1] Evarts to Hayes, Aug. 10, 14, 20, 1879, Hayes Papers.
[2] *Harper's Weekly*, Aug. 16, 1879.

special concern was to accumulate a delegation pledged to the machine candidate, Alonzo B. Cornell.

Shortly before the convention, added difficulties faced Conkling and his lieutenants when their chief became a principal in a newspaper scandal. Early in August, ex-Senator William Sprague of Rhode Island had come to his home at Narragansett Pier and found his wife entertaining several guests, among whom was Roscoe Conkling. After becoming drunk, he had ordered Conkling to leave, and, a bit later, pursued him, armed with a shotgun.

At first there had been an effort to deceive the public by a pretense that Sprague held a violent dislike for a German tutor, and that Conkling incurred his displeasure only when he interceded on the tutor's account. But there was, in fact, no reason to doubt that Conkling and Mrs. Sprague, famous daughter of Salmon P. Chase, had for years been friends in Washington, that their intimacy had attracted the attention of malicious gossips, and that Sprague had, perhaps, acted like an insane man, but had been moved by a long-growing jealousy. In thus treating Conkling, Sprague had severely injured the public standing of the man on whose legal advice he had frequently relied.

Conkling's lieutenants in New York sought to mitigate the unfavorable effect of their chief's misfortune upon their political campaign. They got several New York newspapers to suppress the story until further silence was seen to be useless. One of them was said to have concocted the yarn about the German tutor, and all urged the Senator to stay in the background until the affair should blow over. Not until the eve of the Saratoga convention did Conkling emerge; then, with Arthur and his lieutenants, he moved on the city at the head of a determined phalanx.[1]

The convention which Conkling himself called to order was so important for the fortunes of the party that every prominent Republican leader except old Thurlow Weed was there.[2] For three days, the machine had labored with individual delegates and secured pledges to Cornell, until they had a small but certain majority. The opponents were divided, supporting four important rival candidates. Speeches and platform were brief and dwelt primarily on New York's relation to national Republican success, and the evils of Democratic

[1] See Cincinnati *Gazette*, Aug. 12, 20, citing Washington *Post* and Philadelphia *Times*.
[2] Alexander, *Political History of the State of New York*, Vol. III, p. 412.

rule. When the first ballot was taken, it was expected that Cornell
would be far in the lead, but it was not known until the end that out
of the 450 votes, he had a bare nominating majority, 234.[1] The result
evoked little enthusiasm.

The convention, however, went on to name a whole slate of Conklingites. Arthur became chairman of the State committee; the machine was still in the saddle.

It was not long before the rumblings of discontent were loudly heard.
Curtis, whose "no" had been barely noticed in a vote at the convention
to make Cornell's nomination unanimous, was able to reach a wider
audience through the editorial columns of *Harper's Weekly* in the weeks
which followed. He had no hesitation in calling the nomination a grave
mistake, and in suggesting that to Republicans in other parts of the
country it would indicate the likelihood of renewed "Grantism" after a
successful Presidential election in 1880. He opposed bolting the Republican ticket but urged that Cornell's name be "scratched" as an
indication of loyal Republicanism unwilling to accept continued machine domination.[2]

Republican success, although seriously endangered by the
"scratchers," was made almost certain by a division among the
Democrats. John Kelly, Tammany boss, had broken with Governor
Lucius Robinson before the Democratic convention met at Syracuse.
When Robinson was renominated, Kelly and the Tammany delegation
"bolted" the convention. In a hall dedicated to Shakespeare, Kelly was
nominated for Governor by his loyal adherents, on an Independent
Democratic ticket, the rest of which coincided with the regular slate.[3]

The New York campaign was fought over national questions, chiefly
the Southern issue. Hayes's Administration had betrayed some interest
in the nominations; in the election itself it took a prominent part.
Evarts, the New Yorker of the Cabinet, came to New York City for
a speech against "scratching," "Voting in the Air," which Curtis denounced as "unspeakable." [4] But Evarts had not participated in the
election in time to secure a nominee whom he could well uphold. Having urged Cornell's removal from the naval office, he could not speak
very heartily in his behalf for Governor.

[1] Alexander, *Political History of the State of New York*, Vol. III, p. 416.
[2] *Harper's Weekly*, Sept. 20, 27, Oct. 4, 1879.
[3] *Appleton's Annual Cyclopedia*, 1879, p. 679.
[4] Edward Cary, *George William Curtis*, p. 269; *Harper's Weekly*, Nov. 8, 15, 1879.

John Sherman, on the other hand, had beaten Conkling over the removals, was regarded as forceful and energetic, and was an avowed aspirant for his party's presidential nomination in 1880. His abilities and his ambitions prompted some active share in the canvass. Letters from New York Republicans urged him to take over the leadership of Administration Republicans there.[1] John B. Haskin, an ex-Congressman and a Sherman admirer, suggested that the Secretary take the occasion of a serenade in Washington to "give Cornell—and *your party*—a proper send-off." [2] Sherman agreed to the propriety of so doing; [3] but before long he was exerting himself even more fully in the New York struggle.[4] He wrote to friends in New York of his desire that Cornell be elected and eventually accepted an invitation from Arthur to speak to the voters.[5] It undoubtedly gave the ex-Collector satisfaction that, under his direction, Sherman was to appear in Cornell's behalf. It was recognized by Sherman that this must look like a humiliation of the President, but, despite some doubts, he did not agree that it actually was,[6] and wrote John Jay to that effect. The Independent Republican organization, and the "arch-scratcher," George William Curtis, were averse to Sherman's speeches, but he decided that to offend them was less objectionable than to lose the election.

When Sherman went on to New York on October 27, he dined as the guest of Whitelaw Reid with Cornell, Merritt, and one or two others, Arthur apparently knowing nothing about it.[7]

Arthur had run Sherman into something of a trap, one which Sherman must have foreseen and of which he was warned. Anything he might say in behalf of Cornell was likely to be served up in 1880 as evidence that the Hayes Administration had in its removals been simply persecuting Conkling lieutenants. To Wayne MacVeagh, Sherman's trip was a source of deep indignation. "A dignified reticence was so plainly the true policy," he wrote to Hayes, "that I can only ascribe

[1] A. N. Cole to Sherman, Sept. 13, 1879; Simon Stevens to Sherman, Sept. 14, 1879, Sherman Papers.

[2] Haskin to Sherman, Sept. 17, 1879, Sherman Papers.

[3] *Ibid.*

[4] What may have been the effect of a potential investigation of the Treasury Department, designed to undermine his popularity and put him on the defensive, one can only conjecture. See Special Agent George C. Tichenor to Sherman, Sept. 20, 1879, and L. P. Morton to Sherman, Sept. 20, 1879, for warnings, Sherman Papers.

[5] Sherman to Arthur, Sept. 29, Oct. 15, 1879, Sherman Papers.

[6] Sherman to Willard Warner, Sept. 29, 1879, Sherman Papers.

[7] Reid to Sherman, Oct. 20, Oct. 23, Oct. 24, 1879, Sherman Papers.

what has been done to the buzzing of presidential bees in bonnets." [1]
Sherman's speeches dealt with national issues, and it is to be doubted
that they had so much influence on the result as his mere presence in
Cornell's behalf, an indication of the Administration's attitude.

The canvass was a bare success for Cornell. Curtis insisted that it
was Tammany who had elected him, having in mind either that Kelly
had subtracted 77,566 votes from Robinson, or that there had been a
bargain between the Republican machine and Tammany by which
Democratic votes in New York City went to Cornell. The Republican
"scratchers" caused Cornell to run some twenty thousand votes behind
the rest of the ticket. But he was elected, and so were all but one of
his Republican associates on the ticket. Conkling was dominant in the
State; Arthur in the metropolis. [2]

As soon as Cornell's election was an assured fact, Arthur began to
be thought of for the Senatorship falling vacant at the expiration of
Kernan's term in March, 1881. He was the organization man with the
most obvious "claims" to the new dignity, and, should the machine retain its grip, his election would be guaranteed. [3] But it could wait, while
in January, a Republican legislature was to assemble at Albany and
organize for the work of the session. For the Conklingites, George H.
Sharpe of Kingston, a personal friend of Arthur's, sought the Speakership.

When the legislature assembled, Arthur was in Albany, actively engaged in establishing a majority for Sharpe. [4] He had left his wife in
New York, in low spirits and health. Her mother had died in France
in April, 1878, and besides the shock of the bereavement she had had
the fatigue of a journey to bring the body back to the United States.
Although worn down, she was threatened by no disease when Arthur
left her to go to Albany. In the midst of his work there, on January 11,
he received word that she had been seized by pneumonia, and was
critically ill. It was a Sunday; passenger service was curtailed, so he

---

[1] Wayne MacVeagh, Oct. 29, 1879; Nov. 10, 1879, Hayes Papers.
[2] The extent of Arthur's power is suggested by a published letter from Col. George C.
Bliss to General Arthur, written in November, 1879, urging reform. Bliss described the
membership rolls of the New York City district associations as "deceptive," full of false
names, while good Republicans were excluded. "A word from you," he wrote, "will accomplish it. I mean an earnest word which will make the henchmen understand that you
really mean it." (See 46th Cong., 3rd sess., *House Exec. Doc. No. 94*, pp. 55–6.)
[3] The N. Y. *Semi-Weekly Times*, Jan. 2, 1880, printed a four-column sketch of Arthur,
possibly a preparation for his Senatorial campaign.
[4] N. Y. *Times*, Nov. 19, 1886.

made a slow journey by milk train and reached the city at midnight. He found her beyond hope of recovery; in less than twenty-four hours, she was dead. Arthur was inconsolable.

Ellen Herndon Arthur's funeral was appropriate for the wife of a public figure. Not only were many prominent persons at the Church of the Heavenly Rest, of which she had been a communicant, but when the coffin was taken to Albany it was met at the station by Governor Cornell and his staff, and by delegations from both branches of the legislature. They escorted the cortège to the Rural Cemetery in sleighs, and remained with General Arthur until his wife lay buried beside his parents in the family lot.[1] There were many to whom her death meant the loss of a fine personality.[2] To Arthur, with mother, father, and now wife, gone, it was as if his world had suddenly collapsed upon him. Life seemed purposeless.

[1] Albany *Express,* Jan. 16, 1880.
[2] The Mendelssohn Glee Club, contrary to its custom, sang at the services in New York.

REPUBLICAN success in New York in the autumn of 1879 resulted from the priority of national over State interests. A hopeful interpretation was placed on the outcome by Republicans looking ahead to the Presidential contest of 1880. They believed that in the absence of any other real issues,[1] the Democratic insistence on suppressing the Negro vote could be made a costly policy. It created a "solid South," to be sure, but at the price of preventing thorough working unity between Northern and Southern Democrats, of outraging the independent voters, and of strengthening the Republican Party. The New York machine was especially pleased by the emergence of this issue. Conkling's organization, with Arthur as staff officer, had been responsible for Cornell's nomination for Governor, but only the national situation had made possible his election. What was more, the protest against Conkling's leadership and his flat defiance of reform sentiment indicated that the triumph of 1879 could not be repeated unless national questions were again brought into service.

Exactly fitting these requirements was the opportunity to return General Grant to the Presidency by the election of 1880. After his second term had ended, Grant had set forth on a world tour of over two years. In September, 1879, a series of brilliant receptions along his homeward route began at San Francisco. The press was full of news about the Grants. The whole country rejoiced, it appeared, in the return of its first citizen. The maladministration of his Presidency seemed, for the nonce, forgotten; what was remembered was his resolute strength at the head of the Union armies. When the autumn elections of 1879 brought forth scathing attacks on the "Southern brigadiers" in Congress, it was again said that the country needed "a strong man" in the Executive Mansion; Conkling even procured such expressions from representatives of the Hayes Administration.[2] Whatever Grant was not, he certainly *was* "strong." More and more mention was made of a third term, a subject on which he made

[1] See *The Nation,* April 1, Sept. 30, 1880; a contemporary pamphlet in the New York Public Library, *Arthur and the Ghost* (1883), by Lawrence Goulding; E. B. Andrews, *The Last Quarter-Century, 1870–1895,* p. 312.

[2] Alexander, *Poltical History of the State of New York,* Vol. III, p. 427.

no comment.

Not only in New York, but in Pennsylvania and Illinois, the machine leaders saw in Grant the means of renewed personal strength in their own States. In Pennsylvania, J. Donald Cameron, Simon's son, took the lead; in Illinois, John A. Logan strove to secure a Grant delegation at Chicago. With Conkling, they formed a triumvirate of Senators, "practical politicians" all, identified completely with the methods and objectives formerly designated as "Grantism."

The Conkling group in New York was faced by two main opposing forces. The first was the increasing number of independents and reformers, particularly those who sought to take the civil service out of politics. Some strength was added to their cause by the appearance in January, 1880, of Dorman B. Eaton's book, *Civil Service in Great Britain,* which had "an excellent reception." [1] Much was being said of the economical administration of the Custom House by Collector Merritt since Arthur's retirement and the restoration of civil service examinations there; much also of the work of Thomas L. James as Postmaster of New York. The other opponents were the genuine Republicans favoring other candidates than Grant for the nomination. John Sherman had been "mending his fences" assiduously, and in New York had a substantial following among those who approved his conduct of the country's finances. Elihu B. Washburne had missed no opportunity to advance his own fortunes.[2] Stronger than either was Blaine, transferred to the Senate and recovered from his "sunstroke" of 1876, but not entirely recovered from the "Mulligan letters." He had flayed the "brigadiers" with the best of them and was said to have renewed the Southern issue in its latest form,[3] to which the term "Stalwartism" was currently applied. Soon the label was monopolized by those who made the Southern question a reason for reëlecting Grant; Blaine's large following were called the "Half-Breeds."

Blaine's New York friends had been suppressed in 1876 by the insistence that Conkling have a united New York delegation. In 1880, they proposed to get as large a part of the State's representation as they possibly could. When Grant again left the country for a two

<hr/>

[1] Curtis to Hayes, Jan. 20, 1880, Hayes Papers.

[2] See letters to Washburne from Elliott C. Cowdin, James Milliken, D. D. T. Marshall, Thurlow Weed, and George Jones, running from Jan. 16 to Apr. 30, 1880, Washburne Papers (Library of Congress).

[3] *The Nation,* Jan. 15, 1880.

months' trip, it became clear that the fervor with which he had been welcomed home differed from the feeling with which his return to the White House would be greeted. His popularity as a presidential candidate was very low indeed. In New York, it may have been greater than that of his campaign managers,[1] but it was not enough to carry the state against a Democrat.[2] Yet, following the example of Don Cameron in Pennsylvania, Conkling, Arthur, and their associates prepared to force the choice of Grant delegates at a convention summoned before his popularity should have ebbed.

Arthur, acting for the State committee, summoned the usual convention for electing and instructing delegates-at-large to meet at Utica on February 25, an unprecedentedly early date. Thanks to careful, if sometimes questionable, preparations,[3] little difficulty accompanied the choice of delegates-at-large; Conkling's control of the convention was evinced in the selection of himself, with Arthur, Cornell, and James D. Warren, as the four men. The real struggle came over a bold attempt of the Stalwart majority to use this convention to whip the minority into line as in a party caucus. Instructions were phrased not merely for the delegates-at-large but for all those chosen in separate districts, "to use their most earnest and united efforts to secure the nomination of Ulysses S. Grant." The question at issue was, consequently, whether the State convention or the local district convention had superior authority to determine the action of a delegate. When the convention adopted instructions for all delegates from New York, by a vote of 216 to 183, and required each delegate individually to record his acceptance, it at once became the target of bitter censure from all anti-Conkling, and especially from all pro-Blaine, Republican organs.[4]

Even the aged "boss," Thurlow Weed, was disgusted. "You have the results of our State convention," he wrote privately to Washburne. "With a good leader the result might have been widely different. The old leaders (Conkling, Arthur, Cornell, etc.) hold control simply because no capable men challenge their right to mislead. And

[1] So declared George Jones, of the N. Y. *Times,* in a letter to Elihu B. Washburne, Feb. 28, 1880, Washburne Papers.
[2] According to Thurlow Weed, writing to Washburne, Feb. 27, Apr. 30, 1880, *Ibid.*
[3] *The Nation,* Feb. 12, 1880.
[4] *Harper's Weekly,* Mar. 13, 20, Apr. 3, 1880; *The Nation,* Apr. 1, 1880; N. Y. *Tribune,* Feb. 26, 1880. Other newspapers in opposition were the *Evening Post,* the *Commercial Advertiser,* the *Journal of Commerce.*

they are strengthened by the application of the wretched 'Civil Service Reform' doctrine. Cornell's removal without cause from the Naval Office made him Governor. The removal of Arthur may possibly make him United States Senator. . . . If General Grant becomes a candidate under the bull-dozing process of Cameron and Conkling, he will be beaten. . . . If things should remain as they are till April or May, I shall make an effort to satisfy Arthur, Postmaster James, and a few others that they cannot afford to take the responsibility that will deprive the country of a Republican President. . . ." [1] *The Nation* was particularly bitter.[2] Such a state of public opinion furnished an inviting field for counsels of rebellion.

On May 6, the Albany *Journal* published a letter from William H. Robertson, delegate from Westchester County, which proved to be the insurgents' rallying cry, bringing out other rebels from protective retirement. Robertson, who had not gone to Utica, announced that he intended to vote for Blaine "on the first roll call at Chicago and on each subsequent one until a nomination shall be made." [3] Next day, during the session of the State Senate, William B. Woodin, who had been at Utica and had there agreed to follow the instructions, announced that he would yield to an alternate, who would vote for Blaine, as their district desired. Two other State Senators followed Woodin, and before June, the insurgents numbered nineteen, two of whom were for Sherman.[4]

Public sentiment against the nomination of Grant attained such earnestness that "anti-Grant" clubs were organized during the spring and represented in St. Louis by a national convention, in advance of the Chicago assembly, under the name of "Anti-Third-Term Republicans." They formally resolved: "That as Republicans we cannot be hero-worshippers; and we demand from a party without a master, the nomination of a candidate without a stain." Grant's record as President was so vulnerable that Thurlow Weed felt confident of his defeat, should he be nominated, but the alternative candidates were too numerous. "Anything to beat Grant" had become a slogan among some Republicans, but the wide diversity of their proposed "anythings" gave every advantage of unity to the Grant men.

[1] Feb. 27, 1880, Washburne Papers.
[2] Feb. 19, Apr. 1, 29, 1880.
[3] Letter reprinted in *Appleton's Annual Cyclopedia*, 1880, p. 575.
[4] Alexander, *op. cit.*, Vol. III, pp. 435-7.

Grant's managers had reached a clear understanding to assure united action. Their success was thought to rest upon adoption by the convention of the "unit rule," according to which each State's entire vote would be cast for the candidate approved by a majority of its delegates.[1] This arrangement would bring into Grant's column the votes of several minorities and thus furnish the 389 required for a nomination. It was so certain to bring victory that they were prepared to use their power in the permanent party organization to impose the rule upon the convention by a sort of *coup d'état*, before the delegates could object.[2]

Consternation struck all the opposing leaders when the scheme leaked out. In their helpless division they found it impossible to co-operate for the defeat of such a project until James A. Garfield arrived in Chicago for the preliminary meetings of the national committee. He was leader of the Ohio delegation and the Sherman forces, but he soon rallied all the anti-Grant groups in opposition to the unit rule. Garfield probably knew of Sherman's antipathy toward the rule,[3] he was opposed to it in his own judgment,[4] and he found a majority of the national committee willing to sustain him in demanding a compromise from the Grant leaders, foremost of whom was Conkling. By threatening to depose Cameron from his chairmanship of the national committee, he secured an agreement to make George F. Hoar of Massachusetts temporary presiding officer of the convention. Senator Hoar preferred none of the three—Grant, Blaine, or Sherman—but gave his initial support to George F. Edmunds, the independents' favorite. He would permit the convention to determine for itself whether it would adopt the unit rule. In accepting this com-

[1] In 1876, the Republican national convention at Cincinnati, after prolonged argument, had voted against the unit rule. Four delegates from Pennsylvania had been allowed to vote contrary to the instructions of their State convention, in response to the wishes of their districts, by a vote of 353 to 395. Because of their attitudes in the convention of 1880, it is interesting to observe the following votes on the question in 1876:

	Favoring Unit Rule	Opposed to Unit Rule
Connecticut	9	3
Illinois	4	*38*
Indiana	29	1
New York	54	15
Ohio	*30*	14
Pennsylvania	57	1

See the *Proceedings of the Republican National Convention of 1876* (Concord, N. H., 1876), pp. 88–99.

[2] See Rhodes's account, *op. cit.*, Vol. VIII, pp. 115–27.

[3] Sherman to George H. Foster, Feb. 23, 1880, Sherman Papers.

[4] T. C. Smith, *Garfield*, Vol. II, p. 959.

promise, the Grant men relinquished a scheme which was sure to give them victory, but which would have so divided the party as to make defeat at the polls inevitable. They undertook to persuade the convention to adopt it rather than to use it against the assembly's will.

Arthur had been a zealous partisan of the unit rule, arguing that the power of a State in the final electoral vote ought to be paralleled in the nomination of the candidate.[1] But when the compromise was reached, he defended it against anti-Grant extremists, giving assurances, with Conkling, Senator Jones of Nevada, and other Stalwarts, that Cameron would keep his word.[2] The struggle over the unit rule was, in consequence, transferred to the floor of the convention, and there Arthur restrained Conkling from departing from the agreement in even a minor matter.[3]

To the convention, the majority of the rules committee reported through Chairman Garfield the following provision:

In the record of the vote by States, the vote of each State, Territory and the District of Columbia shall be announced by the chairman; and in case the votes of any State, Territory, or the District of Columbia shall be divided, the chairman shall announce the number of votes cast for any candidate, or for or against any proposition; but if exception be taken by any delegate to the correctness of such announcement by the chairman of his delegation, the President of the Convention shall direct the roll of members of such delegation to be called, and the result recorded in accordance with the votes individually given.[4]

The minority report was offered by George H. Sharpe of New York on behalf of committeemen from nine States; they recommended the substitution of the rule of the previous convention, which contained no reference to possible disagreement with a delegation.[5] On a *viva voce* vote the minority report was lost, and, on a similar vote, the Garfield report was carried. Majority sentiment was clearly opposed to the unit rule.

The platform was reported by Edwards Pierrepont of the New York delegation. After reciting the party's record, it pledged support to proposals of Federal aid to common school education for the over-

---

[1] Gail Hamilton, *James G. Blaine,* p. 483, citing telegram from Eugene Hale to Blaine.
[2] *The Nation,* June 3, 1880.
[3] William E. Chandler's address at the unveiling of the Arthur monument at North Fairfield, Vt., Aug. 19, 1903.
[4] Edward McPherson, *Handbook of Politics,* 1880, p. 189.
[5] *Ibid.*

coming of illiteracy; urged a constitutional amendment forbidding States to appropriate public money for sectarian schools; declared that "duties levied for the purpose of revenue should so discriminate as to favor American labor"; that no further grants of public lands should be made to railroad or other corporations; that polygamy "must die in the territories"; that naturalized citizens should receive the same protection as native citizens from the Federal government; that Chinese immigration should be limited; that seacoasts and harbors should be improved and developed, but that this should be accomplished without subsidies to private interests.

From the floor, James M. Barker of Massachusetts offered an additional paragraph demanding Congressional legislation to establish civil service reform. In indignation, Flanagan of Texas arose to combat this suggestion. "What are we up here for?" he asked. "I mean that members of the Republican Party are entitled to office, and if we are victorious, we will have office." Nevertheless, as finally adopted, the civil service reform plank read: "The Republican Party . . . adopts the declaration of President Hayes that the reform of the civil service should be 'thorough, radical, and complete.' To this end it demands the coöperation of the Legislative with the Executive Departments of the Government, and that Congress shall so legislate that fitness, ascertained by proper practical tests, shall admit to the public service." A provision looking toward removal only for cause was rejected by the convention on the ground that it would promote life tenure and an officeholding class.[1]

Following adoption of the platform, the nomination of candidates began. In a famous speech, Conkling laid Grant's name before the convention with rhetorical power but in a spirit which antagonized rather than conciliated—which brought admirers of Grant to their feet with enthusiasm but won him not a single new vote. Garfield followed with a masterly presentation of John Sherman. The speech revealed Garfield himself as the outstanding leader of the conciliatory group, opposed inflexibly to Grant, but seeking the cohesion of the entire party. Combined with his other work in the convention, it made him a person upon whom the anti-Grant forces might later converge. Blaine was a more serious contender than Sherman, yet the speech

[1] *Proceedings of the Republican National Convention of 1880* (Chicago, 1880), pp. 160 ff.; Edward Stanwood, *A History of Presidential Elections* (3rd ed., Boston, 1888), pp. 356–60.

nominating him was far inferior to Garfield's,[1] a marked contrast to Ingersoll's oratory of the preceding convention, and a deep disappointment to his adherents.

For twenty-eight ballots on June 7, 1880, the convention was unable to break a deadlock. Grant lacked approximately seventy votes of those necessary for a nomination. Blaine and Sherman followed, and had their support been combined, either might have been chosen. The Blaine men, however, were for Blaine first and various different candidates second, and could not be induced to shift to Sherman without great risk of losing enough votes to nominate Grant. Sherman's following could not be delivered to Blaine without the same result.[2] The Grant supporters were entirely hostile to Blaine, while Cameron,[3] Conkling, and Arthur could never be expected to aid Sherman, and Logan, the Illinois "boss," could not have accomplished his nomination without them.

Wearily the delegates reassembled on June 8. While 306 Stalwarts stood by Grant to the bitter end, the opposing forces suddenly concentrated upon their outstanding member, James A. Garfield. The thirty-sixth ballot produced 399 votes for Garfield, 306 for Grant, 42 for Blaine, and 3 for Sherman. The choice had been made.

Although Garfield retained the good will of John Sherman,[4] some of Sherman's admirers were hostile,[5] while the Stalwarts were in an ugly mood. None accepted failure with less grace than Conkling, whose support was deemed essential to party success in the autumn. In designating a candidate for Vice President, Garfield's friends, having assumed command, sought to make Stalwart aid sure by choosing one of that faction. Their first choice appears to have been Levi P. Morton

[1] His followers must have listened in chagrin as the orator (James F. Joy of Michigan) concluded somewhat as follows: "I now have the pleasure and honor of proposing as the candidate of this convention that eminent statesman, James S. Blaine." Probably everybody else in the hall knew that that middle initial was "G" and sought to tell him so, according to Chauncey M. Depew, who relates the story. *My Memories of Eighty Years*, p. 121. He is corroborated by Melville E. Stone, *Fifty Years a Journalist*, pp. 103–4.

[2] Sherman Papers, *passim*, containing telegraphed dispatches to Sherman from his managers at Chicago.

[3] His antipathy is said to have been based upon Sherman's refusal as Senator to confirm the nomination of his father, Simon Cameron, as Minister to Russia. See Royal Cortissoz, *Whitelaw Reid*, Vol. II, pp. 19–20.

[4] Sherman promptly sent congratulations over his special wire to the convention and declined (till years later) to suspect Garfield of having been lukewarm in his behalf. Telegram, June 8, 1880, Sherman Papers; Sherman to Charles Foster, June 30, 1880, Sherman, *Recollections*, Vol. II, pp. 776–8.

[5] Rhodes, *op. cit.*, Vol. VIII, p. 126; Smith, *op. cit.*, Vol. II, p. 989.

of New York City. Morton, like Chester A. Arthur, was the son of a Vermont clergyman; he had become a wealthy banker and importer, and in 1876, at the invitation of the Republican organization, had entered politics as the congressional candidate from his district, and lost. Returning to the contest in 1878, he had won by a large majority and, in the special session of 1879, had gained the reputation of being a strong advocate of "sound money." [1] He was a member of Grant's "306" supporters but, not being a professional politician, had the confidence of both Eastern business men and Half-Breeds. There had been talk of nominating him with Grant; as a running mate for Garfield, he seemed equally desirable. When overtures were made to Morton, he at once consulted Senator Conkling, who expressed doubts that Garfield could be elected but advised discussing the matter with Boutwell of Massachusetts. The latter thought acceptance unwise,[2] so Morton declined.

During the recess of the convention, the New York delegation held a meeting over which, under normal circumstances, General Arthur would have presided. In his absence, they agreed that he should be regarded as the choice of his New York associates. Arthur, like Garfield, had been an active delegate at the convention. In the caucuses of the Grant delegates, he had been second only to Conkling among the New York Stalwarts. From time to time, in Conkling's absence, he had announced the vote of his delegation, always making a pleasing impression. Newspaper men found him courteous and obliging, in marked contrast to Conkling, and considered him a person of great ability.[3] As a leading supporter of Grant, a widely known Republican, and a man who had antagonized no element save the civil service reformers, he was most "available."

When the convention reassembled shortly after five o'clock on June 8, "it was understood that the Conkling men in the New York delegation would propose ex-Collector Arthur for Vice President." [4] It was not realized that, in allowing his name to be presented, Arthur had defied the Senator.[5] A plausible description of the conference in which Arthur and Conkling discussed the matter represents it as oc-

[1] Robert McElroy, *Levi Parsons Morton*, p. 70 ff.
[2] *Ibid.*, pp. 105–6.
[3] A. K. McClure, *Recollections*, pp. 118–19.
[4] N. Y. *World*, June 9, 1880.
[5] A. R. Conkling, *Life and Letters of Roscoe Conkling* (N. Y., 1889), pp. 607–8; Alexander, *op. cit.*, Vol. III, pp. 443–4; McClure, *op. cit.*, p. 119; McElroy, *op. cit.*, p. 107.

curring in the press room of the convention hall, deserted by all save one reporter and the perturbed Conkling, pacing up and down the floor. Arthur met Conkling in the middle of the room.

" 'I have been hunting everywhere for you, Senator,' said Mr. Arthur.

" 'Well, sir,' replied Conkling. . . . There was a moment of hesitation under the uncompromising attitude of the Senator. Finally, Mr. Arthur said: 'The Ohio men have offered me the Vice Presidency.'

"The Senator's voice rang out in indignant tones: 'Well, sir, you should drop it as you would a red-hot shoe from the forge.'

"There was a flash of resentment in the eyes of Arthur as he replied: 'I sought you to consult, not—' Conkling broke in on him:

" 'What is there to consult about? This trickster of Mentor will be defeated before the country.'

" 'There is something else to be said,' remarked Arthur.

" 'What, sir, you think of accepting?' fairly shouted Conkling.

"Arthur hesitated a moment and said slowly, but with emphasis: 'The office of Vice President is a greater honor than I ever dreamed of attaining. A barren nomination would be a great honor. In a calmer moment you will look at this differently.'

" 'If you wish for my favor and my respect you will contemptuously decline it.'

"Arthur looked Conkling straight in the eye and said: 'Senator Conkling, I shall accept the nomination and I shall carry with me the majority of the delegation.'

"The Senator looked at him for a brief moment and then in a towering rage turned and walked away. For another moment, Arthur looked after him regretfully," and then the man who a year later was to become President turned and walked out of the room.[1]

At five-thirty, the convention was called to order; it listened to a male quartet sing "My Country 'tis of Thee" and as an encore, "Old Shady," and then proceeded to the nomination of a candidate for Vice President. General Stewart L. Woodford, "in behalf of many of the New York delegation," presented Chester A. Arthur, whose name was seconded by Governor Dennison for Ohio, and by spokesmen from seven other delegations. The convention balanced his qualifications

[1] W. C. Hudson, *Random Recollections of an Old Political Reporter* (N. Y., 1900), pp. 96–9.

against those of Elihu B. Washburne of Illinois, Marshall Jewell of Connecticut, and several others. Washburne was the leading opponent. He had been before the convention for President, running far behind Grant, Blaine, and Sherman. Though he possessed personal qualifications, his "availability" had been badly curtailed by his presidential candidacy. As a close friend of Grant, he had tried unsuccessfully to prevent his own following from diminishing the Grant contingent at Chicago. Keenly disappointed Stalwart leaders, especially Logan, were charging him with disloyalty. To many in the convention, therefore, Arthur appeared more likely to bring the Grant faction into harmony with the rest of the party.[1] But against Arthur, a seconder of Washburne said: "Let us not do a rash thing in this convention. The convention has passed a resolution favoring civil service reform. Let us not stultify ourselves before the country. (Great cheers.) Let us remember that the people will review our action calmly and coolly by their firesides." At one point, voters for Arthur were hissed.

The roll was soon called. Arthur received 468, Washburne 199, Jewell 43, and all others 65. Particularly gratifying to Arthur was the New York vote, 69 for him and 1 for Washburne.[2]

The outcome was most surprising. Garfield had for months been thought of as a likely compromise candidate and went to the convention with an understanding on the subject between himself and Sherman. But that Arthur should be named to represent the Grant contingent was utterly unexpected by anyone. Sherman chose to consider his nomination as the outcome of his removal from the Custom House but it is fairly clear that the selection was made by his own New York associates, was the fruit of his close relationship to Conkling, and was made more with an eye to the future than to the past. Godkin declared that for Conkling to accept Arthur for Vice President instead of Grant for President was "very like taking a suit of old clothes in lieu of the English mission." [3] But Conkling, his followers thought, was more likely to be satisfied with old clothes than with nothing at all; and Arthur, if anyone, could enlist his aid in the election.

[1] Illinois votes cast for Washburne were gratuitous rather than solicited. Grant, nevertheless, always blamed Washburne for disloyalty. See Gaillard Hunt, ed., *Israel, Elihu and Cadwallader Washburn* (N. Y., 1925), pp. 267–83; Washburn Papers, *passim*.
[2] McPherson, *Handbook of Politics*, 1880, p. 192; N. Y. *World*, June 9, 1880.
[3] *The Nation*, June 17, 1880.

As soon as he could, Arthur set forth for New York. The heat bothered him, and the incessant congratulatory handshakes made it necessary to file off a ring on his right hand. After so many days of nervous tension, the journey seemed a relief. As the long train rolled into the old Grand Central Depot early in the evening of June 11, it passed over seventeen torpedoes to yield a Vice President's salute. From the last car, Arthur stepped off with both hands full of "linen duster, satchel, umbrella, and cane" to find about fifteen hundred welcoming admirers, shouts and cheers, and calls for a speech. He made a few remarks, drowned out by the commotion, and then strode down the platform to a private carriage, his head "towering above all others." [1] At home, his household had been plunged in gloom at the failure of Grant. When the news came, his sister Regina went to the dining room, and drawing the old family servant to the sideboard, said: "Bridget, let us cry together, for the nomination is made at last, and Grant hasn't got it." Bridget looked at her in a bewildered way and said: "Isn't that divilish mean?" [2] But the news that Arthur had been nominated for the Vice Presidency changed their sadness to jubilation. Let his sister tell the story of his arrival:

June 11, 1880.
Mrs. Roosa's son called this afternoon to say that Chester was to be met at the station by his friends with music and escorted home, and there would probably be a great crowd about the house. As the time drew near, I looked out to see if there were any signs of their coming and saw Chester, Alan [Arthur's son], and Arthur [Masten] getting out of a carriage at the door. 'That and nothing more.' The crowd were at the station but Chester's friends thought it best to get him quietly home and give him a chance to rest for one night after his hard work at Chicago, and he had a chance to eat his dinner, only leaving the table once.

Nell [Arthur's daughter] asked her Aunt Molly [McElroy] what she could do for her father by way of congratulation and was told she could get some flowers. When they were brought on to the table and Chester called little Nell to him to kiss her, he completely broke down and said: 'There is nothing worth having now.' We knew what was in his heart without his saying it and

[1] N. Y. *Times,* June 12, 1880.
[2] Regina Caw to Alice Jackson Arthur, June 11, 1880, William Arthur Papers.

very much dreaded his first hours at home, but on the whole, and before people, he got along very well. There were a number in in the evening, among others Dr. and Mrs. Roosa, and I heard Chester telling Mrs. Roosa how different all would have been for him if only Nell [his wife] had been here.[1]

For the next evening, a serenade was arranged, not at Arthur's home but at the Fifth Avenue Hotel. About twenty-five hundred Republicans gathered without much organization at Union Square and, at 10:30 o'clock, marched over Seventeenth Street and up Fifth Avenue behind a band to the hotel. There they found Arthur, who had left the house shortly before with his son and nephew, "very nervous," in the company of many friends. John D. Lawson presented him to the crowd, with "three cheers and a tiger," and Arthur spoke very briefly, as was his wont. Chauncey Depew and three other public men entertained the crowd in the spirit of a Republican rally until midnight.[2] It was the last of such greetings. When New York's leading Republicans, most of them fellow members in the Union League Club, invited Arthur to a testimonial dinner on July 3, 1880, he declined for private reasons, being still in mourning for his wife.

Letters of congratulation, eulogistic editorials, serenades, and testimonial dinners were pleasant to receive, but Arthur knew that he would soon be subjected to particularly bitter misrepresentation from the Democratic press. Godkin might write with his usual humor, but others would surpass his irony and deal sledge-hammer blows. To Massachusetts voters, for example, Arthur was soon pictured as "personally the soul of honor. . . . (his word is as good as his bond)" but also as believing that "all is fair in politics," hesitating at no trickery to defeat his foes, and deserting his political companions if need arose.[3]

Garfield mediated between the Blaine and Sherman wings and was expected to command their support; Arthur's function was that of placating the Stalwarts without antagonizing the others. The immediate response to his nomination was not reassuring. Sherman wrote his principal supporters in Ohio in great disgust over it, although he declared that he would support the ticket.[4] Sherman's friends, sending

[1] Regina Caw to Alice Jackson Arthur, June 11, 1880, William Arthur Papers. Daniel B. St. John Roosa, eminent eye and ear specialist in New York City, was an intimate friend of the Arthur family. From 1873-6, he was president of the American Otological Society.
[2] N. Y. Times, June 14, 1880.
[3] Boston Herald, June 13, 1880.
[4] Sherman to Warner M. Bateman, June 9, 1880, said: "The nomination of Arthur is a ridiculous burlesque and I am afraid was inspired by a desire to beat the ticket"; to

their regrets over the presidential nomination, discreetly avoided mention of the choice of his recent opponent for the second place. Blaine, having defended Arthur at the time of his removal, was not in a position to attack his nomination, although showing no enthusiasm.[1] But from New York came warnings that Arthur's popularity could not offset Tilden's strength [2] and that it was by no means certain that Conkling's machine would be set in operation in his behalf.[3] Arthur and Cornell were at odds,[4] and the Democratic New York *World* [5] stated that he had had "a bitter quarrel, as is perfectly well known in his own State, with those machinists who control the State administration."

Many of the independents wrote to *The Nation* asking how it was possible to vote for Garfield but not for Arthur. Godkin, the editor, reassured them by writing that, although "scratching" Arthur was impossible, "there is no place in which his powers of mischief will be so small as in the Vice Presidency, and it will remove him during a great part of the year from his own field of activity. It is true General Garfield, if elected, may die during his term of office, but this is too unlikely a contingency to be worth making extraordinary provision for." [6] At the outset of the campaign, therefore, it was by no means certain that Arthur's nomination would bring Garfield the Stalwart vote or that it would not completely alienate the party's reform element. At the same time, there were well-founded doubts that he could even win his own State, which was deemed absolutely necessary for Republican victory.

Cincinnati was the scene of the Democratic national convention of 1880. It turned out to be much less contentious than the Republican gathering, and much less exciting than might have been expected. The party could no longer nominate Samuel J. Tilden as a reform candi-

William Dennison, on the same day, he wrote: "While it was very natural for Ohio to look to New York for a Vice President, yet I believe sincerely that the nomination of Arthur was inspired with a view to defeating the ticket. Arthur has no standing whatever that would justify such a nomination"; on June 12, he declared to James M. Hoyt, "I have no regrets for the result of the convention and can heartily support Gen'l Garfield. As for Arthur, I suppose he is connected with the ticket and we must vote for him, although it is rather a scandalous proceeding. The only reason for his nomination was that he was discharged from an office that he was unfit to fill." Sherman Papers.

[1] Gail Hamilton, *op. cit.*, 517.
[2] N. Y. *World*, June 9, 1880.
[3] *The Nation*, June 10, 17, 1880.
[4] Regina Caw to Alice Jackson Arthur, June 11, 1880, William Arthur Papers.
[5] June 9, 1880.
[6] June 17, 1880.

date seeking to relieve the country from Republican corruption. Hayes's Administration could boast great reform pretensions and substantial accomplishments, so that the Republicans could not be exclusively identified with great existing evils; while, since the days of the Electoral Commission, the "cipher dispatches" had robbed Tilden of any sanctity. The seating at Cincinnati of a New York delegation united in Tilden's support did not truly represent his relation to New York Democrats, for he was still at feud with John Kelly and Tammany Hall.[1] Yet the strongest candidate the party might have chosen seemed to many, including Tilden, to be Tilden again, this time seeking vindication for the alleged fraudulent manner in which he had been deprived of the office in 1877. To this end he had entrusted to friends a letter declining to seek the nomination but so phrased as to provoke the old issue of "the fraud of 1876" and thus to guarantee his selection.[2]

The convention, however, made the mistake of taking Tilden at his word; on the second ballot, it assigned the party standard to the hands of Winfield Scott Hancock of Pennsylvania, a handsome, gallant Civil War veteran, with a good military record but no great experience in civil leadership. With him, as running mate, went William H. English from the "doubtful State" of Indiana, rival of New York for the decisive influence in the election of 1880. The Democrats' platform, prepared by Henry Watterson, had the merits of brevity, dash, and ambiguity on some important points.[3]

The two major parties had by 1880 reached an almost equal strength, making it imperative for victory that each muster its full roster and win new voters to its ranks. Garfield recognized how pressing was the need of party harmony,[4] and rejoiced that Cameron and Logan were soon enlisted in his service. Conkling, however, whose personal fortunes as a political leader had required success in the third term venture, played the sulky Achilles, taking no part in the canvass and seemingly content to let the party take defeat. It was Arthur's difficult problem to elicit his active support, and the nature of the struggle precluded

---

[1] Alexander, *op. cit.*, Vol. III, ch. xxxiv.
[2] Printed in John Bigelow, *Life of Samuel J. Tilden,* Vol. II, pp. 266–70.
[3] Stanwood, *op. cit.*, pp. 367–9.
[4] Writing to John Russell Young, Grant's warm personal friend, he said: "I hope all our friends will join in burying the asperities of feeling which were engendered by the convention, and work together in harmony." June 25, 1880, John Russell Young Papers (Library of Congress).

the sacrifice of a Patroclus.

Conkling distrusted Garfield, even when bearing gifts; yet gifts or promises were alone capable of obtaining the New York Senator's assistance. Garfield was unwilling to limit his freedom of action as President by incurring any obligations which would subsequently prevent him from coöperating with other Republican groups in New York. So the matter stood through the early summer. Meanwhile Garfield went about his preparations, visiting Washington in June to arrange his affairs there, narrowly missing a conference with Conkling; [1] while Arthur, who had been asked by some of Garfield's friends to come to Washington to meet him, went fishing, instead. When Garfield invited Arthur to consult with him at Mentor about their letters of acceptance and the revision of the personnel of the Republican national committee,[2] he promised to go some time, but urged Garfield to come to New York. That, however, was more than the presidential candidate was yet willing to do. As a mediator between Garfield and the Stalwarts, Arthur in July appeared ineffective.

But the letters which each candidate wrote accepting the nomination served to put Arthur before the country in a more favorable light than theretofore. To an invitation to make suggestions regarding Garfield's letter he had replied: "I have no suggestions to make and am sure that none are needed." In his own, independently drafted,[3] the ring of frank straightforwardness brought favorable comment from even *The Nation*.[4] "Looked upon, if not exactly as the wicked partner, at least as the poor relation" in the Garfield and Arthur combination, he appeared to Godkin less vague and more courageous than his colleague. In respect to the currency he wrote: "There must be no deteriorated coin, no depreciated paper; and every dollar, whether of metal or paper, should stand the test of the world's fixed standard." Civil service reform received his distinct approval, to the surprise of those who associated him with "machine politics" and nothing else. Like Garfield, he objected to the extreme character of Hayes's executive order forbidding officeholders to take any other part in politics

[1] Smith, *Garfield*, Vol. II, pp. 996–7.
[2] Printed, *ibid.*, Vol. II, pp. 997–8. Letters to and from Arthur are in Garfield Papers, July 8 and July 11, 1880, respectively.
[3] Dated July 15, 1880 and addressed to George F. Hoar, chairman of the convention. Printed in *Proceedings of the Republican National Convention of 1880* (Chicago, 1880), pp. 302–04; and in newspapers, July 18.
[4] July 22, 1880.

than to vote, but he favored measures, including stable tenure of office, intended to make the conduct of public business more akin to that of successful private business.[1] On other matters he was simply orthodox, especially in his attack on the Southern control of the Democratic Party.

Garfield's letter, after demanding equal civil and political rights for all, affirmed the merits of pensions, specie resumption, a protective tariff and rigid economy. He thought, however, that new sums should be spent to make the Mississippi safe for navigation. Chinese immigration should not continue to undermine American labor, but should be stopped, if possible, by diplomatic negotiations. On the other hand, Congress could wisely legislate at once to effect civil service reform. Such were the policies to which Garfield subscribed and which Arthur was to inherit.[2]

The Republican problem in 1880 was succinctly outlined in a sarcastic letter composed by William E. Chandler of the national committee for the eyes of President Hayes.[3] The committee decided it must expect a solid Democratic South with 138 electoral votes, to which the addition of New York's 35 and Indiana's 15 would give a total of 188 —three more than Hancock needed for election. Recognizing how doubtful New York and Indiana were, the committee looked for a Southern State with four votes which might be captured by the Republican candidate. Either Florida with 4, Louisiana with 8, or South Carolina with 7 electoral votes would be sufficient but, Hayes was told, the committee had not yet discovered how to carry any one of them and would welcome assistance from the President who had so recently secured the votes of all three.

By the end of July, a part of which Conkling spent with Arthur fishing on the Restigouche River, the New York Stalwarts were clearly sulking. It was not that Conkling and his followers were inconsolable over their failure to nominate Grant; their fear that Garfield's election would lead only to their downfall in New York was probably more potent. A plan was finally conceived for a consultation

---

[1] N. Y. *Times,* July 18, 1880, strongly approved Arthur's letter and said of its civil service paragraphs: "While not expressing that complete attachment to the reform which [its friends] . . . would be glad to see, it shows a more intelligent appreciation of its real aims and a clearer conception of its methods" than Garfield's letter.

[2] Letter printed in *Proceedings of the Republican National Convention of 1880,* pp. 298–301.

[3] July 3, 1880, Chandler Papers.

between Garfield and their leaders in New York City, at a general gathering of Republican chiefs. Garfield was reluctant to go. Hayes had been warned against a similar encounter with the New Yorkers, during the campaign of 1876, by Carl Schurz, who assured him that he would "be exposed to all sorts of embarrassments." [1] But Garfield's position was desperate, and at the urgent request of Senator Stephen W. Dorsey, secretary of the national committee, of Marshall Jewell, its chairman, and of William E. Chandler, Garfield started east from Mentor Farm on August 3, 1880.[2] The conference to which he was going was to be the decisive point in the campaign and a source of infinite trouble after his election.

Garfield's train made about twenty stops between Buffalo and New York City, at each of which the candidate made short speeches and acquired more traveling companions. Among them were Cornell, Arthur, and Depew.[3] Upon arriving in New York, he was taken to the Republican stronghold, the Fifth Avenue Hotel. That evening, "at a private residence," he met a group of New York Republicans of wealth and standing but with no professionally political connections. He explained the critical aspects of the campaign and designated New York as "the darkest spot." It was agreed that a special fund be raised to carry New York and that Levi P. Morton be made its treasurer. The meeting and the decision were kept entirely secret; the funds were to be administered completely apart from those of the Republican national committee, of whose finance committee also Morton agreed to be chairman.[4]

The better known conference opened at noon of August 5 in the parlors of the Fifth Avenue Hotel, with speeches from Blaine, Logan, Sherman and many others of the two hundred present, but with Roscoe Conkling conspicuously absent.[5] Garfield wrote in his journal of Conkling's absence: "His friends were embarrassed and somewhat indignant. If he intends to take actively hold of the campaign, it is probably best that he does not call on me here. I think his friends are showing zeal and enthusiasm and will work whether he does or not.

---

[1] Schurz to Hayes, Oct. 21, 1876, Hayes Papers.
[2] Garfield Journal, Aug. 3, 1880, Garfield Papers; T. C. Platt, *Autobiography*, p. 127; Jewell to Chandler, July 21, 1880, Chandler Papers.
[3] Hamilton, *Blaine*, pp. 487–8, containing letter from Garfield to Blaine, July 30, 1880.
[4] Robert McElroy, *Levi Parsons Morton*, pp. 109–11, is authority for this private meeting.
[5] Garfield Journal, Aug. 4, 1880, Garfield Papers.

There shall neither be nor appear to be, if I can prevent it, any mort-
gaging of my future freedom." Years later, Thomas C. Platt wrote:
"Garfield came as arranged. But his chagrin, mortification, and indignation, which were manifested (only, of course, to the inner circle)
when he found that Conkling was absent and would not be present,
are left to the imagination." [1] Following conferences with Jay Gould
and old Thurlow Weed, "a remarkably wise and well preserved man,"
Garfield "had in the afternoon [of August sixth] a long interview with
Morton, Cowles [Crowley], Arthur, and Platt," [2] and left next day for
home, stopping over Sunday [August eighth] at Chautauqua, N. Y.
On Monday, he arrived at Mentor, "very weary but feeling that no
serious mistake had been made and probably much good had been
done. No trades, no shackles, and as well fitted for defeat or victory
as ever." [3]

Such was not the understanding of the New Yorkers, as Platt recalled it. The all-important conference which he and his friends had
with Garfield was held "on the morning of the second day after Garfield's arrival," in Morton's rooms in the Fifth Avenue Hotel. The
dramatis personae both Garfield and Platt agree upon, but from the
latter comes a wealth of interesting details noticeably absent in the
Journal. "There were three primary motives for the consultation: one
to pacify Garfield for Conkling's absence; another to have an understanding with General Garfield as to his future relations to and intentions toward the controlling power in the State of New York, *viz.*,
the Grant-Conkling machine; and thirdly, if the former were arranged
to the mutual satisfaction, to adopt ways and means for procuring
money to carry on the canvass for the latter purpose." [4]

At the outset, Garfield, we are told, was pacified by the explanation that Conkling's friends were fully authorized to act for him, and
because "no charge of bargain, trading, or treaty of peace could be
charged with him absent." Next they proceeded to strike a bargain,
trade, or treaty of peace satisfactory to the New Yorkers, who were
not willing to "bear the brunt of the battle in the campaign" unless
secure from being "recognized" and "rewarded" in the same misguided
fashion as that adopted by President Hayes. This assurance, accord-

[1] Platt, *op. cit.*, p. 127 ff.
[2] Garfield Journal, Aug. 6, 1880, Garfield Papers.
[3] *Ibid.*, Aug. 9, 1880.
[4] Platt, *op. cit.*, p. 128.

ing to Platt, was given in the form of a pledge by Garfield that if they "worked hard for him" and his election resulted, "the wishes of the element of the party we represented should be paramount with him, touching all questions of patronage. While it should be his duty to give such decent recognition of and show proper gratitude to the rebellious element [of the New York delegation, led by Judge William H. Robertson] at Chicago that had rendered his nomination possible, yet, in dispensing those favors, he would consult with our friends and do only what was approved by them. These assurances were oft repeated, and solemnly emphasized, and were accepted and agreed to by all those present."[1] "A gentleman who was present" phrased the agreement as follows: Garfield declared his intention to appoint one Cabinet member from New York and to consult and be guided by the State organization, the Senators, Governor, Congressmen, *etc.*, in making all appointments of Federal officials within the State.[2]

Upon his return, Garfield wrote to Whitelaw Reid, asking: "Do you know how Arthur, Platt, or Cornell are feeling since the conference? I do not hear from either of them. My letters indicate that the New York trip did no harm and much good."[3] Does this request imply that Garfield thought he had not arranged any contract with these men, since he would not have been worried over their response if a contract had been settled? It might also imply that Garfield wished to make sure that these men would keep their part of a bargain— that they still felt what he had offered them was worth the price of their activity. Would not such anxiety be natural to a man who felt that he was getting much the better side of a bargain?

There can be no doubt that Garfield knew the sort of men with whom he was dealing in New York. They made no pretense of requiring less of him than a guarantee of their full control over Republican politics in New York in so far as it might be based on Federal patronage. Unless they had become transformed, their new activity after conferring with him arose from their belief that his victory would lead to the only reward for their efforts which they were inclined to value, control of "the offices." While it is remotely possible that they took a risk, that they "went to work" in the mere hope that Garfield would reward them as they desired, it is much more likely that they

[1] Platt, *op. cit.*, p. 131.
[2] A. R. Conkling, *op. cit.*, p. 612.
[3] Smith, *op. cit.*, Vol. II, p. 1015.

received assurance from him. They conferred with him, and it is inconceivable that they should not have attempted to pin him down to a trade or promise. If, as he confided to his journal, he did not make a binding agreement, he succeeded in making them think that he had. If, as Theodore Clarke Smith conjectures,[1] he interpreted a promise to "consult" as little more than a promise to notify of his conclusions, while they interpreted a promise to "consult" as an obligation to seek their advice in every New York appointment and not to contravene it, we cannot dismiss this as simply a case of self-deception by the New Yorkers. They were not the kind to give something for nothing, and there was no reason to believe that they had done so in this case. If they thought Garfield's promise to "consult" them was something more substantial than what he intended to bind himself to, he must have realized it and been willing to profit by it, as most men in his position would. One may imagine that he satisfied his conscience with a resolution to treat them in a manner which seemed just to him, even if not to them.[2]

When the Fifth Avenue conference was over, the Stalwarts in New York began to exert themselves anew. Arthur was chairman of the Republican State committee and Platt of its executive committee. They devoted themselves to organization. Platt raised money from Federal employees; Arthur arranged speaking tours; Morton obtained large sums for the two funds in his charge. "At last Lord Roscoe has visited the rooms," wrote one of the national committee to William E. Chandler,[3] a week later. "He did not see Jewell but had a long session with Dorsey and promised to take part, after his own fashion, in the campaign. He will (perhaps) warm up when he gets on the stump, and do good work." Conkling spoke at the Academy of Music in New York on September 17, and later to other audiences, all large. His first speech opened with a sneer at Hayes for affecting "superior sanctity," ran over several issues, dwelling most upon the Southern situation in the old vein, and closed with an appreciation of the candidates, especially Arthur, "one of the most genuine, patriotic, and honorable of men . . . a high-souled, honorable man—honorable in every position in which he ever stood—a man to be trusted in every relation of life," which

---

[1] Smith, *Garfield*, Vol. II, pp. 1016–17.
[2] My conclusions on the basis of available evidence agree with the suspicions of E. L. Godkin, ironically expressed in *The Nation* of Oct. 21, 1880.
[3] R. C. McCormick to Chandler, Aug. 13, 1880, Chandler Papers.

was enthusiastically applauded.[1] Garfield was not pleased with this form of assistance [2] but received more valuable aid in Ohio on September 28, just after news of defeat in Maine made his situation more critical than ever.

At Warren, Ohio, a giant mass meeting was arranged, which Conkling was persuaded by his New York friends to address along with General Grant.[3] This meeting, attended by several thousand people, made a deep impression throughout the country. "Conkling's speech at Warren was an event of considerable importance," observed Garfield in his journal; even more noteworthy was the visit to Mentor Farm paid by Grant, Logan, Conkling, Morton, and some fifteen other Republicans enroute to Cleveland from Warren. It was a social call, not a political conference, but was interpreted as a gesture of friendly support from the Stalwarts' idol.[4]

A little later, however, the Republican headquarters were indulging in dismal prophecies. "None of us are very cheerful over the outlook," wrote R. C. McCormick. "Tom Platt says New York never looked better but Ellis H. Roberts [Utica editor] has just written Jewell that in his part of the country it never looked worse. . . . Arthur is very hopeful." [5] West Virginia was reckoned among the lost, and Ohio among the wavering. Dorsey, who had quarreled with Marshall Jewell and had left headquarters to lead the battle in Indiana, wrote doubtfully at the end of September. The discord among the campaign leaders continued through October,[6] diminishing only as the final weeks arrived. Indiana workers were "clamorous for money" and Jewell thought that all the funds raised in New York by Morton's special committee had been sent to Dorsey.

While Grant and Conkling were rendering assistance of more than

[1] N. Y. *Tribune,* Sept. 18, 1880.
[2] Journal, Sept. 24, 1880, Garfield Papers.
[3] Platt, *op. cit.,* p. 133.
[4] *Ibid.,* pp. 134–5; Platt's description of a scene allegedly occurring upon their arrival is incredible. Garfield rushed out bare-headed in the pouring rain to clasp Conkling in his arms as he alighted from a carriage and exclaim "pathetically": "Conkling, you have saved me. Whatever man can do for man, that will I do for you!" Whereupon his magnanimous benefactor extracted a rigid promise to make no appointments for New York unless approved by Conkling and his leading associates. Then they went in out of the wet. Theodore Clarke Smith has adequately exploded this fantasy and shown that no such colloquy could have occurred. Smith, *op. cit.,* pp. 1032–34. Cf. A. R. Conkling, *op. cit.,* pp. 623–25; George S. Boutwell, *Reminiscences of Sixty Years,* Vol. II, p. 272; Thomas Beer, *Hanna,* p. 97 ff.
[5] R. C. McCormick to Chandler, Sept. 27, 1880, Chandler Papers.
[6] *Ibid.,* Oct. 5, 1880, Chandler Papers.

local importance in Ohio, Arthur thought his principal contribution should lie in winning New York for the Republican ticket. After doing his best to bring about an understanding at the Fifth Avenue conference, and, so he thought, succeeding, he next turned to the machine work which he deemed most necessary. Victory in New York depended on either winning New York City and King's County, or on so reducing the Democrats' normal margin there that the up-State Republican supremacy would not be overbalanced. Being no orator, he devoted himself without stint to the work of organizing a more than usually intensive campaign in New York and Brooklyn. In the autumn of 1879, he had elected Mayor Edward Cooper by arranging a fusion of city Republicans with anti-Tammany Democrats. In 1880, Tammany made overtures to the Irving Hall Democrats, agreeing on William R. Grace as a compromise candidate for mayor. They seemed likely to present a united front, until a defection from Irving Hall brought out William Dowd as a rival Democratic nominee. Arthur persuaded the Republicans to accept Dowd rather than to set up a third candidate, and got so many out to vote that he failed of victory by only three thousand.[1]

Arthur's own candidacy proved somewhat of a burden for the Republicans to carry. Union College alumni were organized to support him,[2] and his Irish-American extraction was capitalized.[3] But as the campaign progressed inquiries were received by President Hayes, asking if Arthur had been removed from the Collectorship for dishonesty,[4] and such a question was asked point-blank of John Sherman when he addressed a large audience in Cincinnati. Sherman's answer was disingenuous: Arthur had been inefficient, not dishonest. His nomination was inadvisable but Sherman would vote for him a million times before he would vote for William H. English.[5] Evarts found it possible to praise Arthur and ask for his election,[6] and even John Jay supported the Republican ticket.[7]

In August, *The Nation* had hailed the return of Ben Butler to the Democratic Party. "He will," the editor declared, "be a very amusing

[1] Grace, 101,760; Dowd, 98,715.
[2] See *Union Alumni Monthly* (Schenectady, N. Y.), Vol. XV, No. 10, *passim*.
[3] See pamphlet "Questions for Irish-American Voters," in Boston Public Library collection on election of 1880.
[4] Three letters of Sept., 1880, Treas. Dept., Exec. Files.
[5] Cincinnati *Gazette*, Aug. 31, 1880.
[6] N. Y. *Times*, Sept. 30, 1880.
[7] *The International Review*, Sept., 1880.

Democrat, and thus meet one great need of the Democratic Party—
that of 'a funny man.' " [1] That need was not so pronounced near the
end of the canvass. The tariff had taken the lead as an issue between
the parties; while the Republican Party proclaimed the inestimable
virtues of protection,[2] the Democratic platform has somewhat casually
urged "a tariff for revenue only"; [3] and Hancock, who was not a free-
trader, laid himself open to ridicule by insisting that the tariff was "a
local issue." Thomas Nast's pen aided the Republicans materially by
seizing on this seeming ignorance of Hancock's. His cartoon showing
Hancock on a speaker's platform, whispering in a companion's ear:
"Who is Tariff and why is He for revenue only?" was a damaging
blow to the Democrats.[4] It was but one of the many shafts of deri-
sion which cost the Democratic Party needed votes in "doubtful"
Indiana. There, the expenditure of considerable money by the Republicans supplemented the tariff argument in winning Republican
victory in the October State elections.[5] Ohio also went Republican in
October.

At the end, the desperate Democratic ruse of the "Morey letter," a
forgery in which Garfield appeared to approve of continued Chinese
immigration, not merely failed to discredit Garfield but produced a
reaction against the Democrats. In November, New York and the
country gave Republican majorities. New York's vote was very close,
555,544 to 534,511, but that of the whole country was even closer,
4,454,416 for Garfield and Arthur to 4,444,952 for Hancock and English. The electoral count, however, was 214 to 155, without dispute.
The Republicans had again staved off defeat.

[1] *The Nation,* Aug. 26, 1880.
[2] See Republican pamphlet *"Politics and Industry. Plain Talk with Working-men"*
(N. Y., 1880), in Ford Collection, N. Y. Public Library.
[3] Stanwood, *op. cit.,* p. 367.
[4] A. B. Paine, *Th. Nast: His Period and His Pictures,* p. 438.
[5] *The Nation,* Oct. 21, 1880.

CHESTER A. ARTHUR passed the day after election in joyous relaxation at the Fifth Avenue Hotel. A stream of congratulatory telegrams poured into his rooms. Then, and in the weeks which followed, his course of action was not materially altered by his new station. With Garfield it was different; he was soon immersed in the vexatious problem of welding his disunited party into a harmonious whole by the selection of suitable Cabinet officers. The responsibility for restoring Republican unity was his. Arthur could continue to think of himself as a New York politician with Washington connections, and to confine his interest to New York matters.

As soon as the election was over, Conkling and his group were occupied in regaining the party mastery in their State. The Half-Breeds were equally interested in developing the anti-Conkling wing to a point where it could either overthrow the whole machine, or be included in it under new leadership.[1] Both factions, recognizing that control of the party organization was to depend on the Federal patronage, concentrated their attention on the Cabinet which Garfield was forming and on the New York Senatorship to be filled by an election in January.

Garfield's difficulties with respect to a New York member of his Cabinet arose from his sincere desire to satisfy both factions, one responsible for his nomination, and the other for his election. Both must be made to work together if the party supremacy in New York was to survive. A third group increased the President-elect's embarrassments by insisting that appointments to office be entirely divorced from politics. These Independent Republicans, led by George William Curtis and instructed by Godkin, could be relied upon to denounce all instances in which purely political considerations prevailed in the distribution of offices. Finally, there was the understanding created by the Fifth Avenue conference during the campaign, causing endless troubles in the Cabinet-forming process.

At the end of November, Garfield went to Washington for five days, stopping over for lunch with Senator Cameron at Harrisburg. He was given to understand that the Pennsylvania Stalwarts could easily be

[1] Royal Cortissoz, *op. cit.*, Vol. II, p. 51.

brought to support the Administration.[1] At the capital, however, he found Levi P. Morton assiduously attentive, and after seeing him on three occasions, wrote in his diary: "I am annoyed very much at a misunderstanding between Morton and myself in regard to a conversation had in New York in August." In a separate notebook he explained that to give the Secretaryship of the Treasury to a man from New York "was not my understanding and wholly inadmissible. It would be a congestion of financial power, at money center, and would create great jealousy at the West. Collection and management of revenues should be kept as far apart as possible." [2] When he found Morton in his path again next day, he concluded a consultation "with the following points: *First.* I will not make and declare any particular choice of Cabinet ministers for a month or two yet. *Second.* I will not tolerate nor act upon any understanding that anything has been pledged to any party, State, or person." [3] Thus was begun the struggle of the New York Stalwarts to get into their hands the Treasury Department, with its plentiful patronage. The problem was not to be settled until after many hours of consultation and growing antagonism, the first bitter fruits of the Fifth Avenue conference—but by no means the last.

Of the three chief candidates at the Chicago convention, Grant, Sherman, and Blaine, Garfield selected the last to come into his Cabinet as Secretary of State. Blaine accepted the offer in an expansive letter, the receipt of which was noted by Garfield in his journal on December 23. Once this appointment had been determined upon, the choice of others was made far more difficult. The Conkling machine became more determined than ever that Morton should head the Treasury Department. Garfield satisfied Logan and Cameron by the inclusion of Robert Lincoln and Wayne MacVeagh in his official family. But Conkling he could not please by the selection of any other man than Levi P. Morton, nor by the selection of any other place for him than the Secretaryship of the Treasury. On December 13, Governor Cornell, Congressman Richard Crowley, and Louis F. Payn urged this appointment during a visit to Mentor.[4] When Garfield proposed to satisfy Conkling by inducing President Hayes to fill a vacancy in his Cabinet by making Morton his Secretary of the Navy, with the promise that

[1] Garfield Journal, Nov. 23, 1880, Garfield Papers.
[2] *Ibid.*, Nov. 27, 1880, Garfield Papers.
[3] *Ibid.*, Nov. 28, 1880.
[4] *Ibid.*, Dec. 13, 1880, Garfield Papers.

Morton would be kept there when Garfield took office, the suggestion was refused.[1] So matters stood when the new year began, the legislature met at Albany, and its choice of a Senator was at hand.

The elevation of Arthur to the Vice Presidency opened the way for other Stalwarts to seek the Senatorship to which he had earlier aspired. Several candidates came eagerly into the field, of whom the four outstanding were Levi P. Morton, Richard Crowley, Thomas C. Platt, and Chauncey Depew. Crowley and Morton were in Congress; Platt and Depew in business. Depew and Morton lived in New York City, while Crowley and Platt were nominally "up-State men." All but Depew were affiliated with Conkling's organization.

In December, Blaine had come to New York and there persuaded Depew that he must run for the Senate as an unqualified supporter of the Administration.[2] On New Year's Eve, "Blaine, Depew, William H. Robertson, and some others" were guests of Whitelaw Reid at dinner. They determined to open the year with a fight against Conkling. Reid was to go to Albany to tell all Half-Breeds "that they'll be defended if they defy Conkling, and that they won't lose the good graces of Garfield." [3] For the editorial page of Reid's New York *Tribune*, Blaine wrote a public announcement that the new Administration intended to coöperate with all elements of the Republican Party in New York. It appeared with the heading, "By Authority," in the issue of January 3.[4] Anti-Conkling men were to rally to Depew in the senatorial contest and fear no evil at the hands of the Administration. They hoped, also, to control the Assembly by wresting the Speakership from George H. Sharpe.[5]

The machine, for once in its history, was badly divided. Sharpe was readily elected Speaker because of his personal popularity, but the senatorial contest revealed the split. Crowley, Platt, and Morton each had claims to machine support—the two former as seasoned lieutenants, the latter for his generous contributions and steady regularity. Ordinarily, Conkling would have designated one of them as his preference and tried to satisfy the others in some other way. But when Morton

---

[1] Garfield Journal, Dec. 20, 1880.
[2] Chauncey Depew, *My Memories of Eighty Years*, p. 112.
[3] Royal Cortissoz, *Reid*, Vol. II, p. 45.
[4] *Ibid.*, Vol. II, p. 47.
[5] Alexander, *op. cit.*, Vol. III, p. 464.

abruptly asked the Senator to request the organization to concentrate on him, or at least to induce Platt to withdraw in his favor, he received the reply (dated Jan. 10, 1881):

I regret exceedingly the perplexity and vexation of the senatorial and cognate affairs, but it seems to me wholly inadmissible for me to attempt by my request to prevent any friend who pleases from submitting his claims to party friends.[1]

Conkling stood aside but, as he had probably long foreseen, Arthur urged Crowley's election while Governor Cornell supported Platt. The conflict developing between Arthur and Cornell was more clearly emphasized when, on January 10, Arthur went up to Albany in Crowley's behalf. In some parts of the country, for the Vice President-elect to participate so openly in electioneering was deemed an impropriety; but Arthur still thought of himself as a New York Republican leader, bound to fulfill political obligations and maintain organization supremacy.

The legislature was Republican by a wide majority so that, as usual, the actual election was to occur in the party caucus. A preliminary canvass revealed a deadlock among the four. If the choice should narrow down, Crowley had bright prospects of success. In order to bring pressure in his favor, Speaker Sharpe withheld the appointment of any Assembly committees until the contest should be decided, with the understanding that Crowley's "friends" would receive the best places. Before long, it was apparent that the Half-Breeds would never be allowed to elect Depew, but that they must be somewhat placated by whatever selection was made from outside their number. Platt, who was managing his own canvass, quickly appreciated the situation and went at once to Depew, offering assurances of his willingness to support the Administration if he should be chosen. Platt was believed by the Half-Breeds to be the most independent among Conkling's lieutenants, possibly inclined to set up for himself.[2] To Depew and to Reid, separately, and to a meeting of Half-Breeds at Albany, Platt repeated his pledges of loyalty to Garfield. Depew then dropped out in favor of Platt, and New York had "a tall young man" of gentle manners to represent her in the Senate beside the robust,

[1] McElroy, *Morton,* p. 123.
[2] Royal Cortissoz, *Reid,* Vol. II, p. 49.

domineering, curly-headed Conkling. Reid summed it up in a letter to Garfield on January 16th: [1]

My dear General:

The inside facts as to the Senatorial election are these.

Platt had the most alliances with us, and our people made excellent terms. He gave me personal pledges which insure not only fair but friendly general treatment. To Depew he pledged himself that—

1. He would countenance no effort at crushing or ignoring the Chicago bolters.

2. He would not oppose their getting either from State or Nation their fair share of patronage.

3. He would not oppose their confirmation, if any of them should come before the Senate, but on the contrary, would do all in his power to help it.

4. He would help in the prompt confirmation of your Cabinet—even in so extreme a case as the possibility of its containing the name of Judge Robertson—though much opposed to such a nomination.

5. He would do all he could (not much, probably) to keep Conkling reasonable.

On these conditions, Depew transferred to him twenty votes, and thus nominated him, on the first ballot, by one majority. He has since acknowledged his indebtedness to those votes, and to that agreement preceding, for his nomination.

The senatorial election weakened Conkling's organization in New York. Instead of confronting Garfield with two Stalwart Senators and a Stalwart Vice President, acting together in matters of patronage to restore the machine's strength and crush the Robertson element, Conkling had as a colleague one who was explicitly pledged to sustain nominations made in response to Half-Breed desires. To be sure, Platt was still reckoned among the Grant men by Judge Robertson, who wrote:

With two stalwart Senators and Vice-President from the State, the incoming Administration could in no other way so effectually put our Independent delegates to the Chicago Convention in a political metallic casket, hermetically sealed, as by placing in the Cabinet a stalwart from New York. It would surely give the delegation from the State to Grant, Conkling, or Cornell in 1884.[2]

But the fact remained that Platt could no longer be counted on to

[1] Royal Cortissoz, *Reid*, Vol. II, p. 50.
[2] Robertson to Reid, Jan. 25, 1881, Royal Cortissoz, *Reid*, Vol. II, p. 52.

follow Conkling's lead. Furthermore, Arthur's differences with Governor Cornell were sufficient to threaten trouble, perhaps immediately, but certainly for 1882, when Cornell's term was to end.

In the interim between election and inauguration, Arthur unquestionably impaired his national reputation. His active electioneering at Albany was resented as undignified, but, worst of all, his speech at the famous testimonial dinner to Senator Dorsey not only seemed to be lacking in taste but also exhibited a callous disregard for public sentiment. The dinner was tendered to Dorsey by his New York Republican friends on February 11, 1881, at Delmonico's. Stephen W. Dorsey had served with Grant during the Civil War and, after returning to Ohio for a time, had gone into Arkansas as a "carpetbagger," becoming president of the Arkansas Railway Company. From 1873 to 1879 he had represented Arkansas in the Senate but, instead of seeking reelection, had then become a mail contractor. In the campaign of 1880 he had served as secretary of the Republican national committee, representing the Grant men, to whom the chairmanship had been denied.[1] It was widely claimed that his personal activity in Indiana had converted that State, from a Democratic province to Republicanism. This victory in an extremely "doubtful" quarter had helped in carrying Ohio and New York and, through them, the whole election.

General Grant, as the first of a long list of prominent Republicans, presided at the dinner, with Dorsey sitting on his right and Arthur at his left. With Henry Ward Beecher and others, Grant spoke in praise of Dorsey's accomplishments. So also did the Vice President-elect, but in a fashion most unfortunate for his good name. His remarks were rambling and jocular in tone, verging at times on the silly. He made much, for example, of "the secrets of the campaign," which he did not want the reporters to ascertain for fear of "what they might make of it before the inauguration takes place." Then, after some references to the recent public discussion of his birthplace, he turned to the Indiana campaign:

Indiana was really, I suppose, a Democratic State. It had been put down on the books always as a State that might be carried by close and perfect organization and a great deal of—(laughter)—I see the reporters are present, therefore I will simply say that everybody showed a great deal of interest in

[1] The Stalwarts had wanted T. C. Platt. See Wm. E. Chandler to Garfield, Feb. 17, 1881, Garfield Papers.

the occasion and distributed tracts and political documents all through the State. . . .[1]

The speech received much attention. The inference was freely made that Arthur had condoned the corrupt use of money in Indiana. He later denied any such intention, declaring that the whole idea of his having sanctioned the improper use of funds was a reporters' invention.[2]

On this occasion, Arthur was careless of the impression he was making. For him that was unusual, and one can only guess at the reason. He was habitually dignified, but this speech was rather frivolous, not at all in accord with his usual bearing on public occasions. The language he used in itself hardly sustained the evil interpretation adopted by the press, which was probably suggested by his manner, rather than by his words. Whitelaw Reid, speaking after him, took special care to explain the legitimate character of Dorsey's work in Indiana. Garfield thought the dinner "a curious affair, whose whole significance I do not yet understand." [3] For both Garfield and Arthur, it was later to have an importance that at the time they could not possibly anticipate.

In the fortnight after the Dorsey dinner, Arthur arranged his affairs for an indefinite absence in Washington, and went to the capital to establish himself. A few days before the inauguration, he visited the Senate Chamber, escorted by Vice President Wheeler. They walked to a corner sofa, while the galleries buzzed with interest. For a moment they sat alone. Then Senators Logan, Anthony, and Sharon greeted Arthur. Before long, Conkling was introducing Senator after Senator to the tall and portly newcomer, until the reception in the corner quite overshadowed the official proceedings. Hannibal Hamlin of Maine, Vice President under Abraham Lincoln, sat reading at his desk, oblivious to all about him. Conkling tapped him on the shoulder and told him that Arthur had come. With a smile, Hamlin rose to greet him, and for a few moments three Vice Presidents stood together in conversation. The Democrats were next brought up, among them Senator Cockrell of Missouri, with whom Arthur talked for several minutes. Then Conkling guided his protégé to Hamlin's seat, next his own,

---

[1] N. Y. *Tribune*, Feb. 12, 1881; N. Y. *Semi-Weekly Tribune*, Feb. 15, 1881.
[2] See Melville E. Stone, *Fifty Years a Journalist*, p. 148.
[3] Garfield Journal, Feb. 17, 1881, Garfield Papers.

where Arthur was later greeted by other men. Last to come was George H. Pendleton of Ohio, a defeated candidate for the Vice Presidency twelve years before. To Arthur it was a pleasant experience. He bore himself with an ease and grace which impressed reporters.[1]

Meanwhile, the struggle over New York's representative in Garfield's Cabinet went on. During the last week before the inauguration it came to a climax. Conkling's refusal to be satisfied with anything less than Morton's appointment to the Treasury had not overcome the objections which Garfield once told him were "insuperable." An attempt, despite Blaine's opposition, to make Charles J. Folger New York's Cabinet representative instead of Morton, had been foiled by Folger's refusal.[2] There remained in Garfield's mind the alternative of persuading Morton to take the War or Navy Department or of choosing some third New Yorker. A visit from George H. Sharpe was followed by an offer to Morton of the Secretaryship of the Navy,[3] which, at the last possible moment, he accepted. When Garfield reached Washington and went to the Riggs House on March first, he soon understood that Morton was "pleased with his new place but his New York friends not." [4]

Conkling and Arthur found the situation created by Morton's acceptance intolerable so long as there remained a prospect of getting the Treasury Department in Stalwart hands. They may have wanted it as a "reply to Blaine in the State Department," [5] but they needed its patronage, and they believed the place had been promised to them, through Morton, at the Fifth Avenue conference, and that the promise had been confirmed in conversation between Garfield and Senators Plumb, Dorsey, Simon Cameron, and others.[6] Garfield's desire to satisfy them was evident, and they perhaps felt that by persistent refusal to accept anything else they could force him to give them what they desired. When Morton gave in and accepted the Navy Department, they thought it not merely a weak, but an unnecessary, surrender.

Time was pressing. Early on March 2, Conkling and Arthur sent Congressman John H. Starin to persuade Morton to retract. He brought

[1] N. Y. Times, Feb. 24, 1881.

[2] Folger to Garfield, Feb. 23, 1881, Garfield Papers. Folger would have been made Attorney General.

[3] Garfield Journal, Feb. 25, 1881; McElroy, Morton, p. 127.

[4] Ibid., March 1, 1881. Compare McElroy, Morton, p. 128, who says Morton accepted "in disregard of his personal inclinations."

[5] T. C. Smith, Garfield, Vol. II, p. 1072.

[6] McElroy, Morton, pp. 121, 127.

the excited Morton, whom he had routed out of bed, to the lodgings which Arthur and Conkling shared. In the face of their hot criticism, he wilted, and wrote a letter withdrawing his acceptance of less than a day before.[1]

But Garfield, instead of yielding, was as firm as ever in declining to put a New Yorker over the Treasury Department. He began to cast about for a substitute. Blaine, who had a change of heart, and White-law Reid, who knew his man, persuaded Garfield that Thomas L. James as Postmaster General would solve the problem of New York's member in the Cabinet. Unknown to Conkling, they brought James to New York, introduced him to Garfield, and satisfied the President-elect that James would be trustworthy. Senator-elect Platt was then conducted to Garfield, and induced to say that he could not fully concur in any objections which Conkling might possibly raise against James. Thus Garfield's way was cleared.[2]

Arthur and Conkling were finishing their usual late breakfast when Platt came in from his interview with Garfield. The news he bore brought an abrupt end to their leisurely meal. As they went at once to Garfield's hotel rooms, they must have realized that it was hopeless to expect a New York Stalwart to be made the Secretary of the Treasury. Instead of urging it further, they proposed Timothy O. Howe of Wisconsin for the place, believing that he would both serve their purposes and satisfy the Western feeling about the office. Conk-ling did the talking, possibly a tirade against Garfield, as it has been described.[3] In his diary, Garfield reported the Senator as "full of apprehension that he had been or was to be cheated." [4]

Conkling realized that his New York machine was breaking up. He foresaw that, with Blaine at the head of Garfield's Cabinet, Fed-eral aid and comfort would be afforded to his enemies, the Half-Breeds, and that his own personal domination over the party in New York would be weakened, perhaps ended, unless Garfield proved unexpectedly friendly. If both the new Senator and the new Cabinet officer from his State were pledged to act independently of Conkling

---

[1] Garfield Journal, March 2, 1881, Garfield Papers; T. S. Connery, "The Secret History of the Garfield-Conkling Tragedy," in *The Cosmopolitan*, Vol. XXIII (1897), pp. 152–3; Royal Cortissoz, *Reid*, Vol. II, p. 55.

[2] Royal Cortissoz, *Reid*, Vol. II, pp. 55–6.

[3] See T. C. Smith, *Garfield*, Vol. II, pp. 1093–4.

[4] Garfield Journal, Mar. 3, 1881, Garfield Papers; E. B. Andrews, *The Last Quarter-Century in the United States, 1870–1895*, Vol. I, p. 325.

whenever Garfield demanded, it could make little difference that Vice President Arthur remained his loyal adherent. Conkling would be unseated. His machine would break down. A subservient and powerful Cabinet officer was well-nigh essential to his continuance as Republican "boss" of New York.

THE inauguration day was fairly typical. Crowds swarmed into the capital. Flurries of slushy snow fell during the morning, and Pennsylvania Avenue was coated with "muddy slime."

At ten o'clock, Arthur was at Garfield's rooms ready to go with him to the White House. Three quarters of an hour later they rode out of the White House grounds, Garfield and Hayes in one carriage, Arthur and Senator Pendleton in an open barouche behind them. Arthur was in fine spirits, delighting in the four well-matched white horses, doffing his hat constantly, and looking "ruddy and healthy and beaming" to the interested crowds. Arriving at the east end of the Capitol, he went to the Vice President's room and thence to the Senate chamber.

Arthur entered the hall after President Hayes, President-elect Garfield, and the outgoing Cabinet had seated themselves, and took his place beside Vice President Wheeler. He was carefully dressed in "light trousers, a blue Prince Albert coat, colored necktie, and light gloves," and, with his commanding height, high color, and graceful bearing, was personally impressive. When Vice President Wheeler presented him, he gave a brief address to the Senate as follows:

Senators: I come as your presiding officer with genuine solicitude, remembering my inexperience in parliamentary proceedings. I cannot forget how important, intricate, and often embarrassing are the duties of the chair. On the threshold of our official association, I invoke that courtesy and kindness with which you have been wont to aid your presiding officer. I shall need your constant encouragement and support, and I rely with confidence upon your lenient judgment of any errors into which I may fall. In return, be assured of my earnest purpose to administer your rules in a spirit of absolute fairness, to treat every Senator at all times with that courtesy and just consideration due to the representatives of equal States, and to do my part, as assuredly each of you will do yours, to maintain the order, decorum and dignity of the Senate. I trust that the official and personal relations upon which we are now entering will be marked with mutual confidence and regard, and that all our obligations will be so fulfilled as to redound to our own honor, to the glory of our common country, and the prosperity of all its people. I am now ready to take the oath of office prescribed by the Constitution.[1]

[1] N. Y. *World*, N. Y. *Herald*, Mar. 5, 1881.

This "modest speech" was well received, and from Roscoe Conkling drew somewhat ostentatious evidences of approval. The oath of office followed. When Vice President Wheeler had made his farewell remarks and adjourned the old Senate, Arthur took the chair, called the new Senate to order, and swore in new Senators before adjournment to the outdoor platform for Garfield's oath and inaugural address. Conkling's prominent place directly behind the new President at this ceremony caused much comment.

To equip Arthur for his new duties, his New York friends, regardless of party affiliation, gave him a dinner next evening and presented him with an ivory gavel, ornamented with gold. The gavel would be needed, but for Arthur there promised to be a rôle of even greater importance than simply presiding over debates. The special session of the Senate of the new Congress revealed a curious party division of thirty-seven Republicans, thirty-seven Democrats, one Independent (David Davis of Illinois), and one Readjuster-Democrat (William Mahone of Virginia). Newspapers had prophesied much of Arthur's social cultivation, but even more interest was felt in the possibility that he might frequently be called upon to cast deciding votes.

The Senate convened on March 5 with Arthur in the chair. It had been summoned to confirm nominations to the Cabinet and lesser offices, and to consider treaties awaiting ratification. Difficulties in organization absorbed its energies, after it had approved Garfield's Cabinet, inasmuch as the equal division of the major parties left the balance of power in the hands of two independent Senators, or, if they should divide equally, with the Vice President. Vacancies in four Republican seats deferred the ultimate trial of strength. Senators Blaine, Kirkwood, and Windom resigned at once to enter the Cabinet; Senator Carpenter of Wisconsin had died on February 24; and their successors were not all in Washington until March 18. The Republicans had insisted that as soon as all were present, they would control the Senate.

The Democrats challenged the Republican claims to a majority. On March 10, through Senator Pendleton, they proposed a complete list of Senate committees with Democratic chairmen and Democratic majorities. David Davis, the Illinois Independent, next day announced that he would sustain this Democratic effort at organization.[1] Which party should have ultimate control depended, therefore, on the choice

[1] *Cong. Rec.*, Vol. XII, p. 6.

made by the new Virginia Senator, William Mahone. Mahone had been elected by those who, under the name of "Readjuster-Democrats," opposed the old "Bourbon" control of his State. He was the leader of the party which had attained mastery by efficient organization and a program combining partial debt repudiation with Negro voting. His methods were those of a New York "boss" adapted to a Virginia setting. By joining the Republicans in the Senate, he would throw control into Vice President Arthur's hands; by adhering to the Democrats, he would give them a thirty-nine to thirty-seven majority, and Arthur's vote would be unlikely to determine any questions of importance.

While the Republicans were awaiting the arrival of their new men, they postponed a test of Mahone's allegiance by wrangling over the rules governing consideration of Pendleton's committee list. Arthur accepted Conkling's interpretation, Pendleton appealed from his ruling, and it was debated until, turning to executive business, both sides withdrew the question.[1] The Democrats were so eager to learn what Mahone would do that at the next session, the venerable "Ben" Hill of Georgia undertook to force him into the open. In a vigorous speech, he insisted that the Republicans could offset Davis's independent vote only by acquiring some person, elected as a Democrat, who intended "disgracing the commission he holds." The galleries and floor were crowded with visitors, feeling ran high, and the scenes of confusion defied Arthur's intention of maintaining order. Hill's speech named no one. He professed to disbelieve the Republican claims. He asked for an explanation, doubting that one could be given. "I repel as an insult," he thundered, "the charge made against any Democrat that he would be false to his colors and is intending to vote with you on the organization." [2]

When Hill's speech was over, and as soon as he could obtain the floor, the man whom all had known to be Hill's target rose defiantly to his feet. In a shrill voice, with many sharp thrusts at "the Senator from Georgia" and the rest of the "Bourbon Democracy," interrupted frequently by applause and laughter, and fully mindful of the sensation he was creating, Mahone declared his complete independence of the Democratic caucus, and in a colloquy with Senator Hill denied that by

[1] *Cong. Rec.*, Vol. XII, pp. 7–14.
[2] *Ibid.*, XII, pp. 20–22.

voting with the Republicans he would betray the people who had elected him.[1] The Democrats now knew his decision; they had yet to learn his price.

Action on the Democratic committee list was postponed by Republican dilatory motions until Frye of Maine had taken his seat and the Republican side was full. Then, on March 18, Arthur's deciding vote being twice given, the Democratic program was rejected, and that brought forward by Senator Anthony for the Republicans, adopted.[2] Senator Hill had talked of a bargain; and Mahone's price, or the first payment, at least, was soon revealed. On March 23, Senator Dawes, leader of the Republican caucus, offered resolutions covering the election of five new persons to administrative offices of the Senate. George C. Gorham, nominated for Secretary of the Senate, was a friend of Mahone and an editor of the *National Republican,* published in Washington.[3] Closer to Mahone, and more objectionable to Democrats, was the nominee for Sergeant-at-Arms, Harrison H. Riddleberger of Virginia. He was a Mahone "henchman," sponsor of that measure for scaling down Virginia's debt and arbitrarily reducing the interest rate which was known as the "Riddleberger bill." [4] It was the main embodiment of the Readjusters' financial program. Moreover, he was an ex-Confederate officer who, in the last election, had been a Hancock-and-English elector. A worse claimant for Republican favors could hardly be imagined.

The Democrats at once determined that Gorham, Riddleberger, and the others should not replace the existing officials. For six weeks they resisted Republican efforts to come to a vote, using the very tactics by which the Republicans had just prevented the election of Democratic committees. Similarly, in their reversed situation, the Republicans refused to go into executive session until these officers were appointed, Vice President Arthur upholding that determination by his deciding vote at the beginning of the contest.[5] The resolution of the Republicans was eventually shaken by Democratic persistence. The majority could not forever refuse executive sessions in the face of pressure from President and press. On May 4, they began a series

---

[1] *Ibid.,* XII, pp. 22–25.
[2] *Ibid.,* XII, p. 32.
[3] C. C. Pearson, *The Readjuster Movement in Virginia,* pp. 138, 154.
[4] *Ibid., passim;* Printed in *Cong. Rec.,* Vol. XII, pp. 61–3.
[5] *Cong. Rec.,* Vol. XII, p. 41.

of such sessions in which they ratified the Chinese treaty negotiated the year before and acted on nearly three hundred nominations to office. One of Garfield's nominations was of a special interest and provoked a struggle of momentous consequences.

President Garfield, through patronage, could either maintain or break the supremacy in New York of Roscoe Conkling's machine. Unfortunately neither course, in view of the rising revolt against the Senator, could restore essential unity to the Republican Party there. A concerted revolt against Conkling had already begun, not merely among the Independents but among the Half-Breeds. Could Garfield restore sufficient harmony to preserve Republican control of New York in 1882 and 1884? Could he observe the agreement reached at the Fifth Avenue conference, to "consult" the wishes of the Conkling organization, without offending its enemies? Could he depart from it without a sharp struggle with Conkling himself?

When the President was ready to take up the question of New York patronage, he sent for the New York Senators, as they had a right to expect. He had prepared for the interview by consulting New York Republicans outside the machine, and even the Senators from Massachusetts, George F. Hoar and Henry L. Dawes.[1] Platt was obliged to be in New York, and asked that action be delayed until his return; but Conkling came and spent two and a half hours of a Sunday afternoon going over a long list of Federal offices. "I adopted many of his suggestions," Garfield subsequently wrote, "but I told him I must recognize some of the men who had supported me at Chicago. He wanted me to give them foreign appointments. I said they did not deserve exile, but rather a place in the affairs of their own State." [2] Despite this clash, the two men came to a partial agreement and, with the understanding that Platt concurred,[3] the President sent to the Senate, on March 22, eight New York nominations which were altogether satisfactory to the Stalwarts.

Blaine, very much excited, intruded on Garfield's dinner that evening to vent his distress, and when other numerous callers had left, returned with William E. Chandler for a conference from ten-thirty to midnight. Next day's papers and a sheaf of telegrams complained of the apparent surrender to the "boss," and of the unhappy prospect it

[1] Garfield Journal, Mar. 10, 11, 18, 1881, Garfield Papers.
[2] Ibid., Mar. 20, 1881.
[3] Smith, Garfield, Vol. II, p. 1105.

promised.[1] Unwilling to allow so false an understanding to prevail for more than a day, Garfield, probably on his own responsibility, decided on a bold stroke.

Early in the afternoon on March 23, the Senate was listlessly discussing the propriety of considering legislative matters in a special session called for "executive business." Arthur was toying with his ivory gavel; some of the Senators, among them Conkling, were reading; the atmosphere was calm, even dull, when one of the President's secretaries arrived with a message. Arthur quickly opened it and scanned its contents with sudden excitement. His features became hard and set; he summoned a page and sent the paper to Conkling, who read it slowly, and looked up at Arthur with an expression of outraged fury. Neighboring Senators, observing that something untoward had happened, came up to inquire. Conkling said nothing, but showed them the message and attempted to resume his reading. Soon the debate ended, and, with an air of expectancy, the assembly went into executive session.

The message from Garfield contained several appointments. In Europe, certain friends of General Grant were shifted around to make a vacancy in the Consul-Generalship at London. General Edwin A. Merritt was nominated to that position, leaving, of course, a vacancy at the head of the New York Custom House. For this powerful place, until so recently the stronghold of the Stalwart machine, Garfield now proposed William H. Robertson, an enemy of Conkling since 1872, the leading Republican rebel against him in 1880, an outstanding New York Half-Breed, probably the most objectionable person to the Stalwarts whom the President could have selected.

Robertson was a man of ability, and in politics especially sagacious. Unquestionably he was selected by the President, whom he had never met, on purely political grounds, as "the leader of the New York Independents" at the Chicago convention.[2] He was symbolic of the insurgency in Republican ranks which had prevented the nomination of Grant and produced that of Garfield, and which intended to revamp the party leadership in New York. As such, he was personally disagreeable anywhere to the Conkling group, but in the position for which he was advanced, the Collectorship at New York, he was in-

[1] Ibid., p. 1106.
[2] Garfield to B. A. Hinsdale, Apr. 4, 1881, Smith, Garfield, Vol. II, pp. 1108-9.

finitely objectionable.

From certain attacks upon Collector Merritt's administration,[1] Garfield had foreseen that there would be a drive for his place which might prove annoying unless he acted early. The Collector's term was to end in the midst of the campaign of 1882, when New York would be choosing both a Governor and Congressmen, and the rivalry for the place between the Republican factions would be unusually keen. At Mentor, Garfield had talked with Folger about replacing Merritt at the outset of his Administration and had secured his approval.[2] Conkling was probably aware of Garfield's intention when, at the conclusion of their Sunday conference, he asked: "Mr. President, what do you propose about the Collectorship of New York?" Garfield had answered: "We will leave that for another time."[3] The Senator went away supposing that he would be permitted to discuss the matter before a nomination should be made and, as time passed, came to view Garfield's casual remark as a deliberate promise.

It was not, however, Garfield's failure to consult Conkling about the Collectorship that aroused his fiercest resentment. What lay at the foundation of his bitter hostility was undoubtedly the conviction that Robertson, as Collector, would construct a new machine able to drive his own out of power and existence. The appointment, despite the Stalwart nominations of the day before, indicated to Conkling and Arthur a surrender by the President to Blaine, with whom, as they thought, he planned to coöperate in putting the Stalwarts off the stage altogether. The nomination was widely interpreted as Blaine's act, and Garfield did nothing to show that it was entirely his own.[4]

Naturally, the men with whom Arthur associated were bitterly opposed. Soon he shared their conviction that Garfield had treated Conkling shamefully[5] and joined them in fighting the appointment. Several courses were pursued. Their first effort was to induce the President to withdraw the nomination; the second, if he persisted, to persuade the Senate not to confirm it. Platt, especially, tried to make Robertson decline, but he insisted that, although he had had no warn-

[1] Curtis to Hayes, Dec. 1, 1880, Hayes Papers; request made of Secretary Sherman by the Senate, on motion of Senator Conkling, Feb. 8, 1881, *Cong. Rec.*, XI, p. 1335.
[2] Garfield Journal, Mar. 23, 1881.
[3] George S. Boutwell, *Reminiscences,* Vol. II, p. 273, quoting Conkling's version.
[4] Smith, *Garfield,* Vol. II, p. 1106 ff.
[5] T. B. Connery, "Secret History of the Garfield-Conkling Tragedy" in *Cosmopolitan,* Vol. XXIII, pp. 146–7.

ing whatever of his appointment, he had even less intention of re-linquishing the opportunity thus offered.[1] A fourth method of meeting the situation, one favored by some Stalwarts, was that of "extorting from the President, as a means of placating them, the surveyorship and the naval office" with which to neutralize Robertson's political opportunities in the Collector's office. Among those who believed it wise to submit for such a consideration was probably Governor Cornell.[2] The New York Senate, of which Robertson was a member, unanimously adopted a resolution urging the national Senate to confirm the nomination,[3] and Cornell also reflected the Albany attitude when he advised Conkling not to fight the appointment. The division thus manifested in the Conkling organization was to widen into an irreparable breach within a fortnight.

The campaign to persuade Garfield to withdraw Robertson's name opened with a call from Postmaster General Thomas L. James, on March 25, to submit his resignation. Instead of accepting it, Garfield arranged for an interview with Conkling, Arthur, and Platt in the evening, to which Cabinet officers were also to come. On their way to the White House, Arthur and the others called for Senator Conkling and all were about to start out when a message from Cornell, advising nonresistance, was brought to the boss. In a fit of anger at this "treachery," Conkling refused to go on; Garfield was left wondering why "they failed to come." [4] James, after this episode, felt absolved from any need of resignation.

Three days later, Garfield received from James a written protest signed by himself, Vice President Arthur, and the two Senators. It was their substitute for the appointed discussion at which they had not appeared. Shortly before, Garfield had declared to John Hay: "Robertson may be carried out of the Senate head first or feet first. I shall never withdraw him." [5] He remained unmoved by the document, or by Platt's verbal protest later in the day. "I see no mistake in what I have done *in re* Robertson," Garfield wrote, "unless it be in not having talked with the two Senators beforehand. But that would

[1] See his letter to Reid, n.d., 1881, quoted in Cortissoz, *Reid*, Vol. II, p. 63.
[2] See dispatch from Whitelaw Reid to John Hay, Mar. 27, 1881, stolen from the telegraph service and published after Garfield's death, N. Y. *Tribune*, Jan. 7, 1882, cited in Cortissoz, *Reid*, Vol. II, p. 60.
[3] The copy sent to Senator John Sherman is in Sherman Papers, dated Mar. 24, 1881.
[4] Garfield Journal, Mar. 25, 1881, Garfield Papers; Smith, *Garfield*, Vol. II, pp. 1111-2; Connery, *loc. cit.*, pp. 155-7.
[5] Cortissoz, *Reid*, Vol. II, p. 61.

have made no difference in the result." [1]

Instead of persuading Garfield to yield, therefore, the first part of the Stalwart program had simply strengthened his resolution. His Cabinet gave him "generous support" on April 1, and in Senator Sherman he found an ally who had once defeated Conkling and Arthur and was ready to do so again.[2] Consequently, when Platt sought to escape from his intolerably awkward position by a compromise arrangement—a scheme to give Robertson the post of United States district attorney for the southern district of New York, leaving Merritt in the Collectorship, and sending District Attorney Stewart L. Woodford abroad—Garfield flatly refused.[3] Even Senators like William B. Allison (whom he had invited into his Cabinet), John A. Logan, and William P. Frye could not move him.[4] He insisted on putting the issue before the Senate.

Platt did not cease his efforts when Garfield had declined the first compromise. He next strove to obtain Robertson's acceptance of a transfer to some other office. Such an arrangement would, of course, make it possible for Platt to keep his election promises to Depew, Reid, and others. More than that, and probably of equal concern to him, he could in that way prevent Conkling from wrecking the New York Republican Party. The old chief had probably begun to realize that his days in politics were nearly over. At the end of his term, in 1885, he proposed, instead of seeking reëlection, to resume the practice of law and build up a fortune. During the next four years, he intended, and made no secret of his plan, to use whatever power he possessed to obstruct Garfield's Administration and obtain revenge. If he persisted in his intended course, there could be no doubt that one result would be a cleavage of the New York Republicans into irreconcilable divisions, while another outcome would be a blighted political career for Thomas C. Platt and Conkling's other associates. So Senator Platt persevered in his endeavors to reach an accommodation, while Arthur, perhaps with misgivings, sustained Conkling in his insistence that Robertson must not be confirmed.[5]

---

[1] Garfield Journal, Mar. 28, 1881, Garfield Papers.
[2] Sherman to Merritt, March 31, April 5; Garfield to Sherman, April 3; Merritt to Sherman, April 4, 1881, Sherman Papers; Garfield Journal, April 3, 1881, Garfield Papers.
[3] *Ibid.*, April 5, 1881.
[4] *Ibid.*, March 27, April 5, 6, 1881.
[5] For Conkling's attitude, see Louis F. Payn's account, reported by Reid to Garfield, April 11, 1881, Cortissoz, *Reid*, Vol. II, pp. 63–4.

The people of the United States were witnessing a strange spectacle. The President persistently sought to secure the confirmation of Judge Robertson's nomination to the Collectorship; the Vice President, presiding officer of the body which was to ratify the nomination, and former Collector himself, openly opposed the Chief Executive. Arthur frankly told Garfield his objections and acted throughout with his fellow "machinists." First he signed the document which James submitted, deploring what he understood to be a clear breach of promise, especially of the pledge made in August, for the observance of which he felt in some degree responsible to his own friends.[1] When other resources had failed, he went to Garfield on the evening of April 14 for "a long and earnest talk" in which he sought to convince the President that to appoint Robertson to the Collectorship would "inevitably defeat the party in New York." With the contents of Reid's April eleventh letter in mind, the President answered: "Yes, it will defeat us if the leaders determine it shall. Summed up in a word, Mr. Conkling asks me to withdraw Robertson to keep the other leaders of the party from destroying themselves."[2]

Garfield's analysis was no doubt correct. Conkling, Arthur, Cornell, and Platt could accept the appointment of Robertson and quietly submit to being supplanted by other leaders. They could relinquish their hopes of continued dominance, could let their power be shattered by the Administration, which to them signified Blaine, without opposition. If, on the contrary, they intended to fight for their place of leadership, the ill feeling attending the struggle could not be expected to disappear for years. Robertson's appointment would, therefore, temporarily destroy the party in New York unless the Conkling machine should gracefully accept at once what, of course, it must inevitably come to at some time—the end of its career. Garfield was asking them to commit lingering suicide, and, at the same time, was prolonging the agony by granting them some favors and influence.

The division of New York Republicans was illustrated by the legislature. The Senate unanimously approved Robertson's nomination, but in the Assembly a great majority of the Republicans expressed unqualified objections in a formal resolution. As time passed, public opinion, while sharply conflicting, increasingly favored the President's

[1] Letter of protest is printed in Platt, *Autobiography*, p. 154–5.
[2] Garfield Journal, Apr. 14, 1881, Garfield Papers.

position. The civil service reformers were somewhat disarmed by an article in the Philadelphia *Press* of April 24 authoritatively stating Garfield's determination to allow Robertson, as Collector, to build up no machine "to weaken Mr. Conkling's influence." [1] They also appreciated that in fighting "Senatorial courtesy," the President was on the side of reform. The Stalwarts might rally to Conkling's side, finding their arguments in such papers as the *Sun* and *Herald*,[2] but his real support came from the leaders devoted to Senate control of Executive nominations.

Senators found themselves obliged either to offend the President at the outset of his Administration or to discard the practice which built up their political leadership in their own States, a predicament so unhappy for practically all of them that they spent their first energies trying to evade it by a compromise. The deadlock over the election of Gorham, Riddleberger, and others to Senate offices forestalled an immediate decision. The deadlock, indeed, was probably prolonged for the very purpose of escaping such a decision until the Republican Senators had agreed, in caucus, upon a program permitting of executive sessions without action in the Robertson case. A caucus committee of seven, having been assured by Conkling that if necessary—he would publish a letter by Garfield which would make him "bite the dust," [3] and having met with Garfield's immovable purpose not to yield,[4] adopted a procedure calculated to postpone the issue.

They would resume executive sessions, in which they would first consider treaties, and after that, uncontested nominations.[5] Robertson's appointment, by this scheme, would not be taken up until a definite decision to act on it had been reached. Garfield, when apprised of the agreement, insisted that "there could be no peace by evading the New York contest." He persisted in forcing the Senate to make the disagreeable choice, receiving from his Cabinet "a general hearty approval of [his] . . . course." [6] He had the whip hand.

On May 4, the Republican Senators yielded to Democratic tactics and went into the first executive session since March 23, taking up the

[1] Article quoted in T. C. Smith, *Garfield*, Vol. II, pp. 1120–21.
[2] See especially N. Y. *Herald*, May 11, 1881.
[3] See article by Henry L. Dawes, chairman of the committee, "Conkling and Garfield," in *Century Magazine*, Vol. XLVII, (Jan., 1894), p. 343.
[4] *Ibid.*, p. 344; Journal, Apr. 29, 30, May 2, 1881, Garfield Papers.
[5] Alexander, *Political History of the State of New York*, Vol. III, p. 474.
[6] Journal, May 3, 1881, Garfield Papers.

Chinese immigration treaty. On the following day, they ratified it. Pending nominations were next in order. Senator Conkling, under the caucus agreement, was in a position to have his friends confirmed and Robertson's appointment postponed until autumn. Anticipating this, President Garfield, that same day, did what he had long meditated; he withdrew five Stalwart New York nominations, leaving to be first disposed of those of William H. Robertson for Collector and Richard A. Elmer, a friend of Platt, for Second Assistant Postmaster General. It was a bold act which left the Senate no doubt that it would have to choose.

"Glory to God, Victory is Yours, Sure and Lasting" was Blaine's ecstatic note to Garfield upon learning of the action. "My dear Sir: Stick—The Constitution, the Lord God, and the People are with you," another wrote. More enlightening still was Joseph Medill's telegram: "Hold the fort. Better resign to his henchman Arthur and go back to Mentor than degrade the Presidency by succumbing to the usurping boss." [1]

The issue being fairly joined, Conkling foresaw defeat; although in caucus he continued to have his way, it was only after increasing effort and amid continual difficulty. On May 8, the Republican Senators would grant only temporary delay in the report on Robertson's nomination from the committee on commerce, of which Conkling was chairman.[2] At succeeding caucuses, the number on whom Conkling could rely, even in voting for delayed action, kept falling away. The time for the voting approached, with Platt in an impossible position, plainly caught between two incompatible obligations. Since resignation was his only means of escape, for he could not decline to vote, he suggested to Conkling that they both withdraw and seek reëlection at Albany. "Do not be too hasty about this matter, young man," the lordly chief replied. His mind grew more receptive during the week, however, so that on May 14, after a caucus that sealed his fears of failure, he joined in composing a letter of resignation. On Monday, May 16, the the long document was sent to Governor Cornell, while at noon, at the Capitol, Vice President Arthur laid the notifications before the Senate. They were the day's sensation.

Garfield thought it "a very weak attempt at the heroic. If I do not

[1] T. C. Smith, *Garfield*, Vol. II, pp. 1126–7.
[2] Garfield Journal, May 9, 10, 1881, Garfield Papers; Cincinnati *Gazette*, May 9, 1881.

mistake," he wrote, "it will be received with guffaws of laughter. They appeal to a legislature which they think is already secured. Even in this they may fail. They have wounded the self-love of their brother Senators and may lose by it. . . ." [1] The partisan wife of James G. Blaine reported that she had heard no one in Washington compliment Conkling for his behavior, though she had seen "all sorts of people and of every shade of cowardice." [2] Certainly the Senate, eager to adjourn, waited scarcely a decent interval in mourning for the departed before it had the nomination favorably reported from committee (May 17). Two days after the resignations, in a session lasting only twenty-five minutes, without a roll call, Robertson was confirmed. [3] "This leaves Conkling's attitude ridiculous. His row is with the Senate, equally with me," Garfield wrote in jubilation.

Others agreed that Conkling and Platt had been ridiculous. One newspaper reported that after hearing of their resignations, two orphans in a District of Columbia asylum resigned from the institution because they had not been given enough molasses on their bread. The two ex-Senators were likened also to an Irishman with a scythe over his shoulder, who saw a toad. "Aha," he said, "now I've got you." He aimed the butt of the handle, struck at the toad, and cut off his own head. [4]

Arthur called the Senate to order on May 20 but withdrew before it finally adjourned *sine die*. The session ended without the choice of a President *pro tem*. of the Senate. While Arthur had frequently called different Senators to his place in the chair, no official substitute had been agreed upon; and when, in the last few days, the retirement of the New York Senators had given the majority to the Democrats, he refused to permit the election of Thomas F. Bayard or any other Democrat who had not opposed Robertson's confirmation. [5] None had been chosen, an omission whose serious consequences were later much discussed, and for which he was rightly blamed.

Arthur went to New York to consult with other Stalwart leaders upon their course of action. Platt was eager to go at once before the legislature which only five months before had elected him. Conkling

---

[1] Garfield Journal, May 16, 1881, Garfield Papers.
[2] H. S. Beale, ed., *The Letters of Mrs. James G. Blaine*, Vol. I, p. 199.
[3] Cincinnati *Gazette*, May 20, 1881.
[4] *Ibid.*, May 18, 1881.
[5] Bayard to Schurz, July 7, 1881, Frederic Bancroft, ed., *Speeches, Correspondence, and Political Papers of Carl Schurz*, Vol. IV, pp. 146–7.

was averse, but willing to be guided by his political friends, whom he did not wish to leave in the lurch. The leaders gathered at Arthur's Lexington Avenue house on the afternoon of Sunday, May 22. In addition to Arthur, Conkling, and Platt, the group included George H. Sharpe, Stephen B. French, Louis F. Payn, John F. Smyth, and a few others.[1] It was a serious situation; the preservation of their machine was at stake and counsels were divided. All finally consented to march on Albany, with both ex-Senators seeking vindication and every loyal adherent present to aid them. It was not only the Senators but also the Conkling machine which indirectly in this way came before the State legislature for a popular judgment.

At Albany, Governor Cornell held aloof, not opposing, but not helping, his former associates.[2] Arthur, on the contrary, Vice President though he was, accompanied Conkling to electioneer for him in May as he had for Richard Crowley in January. Needless to say, it was obligation rather than pleasure which brought him to Albany and kept him there under the fire of a bitterly hostile press. He was always extraordinarily sensitive to adverse criticism, but he need not have been thin-skinned to suffer under the shafts of Thomas Nast and John Hay, for example. The former, in his telling way, caricatured the Vice President as a bootblack for Conkling and Platt.[3] Hay, temporarily in charge of the *Tribune*, published an editorial headed "A Public Scandal" and another saying: "The manly figure of the Vice President of the United States still stands at Albany under a sign which reads: 'Political dickering and other dirty work done here.' "[4]

Instead of prompt reëlection, Conkling and Platt entered into a protracted struggle which occupied two weary months.[5] Garfield, although always informed, kept scrupulously out of the fray; but Blaine, recognizing the opportunity, went to New York nominally on business but really to push Depew into the contest again and to enjoin on "the friends of the Administration" some unity of action.[6] The Stalwarts were not surprised; they had been convinced that it was Blaine

---

[1] Platt, *Autobiography*, pp. 159–60; A. R. Conkling, *Life of Roscoe Conkling*, p. 642; Cincinnati *Gazette*, May 23, 1881; N. Y. *Sun*, Sept. 20, 1881.

[2] Alexander, *op. cit.*, Vol. III, pp. 478–9.

[3] A. B. Paine, *Th. Nast, His Period and His Pictures*, pp. 449, 486–7.

[4] Issues of May 27, July 1, 1881.

[5] See H. C. Tanner, *"The Lobby" and Public Men from Thurlow Weed's Time*, pp. 293–7.

[6] Garfield Journal, May 22, 25, 28, June 8, 21, 1881, Garfield Papers; Depew, *Eighty Years*, pp. 113–4.

they were fighting from the day of Garfield's election.

Many Republicans, some of them former Stalwarts, refused to enter the party caucus; it became impossible to muster enough Republican strength for any individual nominee. On the first vote, on May 31, only thirty-nine were for Conkling and twenty-nine for Platt; the rest were scattered among a dozen rivals. At no subsequent balloᴛ did either ex-Senator attain a higher vote.[1] The conference at Arthur's house had utterly miscalculated the sentiment of the legislature and the party.

For weeks the contest went on, a dismal affair, the political death-struggle of Roscoe Conkling, New York's arrogant ruler for ten years past. Arthur, bound by ties of loyalty to the side of his chief, witnessed the spectacle of the dictator pleading for help from men who two years before would have "swung into line" without a moment's delay. Platt did not help matters much by being trapped in a scandalous predicament. Convinced, he said, that "remaining in the field . . . was very much injuring Conkling's chances for reëlection," he withdrew on July 1.[2] Conkling had ruined his own chances, but he fought on, though hopelessly.

Eventually, certain Conklingites proposed a compromise if the Half-Breeds would enter a caucus. Warner Miller, a leading Half-Breed, was selected for Platt's place, and Cornell, had he been willing, could have taken the nomination for the rest of Conkling's term. His refusal, while far from pacifying Conkling, left the field open for Elbridge G. Lapham, a Stalwart who had been "first to desert Conkling." [3] Conkling, after this climax to a chapter of failures beginning in 1876, slowly dropped out of politics and plunged into the practice of law. In the summer of 1881, there was no one both willing and able to take his place at the head of a unified Republican machine.

Arthur remained in office, his national reputation further lowered by his continued adherence to the New York Stalwart group and especially by his recent activities in Albany. Whatever remnants of popularity he may have had were suddenly obliterated on July 2. On that day, an insanely brutal disappointed office seeker in Washington

[1] Alexander, *op. cit.*, Vol. III, pp. 479–80.
[2] *Autobiography*, p. 160.
[3] Alexander, *op. cit.*, Vol. III, p. 481. The choice of the Republican caucus did not become that of the Republican-controlled legislature without a further fight. Not until July 16, when Speaker Sharpe yielded, was Warner Miller elected. The balloting for Conkling's successor was postponed until July 22; then, in the midst of summer heat, the old chief's adherents gave in and permitted Lapham to be elected. N. Y. *Tribune*, July 23, 1881.

OUT-"SHINING" EVERYBODY IN HUMILIATION AT ALBANY

"I did not engage you, Vice-President ARTHUR, to do this kind of work."

shot down President Garfield with the exulting words, repeated everywhere: "I am a Stalwart of the Stalwarts . . . Arthur is President now." [1]

[1] N. Y. *Herald,* July 3, 1881.

As HE stepped from a Hudson River boat on the morning of July 2, 1881, Vice President Arthur was greeted by news of the shooting of Garfield, which had occurred less than an hour before. With ex-Senator Conkling, he had returned to New York City for the usual brief week-end respite from the interminable election struggle at Albany. Both were shocked and hurried to their hotel to be free from the importunities of reporters and other curious people. Much excitement and speculation surrounded them, but no remarks or public statements could be extorted from either man.[1]

In Washington, physicians and Cabinet officers expected the President to die. A telegram urged the Vice President to prepare for all eventualities by coming directly to the capital. It was the summons of duty. Arthur's friend, Senator John P. Jones of Nevada, was then in New York on business. The Vice President, needing advice and companionship in this crisis, and recognizing the impropriety of Conkling's presence, asked Senator Jones to return with him to Washington.[2] They arrived at eight o'clock the next morning, and were conveyed directly to Jones's house, where Arthur remained all day in comparative seclusion, declining without qualification all requests for public interviews. That evening, he called at the White House first to talk with Mrs. Garfield, and afterward to meet the Cabinet.

When Arthur was ushered to the office where the Cabinet were waiting, he paused at the threshold, expecting an invitation to enter. No one moved to greet him; for a moment, all stared in silent hostility. Arthur, in confusion, was on the point of withdrawing when another visitor, who had not seen him, looked up from a far corner, came forward cordially, offered his hand, and drew him into the room. The others then came up to receive him.

The President, during the day, had taken a turn for the better, but it was agreed that Arthur should stay in Washington while he remained in danger. In accordance with this understanding, he returned to Senator Jones's house and, in the succeeding days, waited

---

[1] N. Y. *Sun,* July 3, 1881.
[2] Cincinnati *Enquirer,* July 6, 1881, an interview with Senator Jones.

patiently, conducting himself with dignity and decorum.[1]

Consternation gripped the country as news of Garfield's danger spread. Fantastic fears of dire consequences were expressed by men of experience and wisdom. Ex-President Hayes confided to his diary: "The death of the President at this time would be a national calamity whose consequences we can not now confidently conjecture. Arthur for President! Conkling the power behind the throne, superior to the throne! . . ."

I was in Cincinnati Saturday [wrote one of John Sherman's friends] . . . We learned of the shooting . . . by a special telegram received on the train; and the first remark I heard was from a one-legged soldier, a major, who said: 'I fear that is done to make Arthur President and Conkling Premier Primate of the whole country. At least I think the whole country will so view it.' Then we had not even seen the telegram, and of course not the *printed* dispatches giving the words of the assassin at the time.

Cincinnati was in a profound gloom and fever of excitement. I heard a universal expression of apprehension as to the possibility of Arthur's becoming President with all that would imply.

Returning here [Indianapolis] Saturday night, I find a similar fever. . . . Are we not passing through greater peril than we can comprehend? Is there any safety but prompt resignation of Arthur? Will not the stability of our institutions be in imminent peril if there is a widespread feeling that somehow the murder was *in consequence of* Conkling's course (which few will doubt) and *for the purpose of seating Arthur?* (which millions will believe). These questions bewilder. . . . If Arthur should resign (in event of the President's death) and there being no President *pro tem.* of the Senate nor Speaker of the House, would Chief Justice Waite be acting President till an election?

How fatal a mistake was made at Chicago in the nomination for the second place. The prayer for poor Garfield is *universal*. There is not popular confidence in the possible succession. . . . Yours very sincerely in this hour of apprehension and sorrow.[2]

Sherman wrote Hayes his "strong anticipations of the evil to come" if Garfield should die.[3] The reasons for Sherman's apprehension were not those, perhaps, which moved E. L. Godkin to expressions of alarm. It was with the Dorsey dinner and the Albany electioneering in mind

[1] Smith, *Garfield*, Vol. II, pp. 1179–80; B. P. Poore, *Perley's Reminiscences*, Vol. II, p. 425; Cincinnati *Enquirer*, N. Y. *Times, Sun, Tribune*, July 4–14, 1881.

[2] J. Q. Thompson to John Sherman, July 4, 1881, Sherman Papers. This letter is a fair sample of opinion at that juncture. *Cf.* Gath's dispatch to the Cincinnati *Enquirer*, July 7, 1881, stating that in New York City, sullen opposition to Arthur's succession was more intense than in other parts of the country which might be expected to know him less well. *Cf.* also, E. B. Washburne Papers, *passim*.

[3] Sherman to Hayes, July 8, 1881, Hayes Papers.

that he wrote: "Out of this mess of filth . . . Mr. Arthur will go to the Presidential Chair in case of the President's death." [1] All the alarmists, however, were fearful that Conkling would return to power through Arthur, that the latter, continuing his submissiveness, would be simply an instrument for Conkling's vengeful purposes.[2] As a matter of fact, Conkling was injured rather than aided by the assassination. Saner judgment reassured, in some measure, even the alarmists. During the long, hot weeks in which Garfield's strength first rose, then ebbed, while his serene fortitude won sympathetic admiration, Vice President Arthur acted with great discretion. When Garfield's condition so improved that the attending doctors declared his "gradual progress toward complete recovery" to be "manifest," [3] Arthur returned to New York. He remained, however, in seclusion from all but close friends. There on August 27, he was again warned of impending death when Garfield developed complications that revealed the hopelessness of his case. Practical certainty that Garfield would die during the autumn gave a new turn to the problems confronting his constitutional successor.

From the time when Garfield fell in the Washington station, mortally wounded by Guiteau's bullet, to the day of his death over two months later, he was able to perform only one official act, the signing of an extradition paper.[4] In addition, with great effort, he wrote one letter to his mother and requested that one or two matters be attended to by his friends. No Cabinet meetings could be held and, after his sharp decline on August 26, and 27, no hope for his recovery remained. With the President clearly unable to perform the duties of his office, the Federal Administration simply drifted. The situation was admittedly bad, but the grave difficulty of meeting it with Constitutional correctness was rendered more acute by the recent political turmoil in which President and Vice President had been on opposing sides and from which bad feeling persisted.

The provisions for the presidential succession had been left extremely vague, especially in one particular, by the framers of the Constitution. They unquestionably intended the Vice President to take over the duties and powers of the President whenever the latter left

[1] *The Nation,* July 7, 1881.
[2] A. K. McClure, *Recollections,* p. 120; *Gath* in Cincinnati *Enquirer,* July 7, 1881; *Harper's Weekly,* July 23, 1881.
[3] July 13. See Smith, *Garfield,* Vol. II, p. 1189.
[4] *Ibid.,* p. 1195.

office because of death, removal, or resignation. For cases in which the Vice President should also be either "disabled" or no longer in office, the Constitution explicitly charged Congress with providing, by law, for the substitution of some other "officer" to "act as President . . . until the disability be removed, or a President shall be elected." But in the event that the President should seemingly be unable to "discharge the powers and duties of said office" while the Vice President was living and active, the proper course remained entirely uncertain.[1] Such was the situation created by Garfield's increasing weakness.

Important matters demanded decisive action in the summer of 1881, notably the prosecution of certain post-office swindlers, but Garfield was not informed, and Arthur most reluctant to move. Who could have officially pronounced upon Garfield's condition? Certainly for the Vice President to determine the facts would have been grossly improper, subjecting him to such temptations that his judgment might be at fault. If Arthur had been obliged to decide, his reluctance to assume Garfield's official position would have made it impossible for him to reach a dispassionate conclusion. The Cabinet had no more authority than he, perhaps less, and personal concern in the decision they might reach would have tended to affect their verdict. Moreover, the performance of an act with such sweeping political consequences would inevitably have coupled responsibility with vulnerability to attack. It was said that Blaine, as head of the Cabinet, urged that Arthur be invited to take Garfield's place at the end of August. Since the Cabinet was divided, it seemed wise to discover Arthur's views. Postmaster General James went to New York, and there received the Vice President's emphatic refusal to assume the President's office in such circumstances.[2] Nothing more, it appears, was done with respect to presidential "inability." Arthur awaited Garfield's death with deep apprehension and, as long as the President lived, would probably never have taken over his functions until Congress had set up some procedure possessing general support.

As to that, a letter from George Ticknor Curtis in *Harper's Weekly* [3]

[1] Charles Warren, *The Making of the Constitution,* pp. 636–8.

[2] N. Y. *Herald,* Dec. 20, 1884. This article attempts to show that the fall of the Republican Party in the 1884 election was the responsibility of Blaine, and pictures this Cabinet move as the product of Blaine's overweening ambition to get on with his State Department schemes and to dominate President Arthur from the outset. Regardless of the animus, the story is told with sufficient particularity to produce a denial, had the facts been seriously misrepresented.

[3] August 27, 1881.

was the ablest contribution to a considerable public discussion.[1] Curtis insisted that it would be improper for the Vice President to declare the President's "inability," but did assert that the power of Congress under the elastic clause extended to the situation and gave that body authority to prescribe by law a mode of judicially determining a President's "inability." To avoid awaiting the regular session in December, it was necessary that the President summon Congress in a special session. A President could sign such a proclamation, and be able to do nothing more, and be adjudged so incapable of exercising the executive power as a whole that he ought to be succeeded by the Vice President, according to Curtis. In view of his reluctance to become President, it is likely that Arthur approved Curtis's conclusions.

The summer drew to a close—with Garfield fighting a losing battle. The months of unaccustomed confinement, of continuous anxiety and suspense, were telling on Arthur's health. His friends, in real alarm, tried in every way to divert his thoughts from the subject of his distress. Meanwhile, the press prepared the public for the transfer sure to come. Arthur was pictured as a gentleman of good intentions but small ability, instead of as a low politician of evil objectives and great force. The danger to be expected from his succession, it was said, would be his dependence on Conkling for advice. He himself could look forward to support from his worst critics of the past for every future act in the public interest, but he would be held to strict account. Thus the comment ran, and his heart was heavy when the last warning, and the final news, came.

*   *   *

The oath of office which Chester A. Arthur took late at night on September 19, 1881, he spoke with a firm resolution, and those who knew him well realized that it contained a promise of future accomplishment. By a few, it was also understood that he had prepared for the possible contingency of his own sudden death by writing a proclamation, summoning the Senate in immediate special session, at which it might choose a President *pro tem.*, and sealing it in an envelope addressed to the President in Washington. If he lived to issue a call from the capital, the letter would be delivered to him and destroyed, but should some assassin strike him down, in misguided retribution for

[1] Cincinnati *Gazette,* July 4, August 30, 1881.

the death of Garfield, the Constitutional government of the United
States would not be brought to an impasse by the absence of any legal
means for naming his successor.[1]

Next day, having waited for the arrival of Secretary Blaine, the
new President went to Elberon to join the Cabinet in paying tribute to
Garfield's memory. There was a luncheon conference with the Cabinet
at MacVeagh's cottage, a call upon Mrs. Garfield and, on the next
morning, funeral services before proceeding to Washington. There the
body lay in state and, after impressive ceremonies, it was taken to
Cleveland for public burial.[2]

In Washington, President Arthur went once more to Senator Jones's
on Capitol Hill just beyond the Capitol grounds. It had been decided
that, although his oath in New York, taken at the Cabinet's suggestion,
had been proper in form, it would be well to repeat it before the Chief
Justice. Plans were very quietly made and only about forty high
officers gathered at the Capitol on September 22, for an inauguration
ceremony. Arthur, escorted by ex-President Grant and Senator Jones,
went shortly before noon to the room reserved for the Vice President,
to which the Cabinet and others came almost at once. When the moment
arrived, Chief Justice Waite and Associate Justices Harlan and Mat-
thews entered. The former, attired in full judicial robes, went to the
table in the center at which Arthur had been sitting. The Bible used
by many Presidents was brought forward. All rose while the oath was
administered; then Arthur produced a paper, put on his glasses, and
commenced reading his brief inaugural address:

Men may die, but the fabrics of our free institutions remain unshaken.
No higher or more assuring proof could exist of the strength and permanence
of popular government than the fact that, though the chosen of the people be
struck down, his constitutional successor is peacefully installed without shock
or strain except the sorrow which mourns the bereavement. All the noble
aspirations of my lamented predecessor which found expression in his life,
the measures devised and suggested during his brief Administration to correct abuses, to enforce economy, to advance prosperity, and to promote the
general welfare, to insure domestic security and maintain friendly and honorable relations with the nations of the earth, will be garnered in the hearts
of the people; and it will be my earnest endeavor to profit, and to see that the
nation shall profit, by his example and experience. . . . Summoned to these

[1] George C. Bliss, in N. Y. *Times*, Nov. 21, 1886.
[2] For Mrs. Blaine's recollections one year later, see Beale, ed., *Letters of Mrs. Blaine*,
Vol. II, pp. 52–54.

high duties and responsibilities and profoundly conscious of their magnitude and gravity, I assume the trust imposed by the Constitution, relying for aid on divine guidance and the virtue, patriotism, and intelligence of the American people.[1]

On the day that Arthur read these words to the small group in the Capitol, he was more favorably regarded by the millions throughout the nation than ever before. *The Nation,* which on June 7 and July 9, 1881, had taken an "I told you so" attitude, expressed the extent to which public opinion had been modified. "Today [September 22, 1881] President Arthur receives from all parts of the country assurances of good will and of sincere wishes for his success . . . from men of all political parties and shades of opinion . . . and we have no doubt they are sincerely meant." But, it made clear, these assurances were in advance. Ultimate relations with the people would depend upon what the new President did. The New York *Sun* declared: "While Mr. Arthur is not a man who would have entered anybody's mind as a direct candidate for the office, it is not at all certain that he will not make a successful administration. He is a gentleman in his manners, neither obsequious nor arrogant. His bearing is manly, and such as to prepossess in his favor all whom he meets. Truth in speech and fidelity to his friends and his engagements form a part of his character. He has tact and common sense." [2]

"President Arthur's inaugural address was in all respects what the occasion called for," said *The Nation.* "This, moreover, seems to have satisfied the spectators that he fully realizes the solemnity of the occasion and is sensible of the limitations which the peculiar manner of his accession to the office and the state of popular feeling necessarily impose on him in the use he will make of his great powers and opportunities." [3]

The new Administration, however, started out with its warmest public adherents far from confident of public advantage. With trust somewhat restored by Arthur's conduct during the summer, the public saw possibilities of good in him and hoped for his best. Like ex-President Hayes, his critics thought he should be given a fair trial,

[1] Richardson, *Messages and Papers of the Presidents,* Vol. VIII, pp. 33–4.
[2] N. Y. *Sun,* Sept. 20, 1881.
[3] *The Nation,* Sept. 29, 1881. See in similar vein, N. Y. *Tribune,* Sept. 20, 23, 1881, and *The Writings of James Russell Lowell,* Vol. VI, p. 46; Masten Scrapbook #1, clippings from 18 eastern newspapers.

but they could hardly be considered optimistic of positive benefit from Arthur's leadership.[1]

Immediately after the brief inauguration address, a Cabinet meeting was held. By a proclamation then drawn up and signed, the day of Garfield's burial was declared one of "humiliation and mourning," to be observed throughout the United States. Members of the Cabinet were requested to retain their positions until Congress should meet in December, and it was agreed that a special session of the Senate should be called for October 10, 1881.[2]

In order to be free from the claims of his private business, Arthur held conferences in Washington and New York with his law partners and arranged to be released from all demands upon his time.[3] The White House was not yet ready for occupancy. Meanwhile, he converted Senator Jones's house into a temporary Executive Mansion, with offices on the first floor and living quarters above. The clerical staff of the presidential offices he invited to continue under him. Only one important change was required. Mr. Stanley-Brown declined the invitation to continue as the President's private secretary, and was succeeded by Fred J. Phillips.

[1] For the change in opinion, *Gath's* dispatches to the Cincinnati *Enquirer* in this period are excellent.
[2] Richardson, *op. cit.*, Vol. VIII, pp. 34–5.
[3] N. Y. *Sun,* Sept. 28, 30, 1881.

ARTHUR's most serious problem in his first months as President was the choice of advisers and agents. His most optimistic friends hoped that he would make no mistakes and feared that his health would not withstand the strain of greater responsibilities. Distrustful politicians expected an administration of vengeance led by Roscoe Conkling, while hostile business interests considered him a mere "political" President incapable of statesmanship.[1] John Sherman's friends were apprehensive of a war with Arthur which might injure Sherman's presidential chances in 1884. Murat Halstead of Cincinnati, for example, went to Washington, in the hope that through Senator Jones he could bring "conservative advice" to bear upon Arthur.[2] General Grant had stayed close to the President since Garfield's death, acting as "a sort of Lord High Chamberlain," and this increased the fear of Stalwart reprisals. It was said that first Robertson, then the Cabinet, would be replaced.

Senator Jones, Arthur's host, visited Conkling in Utica during the week after the special inauguration. "Everything is at sea about Arthur," wrote John Hay to Whitelaw Reid, for whom he was substituting at the helm of the *Tribune*. "Perhaps the cable will tell you in a day or two what he is up to. But at present the Cabinet knows nothing whatever of his intentions. The facts are: 1. He is living with Jones. 2. Jones has gone to Utica to confer with Conkling. 3. The Grant crowd seems happy."[3] Reid, returning with his bride, anticipated a battle resembling that which he had left in April, and expected changes to be made in the Cabinet. Undoubtedly such changes were discussed when, on October 8 and 9, Conkling came to Washington for a visit to the new President. The political gossips wrote columns of speculation.

On Monday, October 10, 1881, the Senate assembled in the special session called by Arthur. Harris of Tennessee, having "been requested by a number of Senators on both sides of the Chamber to call the

[1] Cincinnati *Enquirer*, *Gath's* dispatch, Sept. 29, 1881; A. K. McClure, *Our Presidents and How We Make Them*, p. 286.
[2] Halstead to Sherman, Sept. 28, 1881, Sherman Papers.
[3] Cortissoz, *Reid*, Vol. II, p. 76.

Senate to order," took the chair for that purpose, and when the proclamation had been read, recognized Senator Pendleton, the Democratic leader, as he moved to elect Thomas F. Bayard the President *pro tem*. Senator Edmunds, for the Republican side, presented the credentials of the three new Senators who had not yet taken their oaths of office, Warner Miller and Elbridge Lapham from New York, and Nelson W. Aldrich of Rhode Island. Until these three Republicans were sworn in, the Democrats controlled the chamber, with the power of electing Bayard to the place next in succession to the Presidency. They might, having first selected him, adopt dilatory measures to prevent his being supplanted by a Republican, once control of the Senate had passed to the other side. The Republicans tried in vain to cause Bayard's election to be only "for this day," and to have the oaths administered before an adjournment. The Senate adjourned without even notifying the President that it had organized and was ready for his communications.

Next day, however, the first thing done was the swearing in of Aldrich, Miller, and Lapham. The Republicans, now in the majority, promptly installed the Independent Senator from Illinois, David Davis, in Bayard's place as President *pro tem*. Arthur was notified, the Senate was organized with Republican committees, as in May, and the work of the session was taken up as rapidly as possible.

In the temporary Executive Mansion, from which Arthur's letters issued with the heading, "Office of the President of the United States," the new President led a busy existence. He was besieged by callers, many of them office seekers prepared to profit from the supposed return of Stalwart leadership. In the midst of other matters, the centennial celebration of the surrender of Yorktown occurred. It involved ceremonial receptions to the nation's invited guests, descendants of Rochambeau and Steuben, and to the representatives of the French and German governments, with observance of etiquette complicated by the hostility between the two groups resulting from the Franco-Prussian War. On October 19, Arthur went to Yorktown for the exercises, delivering the first public speech since his inaugural. It was merely a brief welcome to the guests of the country, with no political significance. Singularly fitting, as public comment generally recognized, was Arthur's order that the ceremonies conclude with a military salute to the British flag.

Garfield's Cabinet had shown some lack of harmony. Wayne Mac-Veagh and Blaine had been at odds and MacVeagh had considered resigning. Thomas L. James, the Stalwart member, had resisted Robertson's appointment. In Arthur's eyes, moreover, the Cabinet had another shortcoming. The Treasury had been placed under William Windom of Minnesota when the New York Stalwarts, among them General Arthur, thought it had been promised to them. Windom suggested that he recast the Cabinet and secure advisers on whose sympathy and loyalty he could rely, although he might not require an entirely new personnel. Advice of this nature was given him from several quarters, but he was slow to act.[1]

The first to go was Windom, who was eager to return to the Senate.[2] During October, efforts were made to find his successor. Ex-President Grant suggested John Jacob Astor.[3] In preference, ex-Governor Edwin D. Morgan of New York, with whom Arthur had made his political start, was invited to take the post. After he had been confirmed, Thurlow Weed reported an "unpleasant and somewhat excited interview" on the morning of October 25, in which Weed's urgings that he accept the appointment were repelled by Morgan on account of poor health.[4] Finally, unconvinced by legal objections which to Garfield had seemed decisive,[5] Arthur named Charles J. Folger of Geneva, N. Y., on October 27. Both nominations were considered creditable, the Stalwarts being especially pleased. The Cabinet received in Folger an able man and hard worker.[6]

Blaine, whose high hopes of honor and power in the next four years had been given some foundation before Garfield's death, was soon rudely shocked. Arthur may have sought an alliance with him,[7] although Grant was urging Frelinghuysen for his place,[8] but it is most unlikely. From Vienna, William Walter Phelps advised an attempt to combine Conkling and Blaine in the same Cabinet,[9] but according to the Stalwarts, Conkling could take only the Secretaryship of State,

---

[1] N. Y. *Tribune*, Sept. 28, 1881.
[2] Windom had voted for Arthur's removal from the Collectorship in February, 1879.
[3] Grant to Arthur, Oct. 8, 1881, Arthur Papers.
[4] Weed to Arthur, Oct. 25, 1881, Arthur Papers.
[5] For Folger's career, see *Catalogue of the Sigma Phi Society*, p. 228; P. C. Headley, *op. cit.*, p. 79.
[6] Mrs. Richard Crowley, *Echoes from Niagara*, p. 230.
[7] H. S. B. Beale, editor, *Letters of Mrs. James G. Blaine*, Vol. I, pp. 213, 226, 248.
[8] Louis A. Coolidge, *Ulysses S. Grant*, p. 552 ff.
[9] Phelps to Arthur, Sept. 27, Oct. 21, 1881, Arthur Papers.

and that as a "sacrifice." Arthur saved him by rejecting the proposal.[1] Blaine, however, had agreed like his colleagues to retire at the President's convenience, and shortly after Congress met in regular session, Frederick T. Frelinghuysen, of New Jersey, was named to succeed him.

Frelinghuysen was of Dutch stock, a successful lawyer, with a career in the Senate running back to the impeachment of Andrew Johnson in 1868. He had declined the British mission in 1870, and had entered the Senate in 1871 to become an influential member of the Committee on Foreign Relations and, later, a member of the Electoral Commission of 1877. Those who knew him expected a more cautious national foreign policy than Blaine's.[2] He was said to have thought that the American eagle was a mere hen, past middle age. Personally, Arthur found him very congenial. On December 12, Blaine yielded the leadership of the Department and retired to write his eulogy of Garfield, and *Twenty Years of Congress,* with lively political storms before him.

The Attorney-Generalship involved the prosecutions of the Star Route ring, a consideration which ultimately controlled the appointment made. MacVeagh was to have retired at the same time as Windom, but when Morgan declined the Treasury and Folger was substituted, Arthur changed his mind and tried to keep him. He refused, resigning on November 8. He may have withdrawn because he feared that the Star Route cases would no longer be willingly prosecuted and in order to avoid being made a scapegoat;[3] certainly it was his own decision.[4] It was to one of MacVeagh's aides, Benjamin Harris Brewster of Philadelphia, that his portfolio was given.[5] Brewster was a well educated, able, elderly attorney, who had served the Federal government in 1846 as a commissioner to adjudicate the Cherokee claims against the United States, and had been Attorney General of Pennsylvania in 1867. During Garfield's illness, he had become special government counsel in the Star Route cases.[6] "Brewster is made Attorney General. All the Stalwarts are going in, and though the mills of Arthur may seem to grind slow, they grind exceeding fine," wrote Mrs. Blaine.[7]

[1] Mrs. Crowley, *op. cit.,* p. 228.
[2] N. Y. *Tribune,* Dec. 13, 1881.
[3] Robert U. Johnson, *Remembered Yesterdays,* pp. 367–9.
[4] N. Y. *Tribune,* Sept. 28, 1881.
[5] Brewster was confirmed on December 19, 1881.
[6] Headley, *op. cit.,* p. 83.
[7] *Mrs. Blaine's Letters,* Vol. I, pp. 268–9.

Postmaster General James was a Stalwart, who had accepted his place in Garfield's Cabinet in opposition to the wishes of his political associates in New York. They believed that his acceptance deprived Levi P. Morton of the far more desirable Secretaryship of the Treasury. Moreover, he was a member of the Cornell wing of the Stalwarts and had refused to resign along with Senators Conkling and Platt.[1] Arthur had long known him, and may have thought his abilities over-rated,[2] but primarily to balance his own Eastern Secretary of the Treasury with a Western man in another place, he named for James's position Senator Timothy O. Howe of Wisconsin.[3] Howe had been a United States Circuit Judge and from 1861 to 1879, a United States Senator. Garfield had had him in mind for some place in his Cabinet, but had dropped him when Sherman criticized him severely for lack of business capacity.[4] He was a Grant man, had been urged upon Garfield very strongly by Conkling, Arthur, and Platt in the maelstrom of March 3, 1881, and now was appointed Postmaster General without being asked if he would accept or not.[5] Elderly and not very strong, he was not to outlive his term.

From General Grant, President Arthur received some help but even greater annoyance. Invited to the White House from time to time, Grant good-naturedly brought with him the importunities of the countless friends and relatives who made his life burdensome. This burden Arthur did not desire to share. He was obliged to show displeasure or else to attempt evasion. When Grant urged his personal friend, General Edward F. Beale, for the Secretaryship of the Navy, it was generally supposed that Arthur would yield. In appointing Frelinghuysen and Howe, he had named friends of Grant. But Arthur passed over Beale, and chose instead Blaine's intimate companion, William E. Chandler of New Hampshire, whom the Senate had refused to confirm for a less important position under Garfield. Arthur finally nominated Chandler only when the Department of State had repudiated some of Blaine's policies and produced a clash with the former Secretary. While still personally devoted to Blaine, Chandler was also on intimate terms with many Stalwarts and was brought into the Cabinet as one

[1] See above, Chapter XIII.
[2] *Gath's* dispatch to the Cincinnati *Enquirer*, Sept. 29, 1881.
[3] Howe had voted against Arthur's removal in Feb., 1879. He was confirmed on Jan. 5, 1882.
[4] Sherman to Garfield, Feb. 16, 1881, Garfield Papers.
[5] Howe to Adam Badeau, Dec. 24, 1881, Garfield Papers.

who would thus give consolidation politics some added strength. By this argument, Grant was somewhat "mollified" [1] and Platt and Conkling were won over to Chandler's appointment, several months before it was made.

In the Interior Department, Senator Sargent of California had been generally expected to replace Secretary Kirkwood.[2] But on the same day which brought Chandler's nomination, Senator Henry M. Teller of Colorado was named for Kirkwood's place.[3] He had grown up on a western New York farm, and had gone farther west to Illinois and finally, to Colorado. There he had been chosen one of the State's two original Senators after its admission in 1876. His selection for the Cabinet was surprising, for he could not bring to Arthur's Administration the support of a large personal following in the West, and even in Colorado he was strongly opposed. He was able, honest, of austere personality, in politics a consistent Stalwart, but not, apparently, a particular friend of President Arthur. With his induction into office, practically a clean sweep had been completed in seven months, for only Robert T. Lincoln remained of Garfield's group, and he was entirely acceptable to Grant's admirers.

Four Eastern and three Western Republicans comprised Arthur's Cabinet, but of the Westerners both Howe and Teller had grown to manhood in the East. All except Chandler had been "Grant men" in 1880; the Sherman wing had suffered most by the changes,[4] but, indeed, they had expected nothing better. The new President, in these and lesser appointments, however, had by no means submitted to the control of his former leader, Roscoe Conkling, or embarked on a program of political vengeance. He preferred to forfeit his popularity with any one powerful faction if necessary, but in any event to act as President of the whole country according to his own judgment of its best interests. The New York Stalwarts grew particularly bitter because he declined to change what they considered a sorry situation in his own State. His refusal to remove Collector Robertson, who prevented them from using the Custom House patronage to maintain their organization, seemed to them a breach of loyalty. As Platt put it,

[1] Geo. Spencer to Chandler, Dec. 25, 1881, Chandler Papers.
[2] Kirkwood had voted for Arthur's removal in 1879; see also Chandler Papers, *passim*.
[3] He had voted against Arthur's removal in 1879.
[4] Sherman to Hayes, July 2, 1882; Sherman to James M. Brown, Nov. 8, 1882, Sherman Papers.

Arthur refused "to cure the sores from which the Republicans of his own State were smarting." [1] Life continued to be difficult when he could easily have "put them in clover." Even Garfield, after Robertson was confirmed, had made some Stalwart nominations; Arthur, it seemed, could have gone much further in the same direction.

*　　*　　*

Arthur's Administration was expected at once to mete out proper punishment to Charles J. Guiteau, Garfield's assassin. After the preliminary problems of jurisdiction and indictment had been solved, Guiteau was permitted to plead not guilty. On November 14, 1881, his trial, one of the most extraordinary and distressing exhibitions of criminal procedure in the country's history, began in Washington.

Guiteau was defended by his brother-in-law, who bore the burden of the case without assistance because the accused man loudly ordered an associate counsel to "get out of the case" during the first day in court. "An appeal to the legal profession" through the newspapers produced no offers of further aid. On the other hand, District Attorney Corkhill was helped by two attorneys in whose selection President Arthur had taken part, Walter Davidge of Washington and John K. Porter of New York.

Murder, Guiteau had proclaimed some weeks earlier in a statement to the press, always presumes either legal or actual malice, whereas he had acted altogether from public motives and in response to a divine inspiration. He described how he retired early in the evening two days after the resignations of Conkling and Platt and tried in vain to go to sleep. "I was lying in bed," he said, "thinking over the political situation and the idea flashed through my brain that if the President was out of the way everything would go better. . . . I shot the President without malice or murderous intent. . . . I had none but the best of feelings, personally, toward the President." Under irresistible divine pressure, he had made his preparations and sought his opportunity for six weeks before accomplishing his "mission."

The defense took two lines. The religious delusion under which Guiteau had acted, it was alleged, was such as to render him irresponsible, a man insane, while the shot which he had fired into Garfield's back was not necessarily mortal and had resulted in death only because

[1] *Autobiography*, p. 180.

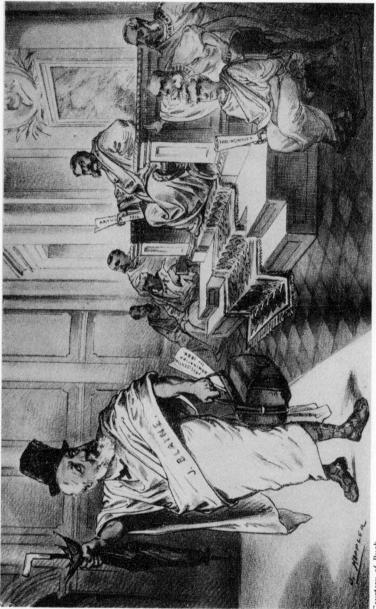

BLAINE LEAVING THE CAPITOL—"I GO—BUT I RETURN"

of subsequent deficiencies in medical care. Against these claims, the prosecution described Guiteau as a disappointed office seeker, self-willed, passionate, egotistical in the extreme, and prompted by un-bridled malice. The injury, they declared, was "necessarily mortal."

To test the sanity of the accused man, District Attorney Corkhill requested the judge to allow him full freedom of action in the court room. The prisoner, not willing to rest his case on the religious seizure, undertook to demonstrate by the most outrageous interruptions and the most obvious contempt of court that he was still insane, while he wrote out for the press long statements which were readily given columns of space. For almost a month, expert alienists testified concerning Guiteau's sanity. With few exceptions they were convinced that his court-room actions were a prolonged pose indicating gross egotism but not insane irresponsibility. When the defense offered to present even the findings of phrenology, the court declined to receive such testimony.

On January 25, the jury received the judge's charge. In less than a half hour they were ready to report and, as darkness fell, filed back into the jury box. As the last man of the twelve pronounced Guiteau "guilty," the condemned man wildly shrieked: "My blood will be upon the heads of that jury. Don't you forget it. God will avenge this outrage." A few days later he was sentenced. He was hanged on June 30. Although the Cabinet deliberated upon his fate, no interposition was offered. There were many who believed that an insane man had thus been put to death.

*   *   *

The Executive Mansion, after the withdrawal of Garfield's family, required renovation. Its use as a hospital for the dying President had prevented normal attention to maintenance and subjected some parts of it to unusual wear. Before President Arthur was ready to move in, he wished it restored to a fitting condition and, inasmuch as such things interested him and offered some relaxation from other problems, he gave the changes much personal attention. After dinner, he frequently was driven over from Senator Jones's to the White House, there to make a thorough inspection of what was being done and to give orders for necessary changes. In addition to the usual refinishing of walls and replacement of worn carpets and rugs, the downstairs rooms received additional furniture. Upstairs, special attention was paid to redecorating the President's library and to placing in all the rooms new, wood-burning fireplaces and brass fire sets. To connect the various floors, the first elevator was installed. The cellars, attics, and storerooms were found filled with the accumulations of many thrifty "first ladies," unwilling to part with articles of potential use. Twenty-four wagon loads were cleared out.[1]

In subsequent years, Arthur made numerous other changes in the interests of privacy, the most striking of which was the Tiffany glass screen set up between the public hall at the entrance and the long corridor connecting the East Room with the dining rooms and the conservatory, a passage which those living in the house had to use in going from room to room. The newspapers gave plentiful space to other improvements made at Arthur's direction. In December the rooms were ready, and the President moved in.

Arthur brought to Washington a French chef who had previously been employed by New York gourmets, and a steward who had spent twelve years in Conkling's service. As a special favor, Stephen B. French loaned the President his own valet, "Alec" Powell. Powell, a striking Negro, soon acquired more airs than all the officials of the capital, and became a well-known member of the President's entourage. When Arthur took him to Newport in the summer of 1884, the New York *Sun* referred to him as "the servant" in one of its columns and received a severe rebuke for not calling him "the messenger." "I hope," the valet's letter concluded, "in the next edition of your paper you will correct the same." [2] More to the President's taste was the loyalty of his old family cook, Bridget Smith. She entered the White House as one of the staff, returned to New York at the end of Arthur's term, and received a small bequest by his will, which described her as "faithful and devoted." With these, and others, the new President moved in, celebrating his first evening by giving an informal dinner to a few personal friends.

Arthur's reputation was much improved by his course in the first few months of office. "Well begun is half done," said the *Evening Mail* in an editorial assessing the first month as "President Arthur's Noble Beginning." [3] *Harper's Weekly* sounded a far more hopeful note than

---

[1] Mrs. Edna M. H. Colman, *White House Gossip*, pp. 154–5.
[2] N. Y. *Sun*, Sept. 1, 1884.
[3] Oct. 18, 1881.

in its earlier statements,[1] and even the caustic Godkin found occasion for praise.[2] Nearly three months after his inaugural, *The Independent* said: "Already, personally, President Arthur commands the respect of the people. If he goes on as he has begun, his Administration will command their confidence." [3] The New York *Sun* was his most unswerving advocate, while even the Half-Breed press, with some exceptions, found it necessary to damn him with faint praise.

With leading politicians, Arthur was not, however, on good terms. Grant was disgruntled, the New York machine exasperated, Blaine and his followers angry, and the Ohio retainers of Senator Sherman distinctly cold. It was the necessary fruit of Arthur's conciliatory policy that, if he failed to delight some factions and deserve the bitter hostility of others, he must, by a middle course, leave all dissatisfied and annoyed. He hoped that the passage of time would bring an alleviation of the first asperities, that once the transition from Garfield to himself had been passed there would be a harmonious general Republicanism. Meanwhile, he turned his attention to the national problems—the meeting of Congress, prosecuting the Star Route conspirators, reforming the civil service, disposing of the government's surplus income from taxes, renovating the national defense, and conducting foreign relations. Compared with Polk or Cleveland, he was not a hard-working President, for he devoted less time to securing information at first hand. He was, however, conscientious, and performed his work with a deceptive appearance of ease.

[1] Oct. 1, 1881.
[2] *The Nation*, Oct. 20, 1881.
[3] Mary Clemmer's letter, Dec. 15, 1881.

In December, the Forty-seventh Congress assembled, with the Republicans having a small working majority in both branches. The Senate had already organized in its October session; the House had to discover new leaders to replace Garfield and Frye. Although J. Warren Keifer of Ohio was chosen Speaker, floor leadership actually passed during the session to Thomas B. Reed of Maine. Reed was to become Garfield's real successor as a party whip.

Arthur's first annual message seemed to indicate that he would play a limited rôle as a leader of national legislative policy. He had been engrossed in October and November with the political aspects of his position, so that he had been forced in this first message to rely upon the recommendations sent him from the executive departments. The message bore the impress of individual convictions upon only three major topics, the presidential succession, the national defense, and civil service reform. On each, and at some length, he urged Congress to deliberate and to enact appropriate legislation.

Arthur's known leadership in legislation lay in his annual messages and vetoes, and was not unusual. With the long first session of the Forty-seventh Congress, which kept him in Washington until August 8, he disagreed on the wisdom of three bills. The first, a measure to restrict the admission of Chinese in accordance with the revised treaty with China, he declared, on April 4, to be "a breach of our national faith." It prohibited the immigration of Chinese for twenty years, although the treaty between the two countries acknowledged the right of the United States to "regulate, limit, or suspend" only for what had been understood to be a briefer period.[1] There was, of course, an outcry that Arthur was offending the California Republicans by his veto; but Congress, after sustaining it,[2] followed his advice with a new measure setting ten years as the period of suspension. The second exclusion act, which he signed on May 6, 1882, and which included among its provisions the denial of State and national citizenship to all Chinese,[3] was passed by a combination of Democratic and Western Re-

[1] Richardson, *Messages*, Vol. VIII, pp. 112 ff.
[2] *Cong. Rec.*, Vol. XIII, p. 2617.
[3] *22 Stat.*, pp. 58–61.

publican votes.

Three months later, on July 1, Arthur returned another bill with his objections, an act regulating the carriage of immigrants to the United States by sea. Designed to apply to steamships the requirements hitherto exacted of sailing vessels in the same service, it had the unanimous approval of the House Committee on Commerce and went through both chambers without a division. They were startled, therefore, to have it returned with some sound and serious objections to the bill's wording, which Arthur knew to be technically at fault and ill-adapted to the purpose for which it had been drawn.[1] In this, as in the case of the Exclusion Act, Congress yielded to the President and passed a new measure meeting his objections. A third effort to regulate immigration, one which Arthur approved, was the act of August 3, 1882, ordering the first generally selective restriction, with the expense of receiving and caring for the newcomers to be defrayed by a "Head Money" tax of fifty cents per immigrant. The method of enforcement was weak, for the Secretary of the Treasury was instructed to make contracts with State governments to execute the law through State officers. It was a relapse to the ways of the Confederation. Experience demonstrated the need for Federal enforcement officers.[2]

Congress failed to make definite provision for the presidential succession, though not for lack of a prompt start. Even before Arthur's message had reached the Senate, Beck of Kentucky offered a resolution, and during the following week another resolution and a bill were introduced.[3] The questions on the subject in the annual message encouraged early consideration; but, after the first week, the Senate turned to other topics and left presidential succession to its Committee on the Judiciary. It was not again referred to until June. Meanwhile, a special House committee made no report.

Troublesome Constitutional questions were in a large degree responsible for this reluctance to come to a decision. There was a sharp difference of opinion as to the appropriate line of succession. One group believed that it should lie through the President's Cabinet, thus insuring the continuance in power of his party; another approved of the arrangement, in an act of 1792, by which it fell to the President *pro tem.* of the Senate and after him to the Speaker of the House of

[1] Richardson, *Messages*, Vol. VIII, pp. 118 ff., July 1, 1882.
[2] Sec. of Treas., *Annual Report*, 1883, pp. lxix ff.; 1884, pp. xlvii ff.
[3] *Cong. Rec.*, Vol. XIII, p. 22, pp. 121–31.

Representatives, although, in taking this stand they were forced to recognize that occasions could arise, as in the summer of 1881, when there was neither a President *pro tem.* nor a Speaker, and that, during the sessions of Congress the Senate or the House could conceivably change its presiding officer from day to day. Still another grave problem for advocates of this line of succession divided them into two groups: those who believed that when both President and Vice President had died, a successor should fill out the entire unexpired term, and those who declared that in such circumstances the successor could hold office only until presidential electors could be chosen and a new President and Vice President named.

Discussions among Congressmen revealed another major field of disagreement,—the nature of the Vice President's authority in case the President's "disability" should be merely temporary. Would the Vice President then simply "discharge the powers and duties" of the President while remaining Vice President in title and rank, or would he also assume the office itself? In the latter event, could he, having once become President, cease to be President before the expiration of the regular term by returning the office to its former incumbent upon the latter's recovery, or must he continue to the end, once authority had been transferred? Equally vexatious was the Constitutional problem as to whether the "inability" of the President should be decided by himself, by the Vice President who would succeed him, or by some third person or designated group. Confronted by such complexities, Congress neglected the knotty subject and turned, instead, to appropriations, in which the surplus revenues tempted them to lavish extravagance.

The prodigality of the Forty-seventh Congress reached its climax in the measure that drew forth Arthur's third veto message, a rivers and harbors bill carrying a total expenditure of $18,743,875,[1] for some members of Congress an ample justification for their whole summer's discomfort. That it was by far the largest sum ever voted for such purposes did not alone cause the President's veto, whose terms any strict constructionist could applaud:

My principal objection to the bill is that it contains appropriations for purposes not for the common defense or general welfare, and which do not

[1] *22 Stat.*, pp. 191 ff.

promote commerce among the States. These provisions, on the contrary, are entirely for the benefit of the particular localities in which it is proposed to make the improvements. I regard such appropriations of the public money as beyond the powers given by the Constitution to Congress and the President.[1]

Without hesitation he spoke his mind on the "peculiar evils" of all rivers and harbors bills, asserting that, as one of those measures "becomes more objectionable, it secures more support." He concluded, however, by denouncing the utter folly of this particular proposal because it required the government to spend twice as much in a single year as would be entirely adequate for all of the approved purposes.

Arthur's message won deserved applause. Old Simon Cameron wrote from Harrisburg, likening the veto to "the act of old Jackson with the Bank."[2] It was more like Jackson's Maysville Road veto in terms but quite like his action in the bank recharter issue in courage, and, indeed, it drew from the country the same sort of grateful response. Newspapers in all sections approved the President's stand.[3] Yet before public opinion had had a chance to exert its pressure, Congress rushed through a reënactment of the bill over Arthur's veto, with party lines ignored and, in the House, the South supplying much the strongest support.[4] The *Tribune,* dubbing the measure "The Big Divide" and "wholesale robbery," warned those Republicans who had voted to override the veto that they would regret it. Arthur, whose veto was based on thorough study of the separate items and a discussion of them in several Cabinet meetings,[5] gained somewhat in public confidence but roused the antagonism of certain party leaders, notably Senator Hoar.

Meanwhile, the people of Washington and, through the press, the entire nation were discovering some of the accidental President's more important personal traits. Unsuspected virtues were revealed through his participation in official society, in which he necessarily assumed a leading position. Those who had known him in New York expected

---

[1] Richardson, *Messages,* Vol. VIII, pp. 121 ff.

[2] Cameron to Brewster, Aug. 3, 1882, Arthur Papers.

[3] See N. Y. *Tribune,* Aug. 3, 1882, which, besides denouncing Congress for rushing to pass the bill over the veto, lists twenty-five different newspapers, of both parties, approving the veto.

[4] The South furnished fifty-six votes for the bill to six against, the other States sixty-six for and fifty-three against. Cincinnati *Enquirer,* Aug. 3, 1882.

[5] N. Y. *Herald,* Dec. 20, 1884; Chandler Diary, July 18, 24, 25, 28, Aug. 1, 1882, Chandler Papers (Concord, N. H.).

not only that he would improve the quality of Executive hospitality but also that he would take an active part in it. They were not mistaken, for, while he persuaded his younger sister, Mary Arthur McElroy, to forsake her husband in Albany during the winter months in order to act as hostess of the Executive Mansion, he himself attended to many details of his state entertainments. He knew exactly what he wished.

Mrs. McElroy's popularity made White House hospitality unusually pleasant. In various ways she made her formal receptions less stilted and established a personal relationship with her guests. Arthur often joined those who remained for tea and to hear from the veranda the music of the Marine Band after her large "afternoons." He would stand among the guests, wearing a hat which, a newspaper felt it necessary to explain, he removed during conversation with the ladies.

With his sister's vigilant aid, Arthur maintained a strict barrier between official and private White House life. The problem was vexing, rendered difficult by the architectural arrangements of that edifice and exceedingly troublesome by the readiness with which newspaper reporters had been able to gratify vulgar curiosity in preceding Administrations. When Arthur determined that no authentic private information should go to them, they published rumors of the most baseless sort. He declined to take notice of foolish reports, but his annoyance was such that he contemplated recommending a separate domestic establishment for presidential households. He is said to have favored the relegation of the White House to official business and state entertainment, and the construction, on the opposite side of Lafayette Square at the site where Henry Adams and John Hay were soon to build, of a presidential residence.[1] On the whole he was fairly successful in shielding those close to him from the public press.

Arthur was thoroughly sociable. During the autumn months before the Executive Mansion had been renovated, and while he was living on Capitol Hill, he was glad to dine out and always reluctant to bring pleasant evenings to a close. "Etiquette requiring everyone to stay till he leaves," wrote a member of the Blaine household, "it becomes an interesting problem how to end a dinner before twelve o'clock." [2] No doubt others beside Arthur were relieved when, early in December,

[1] N. Y. *Tribune,* April 19, 1884.
[2] Gail Hamilton, *James G. Blaine,* p. 546.

PRESIDENT ARTHUR, HIT HIM AGAIN! DON'T LET THE VULTURE BECOME
OUR NATIONAL BIRD

The River and Harbor Bill Veto

he entered the White House with his household.

Arthur worshiped on his first Sunday as President at a Negro church, to which he returned on Thanksgiving Day, but he chose as "the President's church" St. John's, across Lafayette Square. He had already returned to the Episcopal denomination which his father had left to become a Baptist clergyman, and St. John's he associated more- over with his late wife, who had sung in its choir before their marriage. In her memory he gave a window for the little building. There he wor- shiped quite regularly during his four Washington years.

When Congress was in session, Arthur tried to establish a method- ical procedure for every week. He usually rose after nine o'clock, ate a "continental breakfast" while dressing, and went directly to his of- fice. Mondays were kept free from callers on all but the most urgent business, but on every other week day, from ten to twelve o'clock, he received members of Congress, usually in connection with appoint- ments. On Tuesdays and Fridays he went from these consultations to meet his Cabinet at noon; on Wednesdays, Thursdays and Satur- days, he received general callers from noon to one o'clock, before his light lunch, and then attacked the mail. During the afternoons, callers came by appointment until four or five o'clock, after which he went for a drive or, in the latter part of his term, a horseback ride, returning for a family dinner at seven.

Such a program was constantly invaded by special demands—dedi- cation ceremonies, short trips to New York or down the Potomac, state dinners or receptions, and the hospitalities outside the White House which Arthur somewhat freely accepted. To compensate for the interruptions, he often resumed work in the late evening and spent the hours till two or three o'clock reading reports or consulting with political advisers. Quite as often, when business was not pressing, he spent his evenings with personal friends, concluding with a delectable midnight supper in the private dining room he had redecorated to suit himself.

Because of the easy way in which Arthur disposed of his work and the frequency with which he was found at "play," the impression spread that he was indolent. He was deliberate, often procrastinating, in coming to a final decision, and was not punctual in keeping engage- ments, so that, among his secretaries, the tradition developed that he had a "property basket," filled with official looking documents, which he was wont to carry into his office on his way to a delayed appointment to create an appearance of industry although the contents were never disturbed.

Callers at the White House during business hours went to the offices on the second floor. The President was dignified but not forbidding, however trivial their claims to his attention. His costume was invariably immaculate, a braid-bound black Prince Albert coat, buttoned nearly to the chin, dark trousers and gaiters, and a wide black silk scarf, fastened with an onyx pin and partly covering the whitest of standing collars. His commanding stature and expert skill in meeting men made any call upon him an impressive experience; yet, with all his dignity, there was a grace of manner and a consideration of others which disarmed embarrassment whenever he sought to do so. He was gifted with the useful capacity of being talkatively reticent. It saved many a "situation" for those who listened and did so with no cost to him. The cultivated Matthew Arnold carried away from the White House an impression of Arthur's "pleasant, easy manners."

Arthur was an epicure. Many in later years remembered him as a "high liver . . . who ate and drank too much and died young from the effects of overindulgence," though others agreed that his restrained enjoyment of "the good things of life" had caused the tea table to replace the punch bowl "of a past administration." He did gain weight and lose strength during his Washington years, while his high color, cheery affability, and fondness for genial companionship gave some people the impression of a man excessively inclined to drink and frivolity.

He was by no means a total abstainer, but he was unquestionably temperate. The remark is attributed to him, when he received a complaint that a prominent government official had been drunk, that "no gentleman ever sees another gentleman drunk." His own gentility, by sounder tests, was pronounced "innate to the last degree."

Arthur's sedentary life was conducive to corpulence, for he took no exercise and no outdoor recreation beyond driving in the late afternoon. He had been pictured, while Vice President, as driving "to the Capitol every day behind a dappled gray Kentucky mare," covering the distance, one and a half miles, "in exactly ten minutes." After he became President the gray mare gave way to a splendid pair of "mahogany bays" and an equipage described to the public in some detail:

President Arthur's carriage and horses are now in Washington. The establishment . . . is the finest which has ever appeared in the streets of the Capital. The carriage, from the New York Broome Street Brewsters, is a landau of novel design, painted a dark mellow green, relieved with enough picking out in red to show the outline without being conspicuous, the trimmings are of morocco and cloth, the cushions and doors being faced with heavy lace. The harness has been made in keeping with the carriage, and is heavily mounted with plain silver. The dress blankets are of heavy dark green kersey, and the coachman's lap robe of green English box cloth. These are all ornamented with the President's monogram. The lap robe for the inside of the carriage is Labrador otter, beautifully lined with dark green, and having the monogram "C. A. A." worked in silk. The horses, two in number, are magnificent animals—mahogany bays with black points, and without a white spot anywhere. . . . They are matched almost to a hair. . . . They were the President's personal selection, as was also the carriage, and reflect no little credit upon his judgment as a horseman.[1]

During the winter of 1882, there were no state entertainments at the Executive Mansion; Arthur dined out frequently and thus revealed his lighter side to increasing numbers of people. Mrs. Blaine found him shallow and frivolous, his attention centered upon "flowers and wine and food, and slow pacing with a lady on his arm, and a quotation from Thackeray or Dickens, or an old Joe Miller told with an uninterfered-with particularity." Others, similarly blinded by thwarted ambition or jealousy, or moved by malice, took satisfaction in gossip intended to injure him. Thus, his evident partiality for the Frelinghuysen family was described as a hopeless infatuation for one of the daughters, whose husband he made Assistant Secretary of State. Speculation about the photograph in his room before which flowers were placed daily was ended only by the disclosure that it was of his dead wife; yet every year, some newspaper announced at least one rumored romance or impending marriage. The ladies ranged from wealthy widows to a daughter of the British minister. They included even Frances Willard, leading temperance advocate, a suggestion put forward with the comment, "Stranger things have happened." It is possible that Arthur sustained political injury from such gossip, published and unpublished, but there is no evidence of it.

In March, Arthur gave his first state dinner for ex-President and Mrs. Grant, and others soon followed. The new dispensation became

[1] N. Y. *Times,* undated clipping.

the subject of drawing-room discussion. "I dined at the President's Wednesday," wrote Mrs. Blaine to one of her children. "The dinner was extremely elegant, hardly a trace of the old White House taint being perceptible anywhere, the flowers, the damask, the silver, the attendants, all showing the latest style and an abandon in expense and taste. But this is all there is of it." [1]

The change was for the better—but it was soon the occasion for further ill-natured attacks. Chauncey Depew, one of the country's most experienced diners-out, wrote of Arthur that "in all the arts and conventionalities of what is known as 'the best society,' he could have taken equal rank . . . with the Prince of Wales who afterwards became King Edward VII," and John S. Wise declared that "Arthur was a very prince of hospitality, and nothing could betray him into discourtesy." But while Washington society also admired Arthur's taste and manners, some talked and smiled cynically and concluded that, as the bitter Mrs. Blaine said, "this is all there is of it." It was this note which hostile critics emphasized; Arthur, they described as a grown-up playboy.

President Arthur spent as much time as he could with his children. Nell Arthur, not yet in her teens, used occasionally to be his companion on a late afternoon drive, but was usually with her cousins, her French governess, and her aunt. By Arthur's instructions, she was reared in comparative seclusion and with strict simplicity, for he feared the injurious effects of publicity, flattery, and temporary luxury, and in addition may have inherited some of his father's ideas on the subject of children's upbringing. His son was in college and used frequently to appear in Washington.

In April Arthur took them both to Annapolis to see the shaft to their grandfather's memory. In August, when he fled from Washington at the adjournment of Congress, they accompanied him on the *U.S.S. Despatch* to New York and perhaps shared his pleasure in an innovation for which he was responsible, the adoption of a "President's flag."

Arthur's "vacation" was spent in almost perpetual motion. After first calling upon his brother, for some months stationed at Governor's Island, he commenced a round of travels, interspersed with Cabinet meetings at his Lexington Avenue house or in Washington, which took him twice into New England and once to Alexandria Bay. At the end

[1] H. S. B. Beale, *Letters of Mrs. James G. Blaine,* Vol. I, pp. 309–10; Vol. II, pp. 4–5, 8.

of August, he spent a week as the guest of his old patron, Edwin D. Morgan, who had declined to serve in his Cabinet but was glad to introduce him to Newport society. There was a reception followed by a series of entertainments, including a clam bake and a fox hunt in which his son for the first time rode to hounds.

Accompanied by Daniel G. Rollins, Arthur cruised along the New England coast in the *Despatch,* reviewed the North Atlantic squadron off Portsmouth, and spent a short time in the vicinity of Bar Harbor. After a few uncomfortable days, late in September, in sweltering Washington, he went with Robert G. Dun to Alexandria Bay, fishing for bass, putting up at a simple, small hotel, and enjoying leisurely days in the open air. Here on October 5 he celebrated his fifty-second birthday.

Arthur returned to New York to meet the Eastern members of his Cabinet at his home on October 10. That afternoon, with Secretaries Chandler and Lincoln and others, he began a brief trip to Massachusetts for the centennial celebration of Daniel Webster's birthday. At Boston the schools closed, Governor Long and his staff greeted him, he reviewed a parade, and in the afternoon went to Faneuil Hall for a public reception. The old building was crowded with people eager to see the most nearly New England President since Franklin Pierce. Arthur spoke very briefly in appreciation of the welcome accorded him. As soon as he had finished, the crowd burst forward in a truly menacing rush to shake his hand. They were almost upon their prey when the whole presidential party disappeared through holes in the stage to a lower level and escaped somewhat unceremoniously down a rear staircase to the street. Within twenty minutes after arriving at the hall, Arthur was starting back to his hotel. A dinner and a private reception occupied the evening.

Next day a cold, cheerless east wind robbed the trip to Marshfield of much of its pleasure. There, as one of the speakers at the ceremonies on Webster's farm, he expressed, in graceful phrases, his approval of the Webster Historical Society's purposes. That evening he managed to attend two theaters, at one of which the beautiful Modjeska returned his tribute with a bouquet. The audience was enthusiastic.

Early in November, after taking his son to enter Princeton, and casting his vote in New York, he was established at the President's summer residence in the grounds of the Soldiers' Home, to which

Mrs. McElroy had come with the children, and to which many of his own possessions had been sent from New York. The summer "White House" was a stucco cottage of moderate size with open fireplaces in nearly every room and much solid walnut furniture of the type then highly regarded. For the floors, he had sent rugs and carpets salvaged from the Executive Mansion in its sweeping redecoration that summer. For decorations, it had the choicest of White House cast-offs. There were a safe and a telephone and practically no place hunters. It was so comfortable and, besides pleasing Arthur, it so admirably suited the needs of Nell Arthur and the McElroy children that the household remainded there until Christmas week. For the New Year's reception they moved back into the city, where the President's absence had of course caused considerable comment. In the meantime, much of importance had happened; he was deeply involved.

ONE of the first and most difficult of Arthur's presidential responsibilities was a thankless task, that of bringing to justice men charged with defrauding the Post Office Department. Successful prosecutions, while requiring unusual zeal and intelligence, would be of no great political advantage to the Administration or the party. Failure, on the other hand, whether from reluctance or from innumerable obstacles, would furnish ammunition to Arthur's enemies and the Democrats. The clear path of duty was to carry through the prosecutions with vigor and skill. Regardless of the high Republican standing of some of the culprits, Arthur ordered that they be tried.

In the campaign of 1880, one of the men most responsible for Republican success, as we have seen, was Stephen W. Dorsey, ex-Senator from Arkansas and secretary of the National Committee. Garfield was warned by Blaine and William E. Chandler that Dorsey was a man to be watched. Blaine wrote:

I am afraid the true intent and meaning of the Dorsey dinner in New York was to enable him to make demands of the Administration which will in the end modestly center in the Second Assistant Postmaster-Generalship, through which channel, in my judgment, there are cunning preparations being made by a small cabal to steal half a million a year during your Administration. I again beg you to keep yourself free from all possible committals as to the *minor* Cabinet, which in the P. O. D. is even more important than the major.[1]

Chandler prophesied that "the prize of the Star routes" would be the scandal of Garfield's term.[2] After such warnings, Garfield quite naturally ignored all advice from Dorsey respecting the membership of the new Cabinet. We have seen that he named Thomas L. James of New York to be his Postmaster General. His appointment must have caused Dorsey no little anxiety,[3] for the rumors of corruption to which Blaine and Chandler referred were well founded.

Extraordinary demands had been placed upon the postal service

---

[1] Blaine to Garfield, Feb. 13, 1881. See also his warning of Jan. 18, 1881, Garfield Papers.
[2] Chandler to Garfield, Feb. 17, 1881, Garfield Papers.
[3] S. B. Elkins to Chandler, Feb. 16, 20, 1881; George E. Spencer to Chandler, Feb. 19, Mar. 2, 1881, Chandler Papers.

by the rapid growth of the United States in the post-war period, especially in the trans-Mississippi West. Mining rushes presented sudden and fluctuating requirements for mail facilities. Army posts, rather remote from the agricultural areas, needed communication with the East. The persistent onflow of homesteaders required great activity in the Post Office Department. Cattle ranches, dotting the northern plains, poured in their requests. To satisfy all these calls, the Department was obliged to expand its staff and its budget in a comparatively brief time. Congress and President Hayes were inclined to be liberal, extending postal service with an eye to future as well as immediate requirements.[1] They placed considerable discretionary power by law in the hands of the Department, and granted generous appropriations.

Until the Western railroads could turn from building transcontinental main lines to the construction of branches, mail was distributed to inhabitants of the intervening areas by a class of mail service known as the "Star routes," by men, horses, and wagons or stagecoaches. The carriers were under four-year contracts to transport the mails with "certainty, celerity, and security," words which came to be represented in the contract blanks by asterisks, and thus to give the name "Star routes." Specifications respecting the weekly number and the speed of trips between the terminals on each route, while forming a part of each contract, might, within the discretion of the Second Assistant Postmaster General, be altered to meet changed conditions and the compensation modified proportionately, according to an index fixed by statute. It was an arrangement designed to meet a shifting volume of needs with the least possible delay.

President Arthur found, upon assuming office, that investigation had revealed extensive frauds in the "Star service." The leading Federal official implicated was Thomas J. Brady, Second Assistant Postmaster General, whom Grant had appointed on July 24, 1876. After about three years in office, Brady had been obliged to call for a deficiency appropriation of $2,000,000 for inland transportation of mails, and had then weathered a storm of criticism and investigation by members of Congress.[2] But Garfield, not satisfied with Congress's earlier investigations, had commissioned James to search the records of the contract office for evidence of corruption. The Postmaster General had charged

[1] C. R. Williams, ed., *Diary & Letters of R. B. Hayes*, Vol. IV, p. 13.
[2] *Cong. Rec.*, Vol. X, pp. 2008–13; pp. 2048–49, March 31, April 1, 2, May 4, 1880.

PRESIDENT ARTHUR, THE FISHERMAN, AT ALEXANDRIA BAY

P. H. Woodward, a special agent, with the task, and one month later had come to Garfield to report astounding discoveries.

The Republican Party was already being split over the Robertson case when, on April 9, 1881, James and Woodward went to the President with the initial fruits of the investigation. Ex-Senator Dorsey and certain associates appeared to be guilty of defrauding the government of thousands of dollars through "Star route" contracts. Despite the certainty of further damage to Republican strength, Garfield insisted that criminal prosecutions be prepared. Brady and other important subordinates were replaced by men deemed trustworthy; the contract office was reorganized; fraudulent contracts were canceled. Brady retaliated by publishing Garfield's injudicious letter to Jay Hubbell, Republican campaign leader in 1880, countenancing assessments of the government clerks, thus opening what became an unceasing attack upon the Administration in his Washington newspapers. Dorsey began a series of letters to Garfield, demanded a special investigation outside of court, and eventually gave long newspaper interviews complaining of persecution.

With matters at this stage, actual prosecutions were delayed by the shooting of Garfield. Postmaster General James and Attorney General MacVeagh were forced to act upon their own responsibility. As legal counsel, they retained Col. George C. Bliss of New York and Benjamin Harris Brewster of Philadelphia, both outstanding lawyers, chosen, among other reasons, because they "had heretofore maintained cordial personal and political relations with Mr. Arthur." [1] Brewster and Bliss began to master the infinite details of the case, to prepare evidence for the grand jury, and to decide upon their methods of prosecution. Final steps awaited Garfield's death or recovery.

During the summer of illness, although the situation cried for action, no unauthorized prosecutions could be begun. At Arthur's accession, no evidence had been laid before the grand jury. The defense had been rendered stronger by the delay.

In the first few weeks of his Presidency the problem of personnel was uppermost. Who should conduct the government's case? Many conflicting influences were brought to bear upon the new President,

---

[1] Eugene C. Savidge, *Life of Benjamin Harris Brewster* (Philadelphia, 1891), pp. 148–150. See also the report of the "Springer Committee" listed as 48th Cong., 1st sess., *House Misc. Doc. No. 38,* part 2.

who refused to be hurried into a mistake. To William E. Chandler, who was apparently eager to direct the attack, one of his friends wrote:

I got back here [New York City] yesterday p.m. and read your letter to "R. C." He said go straight to C. A. and let me know what he does. T. C. P. was present and said C[handler] must be put into charge of case at once. I said probably the best way is to have the counsel report to him for consultation. R. C. wanted to know what practice you had had in criminal cases. I said probably none since he was Dist. Atty. during the early part of the war in N. H.

I saw C. A. and found him just going out to dine—says Porter and Rollins are both going into case and wanted me to return at 11 p.m. and talk it over. I did not show him letter then. I went back at 11:30 p.m. but McVgh and Geo. Bliss were there and I sat around till 1:15 a.m. and McVgh was still in whining and begging and trying to be let out with a "Karacther," like an Irish biddy. He (McV) looks very blue this a.m. so I suppose he has not made anything—I will see "A" this p.m. and write you. . . .[1]

MacVeagh, after vainly seeking presidential approval of his resignation, nevertheless withdrew. Arthur then appointed Brewster, largely because of his previous work in preparing prosecutions, but his enlarged responsibilities required him to relinquish more and more of the detailed work to Colonel Bliss.[2] Bliss was aided, therefore, by the appointment [3] of Richard T. Merrick of Washington as "Special Assistant Attorney General for the Star Route Trials."

Merrick was professionally qualified to take a leading part in court, but his selection was probably influenced by the fact that he was also a prominent Democrat, having argued for the Democrats before the Electoral Commission of 1877, and, should the prosecutions fail, his participation would preclude charges of party favoritism to Republican defendants. Similarly, W. W. Ker was appointed to draft the indictments; his Democratic affiliations forestalled any subsequent assertion that for partisan reasons the indictments had been deliberately imperfect. With Attorney General Brewster supervising, Bliss, Merrick, and Ker went ahead with the prosecutions as rapidly as possible. For evidence, they were constantly under obligation to Postmaster General James and Special Agent Woodward.

[1] W. H. Painter to Chandler, November 10, 1881, Chandler Papers. R. C. is probably Conkling; C. A., President Arthur; C., Chandler; T. C. P., Platt.

[2] Bliss and Dorsey had both been active in the campaign of 1880 and had jointly urged Folger for the Cabinet rather than James.

[3] March 28, 1882.

The method of defrauding the government rested upon an administrative system established in a series of Federal statutes and Post Office Department regulations.[1] Complete charge of the service on all "Star routes" had been placed in the hands of the Second Assistant Postmaster General. Congress determined the routes for the entire country; the department divided the country into four regions and each year arranged for service on the routes of one region by contracts running for four years thereafter. The Second Assistant Postmaster General let the contracts, after advertisement and competitive bidding, to the lowest responsible applicant. He determined what type of service should be given on each route and caused appropriate specifications to be put in each contract, but if circumstances should warrant a change after a contract had been let, he was empowered to authorize alterations in both service *and compensation*.

What Woodward had discovered was that Brady, for the past three years, had been recklessly ordering improved service, accompanied by maximum increases in compensation, on routes for which a small group of men held the contracts, and that the inducement to issue the orders could not have been *bona fide* needs.

Woodward's evidence convinced Garfield and Arthur that the culprits ought to be punished, but it was another matter to convince a Washington jury. The government felt justified in publishing a list, in April, of ninety-three routes which it believed showed evidence of a fraudulent conspiracy between Brady and the contractors, but it needed witnesses to show that Brady had received a share of the money he awarded so prodigally to others. Difficulties were increased by two government investigators, unfortunate legacies from Garfield's Administration, who betrayed the Administration's plans to the "ring." Another embarrassment was the slipperiness of certain witnesses, particularly the unreliability of Montfort C. Rerdell.

Rerdell had become alarmed in June, 1881, and had sought to save himself by making a clean breast of his participation in the frauds.[2] He was, he confessed, the secretary of Stephen Dorsey and one of a "ring" whose members he named. He knew of a ledger account, under aliases, of the sums owed and paid to Brady at a fixed rate of one third of the first year's increased compensation on each mail route

---

[1] See Sections 3941–61 of the *Revised Statutes.*
[2] He had told his story to James and Woodward and repeated it to MacVeagh.

and one half of all fines and penalties remitted by Brady's order. He could produce the ledger by obtaining it from Dorsey's New York office, and to get it, he made a trip there and back on the same trains with Postmaster General James. A few days later, however, he made a signed recantation of all his statements.

Prior to Rerdell's disavowal, Dorsey had spent some very uncomfortable days. Looking distraught, he came one evening into a hotel room where ex-Senator Spencer of Nevada and S. B. Elkins, a recent territorial delegate from New Mexico, were conversing. He begged for help and said that his clerk had "squealed." Four days later, seeing Spencer, he seemed much more cheerful and reported that everything had been made all right, that Rerdell had repudiated his confession. The government desired to put the substance of the confession before the jury and to support it with testimony concerning Dorsey's behavior. Not only had Rerdell failed them, but Spencer then disregarded a subpoena until the trials were over and successfully defended himself from the charge of contempt of court by showing that the subpoena had been illegal in form, a fact which Roscoe Conkling had pointed out to him. Thus the prosecution lost two shifty witnesses.

Faithful men, who came on from the Southwest ready to assist the government's case, became discouraged by the necessity of waiting for weeks while the lawyers argued fine legal points. They lost their jobs; they found government allowances inadequate for the expenses of travel and of living in Washington; indeed, to save some of them from destitution, special appropriations had to be put through Congress.[1] Finally, many potential witnesses were deterred from aiding the government by the outrageous abuse to which Brady's newspapers subjected the entire prosecution, day after day.

Impressive legal obstacles had also to be surmounted before the dishonest men could be punished. The only crime with which they could be charged was conspiracy to defraud the government, one of the most difficult of crimes in which to establish guilt. When the investigations had yielded enough evidence to attempt to secure indictments, and when the counsel were prepared to go before the grand jury, District Attorney Corkhill, either because of a misunderstanding or from ulterior motives, suddenly discharged the grand jury. Before it could be again convened, the statute of limitations threatened to intervene

[1] 22 *Stat.*, pp. 386, 403.

for most of the defendants.[1] An attempt was therefore made to proceed by information instead of indictment, but this was declared illegal on the ground that, in the District of Columbia, conspiracy to defraud was an "infamous crime" which required indictment.[2] Finally, after much argument had proved a first indictment to be defective, another was obtained on May 20, 1882.

Against John W. Dorsey, John R. Miner, John M. Peck, Stephen W. Dorsey, Harvey M. Vaile, M. C. Rerdell, Thomas J. Brady, and William H. Turner, the indictment charged conspiracy to defraud the Federal Government. On May 29, all except Peck appeared in court to plead not guilty. Two, Brady and Turner, had been officers in the Post Office Department; the others were former mail contractors. On June 1, little realizing how strenuous a summer lay before them, an imposing array of counsel, jurymen, witnesses, and defendants began the first trial in the Supreme Court of the District.

From the outset, the government lawyers were beset with difficulties. Merrick conducted himself with a solemnity in marked contrast to the confident gayety of the galaxy of ten opposing lawyers. There were able men among them. Most prominent was Robert G. Ingersoll, ex-Senator Dorsey's counsel; another was Enoch Totten, son-in-law of Postmaster General Howe. The government, after long wrangling, was allowed three peremptory challenges, while four were granted for each defendant. The jury was swiftly selected and sworn in on the first day. Then, after a succession of opening addresses by counsel, examination of witnesses continued without important interruption until September 8, through sizzling heat and true Washington humidity.

The first attempt of the government to get Rerdell's confession before the jury precipitated a long legal wrangle ending in defeat. It could not be admitted in evidence at that point.[3] The government provoked another protracted discussion when it put Albert E. Boone, an alleged ex-member of the "Dorsey ring," on the stand to testify to acts by which the conspiracy was organized in 1877. The indictment had named May 23, 1879, as a day when the conspiracy had been in effect.

---

[1] Within three years prosecutions must have been begun in all cases of alleged crime against the United States.

[2] Information was filed on Sept. 30, 1881 and dismissed on Nov. 10, 1881.

[3] Later, the versions of both MacVeagh and James were received. Proceedings in the Trial of the Case of the United States *vs.* John W. Dorsey and others, hereafter referred to as *Star Route Trials* (3 vols., Wash., 1882), Vol. II, pp. 1807–38.

The prosecutors planned to trace the growth of the "ring" from its origins to the date set in the indictment, but the defense insisted that all such testimony was irrelevant unless a conspiracy on the designated day were first proved. When the court ruled against them, they took exceptions.[1]

Defense attorneys kept up a persistent barrage of objections to the order of testimony, the admission of documents, and the form of questions. They fired at every loophole which offered an opening through which to embarrass and delay and confuse the government's case. Again and again testimony was stopped by a debate concerning admissibility, based on demands that evidence of the conspiracy must pertain to joint, not individual, acts. If testimony concerning a single defendant were admitted, they always took exceptions.[2]

For over two days they carried on a persistent and sometimes acrimonious struggle with Bliss, Merrick, and Ker over admitting the testimony of John A. Walsh, another mail contractor, who wished to swear that he had paid money to Brady and that Brady had informed him of his participation in such a conspiracy as was charged. Ingersoll summed up the position of the defense as follows: "Now, in order to make the declaration [of Brady to Walsh] evidence, there must first be a conspiracy; second, the man making the declaration must have been proved to be one of the conspirators, and what more? He must make the declaration while he is carrying out the conspiracy. It must be a part of the *res gestae*. It must belong to and be a part of the act that he is then doing, and that act must be in pursuance of the conspiracy."[3] When the court declared Walsh's testimony admissible as against Brady, but not the others, another exception was taken by the defense.[4]

The case of the government was based upon nineteen contracts of the 134 held by the "Dorsey ring." In two years, Brady had made 138 orders increasing the compensation on all those routes for one alleged reason or another.[5] Instead of proceeding in the simplest possible way to demonstrate fraudulent conspiracy, the government selected

[1] *Star Route Trials*, Vol. II, pp. 1443–63.

[2] *Ibid.*, Vol. I, pp. 355–62.

[3] *Ibid.*, Vol. II, pp. 1608 ff.

[4] *Ibid.*, Vol. II, pp. 1697–99. Col. Ingersoll had before the trials written to Postmaster General James: "I concur with you that there have been great irregularities in the past in relation to mail contracts . . ." Post Office Dept. Files, *Letters of the Postmaster-General*, Vol. XIV, p. 43.

[5] *Ibid.*, Vol. I, p. 104.

the nineteen routes and proved, in connection with each, facts which alone and by themselves might have seemed to show innocent blunders but which, in conjunction with one another, were believed to be convincing proof of an organized, corrupt understanding between Brady and the "Dorsey ring." [1]

This method was confusing rather than convincing unless patiently studied and carefully followed. It was, however, almost unavoidable because only one witness, John A. Walsh, could be induced to testify to having made an actual payment of money to Brady.[2]

Evidence for the defense began on Monday, July 31, 1882. It supported the plausible position that orders issued by Thomas J. Brady for changes in mail service with increased remuneration were of three kinds —first, those demanded by the rapidity of increase in population or by special requirements of the army in the West; second, those made in response to the influential requests of members of Congress; and third, those issued because of misinformation or of mistaken, though honest, judgment. It was emphatically denied that any money had been paid to him for the orders. The organization of the "ring" they explained as legitimate and for honest purposes.

The validity of Rerdell's confession had first to be completely destroyed. Although the versions of James and MacVeagh had been somewhat corroborated by ex-Senator Clayton,[3] the defense endeavored to show that Rerdell had an ulterior motive ior making a supposed confession. He had wished to protect a steamboat mail contract of his own. They likewise put on the stand Harvey M. Vaile, who described the acts portrayed in the confession as those of a lawful combination. On the other hand, a construction similar to Rerdell's was given to those early acts by one of the government's witnesses, Albert E. Boone, who had been frozen out of the "Dorsey ring," and Rerdell's testimony as to Brady's criminally dishonest relationship was in accord with that of John A. Walsh.

The Arthur Administration laid itself open to the charge that it did not desire a conviction when Secretary Teller appeared as a witness for the defense and testified that, as Senator from Colorado, he had fre-

---

[1] Bliss preferred this method, knowing that it was the way in which Boss Tweed had been convicted in New York. See *Springer Committee Report*, pp. 159–61; Bliss's testimony.

[2] Rerdell's confession was weak testimony, especially when he recanted and refused to substantiate it in court.

[3] *Star Route Trials*, Vol. II, pp. 1839–42.

quently urged the Post Office Department to increase mail facilities in the West. It was his theory that the government owed to Western settlers the same quality of postal service as to Eastern residents, irrespective of the difference in cost.[1] Another member of Arthur's Cabinet, Postmaster General Howe, showed no enthusiasm for spending department funds to indemnify government witnesses. In every other way, however, his support seems to have been given to the Administration.[2]

General William Sherman, ranking officer of the army, also testified for the defense. He explained that the very expensive Route No. 35051, from Bismarck to Tongue River, Dakota Territory, a route much stressed by the prosecution because of the insignificant revenue and the large expense, he had urged the Post Office Department to create because it would bring mail to Fort Keogh at three- or four-day intervals instead of much greater periods. Its usefulness, moreover, had been even greater because of its indirect aid in policing the unpopulated region through which it ran, by its series of stations at twenty-mile intervals.[3]

Near the end of the trial, there was great excitement when Judge Wylie informed the jury that more than one of them had reported being approached with offers of bribes. Such offers he denounced as an insult to their honor. William W. Dickson, the foreman, then promised that after the verdict he would lay all the facts in his case before Judge Wylie. Defending counsel [4] demanded an immediate investigation.

Although the Judge charged the jury before their retirement (September 8, 1882) not to allow the attempt at "jury fixing" to prejudice their views and not to take into the jury room any papers, Dickson read an affidavit to the jury in which he described an alleged attempt of a government agent to bribe him to secure a verdict of guilty.[5] It is

[1] *Star Route Trials,* Vol. II, pp. 2021 ff.
[2] Post Office Dept. Files, *Letters of the Postmaster-General,* Vol. XIV, p. 135, p. 140; Vol. XV, p. 89. To Attorney General Brewster, he wrote on November 8, 1882, denying remarks attributed to Bliss which implied neglect on the part of his Department. He stated that all the Post Office Department could offer was its records and its officers, which had been freely given to the Department of Justice, even to the extent of using Post Office inspectors instead of United States Marshals for the summoning of witnesses.
[3] *Star Route Trials,* Vol. III, pp. 2074 ff.
[4] Henkle and McSweeny. *Star Route Trials,* Vol. III, pp. 3156–57.
[5] Department of Justice Files, *Star Route Trials;* Affidavit of Juror Edwin McLain, Nov. 21, 1882.

inconceivable that this did not have its effect upon the jury.[1]

The verdict was reached by means of twelve ballots, interspersed with long periods of discussion and argument. The first vote was informal, its object being to discover how all stood on the general question of the guilt of all defendants. It resulted in an eight to four division favoring conviction. Then a second ballot was taken as to the proof of the overt acts described in the indictment, with the following results:

	Guilty	Not Guilty
John W. Dorsey	9	3
John R. Miner	10	2
J. M. Peck	4	8
S. W. Dorsey	8	4
H. M. Vaile	9	3
M. C. Rerdell	10	2
T. J. Brady	8	4
William Turner	0	12

A formal vote was immediately taken acquitting Turner. Next day, formal votes convicted Miner and Rerdell and exonerated Peck. In time, a fourth ballot was reached in which Juror Holmead favored the acquittal of the four remaining defendants but the other eleven jurymen were variously divided. On Sunday, September 10, 1882, the jury six times voted without change. There was no prospect of agreement, so the verdict was reported, with entire inconsistency, to be: William H. Turner, not guilty; John R. Miner and M. C. Rerdell, guilty; John W. Dorsey, S. W. Dorsey, H. M. Vaile and Thomas J. Brady, a disagreement.[2] It was absurd that two men of a group should conspire with four others who supposedly did not conspire. The court, accordingly, at once ordered a new trial for all but Turner and Peck.[3]

The second trial began on December 7, 1882,[4] after three months of activity by the government divided between getting new witnesses, in-

[1] The jury consisted of the following: William Dickson, foreman; John W. Hayes, John B. McCarthy, Edwin J. McLain, William K. Brown, Edward D. Doniphan, Henry A. Olcott, William Holmead, Thomas Martin, George W. Cox, Hugh T. Murray, and Zacharias Tobriner.

[2] The court had been satisfied that Peck was dead.

[3] *Star Route Trials*, Vol. III, pp. 3235 ff.

[4] *Proceedings in the Second Trial of the Case of the United States vs. John W. Dorsey and others for Conspiracy* (4 vols., Washington, 1883).

vestigating bribery charges, clearing the government service of obstructing friends of the defendants, and trying to fortify Rerdell. He was a weak reed. Having made his confession in June, 1881, and subsequently retracted it, between the first and second trials he again seemed to be smitten with remorse or the desire to save himself by turning state's witness. Again, however, he denied his confession after he had been excoriated for disloyalty by his former associates and encouraged, by harangues from their attorneys, to expect acquittal.

On December 26, 1882, the Washington *Evening Star* called attention to a rumor that Rerdell was at last to testify for the government and to the undoubted fact that Colonel Ingersoll, in his opening, had tried to protect the defendants from such a contingency. Rerdell publicly denied this report next day, but, on February 15, he changed his plea to "guilty" and threw himself on the mercy of the court. Both he and his wife took the stand for the prosecution, as did James W. Bosler, who had paid money to Brady. More than a score of the witnesses had not appeared in the first trial.

To repulse this new attack, the defendants at last testified in their own behalf and were aided by a dozen new witnesses, including General Nelson A. Miles. For several weary months litigation dragged on; then, on June 14, 1883, an exhausted jury pronounced each of the defendants "not guilty."

With this jury, the defense had probably tampered. Its foreman's business partner had served as a link between him and one of the defense counsel, notorious in Washington courts as a "jury fixer." [1] Although investigations furnished evidence of this outrageous performance, neither the corrupted jurors nor those who bribed them were indicted. Attorney General Brewster was so eager to bring the whole mess to a satisfactory conclusion that he urged Woodward in a series of letters, late in 1884, to hasten the prosecution of the culprits. In reply, Woodward wrote:

I have developed enough facts already to convince any man whom it may be desirable to satisfy. Many facts could not be used in court, and others still would lose their force through the necessary withholding at the time of trial of correlated facts. If taken into court, the entirety of the case as regards evidence would be lost. *The results were accomplished by many distinct crimes converging to a common end.* If presented, each would have to stand or fall

[1] Affidavit of James A. Nelson, Mar. 7, 1884, in the records of the Department of Justice.

by itself and thus the stock of evidence, separated into the facts belonging to each particular crime, and broken in its connections, would prove insufficient. As the instruments employed are for the most part kept in ignorance of what their associates are doing, it is exceedingly difficult . . . to develop a complete chain of legal proof.

The guilty men were never brought to justice! [1]

Criminal prosecutions for conspiracy failing, civil suits were begun. Preliminary steps to recover the sums illegally obtained by some of the larger mail contractors had been taken before the second conspiracy trial ended in failure. When Walter Q. Gresham succeeded Howe, he encouraged their continuance. Bliss would gladly have conducted these civil suits, but his fees were considered exorbitant, and since the money for any other skillful, experienced lawyer was not then available, the cases were assigned to the Federal attorneys in each district where the mail routes in question lay. Nothing was accomplished by that arrangement and eventually, in November, 1884, all these prosecutions were put in the care of a special Assistant Attorney General, George L. Douglass.

Douglass's work in court did not begin until, in May, 1885, he pushed to a conclusion the cases of which United States *vs.* Cosgrove [2] furnished the recorded opinion. The Circuit Court at Topeka insisted that to warrant recovery by the government of payments which had exceeded legitimate compensation, it must be shown that fraud was responsible for the over-payments. Juries declined to see in Brady's flagrant prodigality anything but the result of errors in fact or judgment, so the defendants were exonerated from liability to restore any of the money.

Against another "ring" the government subsequently carried its case to the Supreme Court and won a substantial victory. Fraud, the highest tribunal said, was not essential in order to render the government's excess payments recoverable. If unduly large compensation had been ordered on the basis of errors of fact (not errors of judgment), the government could demand restitution. [3] This was the only victorious

---

[1] Savidge, *op. cit.*, p. 170, contains this letter and others of the same purport. See also Woodward to Brewster Cameron, Apr. 7, 1884, in the records of the Department of Justice.

[2] 26 *Fed.*, p. 908.

[3] U. S. *vs.* Voorhees, 135 *U. S.*, 550 (1890); U. S. *vs.* Piatt and Salisbury, 157 *U. S.*, 113 (1895); U. S. *vs.* Salisbury, 157 *U. S.*, p. 121 (1895).

"Star route" prosecution, productive of merely a partial indemnification for the millions lost through Brady's dishonesty.

Contemporary opinion ascribed failure to the half-hearted nature of the Administration's efforts. The defendants were reported at one time to hold the theory that "the Attorney General is in earnest on the Star route case. But the head of the Administration and Mr. Bliss are only making a sham fight." [1] This theory has been adopted by others and has some plausibility in view of the friendly personal and political relations, prior to the trials, between the President, Secretary Folger, Colonel Bliss, and some of the defendants. But whatever the President's inclinations may have been, they could have been exercised only through the Post Office Department or the Department of Justice. With the latter's energetic activities in mind, it is necessary only to discover if they had the interested support of the President.

Both before and after the trials, Attorney-General Brewster stated that Arthur's instructions and counsel had been directed toward successful prosecutions, carried on "with diligence and with earnestness to a practical result." Before the "Springer Committee," investigating his department in 1884, he reported Arthur's words to have been:

I want this work to be done as you are doing it, in the spirit in which you are doing it; I want it to be done earnestly and thoroughly. I desire that these people shall be prosecuted with the utmost vigor of the law. I will give you all the help I can. You can come to me whenever you wish to, and I will do all I can to aid you.

"And," Brewster continued, "he did so all the way through; without a moment's hesitation—always stood by me and strengthened me and gave me confidence." [2]

Arthur could distinguish certain happy results of real importance. The accused men were driven from the government service; the Post Office Department improved in personnel and saved some $500,000 per year. Public opinion was aroused against corruption in office and impetus given to the movement for civil service reform. Statutory changes put an end to the unsafe features of the old method for adjusting com-

---

[1] F. H. Fall to Brewster Cameron, July 17, 1882, Records of the Department of Justice. See also A. K. McClure, *Our Presidents and How We Make Them*, p. 286.

[2] *Springer Committee Report*, pp. iii, 847; Richardson, *Messages*, Vol. VIII, pp. 53, 143, for Arthur's public statements.

pensation on Star routes. Before many years, the railway mail service had expanded and the Star routes declined precipitately in numbers and in mileage. But in the trials, the Arthur administration had seemed to fail; politically, their outcome was injurious to the President's hopes.

APPARENTLY, when Blaine had retired from Arthur's Cabinet into private life, some of his foes decided it would be well to keep him there. His conduct of foreign relations had been marked by extraordinary aggressiveness, looking to the eventual acquisition of the Hawaiian Islands, Galapagos Islands, and even perhaps St. Pierre and Miquelon. In Central America he fostered the effort to reëstablish a political union of the several states, and in South America he undertook two notable enterprises which his opponents at once attacked. He attempted to end the War of the Pacific, in which Chile was overwhelming Bolivia and Peru, by sending a special diplomatic mission under instructions which threatened, in certain circumstances, armed intervention by the United States. To promote friendly relations among the American countries, he invited them to send delegates to an American International Conference in Washington. The unprecedented initiative shown in these plans was assailed as rash, aggressive, and dangerous by persons desiring to discredit the brilliant ex-Secretary.

In January and February, 1882, Blaine's enemies opened the attack.[1] Arthur and Frelinghuysen aided them by recalling the special (Trescot) mission and indefinitely postponing the conference. An investigation in the House Committee on Foreign Affairs attempted to impugn his motives in dealing with Chile and Peru. Naturally, he struck back, denouncing Arthur's withdrawal of the conference invitations, protesting against newspaper publication of his instructions to Trescot, and in the committee investigation turning on some of his questioners with angry retorts.[2] He was on the defensive, charged with resemblance to Aaron Burr, "a disappointed politician" planning imperial schemes.[3]

Blaine could not fail to resent the new Administration's part in undermining his popularity. His friends were angered at what they considered a Stalwart attack upon their idol, but thus far no clear evidence has arisen to show who was personally responsible. Arthur, embarrassed by the attacks, tried to show his friendly attitude in various ways.[4] But

[1] See N. Y. *Herald,* Jan. 27, 1882; *Mrs. Blaine's Letters,* Vol. I, pp. 293–7.
[2] See 47th Cong., 1st sess., *House Report No. 1790.*
[3] N. Y. *Herald,* Feb. 2, 4, 1882; Phila. *Times,* Feb. 11, 1882.
[4] H. S. B. Beale, editor, *Letters of Mrs. James G. Blaine,* Vol. I, p. 297; Stanwood, *James G. Blaine,* pp. 250–1; Gail Hamilton, *James G. Blaine, passim.*

he had assented to the conference invitations and the Trescot instructions before Blaine's withdrawal, and it remains impossible to understand how he could withdraw his approval of both unless from factional motives or ignorance. Half-Breeds determined that he should suffer for it.

Further evidence that the Stalwarts were in the saddle came in February, 1882. When Justice Hunt of the Supreme Court was retired by special act of Congress, Arthur appointed Roscoe Conkling to the vacancy [1] and had the nomination confirmed. Conkling declined the place, and after Senator Edmunds had also refused, Arthur appointed Samuel Blatchford of New York, who accepted. The appointment of Conkling was hardly defensible, even though, according to the politicians' code, it may have released Arthur from further unwelcome obligations to his former chief. The ex-Senator did not possess the requisites of a good judge. He was by nature partisan. When it was suggested that the whole procedure was complimentary, that Conkling's refusal had been expected, critics very properly denounced the use of Supreme Court nominations to pay such compliments.[2]

A year after Arthur's accession, the Administration had gone far toward control by the Stalwarts, for the most part by gradual steps. John Sherman wrote to ex-President Hayes:

It seems the purpose of the Adm'n not only to undo all you did, but to remove from office all your appointees. I feel this more keenly than you, for I am . . . powerless to prevent it. . . . The Democratic Senators support Arthur in every instance and are paid for it by personal appointments in their interests. Republican Senators, hopeless of success, acquiesce in removals they cannot prevent. . . . Three or four Senators control most of the appointments at large while local appointments are made by Congressmen. This rule is not applicable to Ohio, for most of us (I especially) are ignored.[3]

Hayes replied:

I am very glad to get your letter and to hear the exact condition of affairs. I have suspected for some time that "to get even" was the key to the Conkling-Arthur policy. No merit will save any officer who was a friend of the Hayes Administration. Only fear of public opinion spares those who are left. . . .

---

[1] See letter reproduced in A. R. Conkling, *Life of Roscoe Conkling*, p. 676.
[2] *The Nation*, Mar. 2, 1882.
[3] July 2, 1882, Hayes Papers.

There are no Arthur men in this region except a few who want place at any price.[1]

A month later, Sherman was more convinced than ever of Arthur's proscriptive policy in Ohio, writing Hayes that "every appointee of yours and nearly every officeholder from Ohio is replaced when his office lapses." [2] As the elections of 1882 approached, therefore, Arthur's Administration had antagonized both Half-breeds and Sherman men. In New York, Collector Robertson remained in office as a symbol of the new President's supposed desire to harmonize the party. But the failure to remove him had exasperated many of Arthur's New York associates and deprived his Administration of the powerful support they could give. It had won him no new followers.

Such was the situation when Congress adjourned, its members returning home to receive limited approval from even the regular Republican press, and sharp attacks from the Democrats for their lack of creditable accomplishment. The legislative record was vulnerable. Charges of extravagance and procrastination had evident truth. The outstanding instance of prodigality, the rivers and harbors bill, was described as "like a jack-pot with everyone in." [3] Disapproval was widespread. When Congressman William W. Crapo of Massachusetts, who had voted to override the veto, failed to secure the nomination for Governor, his failure was ascribed to that vote.[4] As a lesser waste, lavish pension doles were allowed to continue in circumstances permitting fraud despite Arthur's recommendations to the contrary.

As effective as the imputation of extravagance was that of antipathy to civil service reform. At the end of the first session, there seemed to be "no prospect whatever" that the Pendleton Act would ever be adopted.[5] The neglect of the measure had been emphasized by scornful remarks in Capitol corridors, but agitation in its behalf persisted.[6] More serious in the public mind was the continued raising of Republican campaign funds by levying assessments upon officeholders' salaries. The law prohibiting the solicitation of such funds from one officer of

[1] July 5, 1882, Hayes Papers.
[2] Aug. 3, 1882, Hayes Papers.
[3] Cincinnati *Enquirer,* Aug. 3, 1882.
[4] *Ibid.,* September 21, 1882.
[5] N. Y. *Tribune,* September 12, 1882.
[6] *North American Review,* CXXXV (1882) had articles in four issues out of six dealing with this subject.

A POPULAR MELODY APPLIED.

We never speak as we pass by,
Altho' a tear bedims her eye; * * *

The spell is past, the dream is o'er,
And tho' we meet, we love no more!

the United States by another, was egregiously evaded by the Republican congressional campaign committee in the elections of 1882. An opinion was elicited from Attorney General Brewster stating that Congressmen were not *officers* in the sense contemplated by the law of 1876, so that Chairman Hubbell of the committee might receive contributions lawfully. Though gifts in name, the vigorous mode of solicitation made the returns in fact, assessments. Democrats in many States assailed this violation of law and induced the public to regard money thus raised as little better than a corruption fund.[1]

Arthur's Administration tried to foster the opposition rising in the South against the dominant Democratic factions. Wherever possible, it encouraged the coalition of Republicans with "anti-Bourbon" Democrats by its distribution of Federal patronage, hoping thus to develop organized resistance of enduring strength.[2] Had the plan succeeded, the actual end of the old Southern economic sectionalism might have found expression through a revived, two-party system in politics. But it failed, largely because of the failure of Southern Republicans to co-operate as the Administration desired. The election of 1882 tested the program and showed it to be far from adequate until more thoroughly applied. The election of 1884 was to be even more conclusive.

The congressional elections of 1882 resembled the off-elections of earlier years in that they were much influenced by local as well as national considerations. In some normally Republican States, local problems of party leadership or such local issues as State railroad taxation, prohibition laws, and Sunday regulation, either divided the party or gave even more strength to the Democrats than national questions could have afforded. As in 1878 and 1874, the Democratic Party made gains in the House which cannot be explained except by the existence of large numbers of voters in many States who trusted the Democrats of their own State but not those of the rest of the country; who preferred a Republican President but a Democratic State administration and congressional representation. The combined effect of the various factors produced a Democratic "landslide" in 1882.

Among the States with large populations, Pennsylvania was the scene of an Independent Republican movement, a revolt from the Camerons'

[1] See the platforms of Ohio, Illinois, Michigan, and Pennsylvania Democrats in *Appleton's Annual Cyclopedia* for 1882.
[2] General Longstreet to Arthur, June 27, 1882, Arthur Papers; P. B. S. Pinchback to W. E. Chandler, Oct. 26, 1882, Chandler Papers. Chandler was most active in this effort.

"regular" leadership which split the party and delivered control to the Democrats led by Governor R. E. Pattison, a well-known reformer. Ohio was diverted by local issues on which Republicans differed, and they lost by a plurality of nearly twenty thousand.[1] In California, the Republicans were on the unpopular side in favoring Sunday "blue" laws, on the defensive over their Railroad Commission's activities, and unable to win public favor on the score of Chinese exclusion because the issue had been merely shelved for ten years, not settled. The result was a Democratic sweep. In Indiana, Illinois, and Michigan, national issues were most prominent in the party platforms, and the Democrats won substantial gains but not complete victory. In Massachusetts, Ben Butler, of all persons, was chosen by the combined Democratic and Greenback Parties to carry out a program of *reform*. The Republican rout was strikingly widespread.

Fortunately for the Republicans, senatorial elections in wavering States fell where they retained control of the legislatures. As a result, the Senate of the Forty-eighth Congress was to consist of thirty-nine Republicans, aided by Senator Mahone and opposed by but thirty-six Democrats.[2] In sharp contrast to the Senate, the House of Representatives experienced an astonishing overturn. It had been enlarged by the Reapportionment Act of February 25, 1882,[3] from 293 to 325 members. Democratic mastery was assured by a party alignment of 201 Democrats, 119 Republicans, 4 Independents, and 1 Greenbacker. Extravagance and procrastination, as well as factional division, caused the Republican defeat.[4]

The prestige of Arthur's position was sadly diminished by the stinging blows which deprived his party of its control of Congress. But more disastrous to his ambition to secure the Republican nomination in 1884 was the overwhelming repulse which he received in New York. In order to develop an Administration wing of the Republican Party there, he undertook to put in office a Governor of his own choosing, for the first

[1] Washington *Evening Critic,* October 14, 1882, contains explanation of Ohio elections by Judge William Lawrence, First Comptroller of the Treasury.

[2] Four Republicans and ten Democrats were reëlected; eight Senators were replaced by others of the same party; the Democrats gained a seat in Louisiana but lost one each from Virginia and Oregon. Shelby M. Cullom, a Republican, replaced David Davis, Illinois Independent.

[3] 22 *Stat.* 5–6; McPherson, *Handbook of Politics,* 1882, p. 39–44.

[4] This conclusion rests upon a check of the record of sixteen Republicans defeated for reelection in six scattered States. Every one voted to carry the Rivers and Harbors Act over Arthur's veto; all but one voted for the Tariff Commission Act.

time attempting independently to lead his party in his own State. A marked coldness had arisen between the Conkling-Arthur group and the adherents of Governor Cornell in the course of the fiasco of 1881 at Albany.[1] Arthur's subsequent succession to the Presidency had produced no great dispensation of bounties among his New York associates, many of whom considered him ungrateful. Although the State convention in October, 1881, had passed a resolution supporting him, its nominations had gone to Half-Breeds.[2] Clearly, no half-hearted efforts could yield mastery to Arthur and the few Stalwarts who would "work" with him.

When Congress adjourned in August, 1882, the President went with his children to New York City by boat, and later on, cruised along the New England coast with Secretary Chandler, apparently oblivious of political problems. Actually, he had already begun quiet efforts to secure delegates to the Republican State convention.[3]

Arthur's leadership depended upon the nomination of Secretary Folger for Governor of New York. Folger's candidacy had been under discussion in the spring; and, in answer to an inquiry, one of his associates, the Treasury Department's appointment clerk, had replied:

. . . As near as I can learn, Secretary Folger does not seek or desire the nomination for Governor. He does not approve of anybody getting a delegation for him, or asking for him influence in any convention. He will never consent to go into a convention as a candidate of any wing of the Republican Party as against the candidate of any other wing. This is about all I can say to you in regard to the matter in question. . . . Speaking for myself, as if I were in his place, . . . [I would] say that, if the convention should extend to me unanimously the nomination for the Governorship, I would promptly accept it. The Secretary may have a good deal of this human nature in him and may or may not be moved similarly. . . .[4]

Of course this was sparring. It was too early to announce a candidacy. But the Secretary's decision to seek the nomination was reached prior to August 14, since on that date he wrote to Arthur for assistance in obtaining friendly delegates to the convention.[5] How he was induced

---

[1] N. Y. *Semi-weekly Tribune*, August 29, 1882, says that only Conkling, not mutual confidence, had kept Cornell and Arthur together.

[2] N. Y. *Sun*, Oct. 6, 1881.

[3] Folger to Arthur, Aug. 14, 1882, Arthur Papers.

[4] James B. Butler to H. D. Cunningham, May 22, 1882, Butler Papers. (New York Public Library.)

[5] Folger to Arthur, Aug. 14, 1882, Arthur Papers.

to run remains uncertain.[1]

One of Arthur's friends asserted that the President took no part in the Folger campaign, preferring him to others but doing nothing to aid him, and so incurring his indignation.[2] Others later declared that Arthur opposed Folger's candidacy until convinced that no other Republican could carry New York and then insisted upon it, even when it seemed that no Republican could win.[3] By September, the Secretary had long since abandoned any unwillingness to take the nomination. He was zealously engaged in forwarding his candidacy, and finding the President's noncommittal attitude embarrassing, wrote as follows:

My dear Arthur:

I have seen several people here who seem disturbed and irresolute, for the reason that they do not know, as they say, what it is that the Administration wishes in regard to the nomination for Governor. There is an impression that Mr. Conkling, T. C. Platt, and others of like position are for Clarence A. Seward. It is doubted whether or not you are in favor of him. It is represented as desirable that you let some one, as, for instance, Pierre C. Van Wyck, say what you wish.

I have no doubt myself what your desire is. I should have to lose my respect for you, if I did doubt and I write to you the foregoing in plain words, for your consideration whether it is or is not politic for you to authorize Van Wyck or other person to speak in a quiet way for you on the subject. I have no suggestion to make as to the policy, and no wish that you act in one way or the other.

There are several things upon which I would like your views—especially the appointment of Inspectors of Steam Vessels (foreign),—but I do not learn that you are to be here soon, and if you are really quiet and resting would not have you come.[4]

Folger had some misgivings before the convention. At his home in Geneva, N. Y., in early September, he wrote to Butler:

You have no idea of the bitterness in this region towards all Stalwarts and persons supposed to be in harmony with the Administration. Old personal friends and clients of mine declare that they will not vote for me, if nominated, not, they say, that they dislike me but those behind me. It is doubtful

---

[1] His daughter has declined to open the papers to historians for any purpose, particularly a biography of Chester A. Arthur.
[2] N. Y. *Herald*, Dec. 25, 1882.
[3] *Ibid.*, Dec. 20, 1884.
[4] Arthur Papers.

if Cornell does not carry this county, Ontario, my own county, on that ground alone.

"Gould and Conkling," "Gould and Conkling," that is the cry and it seems to set men mad. The N. Y. *Herald* of Saturday, in its correspondence gives one a good idea of it. . . .

Keep what I have said to yourself. It worries me much.[1]

Cornell and Jay Gould had engaged in a long newspaper altercation in August which had not revealed the Governor in the most favorable light but had assisted his popularity because Gould and his attorney, Roscoe Conkling, were so widely hated.[2] Butler wrote confidently to his chief, minimized the effect of the Gould affair, and assured him that, after his nomination, the newspapers and the Cornell adherents would fall into line. Meanwhile, Treasury Department patronage was used to the full in Folger's behalf.[3] When the convention assembled at Saratoga on September 20, there was no doubt among the delegates and little in the press that Folger was "the Administration's man" and was to receive the support of practically all the Stalwarts save the Cornell wing. Even General George H. Sharpe, who had deserted Conkling in the reëlection struggle at Albany, was working with Arthur.[4]

The principal contest lay between Folger and Governor Cornell, who sought renomination after a creditable but not brilliant term. Folger was respected as a man of ability and character, but was somewhat more closely identified with the remnants of Conkling's following. Cornell's principal agent in the convention was Senator Warner Miller, an adherent of Blaine. The Administration forces barely beat Cornell's. On the second ballot, amid great excitement, Folger was nominated by a majority of only 17 in 497 votes.[5] It was a Pyrrhic victory.

In the weeks that followed, the voters learned that Folger managers

---

[1] Sept. 11, 1882, Butler Papers.

[2] N. Y. *Herald,* Aug. 20, 22, 25, 1882.

[3] Butler to Folger, Sept. 12, 14, 1882, Butler Papers.

[4] Other Stalwarts divided as follows: for Folger—Geo. C. Bliss, Richard Crowley, T. C. Platt, J. D. Warren; for Cornell—A. E. Daggett, S. B. Dutcher, and Louis F. Payn. Folger had deprived Daggett of a lucrative hauling contract in Brooklyn. Daggett to Chandler, Apr. 26, 1882; Chandler Papers.

[5] First ballot: Folger 223, Cornell 180, Wadsworth 69, Starin 19, Robinson 6; second ballot, Folger 257, Cornell 222, Wadsworth 18. For description see N. Y. *Tribune,* Sept. 21, 1882.

had used two fraudulent proxies in a meeting of the State Committee to assure the choice of one of their number for temporary chairman and through him control the organization of committees.[1] Federal officeholders among the delegates were declared to have been dragooned into voting for Folger that they might retain their jobs. "Presidential bossism" was earnestly denounced. On September 26, the New York *Herald* proclaimed that it would support Grover Cleveland in view of the circumstances of Folger's nomination. Folger began his campaign with an apologetic acceptance,[2] and the whole tone of his protagonists was defensive.[3]

Against Grover Cleveland, Folger's candidacy steadily lost ground. Despite his care to avoid offending Blaine,[4] many Half-Breeds either supported Cleveland or determined not to vote at all. Republican efforts to propitiate the labor vote, the Jews, and the French-Canadians in northern New York met scant success. Near the end of October, Folger leaders were trying to get Democratic votes for him, and the candidate himself suggested:

. . . If the men want to show disgust at *machine,* etc., they can do so without cutting off the *head of the ticket,* to whom they do not object.
Let them *go to the polls* and *vote for F.* at all events.[5]

As his note indicates, the independent and opposition press had taken the stand that the bosses were trading on Folger's good name, and that his defeat should be made a rebuke to *them* rather than to him.

The popular verdict rendered on November 5 was so emphatic that even the Democrats were startled. Cleveland's vote was 535,318; Folger's, 342,464. Explanations varied, but the consensus of opinion in both Republican and Democratic ranks blamed Chester A. Arthur for interference; first, on the ground that the Administration's record made his candidate subject to some popular antagonism; and second, because the President was required by the people to rise above the open management of State politics. Arthur was advised to stand firmly

[1] Cincinnati *Enquirer,* Sept. 21, 27, 1882. One of these proxies from W. H. Robertson to S. B. French, was possibly a trap set by Robertson. Hugh Hastings to Butler, June 27, 1883, Butler Papers.
[2] New York papers of Oct. 4, 1882.
[3] See for example A. W. Tenney, *The Situation,* a speech given in Brooklyn on October 2, 1882, wholly concerned with defending the Folger men at the convention. (Reprint in Ford Collection, N. Y. Public Library.)
[4] Butler to Folger, Sept. 24, 1882, Butler Papers.
[5] Butler Papers, *passim,* and Folger to Butler, Oct. 27, 1882.

on his own feet, abandoning political colleagues of whom New York was heartily tired.[1]

The unprecedented size of the Democratic majority could never have been attained had its candidate not commanded the confidence of thousands who usually voted in the Republican column. Their protest was not expressed in a refusal to vote or in "scratching," as in former years, but in a solid transfer of their support to a man of promise.[2] In addition to the personal claims of Cleveland, he and his party profited from the rising tide of anti-monopoly sentiment in the State, which neither Folger nor his party bothered themselves to placate or attract.[3] The combination of Republican deficiencies and Democratic superiorities served to humiliate Folger in a way that was totally unjust to his personal character and abilities.

To Arthur, the outcome in New York was a political reverse of the first order. It is possible that he deserved it. Certainly it rendered his nomination in 1884 doubtful. Already, news of a Blaine-Logan combination had been circulated, explaining that, by mutual agreement, whichever was stronger in 1884 should have first and the other second place on the Republican ticket. Logan's action was declared to be but one of the numerous withdrawals by Stalwarts from Arthur's support.[4]

[1] N. Y. *Tribune*, Nov. 10, 1882; Washington *Evening Star*, Nov. 8, 1882; Breen, *Thirty Years of New York Politics* (N. Y., 1899), p. 682. *Cf.* Gath in Cincinnati *Enquirer*, Feb. 21, 1883, stating that Folger forced himself into nomination but managed to make it appear that the Administration had "pushed him into the gap."

[2] Two years later, with Blaine men at the helm in New York Republican Party affairs, Cleveland's lead dwindled to nothing, or less than nothing.

[3] Henry E. Tremain, *Fifty Papers* (N. Y., 1909), No. 6, "Historical Sketch of the Anti-Monopoly Movement."

[4] Washington *Evening Star*, October 30, 1882; N. Y. *Herald*, October 30, 1882. Blaine's idea of second place was said to be the Secretaryship of State.

THE sharp reverse suffered by the Republican Party in the elections of 1882 was partly the fruit of public indignation over the refusal of Congress to promote civil service reform. Its actions had justified the belief that there was "no prospect whatever" that it would adopt the bills proposed by Senator Pendleton, or any others truly conducive to reform. The sentiment for improvement, persistently expressed by local and national organizations, by the independent press, notably *The Nation, Harper's Weekly,* and the *North American Review,* and by a nonpartisan minority of Congress, had been developing power for years. It reached in the autumn of 1882 a force that could no longer be dismissed with sneers at "visionary fanaticism."

For years, the national government had been controlled by what James Russell Lowell termed the "majority manufacturers," professional politicians at the head of party organizations made up, in the influential positions, of government officeholders and, in the mere rank and file, of unquestioning, loyal voters from every walk of life. The chief danger to the country, demonstrated by the career of Conkling's machine in New York, was the development of a bureaucracy. It was necessary that the civil service of the government be dissevered from politics and become more truly responsible to the public whose servants its members nominally were, and that the popular will which chose candidates and elected them to office be that of the nonofficial classes. Leadership, it was believed, would then approach the real problems of general welfare. Instead of satisfying an organization of officeholders who supplied the campaign funds and whose principal object was to hold office, the heads of the parties would be obliged to keep the approval of a public interested in economic and social legislation, in efficient administration of the laws—in short, in questions of statesmanship. The civil service reform movement, then, was not only a drive for honest and capable public servants; it was a crusade for genuinely republican government.

When Garfield lay dying, the reformers hastened to turn the emotions of the public mind to civil service reform, to picture the existing system as a moral evil, and to arouse that fervor which even the most cynical Congressmen recognize as an inescapable mandate. Local reform clubs had previously been united into a National Civil Service Reform League, with George William Curtis for its president. The movement had thus made several strides forward when Garfield's short Administration came to its end.

With Chester A. Arthur as Garfield's successor, the last thing the public expected from the President was leadership or sincere support of the civil service reform cause.[1] His record as a machine politician, one who had been removed from office after an investigation and despite the protection of his "boss," sinister rumors charging his participation in political corruption, his electioneering at Albany after his election to the Vice Presidency, and finally, the fact that he was thought to have shown not the slightest favorable interest in reform—all augured ill.

When the first civil service examinations had been attempted under Grant, Arthur was Collector at New York, dispensing patronage on a large scale. After the new tests had been in force for some time, he made a report which afforded no satisfaction to his political associates but which represented his own convictions. "No one in any degree acquainted with the necessities of the Customs Service," he wrote in 1873, "can doubt the propriety of some kind of examinations for admission to it. . . . [The new system] has excluded many unfit persons and deterred a much larger number from applying. . . . [In promotions, it] has been of inestimable value." [2] When Grant ceased to support the merit system, Arthur returned to the older method of selection, but tried always to merge the objectives of both the merit and spoils systems. The resulting compromise only partly succeeded in eliminating the unfit.

In 1881, his old report was forgotten, while his position in the Conkling machine gave no indication that he would ever object to government of, by, and for the officeholders and professional politicians.

Arthur's letter accepting the vice presidential nomination, to nearly everyone's surprise, included frank statements favoring civil service

1 Old subordinates in the New York Custom House wrote to him, when President, to obtain his "influence" as an aid in retaining their places, obtaining promotions, getting reinstated, etc. Treas. Dept., Exec. Files, 1881–5, *passim.*
2 Cited by Dorman B. Eaton, *The "Spoils System" and Civil Service Reform in the Customs House and Post Office at New York* (N. Y., 1882), pp. 31–32.

reform, and prescribed principles which he thought should govern appointments, tenure, promotion, and removal; but it did not commit him to any given method of applying those principles.[1] His first annual message explained even more fully his favorable attitude toward reform legislation. Fully one seventh of it was devoted to the subject, approving the purpose but urging caution in choice of methods. Hayes thought that Arthur revealed "no faith in reform" but was simply yielding to public sentiment.[2]

In the summer of 1882, during the congressional campaign, the national capital was the scene of much assessment-levying upon the government clerks.[3] Arthur had announced in July, possibly after Cabinet consultation,[4] that government employees might freely give, or refuse to give, to campaign funds; in either case, their security would be unaffected.[5] There was, however, no confidence that he could carry out this policy. Accepting Attorney General Brewster's interpretation of the law, the congressional campaign committee collected large sums. But in New York, General N. M. Curtis of the State Committee was convicted of violating the statute; and President Arthur refused the request of Edwin D. Morgan that Curtis be pardoned.[6] When the Supreme Court gave its decision on appeal on December 17, Chief Justice Waite said: ". . . The managers of political campaigns, not in the employ of the United States, are just as free now to call on those in office for money to be used for political purposes as they ever were, and those in office can contribute as liberally as they please, provided their payments are not made to any of the prohibited officers or employees. . . ."[7] Curtis, however, was within the prohibited group and paid the penalty.[8]

During the campaign of 1882, the Secretary of the Navy, having Arthur's approval, went to New York with members of Congress to raise campaign funds.[9] The Treasury Department was drawn upon by the congressional campaign committee for available patronage in

---

[1] Richardson, *Messages,* Vol. VIII, p. 60.
[2] C. R. Williams, ed., *Diary & Letters of R. B. Hayes,* Vol. IV, p. 52.
[3] Washington *Evening Star,* Oct. 21, 31, 1882.
[4] Secretary Teller later denied that the Cabinet had taken up the subject, *Cong. Rec.,* Vol. XIX, pp. 9152–3; but this is in conflict with Secretary Chandler's diary for July 22, 25, 1882. Chandler Papers (Concord, N. H.).
[5] Richardson, *Messages,* Vol. VIII, p. 147.
[6] Morgan to Arthur, June 9, 1882, Arthur Papers.
[7] *Ex parte* Curtis, 106 U. S., p. 373.
[8] Washington *Evening Star,* Oct. 24, Dec. 18, 1882.
[9] D. B. Henderson to Chandler, Sept. 27, 1882, Chandler Papers.

all parts of the country.[1] In the New York struggle, Folger's department did whatever it could to win support by dispensing plums.[2] Some indications of these activities reached the public, but the criticism in George William Curtis's first annual address to the National Civil Service Reform League on August 2, 1882, was directed primarily at Arthur's refusal to reappoint practically half the officers whose terms had expired, a practice which Curtis branded as equivalent to removal from office, and as a violation of Arthur's expressed belief that "tenure of office should be stable." Even more severely, he denounced Congress's appropriation of only $15,000 to revive Grant's old commission.[3]

Congress reassembled in December, 1882, the Republicans thoroughly chastened by the recent elections and aware that in three months more the House (not the Senate) would be under Democratic control. Arthur's message assured them that public opinion demanded civil service reform and that "action should no longer be postponed." He grasped this opportunity, by presenting statistics, to show that his own use of the appointing power had been governed by the principles he approved, in that he had made comparatively fewer removals than his predecessors.[4] Moreover, he promised executive approval of all legislation designed to prevent assessments on the salaries of public officials, even in the guise of fictitious donations.

Civil service reform was almost the first problem to be taken up in the Senate. Pendleton opened discussion of it in a speech of December 12,[5] in which he emphasized the mandate of the late elections. Discussion was very inadequate. Opponents scoffed at it in the vein of Conkling's epithet, "snivel service reform." Senator Brown of Georgia insisted that the provision for admission to the service in only the lowest grade of positions was nothing but a nefarious device to keep Democrats out of better places, now that the Republicans were losing their grip. Senator George of Mississippi insinuated that if the Republican Administration required shackles to keep it from wrongdoing, Congress should oblige.[6] One Republican, Ingalls of

[1] See James B. Butler Papers, *passim*, for many letters from D. B. Henderson, secretary of the committee.
[2] Butler to "Bob" McCord, Jan. 5, 1883, Butler Papers.
[3] C. E. Norton, ed., *Orations and Addresses of George William Curtis*, Vol. II, pp. 205–24.
[4] Richardson, *Messages*, Vol. VIII, pp. 145–7.
[5] *Cong. Rec.*, Vol. XIV, pp. 204 ff.
[6] *Ibid.*, XIV, p. 321.

Kansas, branded the whole scheme as nothing but an instrument with which each party expected to cheat the other. Voorhees of Indiana and Maxey of Texas, both Democrats, declared the Pendleton Act a paltry response to the ardent demand for real reform.[1]

Truly serious objections were raised on only two grounds, the lack of limitation on the removal of civil servants who were honest and able, and the creation of a new and somewhat expensive commission. In answer to the first, several advocates, notably Hoar of Massachusetts, insisted that the political incentive to remove an official was virtually eradicated by lack of control over the choice of his successor.[2] The second objection they countered by sound arguments in behalf of both centralized control and centralized responsibility for the maintenance of the merit system.

With 33 Senators absent, of whom 22 were paired, the final vote on December 27, 1882, was 38 to 5 for the Pendleton bill. The House, having made New Year's resolutions to waste no time, begrudged it thirty minutes of unimportant debate and finally passed it on the same day that it was reported from committee,[3] 155 to 47, with 87 not voting. On January 16, 1883, by virtue of Arthur's signature, the Pendleton Act became a law. The first great step toward a merit system had been taken.[4]

The new law embodied the benefits of experience. Subject to Senate confirmation, the President was to appoint a small, bipartisan commission to aid him in making and executing rules and regulations covering appointments to the Federal civil service. Flexible but not blanket authority was given to the commission, for the act laid down eight "fundamental provisions" to be embodied in its rules. The necessary prelude to all appointments was to be a competitive examination, or, where competition was impracticable, a qualifying test. Promotions were to be only from one grade to the next higher. Every appointee was to be on probation for a reasonable time in which to subject his theoretical fitness to a practical test. The only recommendations which the commission might receive from members of Congress should be as to character and residence. The rules, however, were to apply to

[1] *Cong. Rec.*, Vol. XIV, pp. 355–60.
[2] *Ibid.*, XIV, p. 210.
[3] *Ibid.*, Vol. XIV, pp. 860–67.
[4] A synopsis of the civil service reform movement appears in the *Fifteenth Annual Report* of the Civil Service Commission, dated Nov. 1, 1898.

neither the highest nor lowest offices, neither to laborers nor those customarily appointed by the President with the Senate's approval.

A chief examiner and subsidiary examining boards, each with a clerical staff, constituted the machinery of enforcement. The commission was to keep records, investigate alleged infractions of its rules and regulations, and make annual reports to Congress. Serious penalties were established, particularly for levying political assessments upon Federal officials' salaries.

President Arthur at once took up the selection of three persons for the new civil service commission. Senator Pendleton was eager to name the Democratic member [1] and Arthur accordingly accepted his recommendation of Leroy D. Thoman of Youngstown, O., a young lawyer and probate judge, thirty-two years of age.[2] This was evidence that Arthur planned to put the enforcement of the new law in the hands of its friends.[3] More emphatically demonstrating Arthur's "good faith" [4] was the selection of Dorman B. Eaton, Hayes's protégé and the author of *Civil Service in Great Britain,* a fountain of reform doctrine. The third nominee was an old boyhood and Union College friend, John M. Gregory, pioneer Regent, from 1867 to 1880, of what later became the University of Illinois.

In the choice of the Chief Examiner, Arthur thought it possible to accomplish two satisfactory ends with one appointment. He named Silas W. Burt, who as deputy Naval Officer at New York had conducted the first civil service examinations outside Washington, and whom Hayes had appointed to the place from which Cornell was removed in 1878. As a leading light among the reformers, he seemed an admirable selection. On the other hand, he was unpopular in the Custom House with friends of the Administration. They considered him a charlatan, since, as a special report on his appointments revealed,[5] he had violated his own "school-boy rules" at the outset of his term, although he was subsequently enough of a reformer to be exasperating. Shifting him to Chief Examiner at the end of his term as Naval Officer was as satisfactory to the enemies as to friends of the reform. When he declined the new place, he was not continued in the

---

[1] George F. Edmunds to Arthur, Jan. 17, 26, 1883; Joseph R. Hawley to Arthur, Jan. 18, 1883, Arthur Papers.
[2] See sketch in *Harper's Weekly,* Mar. 17, 1883.
[3] Cincinnati *Enquirer,* Feb. 21, 22, 1883.
[4] Edward Cary, *George William Curtis,* p. 278.
[5] Butler Papers.

old.[1] Despite the Burt incident, the Civil Service Commission held its first meeting in Washington on March 9 and commenced its work with assurances of Arthur's support.

The first rules and regulations of the new commission were promulgated on May 7, 1883.[2] Much foresight had been shown, but the commission learned as it went, and its rules became more and more specialized as its experience grew. During the first year, it controlled the appointments to 13,924 offices, about one third of those to which the merit system might appropriately apply.[3] In the next, about half the postal officials and three fourths of the customs service were added.[4] The annual reports expressed confidence that good results were being obtained.

In the estimation of many, the most grievous practical evil to be eliminated was the system of party assessments upon officials. The days of "frying the fat" out of those who prospered under the high tariff awaited the ascendancy of Matt Quay and Mark Hanna. Upon administration, the older method was as demoralizing as the later proved to be upon legislation. Denunciation of assessments by Grant's commission had accomplished nothing; the Act of August 15, 1876, was widely evaded or ignored; and it remained for the more drastic penalties of the Pendleton Act, with the readiness of the new commission to prosecute, to offer effective restraints. At the end of the first year, the commission reported a material reduction in the volume of such levies although "a feeling of complete safety in declining to pay" had not yet developed; "the practice of former years, of opening in the great cities, near the public offices, assessment-collection bureaux," had been discontinued, yet no one could fail to observe "the undiminished vigor and enthusiasm of the parties at the late elections." [5] The second year likewise saw improvement but brought recommendations for an expansion of the law.[6]

If the first report of the commission was encouraging, the second was thoroughly enthusiastic. "The enforcement of the civil service act . . . has been found both practicable and effective for the ac-

---

[1] *The Nation*, Apr. 26, 1883.

[2] Richardson, *op. cit.*, Vol. VIII, pp. 161–9, 226–7, 230–1, 233–5, 286–93.

[3] Civil Service Commission, *First Annual Report*, February 7, 1884, pp. 15–16, and note, p. 16.

[4] *Second Annual Report*, Jan. 25, 1885, pp. 7–10.

[5] *First Annual Report*, p. 10.

[6] *Second Annual Report*, Jan. 25, 1885, pp. 52 ff.

complishment of its purpose. Only the continuing support of the Executive and moderate appropriations by Congress are needed for the extension of the new system which the civil service law and rules have established." President Arthur was pleased. "The good results . . . foreshadowed have been more than realized," he stated. "The system has fully answered the expectations of its friends. . . . The law has had the unqualified support of the President and of the heads of the several Departments." [1] Hayes continued to believe that Arthur had been "driven into reform positions by a public sentiment which he dare not resist," [2] but George William Curtis paid a handsome tribute to Arthur and to the Administration as a whole; though he complained of great evils continuing outside the offices to which the new law applied.[3]

Arthur was a practical reformer, not a doctrinaire. When he was once asked if the support of business men did not promise success for Edward Cooper in the mayoralty campaign of 1878, he replied, "very earnestly":

Now you were never more mistaken in your life than to suppose that the business men carry elections. A large vote is brought out when all the men in politics are pleased and satisfied and set to work with enthusiasm for the ticket. They bring out the votes, and if you trusted these elections to business men and *merely respectable influences,* the Democratic Party would get in every time [by default].[4]

He did not lose sight of this fact in his desire to improve the public service. Within the large field of patronage unaffected by the merit system, the Arthur Administration was governed by the same considerations in making appointments that have operated, with temporary exceptions, at least since Jefferson's day.

The President was alternately flattered, coaxed, and menaced by *Harper's Weekly,* the *Tribune,* the *Evening Post,* and those who followed such leadership. He had an opportunity to reward his friends, to punish his enemies, to strengthen the party, and to lay a basis for his own nomination in 1884. They objected if he appointed Stalwarts, however capable, on the ground that they were Stalwarts, while if he

---

[1] Richardson, *Messages,* Vol. VIII, p. 252.
[2] Hayes Diary (MSS.), May 26, 1884, Hayes Papers.
[3] C. E. Norton, ed., *op. cit.,* Vol. III, pp. 257, 274.
[4] Gath, in Cincinnati *Enquirer,* Sept. 11, 1882, reporting an old conversation. (Italics are mine.)

chose Republicans with other affiliations, they were inclined to question their fitness. It seemed impossible to please them. In New York, where he knew the ground, he took care that appointees were trustworthy and capable; and, although he put in men who were not Half-Breeds, several of them were new, young, and of great promise, owing their start to him, rather than to Grant, Conkling, Platt, or any other person.[1]

With the Senate Arthur was on moderately friendly terms, for, though thirty-seven of his nominations were contested, only eight were rejected.[2] His diplomatic appointments were creditable. His Cabinet, necessarily appointed in accordance with political considerations, was neither brilliant nor weak. Of its members, William E. Chandler was the liveliest politician. Yet his correspondence shows that he was concerned not only in the organization and strengthening by patronage of the Republican Party, north and south, but also in rebuilding the navy, in the problems of finance and tariff policy confronting the Administration, and even in the new railroad time map. Brewster, the Attorney General, was an elderly, picturesque figure but not a powerful political leader. His memory was strong; his love of literature had been gratified by extensive reading; and despite his eccentricities, he and Arthur found much in common outside of politics and administration.

Secretary Teller's conduct of the Department of the Interior was harmful to the Administration's reputation for reform. Although he left most of his predecessor's major subordinates undisturbed, he made a clean sweep of the incompetent sectarians whom it had been the custom since Grant's first Administration to appoint to the Indian service. Naturally, the professional friends of the Indian became antagonized. Both Teller and Arthur had expected that. Equal hostility was created in the West by Teller's "soft" policy toward the Indians in sharing their opposition to the "severalty" proposal, in aiding Helen Hunt Jackson's work, and in advocating extensive Indian education. Again, his enforcement of the land laws subjected the Administration to charges of grave laxity. More contestable were the Democratic strictures upon his management of Indian lands. He found, for example, that the established practice of leasing "grazing-rights" on

[1] Among them were Elihu Root and Andrew Sloan Draper, later president of the University of Illinois.
[2] Fish, *op. cit.*, p. 204.

unoccupied Indian lands had led to wide abuses, and, while defending the legality of such leases, asked in vain that Congress grant him authority to regulate them. When Cleveland denied their legal validity and canceled them all, then, as Teller had foreseen, the Indians lost a source of revenue while the lands were put to no use. Near the end of Arthur's term, after negotiations with some of the Sioux had broken down, he ordered the opening of some excess reservation areas to the operation of the homestead and kindred laws. The order was at once denounced by persons who contended that the Indians owned their reservations. They declared it illegal and unjust. Both charges were at least debatable, for at no time had the government granted these Indians any title which they could rightfully assert against the donor. Their lands had been reserved for their use, not submitted to their ownership. Judged by any standards which justify the white advance across the areas formerly Indian, this particular action would not seem harsh.

*   *   *

When Timothy O. Howe died on March 25, 1883, Arthur chose Walter Q. Gresham, a former Stalwart, as Postmaster General, thus elevating Senator Benjamin Harrison's chief rival for party leadership in Indiana. He had already ceased to turn to Conkling or Grant for advice; he had offended Richard Crowley; Senator John A. Logan was likewise estranged; and the choice of Gresham was rightly interpreted as revealing his purpose to develop new Republican leadership.[1] One infers from Arthur's course that he was in truth attempting to "harmonize" the party by attracting into a new alignment men who were formerly identified with Grant or Blaine, or who were new in politics.

Prior to the passage of the Pendleton Act, Arthur used the government offices in New York to care for some of his friends;[2] but after it went into effect, on July 16, 1883, such opportunities were no longer open to him and apparently not sought. The New York Custom House continued to supply places for friends of Secretary Folger, some of whom were granted leaves of absence for political work.[3] Congress-

[1] N. Y. *Times*, May 11, 1883.
[2] S. M. Blatchford to Butler, Aug. 15, 1882; Sept. 6, 1882; Butler to Folger, Aug. 18, 1882, Butler Papers.
[3] A. P. Ketchum to Butler, May 11, 1883, Butler to John W. Corning, Aug. (?), 1883; Butler to Ketchum, Aug. 20, 1883, Butler Papers.

man Henry Cabot Lodge of Massachusetts, prior to the new dispensation, made successful requests of Secretary Chandler for patronage.[1] B·ɪt Thomas C. Platt found himself unable to obtain favors of Secretary Chandler and wrote with asperity:

Permit me to congratulate you on your conversion to the principle of non-interference in local political affairs and to express the opinion, with all due respect, that if you had been an earlier convert, there might have been less friction in the internal politics of this State.[2]

The national convention of 1884 found Platt among Arthur's opponents. There was a sensation in political circles when on March 1, 1883, Arthur nominated Elihu Root to supplant Stewart L. Woodford as United States Attorney at New York City. In this, he acted deliberately. Woodford had nominated him for the Vice Presidency, had been associated with him in the Conkling organization, and so had "claims" upon his friendship. But complaints reached Washington that he was not conscientiously performing his duties.[3] Apparently he refused to follow instructions from the capital, so that the press had reported that both he and Robertson were to be ejected.[4] Robertson remained but Woodford was replaced, antagonizing his friends and giving Arthur's foes another opportunity to condemn his ingratitude.

Robertson continued in the Collectorship but he was prevented from strengthening his own Republican faction by patronage.[5] All nominations to Custom House positions prior to October, 1884, including even those made by Appraiser Howard before his retirement, were examined by Col. George C. Bliss before being acted upon.[6] It was Folger's professed policy to approve all Robertson's nominees unless they could be rejected on grounds of personal unfitness, but the Collector was evidently kept in bounds and occasionally retaliated.[7] "I am a little sorry you did not confirm Murphy right off and ask the reason of his selection at the same time. It don't amount to much but it looks as if

[1] June 24, 27, July 4, 1883, Chandler Papers.
[2] Platt to Chandler, Dec. 3, 1883. See also, ditto, Sept. 25, 1883, Aug. 25, 1884, Chandler Papers.
[3] *Letters of the Postmaster-General* (MSS.), XIV, p. 378, Howe to Attorney-General Brewster, June 7, 1882.
[4] Cincinnati *Enquirer*, Jan. 9, 1883.
[5] *Ibid.*, Sept. 30, 1881, prophesied this course.
[6] Ten letters from Bliss running from Dec. 12, 1881 to Oct. 9, 1884, Butler Papers.
[7] James R. Davies to Butler, several letters in Apr. and May, 1883, Butler Papers.

you thought we were of Robertson's kidney and wanted to slap us every time," wrote one of Arthur's friends in the Surveyor's office to Butler.[1] Again, next day, he said: "Bear in mind, please, that the laborers are skilled men and are appointed by this office and not by the Collector—so you need not rap us over the knuckles thinking you are hitting the Collector." [2]

However much the Custom House may have failed to become a Half-Breed treasury of offices, however much it may have aided the Administration through the new Naval Officer and Surveyor,[3] it remained a very different political agency from the days of Arthur's Collectorship. His old political associates were indignant that he declined to revive their power by a reversion to the old regime. In time, from Conkling, came the title of "His Accidency," and an assignment to somewhat the same category (and ultimate destination) as "His Fraudulency," ex-President Hayes. In their antagonism toward Arthur, the New York Stalwarts were following General Grant, whose friendliness was eventually transformed into both resentment and contempt.[4] Arthur declined to send Adam Badeau, Grant's biographer, to Italy upon the death of George P. Marsh,[5] and near the end of his term, left Frederick D. Grant unsatisfied by an offer of an assistant quartermastership in the U. S. Army.[6] Although the last act of his Administration was the signature of a bill by which the old ex-President, fallen on evil days, became General on the retired list, with full pay,[7] even this did not satisfy Grant, since the long delay meant that his commission was eventually signed by Cleveland.

A notable use of the patronage by President Arthur for political ends lay in his relations with the "Readjuster-Democrats" of Virginia.[8] Where Garfield had divided favors between that party and the Republicans of Virginia, Arthur worked exclusively with Mahone, Rid-

---

[1] S. M. Blatchford to Butler, Apr. 5, 1883, Butler Papers.

[2] *Ibid.,* Apr. 6, 1883.

[3] C. K. Graham to Butler, Nov. 13, 1882; Mar. 28, 1883; June 8, 1883; Dec. 30, 1884; Blatchford to Butler, Apr. 5, 1883, Butler Papers. Graham succeeded Burt as Naval Officer; James L. Benedict became Surveyor, in March, 1883.

[4] L. A. Coolidge, *Ulysses S. Grant,* pp. 552-3.

[5] Badeau to Chandler, July 28, 1882, Chandler Papers; Badeau, *Grant in Peace,* pp. 337, 535-43.

[6] F. D. Grant to Arthur, Nov. 23, 1884; Jan. 18, 1885, Arthur Papers.

[7] A suggestion made by William E. Chandler as early as Nov. 18, 1880. N. Y. *Tribune* of that date contains letter from him containing the proposal.

[8] See attack by Senator B. H. Hill of Georgia, *Cong. Rec.,* Vol. XIII, pp. 84-5.

dleberger, and their followers. He supported what he hoped would be the opening wedge, the first anti-Bourbon group to gain control of a Southern State.[1] Time was to reveal that it consisted of Democrats capable of merely temporary alliance with the black and white Republicans, and then only for debt reduction. As soon as that problem had been settled, they withdrew, leaving the Readjusters numerically inferior and the Republican organization virtually defunct. Arthur's assistance had, at most, prolonged "the Readjuster incident." [2]

Arthur's Administration permitted one evil aspect of the campaign of 1884. Commissioner W. W. Dudley of the Pensions Office, who had been appointed by Arthur and whose resignation was to take effect on November 10, took leave of absence in order to engage actively in the campaign in Ohio and Indiana, both very closely contested. Accompanying him were E. G. Rathbone, chief of the special examiners' division of the Pensions Bureau, and over one hundred special examiners, where the normal force was sixty. Some of them were supposed to be on active duty; some were on leave of absence. All were charged, apparently on ample foundation, with advising claimants of pensions to vote for the Republican "soldier ticket," Blaine and Logan, instead of for the Democratic ticket with "not a soldier on it," if they wanted to do something advantageous for their pension claims. Protests were emphatic, led by the New York *Times* in its issue of October 20, 1884. Arthur could probably have halted this electioneering but preferred to avert further disastrous dissensions in his party.

The Democrats also found something to criticize in Arthur's administration of the Pendleton Act. When Cleveland's election was conceded, the executive departments reclassified their employees so as to curtail the places requiring no competitive civil service examinations, and even the Department of Agriculture, not yet accorded Cabinet status, was so reorganized. The necessary effect was to protect many Republicans in office from removal and to minimize the party ad-

[1] The Richmond (Va.) *Dispatch* of Sept. 13, 1882 charged Arthur with seeking to obtain a solid Republican delegation via Mahone which would support him in the Republican national convention in 1884. Blaine opposed Mahone. (Washington *Evening Star*, Sept. 20, 1882.) Arthur did have the support of most of the Virginia delegation to the end in the 1884 convention.

[2] See William A. Scott, *The Repudiation of State Debts*, pp. 175–89; John S. Wise, *Recollections of Thirteen Presidents*, pp. 155–64; Richmond *Dispatch*, Sept. 12, 1882; N. Y. *Times*, Nov. 20, 1881; John Russell Young Papers (MSS., Library of Congress), Vol. XVI, pp. 3712–13; Mahone to Young, May 23, 1883, saying: We shall win the election in November "but would not if it depended on help at Washington"; Pearson, *op. cit.*, pp. 156, 168.

vantages of Democratic success.[1] Unfavorable criticism, especially in military circles, was provoked near the end of Arthur's term by his appointment of Henry Haynsworth, his brother-in-law, from civil life to the position and rank of quartermaster and captain in the army. Mr. Haynsworth was fitted for the post but at the same time was clearly the recipient of fraternal favoritism.[2]

Nevertheless, at the conclusion of his term, President Arthur could look back on his connections with the reform movement with some satisfaction. Both in legislation and in administration, the cause had been advanced. The Civil Service Commission was the principal agent in this activity, yet it frankly acknowledged Arthur's help. "Our functions cannot be successfully discharged without the constant, firm, and friendly support of the President," it declared. "That support has never failed. The Commission has never asked advice or an exercise of authority on the part of the President which has been refused. . . . As to its own action, the Commission can declare positively, and as to that of the President, it can express its unhesitating belief, that neither discrimination on the ground of political or religious opinions, nor favoritism of any sort has been allowed to defeat, delay, or in any wise impair or improve the chances or opportunities of any person under the civil service act." [3]

[1] See *Cong. Rec.*, Vol. XIX, pp. 9116–7 (Oct. 3, 1888) for remarks by Senator Cockrell of Missouri.
[2] N. Y. *Tribune,* Feb. 27, 28, 1885.
[3] Civil Service Commission, *Second Annual Report,* p. 55.

CONGRESS, after the election of 1882, was confronted by the necessity of decisive action upon the tariff question. Demand for a general modification had been mounting for years. During the period immediately after the war, it had been circumvented by the predominance of Reconstruction issues, which separated the Republicans of the agrarian Northwest from the Southern Democrats and thus prevented a natural coöperation to restore lower duties. Northeastern industrialists had seized and held their advantage. They not only maintained the high wartime rates but, whenever political conditions were propitious, even raised those protecting certain industries. The fact that, on tariff policy, both parties were divided, had aided the protectionists to maintain the *status quo* by preaching party harmony. But economic conditions cried for a change and, by 1882, such considerations as party harmony could not prevail against determined public demand. Even beneficiaries of the existing law admitted that general revision had been postponed as long as it could be. Public sentiment was unmistakable; the three months before March fourth gave the last opportunity to Republican friends of protection to control the change; thereafter, the House was to be dominated by the Democrats.

The census of 1880 forced some striking comparisons of American prosperity in the decade preceding, under a high tariff, with that in the 1850's, when duties had been about one half as great. In both periods, there had been panics, followed by severe business depressions. The rate at which capital had been accumulated, and at which labor, wages, materials used in manufacture, and products of manufacture had increased in value, had been greater under the low than under the higher rates. If, in the 1870's, the protected iron and steel industry had flourished, the woolen industry, likewise protected, had not. The conclusion from these data was inescapable—protection did not guarantee prosperity.

The iron and steel industry was a notorious illustration of the necessity for tariff change. Under protection, it was making profits from the swift spread of railway construction. In 1870, Pennsylvania ironmasters had succeeded in obtaining a duty of $28 per ton upon steel rails. Though the price in England subsequently dropped during the decade to $31 per ton, in the United States it stayed always approximately $30 higher.[1] By 1880, American steel mills were rolling 940,000 tons of rails,[2] not all that the home market could absorb, and their profits were phenomenal.[3] Thus, whenever Andrew Carnegie decided to take a valuable associate into partnership, he was able to set aside a share for him and in a very few years to pay it up out of its proportion of the subsequent profits. When the eccentric manager of his Edgar Thomson Works refused to separate himself from the rank and file of workers by becoming a partner, one alternative seemed to Carnegie appropriate. He paid to him, by agreement, "the same salary that the President of the United States received" plus bonuses, royalties on patents, and other emoluments.[4] The deep reservoir of profits from which such munificent rewards could be dispensed came, of course, from the lavish, protected price for rails which the railroad companies had to pay, an excessive cost eventually reflected in higher charges for transportation.

Tariff reformers of every description, from those favoring free trade to those merely desiring more reasonable and harmonious protection, had been thwarted at every turn since the Civil War. In 1867, the industrialists defeated proposals for a wise, inclusive revision. Thereafter, the only general enactments were the ten per cent. reduction of 1872 and its restoration in 1875. The Liberal Republican movement in 1872 left tariff reformers in the lurch, and from then to 1880, they acquired political strength too slowly to accomplish anything. In 1880, even, the House refused to authorize appointment of a commission of experts to make tariff recommendations to Congress, while Garfield's election gave no assurance of revision, in either his party's platform, his public statements, or his inaugural.

But sentiment for revision was so strong that by 1882 even carefully organized industries no longer opposed it. They merely wished a guarantee that modification would proceed along protective lines and be controlled by their friends. Thus in November, 1881, the Industrial League held a large tariff convention in New York which ap-

---

[1] F. W. Taussig, *Tariff History of the United States* (8th ed., rev.), p. 223.

[2] B. J. Hendrick, *The Life of Andrew Carnegie*, Vol. I, p. 309.

[3] The Pennsylvania Steel Company paid what amounted to 77% in dividends in 1881 and retained undivided profits on its capital of about 120%. See *Cong. Rec.*, Vol. XIII, pp. 3980–81 (May 16, 1882).

[4] Hendrick, *op. cit.*, Vol. I, p. 208.

proved the idea of an expert commission.[1] When Arthur next month sent his annual message to Congress, he felt warranted, despite the delicacy of his political situation, in approving that plan. "The tariff laws need revision," he declared, "but . . . . important changes should be made with caution. If a careful revision cannot be made at this session, a commission such as was lately approved by the Senate and is now recommended by the Secretary of the Treasury would doubtless lighten the labors of Congress." [2]

Wise revision was a complex problem. Industries which had risen under shelter of high tariffs might be ruined if suddenly obliged to meet the price level created by drastic reduction. Due regard for national benefits from such industries, and from changes which a new tariff could induce, demanded a discriminating alteration of the old rates and perhaps the introduction of new. These considerations favored resort to an expert commission, from whom could be expected a tariff measure more systematic and objective than any product of Congressional bargaining. Their work would delay a new law but that very fact brought support from two quarters—opponents of lower duties who wished to postpone revision as long as possible, and others who desired not only an equitable but a lasting change in the interests of business stability. Thus, from various considerations, Congress authorized a Tariff Commission in an act which Arthur signed on May 15, 1882.[3] Revisionists were elated.

With Senate approval, Arthur was to appoint nine civilian "experts" who should "take into consideration all the various questions relating to the agricultural, commercial, mercantile, manufacturing, mining, and industrial interests of the United States, so far as the same may be necessary to the establishment of a judicious tariff or a revision of the existing tariff, upon a scale of justice to all interests." Arthur spent a month in selecting them, seeking a group representative of the great industries, entitled to public confidence, and moderately protectionist. He decided at once to name as chairman, John L. Hayes. Hayes had been for several years the paid secretary and lobbyist of the National Association of Wool Manufacturers, but described himself to Secretary Chandler, after his selection, as unpledged to any interest and "not an advocate of a high tariff" but of protection for all interests, "barely

[1] Ida Tarbell, *The Tariff in Our Times,* p. 100.
[2] Richardson, *op. cit.,* Vol. VIII, p. 49.
[3] For debates, see *Cong. Rec.,* Vol. XIII, pp. 3110–11, 3520, 3566–7, 3687, 3742.

high enough to equalize the conditions of labor and capital here with those of our foreign competitors." [1] Arthur named spokesmen for three other interests. Iron and steel were represented by Henry W. Oliver, Jr., of Pittsburgh,[2] wool by Austin M. Garland of Illinois, and sugar by Duncan F. Kenner of Louisiana.[3] General William H. McMahon of the New York Custom House sat as an expert on tariff administration; Robert P. Porter, of the Census Bureau, as a statistician. The other members were John W. H. Underwood of Georgia, Jacob A. Ambler of Ohio, and Alexander R. Boteler of West Virginia. The commission was manifestly protectionist, though not extreme. Nominations were confirmed on June 20, and work begun a fortnight later. The public, suspicious of Hayes's position as chairman especially, had slight hope that a fair and objective tariff would come of the deliberations.

The Tariff Commission set out to obtain information by public hearings in the principal cities. Between July 6 and October 16, it covered some seven thousand miles, heard over six hundred persons, received written communications from governors of far western States and Territories, and then retired to formulate its findings. From the sort of special pleaders who made up the roll of voluntary witnesses, there was small reason to expect that the commission had obtained material for a meritorious report. In fact, its work was already discounted when Congress assembled, after the Democratic landslide of 1882, and received its report.[4]

Surprise and wide approval then greeted the commission's conclusions. Mindful that they were to curtail tariff receipts with careful discrimination, recognizing, moreover, the fusion of revenue-yielding capacity and general economic regulation that is present in every tariff law, the commission had braved the difficult problem of determining what business interests should be encouraged and what, if any, should be allowed to shift for themselves, or lapse. Instead of devising some entirely new system upon an original and scientifically conceived basis, the commission chose to revise the existing system, treating the exist-

[1] Hayes to Chandler, May 19, 1882, Chandler Papers.
[2] Oliver was an independent and somewhat unstable ironmaster, later associated with Carnegie. In politics, he was identified with the Cameron machine. Joseph Wharton to Chandler, May 22, 23, 27, 1882, Chandler Papers.
[3] Kenner had been a prominent Confederate official. The sugar interest described itself as representing $300,000,000 invested capital and $48,000,000 annual tax revenue to the government. Copy of petition to Folger, dated May 27, 1882, in Chandler Papers.
[4] Printed as *House Misc., Doc. No. 6,* 47th Cong., 2nd sess., in two volumes. Hereafter referred to as *Report of the Tariff Commission.*

ing products of past favoritism in a way to prevent abruptly wrecking their business. On the other hand, having become convinced early in their deliberations that "a substantial reduction in tariff duties . . . [was] demanded not by a mere indiscriminate popular clamor but by the best conservative opinion of the country, including that which has in former times been most strenuous for the preservation of our national industrial defenses," it had deliberately arranged a general reduction totaling from twenty to twenty-five per cent.[1]

The report offered finished drafts of a proposed tariff law, arranged by schedules, and of additional measures intended to improve the system of collection. The draft tariff bill maintained substantial shelter for manufactured articles by reducing duties on raw materials, and cut most deeply the rates on sugar, molasses, and other necessities. Despite its retention of high duties on luxuries, it would diminish the net income of the government about one fifth.[2]

In submitting the report to both branches of Congress, Arthur emphatically condemned the existing tariff system as unnecessarily complex and "in many ways unjust." He recommended, in agreement with Secretary Folger, an enlarged free list, simplified schedules on cotton, iron, and steel, and lower duties upon them and upon silk, wool, woolen goods, sugar and molasses.[3] Unfortunately, he took no position upon the merits of the Commission's proposals. He abandoned leadership to certain members of Congress. Had he acted with the vigor he later showed in connection with his reciprocity program, he might have accomplished some good. Instead, he let others seize the reins. What ensued was a serious national misfortune.

Congress promptly shelved the commission's proposals. In a way which today seems indefensible, the House Committee on Ways and Means commenced the forming of a bill of its own devising, under the veteran protectionist leadership of William D. Kelley. The Senate Committee on Finance not only passed over the report but even disregarded the prospective House bill and concocted a third and separate measure of its own. It was to be attached as an extended amendment

---

[1] *Report*, Vol. I, pp. 5–7.

[2] For the year ending June 30, 1883, the customs duties received were $214,706,496.93 on goods valued at $493,916,384. Estimated receipts from the proposed new law would have made next year's receipts approximately $172,000,000. Actual income from the Tariff Act of 1883 was $195,067,000.

[3] Richardson, *op. cit.*, Vol. VIII, pp. 134–6; Secretary of the Treasury, *Annual Report for 1882*, pp. xxxii–xxxiii.

to a bill for reducing internal revenue which the House had passed and sent to the Senate in the preceding session. Thus a constitutional defect, the origin of tariff sections in the upper instead of the lower house, might possibly be evaded. So far as Congress was concerned, the Tariff Commission had merely delayed, not helped, a general revision of the tariff.

When Congressional committees took up preparation of the new tariff, lobbyists for special interests flocked to Washington. Even John L. Hayes sought to obtain other duties on woolen goods than those proposed in the report he had signed, and found Congressmen more amenable to this scheme than his associates on the late commission. While other interests were securing favors, Hayes would have been considered negligent not to have attended to that of the wool manufacturers. By mid-January, the hotels were said to be crowded with agents of similar mind, whom the press freely condemned as "plunderers." [1] Congressmen and Senators were no less alert in advancing the interests of their own particular sections. Objective, systematic, tariff making had been thrown to the winds.

In both houses, for a time, different tariff measures were being debated at once. The Senate was first, taking up its bill on January 10. In important instances this bill proposed lower duties than the commission. But Democratic Senators frequently forced Republicans who had individually espoused reform to vote as a group against even larger reductions in existing rates. (Reform must not be carried "too far.") These tactics produced personal and rather acid remarks. In a moment of irritation, Beck declared that Hoar reminded him of a sterile tract of ground once described as "poor by nature and exhausted by cultivation." Later, another Senator, expressing surprise that his associates could find anything more to say about the tariff, remarked: "Why there is Senator Beck, who is constantly on his feet, and does nothing but talk. Dear me, when does he give his intellect rest?" Hoar quickly snatched this chance. "When he talks, his intellect rests," he interjected. Such methods and such feeling produced a measure which was anything but objective or well planned.

The House had even less success. On January 25, it began debate upon the "Kelley bill," a committee measure which proposed, less systematically than the commission's report, a general reduction of

[1] Cincinnati *Enquirer*, Jan. 17, 1883; Tarbell, *op. cit.*, p. 113.

about 10 per cent. of the prevailing rates. Party lines soon dissolved. John G. Carlisle assumed the leadership of one Democratic faction determined to have a more drastic reduction, while another followed Samuel J. Randall in aiding the Republican majority. Among Republicans, revision was generally supported, but a minority faction intended it to be more in form than in substance.[1]

The Kelley bill was at once subjected to a separate vote on every item. After ten days, it seemed certain that no measure could be passed before March fourth unless the obstructionists were satisfied or silenced. The matter had completely escaped Arthur's hands.

On February 20, the Senate returned to the House the bill for reducing internal taxes accompanied by its tariff amendments. The latter, passed by a narrow margin, departed from the commission's report in serious ways but was composed of considerably lower duties than the Kelley bill. Nevertheless, it was the high protectionists' one opportunity to regain control of the tariff proceedings in the House. Unwilling or unable to limit debate,[2] they now proposed to silence the opposition by a bold and ingenious parliamentary trick. On February 24, with less than a fortnight before adjournment, they carried in the Republican caucus their proposal for a special House rule calculated to meet their needs. Their procedure bordered on sharp practice.

The regular rules required a two-thirds vote to take a bill from the Speaker's table for consideration. While the protectionists were in a majority, it was not that great, and even among their number, even less were high protectionists.

The special rule authorized a simple majority to take the tax and tariff bill from the Speaker's table. It went further. Unlike a rule proposed a few days earlier by John A. Kasson, which would have permitted either concurrence or nonconcurrence in the Senate amendments, Reed's permitted the bill's withdrawal from the table only for the purpose of objecting to the changes and sending them to conference.

Kelley discovered that under Kasson's proposed rule the House would have adopted the Senate measure.[3] He had accordingly opposed it. Reed's rule forestalled all danger of concurrence and guaranteed, moreover, that any tariff approved in both houses at this session would

---

[1] Tarbell, *op. cit.*, p. 118.
[2] Edward Stanwood, *American Tariff Controversies of the Nineteenth Century*, Vol. II, pp. 208 ff.
[3] Tarbell, *op. cit.*, p. 124.

be the product of a small joint committee. He gave it full support. On February 27, despite varied Democratic efforts to stop its adoption, including an effort to prevent a quorum, it was passed by a vote of 129 to 22, with 140 not voting.

During the debate on the special rule, both Republicans and Democrats had expressed doubts that a tariff measure composed of Senate amendments to an internal revenue tax bill could comply with the Constitutional requirement that the House originate all tax legislation. After the rule had been adopted, the Democratic Representatives supported a resolution completely repudiating the Senate's tariff schedules on those grounds. The Republicans succeeded, however, in forcing the reference of even the Constitutional question to the proposed committee of conference. Next exercising the special rule, they authorized its appointment.[1]

The Senate Democrats tried in vain to prevent the authorization of any Senate conferees, and finally succeeded only in obtaining instructions that Senators should withdraw from the conference if it were not "full and free." [2] Senators Bayard and Beck, the Democrats, refused, on March 1, to remain with Senators Morrill, Sherman, and Aldrich, and the House conferees,[3] taking the ground that, since the House had once definitely resolved that the Senate amendments were unconstitutional, its members in the conference were clearly limited, not free.[4] No other regular Democrats would serve, so Mahone, the Readjuster, and McDill, of Iowa, were eventually substituted for Bayard and Beck [5] before the conference went on with its duties.

In twenty-four hours' time, these ten men revised the Senate's tariff, ultimately producing a report in which some items, notably iron ore and steel rails, bore higher rates than Senate, House, or Tariff Commission had recommended. Despite these advances in protection, John Sherman failed dismally to get the duties on raw wool "up where they belonged" and was so unhappy that he refused to sign the conference report. Had he voted against it, he could have defeated it in the Senate.[6]

The conference report was signed at noon on March second, and

[1] *Cong. Rec.*, Vol. XIV, pp. 3336–50 (Feb. 27, 1883).
[2] *Ibid.*, Vol. XIV, p. 3376 (Feb. 28, 1883).
[3] Kelley, McKinley, Haskell, Speer, and Carlisle.
[4] *Cong. Rec.*, Vol. XIV, pp. 3454–57.
[5] *Ibid.*, XIV, pp. 3466–67.
[6] Sherman, *Recollections*, Vol. II, pp. 851–5.

placed before the Senate at 9:30 o'clock that evening. About midnight, by a margin of one vote, the Senate registered its approval. McPherson of New Jersey, a Democrat, and David Davis of Illinois, an Independent, voted with the Republicans.[1] In the House, a stormy session on the tariff consumed the next afternoon. From one quarter the conference report was denounced because it did not give enough protection; from another, because it did not sufficiently reduce the tariff burden; from a third, because of the Constitutional insecurity involved in its Senate origin; but, most vehemently of all, because it was being carried through by the "Reed rule." Nevertheless, the final vote, 152 to 116, taken at five o'clock, brought the bill before President Arthur. Undoubtedly he signed it with serious misgivings about "scientific" tariff legislation under a government so constituted as ours.[2]

The futility of an objective treatment of any legislative problem so directly affecting individual and sectional prosperity was well demonstrated by the fate of the Tariff Commission's report. Under a government whose members are selected as they are in the United States, in a civilization in which expanded material wealth is so distinctly and uncritically the end of life, no legislation brings out in broad daylight the greedy aspects of human nature so unblushingly as tariff legislation. The United States had, in this episode, witnessed a conflict between the restrained ambitions of intelligent industrialists, set forth in the commission's report, and the unbridled acquisitiveness of the average business man, for whom by the pressure of the lobby the government was made to serve as an agency to fatten profits.[3] On no previous occasion had the conflict been so obvious, while in the future it was to be lessened somewhat only by the disillusioned and cynical resignation of those who, like Arthur on this occasion, might have opposed the greedy. The failure of the Tariff Commission of 1882 to effect what Congress alone could never accomplish was therefore a serious misfortune with a train of evil consequences.

[1] *Cong. Rec.*, Vol. XIV, p. 3586.
[2] *Ibid.*, XIV, p. 3742. See also Tarbell, *op. cit.*, pp. 110–30; Taussig, *Tariff History of the United States* (5th ed., N. Y., 1909), Part II, ch. iv; Stanwood, *op. cit.*, Vol. II, pp. 200–17; N. W. Stephenson, *Nelson W. Aldrich*, pp. 49 ff.
[3] Murat Halstead called it an instance of "plain business jobbery," the fruit of a temporary alliance between the Northeast and the Southeast. Cincinnati *Commercial-Gazette*, Mar. 5, 1883.

GOVERNMENTS, ancient or modern, have seldom had to complain of an embarrassing excess of funds. Yet this was the rather happy perplexity which faced Americans during the eighties until Harrison's Administration brought in our first "billion dollar Congress." A few millions each year would not have been troublesome. But the redundance amounted to much more; indeed, during Arthur's Administration it averaged over $100,000,000, created several grave questions, and caused Arthur the greatest concern.

The most pressing problem was to return the money to circulation. It was not easily solved. Although the law permitted a large portion of the public funds to be deposited in the various national banks, customs receipts had to be retained in the Treasury until expended. Over half the normal income was thus withdrawn from business uses for long periods, sometimes when it was most needed.[1] To deposit Federal moneys more widely in private banks, as Cleveland was to do, would solve this difficulty only by creating another, for it involved a greater risk of government loss, as in 1837, should a sudden panic close many banks. Grant and others urged a different method. If the Treasury would buy government bonds in the open market in times of money stringency, and, to check an excess of currency later, sell them, it would introduce that elasticity in the circulating medium so necessary for business stability.[2] Unfortunately, this process could not relieve the Treasury of the predicament created by a continuing surplus, however well it might serve temporarily. In fact, no matter in what way the problem of returning money to circulation was solved, the surplus would remain, and every argument of sound public finance compelled its destruction.

Arthur's Administration could curtail, or even eliminate, the surplus in four major ways. It could spend it by lavish appropriations, distribute it, as in 1836, among the States, devote it to paying off the public debt, or abolish it by lowering taxes. Arthur consistently supported his two Secretaries of the Treasury in urging the last method.

[1] Sec. of Treas., *Annual Report,* 1882, p. xxvii; Grant to Arthur, Nov. 22, 1882, Arthur Papers.
[2] Grant to Arthur, Nov. 22, 1882, Arthur Papers; G. M. Dodge to W. E. Chandler, Nov. 22, 23, 1882, Mar. 21, 22, July 2, 1883; W. A. Simmons to W. E. Chandler, Nov. 25, 1882, Chandler Papers.

The temptation to squander money was overwhelming; the Rivers and Harbors Act passed over Arthur's veto in 1882 demonstrated how strongly it lay upon Congress. Pensions, another politically ingratiating form of spending, absorbed increasing amounts, although no new general act was passed. Indeed, the Arrears of Pensions Act of 1879, the most vigorous reach into Uncle Sam's pocket up to that time, was still bringing into the Pension Bureau a flood of new claims which threatened to consume one third of all the government's expenditures.[1] This prospect made another general law seem unreasonable, but it did not prevent the passage of innumerable special pensions bills. More measures of .this type than of any other became law, even more than those donating condemned Civil War cannon to municipal parks in the North.[2]

For the national defense, which he had always in mind, and for the Indians, Arthur himself urged increased appropriations. Had his party not been so roundly trounced in the elections of 1882, they might have repeated the extravagance of the Rivers and Harbors Act in other fields as well. But the advent of Democratic control in the House brought determined opposition to Arthur's naval building program and a stronger support for his counsels of restraint. Congress avoided reckless outlays. The annual average of expenditures remained below $260,000,000, a sum slightly less than in the succeeding Administration.

Some voices were raised for a distribution of the surplus among the States. Blaine, resembling Henry Clay, favored it in some form.[3] Virginia and Arkansas even applied for the installment under the Act of 1836 which they alone had failed to receive. But the previous instance of such distribution had contributed to an economic disaster which there was no disposition to repeat, and in repudiating the claims of Virginia and Arkansas, whether in law or equity, Secretary Folger also emphasized the very grave contrast between conditions in 1836 and those of 1883. The major difference was the outstanding public debt of about one and one-quarter billion dollars, bearing an annual interest charge of over fifty millions.[4]

---

[1] Richardson, *op. cit.*, Vol. VIII, pp. 58–59.
[2] Between 1881 and 1885, 814 private pension bills became law; in the next four years, 1871. See W. H. Glasson, *Federal Military Pensions in the United States*, p. 273.
[3] See *post*, pp. 255–6.
[4] Sec. of Treas., *Annual Report*, 1883, pp. xxx–xxxiii.

Courtesy L. C. Handy Studios, Washington, D. C.

PRESIDENT ARTHUR AND R. G. DUN, SEPTEMBER, 1882

When Congress met in 1881 and again in 1882, Arthur urged some relief for the taxpayer. At the polls, this recommendation was warmly sustained by the taxpayers themselves in the interval between those two sessions. He had proposed the elimination of all internal taxes save on liquors and tobaccos and their manufacture, and, in addition, the downward revision of tariff duties. Although diminished receipts were expected from the law which he finally signed on March 3, 1883, the drop of less than one per cent. in the level of import duties unfortunately produced no relief from that source, though a business depression did in a limited degree, while increased returns from the liquor taxes overthrew all calculations and rendered curtailment of the surplus much less than had been anticipated. The proposal, so popular in the Ohio Valley, for extending the period during which liquors might remain untaxed in bonded warehouses, did not prevail. There remained, after the tax revision of 1883 had been given a fair trial, no alternative for disposing of the surplus than that which had thus far been adopted. It had to be spent in paying off the public debt.

In 1881, it was estimated that, at the current rate of redemption, bonds subject to call by the government would all be canceled in a decade. The others, payable in 1891 and 1907, respectively, were selling at a substantial premium. A brilliant stroke of the brief Garfield Administration had placed some $563,000,000 at the call of the Treasury at any time, with interest in the interval reduced to $3\frac{1}{2}$ per cent.,[1] and these offered a wide field for bond redemption without premium payment. But there was strong opposition.

The rapid extinction of these $3\frac{1}{2}$ per cent. bonds spelled the doom of national bank note circulation. Resting as it did upon the government debt for its security, this currency would be necessarily curtailed as the quantity of available bonds diminished. To meet the resulting deficiency, monetary heretics proposed several alternatives. The whole national money question was raised by the policy of rapid bond redemption. In the spring of 1882, during debate over a bill to prolong the charters of the national banks, the correlated issues were well argued.

The charters of nearly four hundred national banks lapsed within the year prior to February 25, 1883. Because of their "capacity for future usefulness," the House Committee on Banking and Currency

[1] T. C. Smith, *Garfield*, Vol. II, pp. 1162 ff. These bonds were called the "Windom bonds."

proposed to authorize extension of their charters for another term of twenty years. The principal object was to forestall enforced liquidation, which would withdraw, at least temporarily, the bank credit underlying a very large amount of business. Opponents of this bill centered their attacks on the national banks' privilege of issuing notes, a practice characterized as the source of swollen profits, and controlled by considerations of private rather than public interest. They described the system as a "moneyed monopoly," and the $12,000,000 of annual interest on the bonds, held as security for note redemption, as a gratuitous "bounty." To extend the charters conveying this privilege was in effect to continue the public debt, Bland of Missouri hoarsely warned his colleagues.

We are paying off the national debt at the rate of over $100,000,000 a year, and unless we cease to pay off this debt, unless this bill means, as I think it does, that when we have continued and rechartered these banks the next legislation asked . . . will be to cease the payment of the public debt in order to maintain the banks, the basis on which national bank currency has rested must shortly pass away.[1]

It was not hard to show that the system was not a monopoly, that the profits from the privilege of note-issue were not unduly large, that the banks bore a substantial burden of Federal and State taxation, and that most of their profits were derived from the millions of deposits which came to them as a result of particular public confidence.[2] Their critics did not resist their continuance as banks of deposit and discount, urging only the early elimination of their power of note-issue; but, to replace their notes, they proposed conflicting alternatives which had one point in common—they provided for a paper currency uninjured by rapid contraction of the national debt.[3]

Arthur favored the national banks, despite their unpopularity. The bankers might be pictured as gathering in frequent conventions, "eating bon bons, and drinking wine, and passing resolutions"; [4] in what was termed the "irrepressible conflict" between them and the advocates of unlimited silver coinage, he was frankly on their side. He desired Congress to foster the banks, and even to repeal the Silver-purchase

[1] *Cong. Rec.*, Vol. XIII, p. 3910.
[2] *Ibid.*, XIII, p. 3915.
[3] The alternatives are clearly set forth by Nelson Dingley, Jr. in his speech on May 17, 1882, *Cong. Rec.*, Vol. XIII, pp. 4050–56.
[4] Dewey, *Financial History of the United States*, pp. 410–11.

Law of 1878. His well-known opposition to silver inflationary measures left no doubt that he would veto anything of that description. While he was strong enough to prevent new legislation, he could not bring about the repeal. In fact, the silverites were responsible for one of the features of the Bank Charter Extension Act.

As finally passed, the law reconciled several opposing views. The Senate inserted a section authorizing three per cent. bonds to be issued to holders of the "Windom bonds" who would voluntarily accept lower interest. In return their new securities were to be called only when no available bonds at higher interest were outstanding. This was not the long-term series first proposed by Congressman Flower, of New York, but it promised a saving in annual interest payments, and provided temporarily for the needs of the banks. Silver advocates were gratified by a section intended to force the banks to cease discriminating against silver certificates. Opponents of bank speculation in government bonds and enemies of currency contraction were alike mollified by limitations upon the monthly amounts in which bonds could be presented by the banks for redemption. In consequence of these compromises, despite opposition coming mostly from representatives from the South and trans-Mississippi West, the extension of charters was authorized and their power of note-issue continued.[1]

Despite the effect upon the banks, Arthur's Administration reduced the public debt by over $400,000,000.[2] The controversies of his term did clarify the issues, but his successor found the major fiscal problems still unsolved. Cleveland had to grapple with rapid bond redemption, extravagant appropriations, and tariff revision, all complicated by excessive revenues and a rising tide of silver. In addition, he had to determine what use he would make of Arthur's favored device for tariff reduction—international treaties providing for commercial reciprocity.

[1] 22 *Stat.*, pp. 162-66, dated July 12, 1882.
[2] Dewey, *op. cit.*, table, p. 432.

IN addition to the Pendleton and tariff laws, the last session of the Republican Forty-seventh Congress added little of importance to the statute book except the regular appropriation measures. Of these, the most significant was to strengthen the national defense.

By 1880, the United States Navy had returned to a state comparable to that before 1812, "a satirical semblance of a navy. . . . The five 'first rate' vessels that we have now," the country was informed, "are now to be classed as obsolete and as 'non-combatants'; . . . Of twenty-seven 'second-rates,' three are 'unfinished on the stocks, rotten, and worthless,' seven are probably not worth repairing, and only nine are in condition for service; . . . of twenty-nine third-rate steamers, six should be broken up, and only fifteen are now fit for service; . . . the six fourth-rate steamers are 'of really no account as vessels of war'; . . . of the twenty-four ironclads, four are 'rotten and worthless,' a number of them unfinished, and the fourteen that are serviceable are all 'fourth-rates,' and carry only two guns each—smooth-bores of five-inch caliber. 'There is not . . . a single rifled gun on our ironclad fleet afloat.' " [1]

The sorry condition of the navy when Arthur became President was not the product of recent neglect. For fifteen years, as the country had been drifting into a state of naval defenselessness, Congress had viewed the process of decay with complacency. There had been complaints in Congress and in the press; but the seriousness of the evil was first definitely pictured for President Arthur in a report submitted by a Naval Advisory Board on November 7, 1881, at the conclusion of a summer's investigations.

The board found in the entire fleet of the United States Navy only thirty-two vessels available for service, of which twenty-four were actually in commission. In sharp contrast, the appropriate numerical strength they established at forty-three unarmored vessels always in commission, twenty-two more unarmored vessels for relief work, and five for possible losses, in addition to five steel rams, five torpedo gun-

---

[1] *The Nation*, Feb. 5, 1880, with reference to a report to the House of Representatives submitted Jan. 30, 1880, which is cited in part.

boats, ten cruising, and ten harbor, torpedo boats. To complete the essential construction, they estimated that $29,607,000 would be required for a building program extending over eight years. To make the navy adequate, they recommended twenty new, unarmored, wooden cruisers of ten knots, and eighteen new, unarmored, steel cruisers of different speeds. All should have full sail power. Supplementing them should be numerous rams, torpedo boats, and torpedo gunboats.[1]

This schedule of construction frankly preferred numbers to individual strength, favoring a large unarmored fleet instead of fewer ironclads because of the high cost of the latter and the necessity of purchasing their armament abroad. Building the stronger vessels, it was thought, could well be postponed until the more essential ships were in commission.

Arthur earnestly supported the board's recommendations. "I cannot too strongly urge upon you my conviction that every consideration of national safety, economy, and honor imperatively demands a thorough rehabilitation of our Navy," he declared to Congress in December, 1881. "For avoiding as well as for repelling dangers that may threaten us in the future we must be prepared to enforce any policy which we think wise to adopt."[2]

Political considerations had much to do with Arthur's choice of William E. Chandler to become his new Secretary of the Navy; but he must also have been impressed by Chandler's young, vigorous energy, energy upon which the renovation of the navy would make great drains if the innumerable serious obstacles were to be surmounted. As the two men lunched together on April 5, 1882, the day before Chandler's nomination went to the Senate, they probably discussed the prospects of obtaining congressional authorization and grants of money to build the vessels so sadly needed. That, however, was but the first of the difficulties.

In response to Arthur's recommendations, Congress, in the naval appropriation measure of August 5, 1882, authorized the building of two new steel, unarmored cruisers and completion of the four double-turreted monitors already begun. Work was promptly undertaken with the general advice and aid of a second naval advisory board, a group of experts now charged with the responsibility of overseeing construc-

[1] Sec. of Navy, *Annual Report*, 1881, pp. 28–47. A minority of the committee submitted a report differing in technical details on the building program.
[2] Richardson, *Messages*, Vol. VIII, p. 51.

tion.[1] Steel vessels were a novelty in the United States Navy, and these first ships were necessarily experimental, yet Chandler pushed the building program as rapidly as Congress would permit. For the next year, for example, he proposed the immediate construction of two more second-rate, steel, unarmored cruisers of thirteen knots, one iron dispatch-boat, and five steel rams, in addition to what had already been begun.[2] On March 3, 1883, the last full day of the Forty-seventh Congress, under Republican control in both branches, appropriations for three new steel cruisers of different grades and for one dispatch-boat received Arthur's approval.

Meanwhile, to save wasteful expense at the numerous, widely separated, and costly navy yards, they were investigated by a special commission preparatory to disposing of what could not be used. Similarly, the problem of supplying from American sources up-to-date ordnance for new vessels was confided to a gun foundry board, appointed by President Arthur on April 2, 1883. Visiting England, France, and Russia, but denied access to the Krupp works at Essen, this board examined the sources of supply and the types of ordnance made in each country. They estimated that three years would be required for the construction of adequate manufacturing plants and the assemblage of necessary tools in the United States. As an initial appropriation for immediate use, they named the sum of $1,800,000 to be spent in building two government assembly plants, one for the navy and one for the army, at Washington Navy Yard and Watervliet Arsenal, respectively. The gun material, they declared, should be purchased from United States steel manufacturers, who should be encouraged to establish plants for the purpose by the prospect of large government orders.[3] Congress, receiving this report with favor, caused the board to reconvene on April 29, 1884, to draft a plan of action.

On May 15, a circular letter was addressed to the steel factories of the United States in part as follows:

---

[1] Commodore R. W. Shufeldt, upon his return from Korea, became the chairman of the second Naval Advisory Board and assisted in the selection of its two civilian members. See his letter and telegram to Chandler, October 30, November 2, 3, 7, 1882, Chandler Papers.

[2] Sec. of Navy, *Annual Report*, 1882, Vol. I, pp. 22 ff. Arthur favored this program, also. Richardson, *Messages*, Vol. VIII, p. 140.

[3] Report submitted February 16, 1884, was printed as 48th Cong., 1st sess., *House Exec. Doc. No. 27*, and also embodied in Sec. of Navy, *Annual Report*, 1884, Vol. I, pp. 255–382. See also Lieut. W. H. Jaques to Wm. E. Chandler, Aug. 5, 11, 18, Sept. 1, 7, 1883, Chandler Papers.

. . . the Board is very decidedly of the opinion that the gun material should be developed in this country, and the object of now addressing you is to request from you such proposals as may guide the Board in its recommendations as to the annual appropriations to be made. . . .

In whatever particular your works may be deficient in the appliances required above, you are requested to consider the outlay necessary to efficiently equip your establishment, and to determine the size of contract for annual supply of gun material . . . that will justify you in incurring this expense for plant, your remuneration to be derived solely from the price paid by the Government for the material after passing the tests required.

As this subject is now before Congress you are requested to provide the information asked for at your earliest convenience. In considering the matter of a plant for the manufacture of gun material the Board suggests that you do not lose sight of its availability for the manufacture of armor, for which a call may be made by the Government. . . .

From the responses to this letter, the board made its supplementary report on December 20, 1884. Responsible steel manufacturers in the United States, it said, were prepared to build plants and bid for contracts to supply material for the heaviest guns if they could be assured of orders. Arthur warmly urged Congress to grasp this excellent opportunity to develop national self-sufficiency.[1]

The Commission on Navy Yards had meanwhile reported its findings on December 1, 1883.[2] Navy yards, it declared, should be located at places already well fortified, such as large cities or naval rendezvous. According to this criterion, some should be closed; the mechanical departments of those retained for construction or repair should be reorganized and concentrated; there should be "one shop in each for the performance of any one class of work and . . . each of the several articles that form part of the outfit of a ship should be made in one yard only." With a navy of about thirty vessels, only five or six needed repairs at a time. To maintain a separate yard for the repairing of each of these vessels, as in the past, would be folly. Instead of having navy yards to care for ships, "ships have been dragging out a protracted existence for the benefit of the navy yards," commented Secretary Chandler.[3] Reforms, however, met with such resistance from

[1] Richardson, *Messages*, Vol. VIII, p. 247.
[2] Printed as 48th Cong., 1st sess., *Sen. Exec. Doc. No. 55*. For suppressed convictions of one of its members see A. B. Mullett to Wm. E. Chandler, Sept. 18, 1883, Chandler Papers.
[3] *William E. Chandler's Reply to Resolutions of Congress for Appointment of Committees on Ordnance and Naval Construction, July 12, 1884* (Washington, 1884). See also his letter to the Senate dated January 11, 1884, listing 92 vessels whose original cost was

those with vested interests that the Secretary was led to insist that until politics and patronage should be taken out of the navy yards (a step which he did little to hasten), construction must be accomplished through private contracts.[1]

Construction was begun under the moderate appropriations of August 5, 1882, and March 3, 1883. These vessels, unlike the monitors being built when the Arthur Administration opened, were not delayed by the inability of American steel manufacturers to supply armor, for they were not heavily armored. Yet they had their own difficulties. While the misfortunes of the monitors were partly due to public belief that vessels of that type were already obsolete, those of the cruisers may be chiefly ascribed to the novelty of their design. They represented the transition from wooden ships with great sail areas and low steam power to steel vessels of high steam power and minimum canvas,—from unarmored vessels with no watertight subdivision and with cast-iron, muzzle-loading artillery, to ships with armored decks, minute subdivision, steel artillery, and secondary batteries of machine guns and torpedoes. It was a leap of great length, made possible only by a study of English and French warships.[2] In their eagerness to commence construction, the Arthur Administration made the leap without sufficient preliminary observation.

The three vessels in the cruiser class which provided the first building experience were the *Boston,* the *Atlanta,* and the *Chicago,* all of which were begun in the Arthur Administration. A fourth vessel, the *Dolphin,* was a supposedly swift dispatch-boat. Under the supervision of the Naval Advisory Board, the designs for each ship were drafted in some haste, but with every desire to utilize the best available knowledge. Photographs and diagrams were published, accompanied by full descriptions, in order to obtain useful criticism.[3] While they may have aided the builders, it offered another means for Democratic attack upon the Administration, rendered the more effective by the eventual failure of the vessels to meet expectations. Deficiencies in design of each vessel either left unprotected the hull or steering gear, or placed obstructions in the way of firing the guns. Moreover, they never attained the speed desired of them.

$40,796,612.92 and whose repairs to that date had cost $41,200,822.13; printed as 48th Cong., 1st sess., *Sen. Exec. Doc. No. 48.*

[1] Sec. of Navy, *Annual Report,* 1883, Vol. I, pp. 17–18.
[2] William Hovgaard, *Modern History of Warships* (London, 1920), pp. 170–74.
[3] R. W. Shufeldt to W. E. Chandler, Aug. 10, 1883, Chandler Papers.

Contracts for the construction of each of the vessels went to Chandler's personal friend, the well-known shipbuilder, John Roach, bringing with them the complaints of the disappointed, the abuse of those who suspected that Roach was dishonest, and infinitely vexatious delays and difficulties arising from the necessity of dealing with both the Department of the Navy and the special, independent, Naval Advisory Board.[1] Plans and specifications were being determined even while the building was in process, instead of being complete before construction was begun.

Once the ships were on the stocks, Roach was eager to finish them promptly. As the work dragged on into the election campaign of 1884, he became eager to finish before the Democrats should get in and, as he said, "destroy the character of the vessels." With thousands of dollars tied up in materials and a pay roll of $30,000 a week, he was held back constantly by disagreements within the Naval Advisory Board, either as to details of design still open to change, or as to matters of construction, such as the approving of propeller shafts and boilers, which must be settled before he could proceed with the building. By December, 1884, with Cleveland's election conceded, he had $556,910 invested in the uncompleted vessels, while a change from steel to iron shafts ordered by the board delayed the construction and held back over $460,000 otherwise due him under the contracts.[2] Even though Secretary Chandler paid over much of this before contract conditions had been met, Roach was eventually bankrupt, his assets "frozen" in the unfinished cruisers.

The *Dolphin*, which had been designed by the government, failed to make the speed required by the contract for its construction; nothing but use could test its "strength" to determine if that were up to specification, and the question arose: if weakness should be discovered, would it be on account of materials and workmanship, or of design? William C. Whitney, Cleveland's enterprising Secretary of the Navy, complained of its vulnerability and declared it a pleasure craft rather than a war vessel. As Chandler's successor, it fell to him to arrange financial details with Roach's assignees, thus to complete the construction of these ships,[3] and also to promote the building of others with the benefit of Chandler's experience.

[1] See N. Y. *Sun,* Aug. 26, 1883, for ugly attack on both Roach and Chandler.
[2] Roach to Chandler, July 3, Dec. 10, 18, 1884, Chandler Papers.
[3] Sec. of Navy, *Annual Report,* 1885, pp. xix ff.

Arthur's recommendations to the Forty-seventh Congress called for the construction of four cruisers and one dispatch-boat. These, the Republican majority sanctioned. The next Congress, politically divided into a Republican Senate and a Democratic House, was unresponsive to his suggestion that it authorize construction of four gunboats and three steel cruisers. The Senate favored building six new cruisers,[1] the House refused to proceed further with any construction program, and disregarded the President's appeal in a special message of March 26, 1884.[2] The two could agree upon nothing beyond an appropriation to maintain the regular naval establishment until the next session.

When Congress reassembled, Arthur urged the authorization of ten vessels, two of which would be cruisers, the others, smaller craft. On his very last day in office, he was permitted to sign a measure appropriating $1,895,000 to commence the construction of two cruisers and two gunboats of "the best and most modern design, having *the highest attainable speed.*" [3] Public opinion was gradually accepting the necessity of a considerable outlay for the restoration of our naval power.

While the country haltingly undertook new ship construction to retrieve its navy from utter impotence, and perfected plans for the domestic manufacture of ordnance and armor plate, tests and investigations led to valuable improvements in machinery, torpedoes, and submarines. Boilers were strengthened and furnaces improved so that steam pressures could be tremendously increased. The torpedo boat *Destroyer,* in whose design Captain Ericsson was much involved, was put through tests before a Navy Department board which reported to Congress. Attention was paid to experiments with submarines, and with use of petroleum for fuel. An Office of Naval Intelligence was established in the Navy Department. An attempt was made to compile records of the available merchant vessels in a Bureau of Mercantile Marine. Plans were devised to render the Bureau of Naval Construction more efficient.[4] The entire foundation was laid and the first steps taken in the rapid development of "the new navy" to be built in later years.

[1] *Cong. Rec.,* Vol. XV, p. 1496 (Feb. 29, 1884).
[2] Richardson, *Messages,* Vol. VIII, pp. 209–10.
[3] 23 *Stat.,* pp. 426–33.
[4] Hovgaard, *op. cit.,* pp. 283–4, 367–74; 48th Cong., 1st sess., *Sen. Exec. Doc. No. 115;* John T. Morgan to Chandler, Nov. 22, 1883, Chandler Papers; Sec. of Navy, *Annual Report,* 1883, Vol. I, p. 38; 1884, Vol. I, p. 14.

In line with his insistence upon adequate defense, Arthur advocated congressional attention to the problem of coast defense works, pointing out in his annual messages that those in existence were either antiquated or insufficient. In April, 1884, having evoked no response up to that time, he sent a special message deploring delay and naming $1,500,000 as his estimate of a proper permanent annual appropriation for the purpose.[1] On July 5, 1884, a grant of $700,000 was made. Not until March 3, 1885, did Congress reach the point of providing for an investigating Board of Fortifications and Coast Defenses.[2] This body, reporting in Cleveland's Administration, thoroughly endorsed the conclusions of the Gun Foundry Board and forced Congress to recognize the country's serious weakness.

The other great branch of national defense, the army, was principally engaged during the Arthur Administration in policing the Far West, protecting settlers from Indians, and reservation Indians from intruders upon their lands, aiding newly arrived immigrants, and maintaining peace and order in new settlements. With the coffers of the Treasury full, Arthur urged the appropriation of money for the enlistment of the army to the full strength of 30,000 men.[3] It was suggested that the cost of the larger numbers would be no greater than that required to shift detachments from place to place to meet changing demands.[4] Neither Congress was willing to make this increase, but placed a limit of 25,000 men in the appropriation bills for the War Department. The President's suggestion that Federal aid to the State militia units should be increased likewise met with little response. Arrangement was made for the issue of heavy ordnance to militia units in coastal States. At that point, Federal aid rested.

Arthur took great satisfaction in every important step toward the renovation of the national defense, especially in the activities of the Department of the Navy. While the work of Secretary Chandler and his subordinates was undoubtedly creditable, it is now abundantly clear that it could have been better. Eagerness to build new vessels was not attended by adequate care to make them of the best type or to construct them in the most efficient way. While Arthur's Administration might claim credit for refraining from extravagance and waste-

[1] Richardson, *Messages,* Vol. VIII, p. 211.
[2] *23 Stat.,* p. 434.
[3] Richardson, *Messages,* Vol. VIII, p. 50.
[4] Sec. of War, *Annual Report,* 1881, p. 4.

fulness in this field, despite the government's large surplus revenues, principal responsibility for this restraint must be accorded to a House of Representatives controlled by Democrats. By withholding authorizations and appropriations until the process of design and construction should have become more familiar, and the commission of serious blunders less likely, that House was of real service to the country. Moreover, while Secretary Chandler frequently denounced the organization of the department as he found it, in particular the inexcusably expensive navy-yard system, he did nothing else of real significance to effect an improvement. His successor, William C. Whitney, found ample opportunity for house cleaning. Chandler, it seems, had been engrossed by Republican politics and the naval building program.

The credit to which Arthur's Administration is entitled for creating "the new navy" is, on the other hand, far more than that which actual ships, guns, and organization would appear to warrant. For, in addition to tangible results, the work of preparation had swept aside barriers of indifference and ignorance, thus clearing the path for subsequent progress toward the enlarged and modern navy. Much laborious preliminary work had been done, its consequences not yet ascertained at the time when Arthur surrendered the Presidency to another.[1] Thereafter, public opinion supported Congress in the more rapid construction of a steel fleet and in the necessarily increasing outlay of tax-raised funds.

[1] "An aggregate of 88 floating craft in various stages of construction or dilapidation may be said to form the navy of the United States," the British Minister then reported. L. S. S. West to Earl Granville, 18 April, 1885, F. O. 5/ 1903 (Public Record Office).

ARTHUR's life as President during the active short session was not all politics. It had other aspects which gave him keen delight, for Washington society in the winter of 1883 was more than usually gay with its succession of official and private receptions, several notable weddings, innumerable dinners, and balls. He enjoyed attending many of them. He continued to dine at the homes of certain Senators, as well as others in public office whom a President more often thus honors, while also giving attentive oversight to White House hospitality.

During the summer, the White House had been thoroughly redecorated, and in Christmas week Arthur moved in from the Soldiers' Home cottage to establish himself in time for his first New Year's reception. At smaller gatherings, he adopted the custom of moving from group to group of guests in the great East Room; but the throngs who came on this occasion forced him to stand, with Mrs. McElroy and the large number of ladies whom she was accustomed to invite to assist her, while the guests filed past.

While Arthur stood receiving the congratulations of his guests, the shocking news was brought to him that in a cloakroom the Minister from the Hawaiian Islands had suddenly dropped dead. The festivities were ended at once.

Early in January, Grant arrived in the capital. A series of entertainments for the ex-President and his wife included, on January 10, a large dinner at the Executive Mansion, in the elaborate fashion to which Washington had become accustomed during Arthur's first season. Three days later, Mrs. McElroy came with her daughters to resume the rôle of her brother's hostess and to care for her niece. During the winter his brother and his sister, Mrs. Haynsworth, made short visits. Beside these members of his family, and his nephew, Arthur H. Masten, and Mrs. Masten, Arthur had other guests almost constantly, most of whom were New York friends.

Washington society was stirred late in January by the arrival of the Marquis of Lorne, Governor General of Canada, who had recently made an extended trip in the Northwest and came to Washington much heralded by the press. For him, Arthur gave a dinner on January 27, one of a series of brilliant gatherings in which the visitor was the central figure.

February 6, the last day before Lent, was crowded with social engagements. At noon Alice Blaine was married at the new Blaine mansion to Colonel John H. Coppinger, while President Arthur, two officers of his Cabinet, Speaker Keifer, and the congressional delegation from Maine withdrew from their official duties to attend. That evening, Mary Brewster, the Attorney General's daughter, was married to Robert J. W. Koons of Philadelphia, in a large church ceremony to which all the Arthurs and hundreds of others went. At its conclusion, the President and Mrs. McElroy had to hasten back to the Executive Mansion for the Army and Navy reception.

Arthur, however, chose to walk back through the sleet, for just before the wedding, and in front of the church, his carriage had been broken in what was almost a grave accident. In the great crush of arrivals, the tongue of a carriage behind his had been driven through the back of his own, had passed between Arthur and his daughter, and had given them both a serious scare. The walk was refreshing, despite the slippery streets, and he faced the stream of guests at his reception with his usual easy dignity.

From a series of vexatious political problems, Arthur went to New York on February 15 for the funeral of his old friend, Edwin D. Morgan, and then returned at once to Washington. His more recent New York political associates were giving him much trouble. They pressed him to oust Robertson and install Marvelle W. Cooper, his personal friend, as Collector at New York, and complained of his choice of General Ketchum to become Appraiser there.[1] Congress, at the same time, was getting into a snarl over tax reduction with only two weeks before adjournment, and the tariff recommendations of his annual message were apparently to go unobserved.

In the midst of the last days of the session, a welcome diversion from even the usual round of entertainments was a concert in the White House given by Adelina Patti on Washington's birthday. Another was his dinner to the Washington members of Psi Upsilon, his college fraternity. On February 28 they came to the White House and spent the evening informally until after midnight. The most notable of the guests on this occasion was the essayist Charles Dudley Warner.

[1] Cincinnati *Commercial-Gazette,* Jan. 2, 4, 1883.

Interspersed among his other engagements were dinners at the homes of various friends, including the venerable historian, George Bancroft. The story is told that Arthur once met Bancroft soon after receiving an invitation to dine at his house, and before an acknowledgment had been returned.

"Mr. President," said the old gentleman, "I trust we are to have the honor of an acceptance?"

"I believe," replied Arthur, "that I am permitted to dine with Cabinet officers, Justices of the Supreme Court, the Vice President, and— Mr. George Bancroft! I shall most certainly come."

To Henry Adams, Washington was full of "confused politicians and idiotic society," the short session of the Forty-seventh Congress seemed "foul" and "revolting," and Arthur, "a creature for whose skin the romancist ought to go with a carving knife." [1] Less exquisite tastes were gratified by the President's political conservatism and social gifts.

Congress breathed its last speech on the legislative day known as March 3, 1883. By a liberal construction of their powers, Congressmen extended the day well into that which the man in the street would have sworn was the fourth of March. The House was the scene of the usual bustling activity, and the whole Capitol, with galleries crowded and floors full, seemed unusually conscious of the flight of time. An all night session went on in the House wing, and there were angry voices among the pressmen whom the Speaker had deprived of their gallery. Over in the Senate, there was less work and more of the spirit of play, with "spreads" in several committee rooms and a certain tuneful jollity apparent in the halls. Arthur arrived at the President's room at ten o'clock and before he left in the early morning had signed about a score of bills. All the important appropriation and revenue bills of the session were approved on this last day, and to Arthur, as well as to Congress, the adjournment brought relief.

No human physique could withstand the strain to which Arthur subjected himself in partaking so freely of the pleasures, as well as the labors, of Washington life. As the winter passed, his friends observed that in the daylight hours his face was lined, his eyes dulled, and his mind less keen than late at night. Then, he seemed temporarily to regain his normal powers. He was gaining weight and losing energy, and perhaps turning more frequently to stimulants to revive a dimin-

[1] Worthington C. Ford, ed., *Letters of Henry Adams, 1858–1891,* p. 346, pp. 348–9.

ishing vigor. By mid-March it was apparent that some steps must be taken to forestall a serious illness. After talk of a trip to Fortress Monroe, Arthur decided to remain in Washington until ex-President Diaz of Mexico had made a ceremonial visit, and then to go to Florida for fishing. Florida was then coming into fashion as a resort for wealthy New Yorkers in the early spring.[1]

While Arthur waited for Diaz, news came during the afternoon of March 25 that Timothy O. Howe, the Postmaster General, had died at his home in Wisconsin. It was the first break in Arthur's Cabinet, the occasion of more than usual embarrassment for him, and it came when he was all but tired out. Charles J. Folger, Secretary of the Treasury, was so ill that he had been obliged to abandon his desk and to rest completely. The newspapers carried daily reports on his health and began to hint at impending general changes in the Cabinet, while advocates promptly swarmed about Arthur to urge various persons for the place so recently vacated.

The President had undoubtedly created serious disappointment among his old New York associates by the series of New York appointments at the end of the session.[2] Many, however, seemed to expect that they would soon be benefited by the elevation of Richard Crowley to some position of influence.[3] It was thought that he might go into Folger's place, although he was also mentioned for the Postmaster-Generalship. For that position, however, Arthur determined to take a mid-Western Republican. Accordingly, on April 3, he appointed Walter Q. Gresham of Indiana, much to everyone's surprise, but amid general approval. Meanwhile, he put a stop to rumors that Folger would be asked to resign and Crowley put at the head of the Treasury Department, in some manner most offensive to the latter. By the second week in April, newspapers were ascribing Crowley's open break with Arthur to various causes, and Conkling's sneer was being widely quoted: "I have but one annoyance with the Administration of President Arthur, and that is, that, in contrast with it, the Administration of Hayes becomes respectable, if not heroic."[4]

On April 5, free at last, Arthur left Washington from the same station in which Garfield had met his death wound, and started south,

[1] Murat Halstead so discovered in Mar., 1883. See Cincinnati *Commercial-Gazette,* Mar. 11, 1883.

[2] N. Y. *Tribune,* Mar. 2, 1883.

[3] Cincinnati *Commercial-Gazette,* Mar. 27, 1883.

[4] *Ibid.,* Apr. 12, 1883, citing Philadelphia *Press,* n.d.

ARTHUR IN YELLOWSTONE PARK, AUGUST, 1883

The party consists of: Seated (left to right), Governor Schuyler Crosby, General Phil Sheridan, President Arthur, Secretary Robert Lincoln, Senator G. G. Vest; Standing, Col. Mike Sheridan, Gen. Anson Stager, Capt. Philo Clark, Judge Daniel G. Rollins, Col. J. F. Gregory.

accompanied by Secretary Chandler, Charles E. Miller, an intimate New York City friend, the private secretary, the valet, the chef, and four reporters. The journey was hot and dusty and marked by many discomforts. An overzealous conductor, for example, insisted on trying to collect fares at one time; at another, the trucks of the private car had to be altered to fit the wider gauge of the rails, and a few hours later, the entire car was left stranded in the countryside for some time at night when its coupler broke loose and the rest of the train went on.

At Savannah, instead of stopping as he had planned, Arthur remained only the minimum amount of time. He reached Jacksonville late on April 6, to be greeted by throngs of people and a temperature of ninety degrees, and to transfer through the crowds to a boat for a ride up the St. John's River to Sanford. He was pleased to have a brief chat with his secretary of the old war days, Daniel G. Tyler, on the wharf at Green Cove Springs, and, late that night, to take aboard his wife's cousin, Mrs. George A. Mercer (Ann Maury Herndon), and two girls, Miss Cope and Miss Bruce, to ride from Palatka to Sanford. A pleasant hotel at Sanford was so attractive that Arthur regretted leaving it in accordance with the original plans. He was irritable and sullen, distinctly out of sorts, when Sanford was left behind and his party started by train for Kissimmee City. Near Maitland, they stopped to visit some orange groves, and after all other means of getting ripe fruit had failed, Secretary Chandler blithely climbed a tree to pick some; but nothing could restore the spirits of the President, who refused to go through with a school picnic and reception program at Orlando and sat indignantly inside a stuffy, hot railroad car while the train stopped, contrary to his wishes, beside the picnic grounds. He was not himself.

From Kissimmee City, Arthur's party went by boat up the Florida Improvement Company's canal, planning to camp on "Gardiner's Island" in the wilderness. Militant mosquitoes, sandflies, and midges drove them back to the mouth of the outlet of Lake Tohopekaliga. Soon the newspapers reported examples of fishermen's luck in Arthur's expedition and revealed that the President was considered an expert angler by competent judges. Francis Endicott called him "the finest amateur caster that I have ever seen," and others described Arthur's measured, accurate cast of seventy-eight feet with a trout-fly and his splendid records in salmon and bass fishing. In a few days, they started north for St. Augustine, where the U.S.S. *Tallapoosa* was to meet them for the journey as far as Savannah, and perhaps further north. They spent a Sunday in the old city, with Arthur attending an Episcopal service in the morning and that of a Negro church in the evening. The President walked about the streets during the next two days practically unnoticed, quietly shopping and observing points of interest. When he began the sea voyage, he was already tanned and somewhat refreshed, although he never flourished in hot weather and had perhaps over-exposed himself to sun and rain.

Arthur returned to the *Tallapoosa* in Savannah harbor on the evening of April 19 after spending the better part of the day and the evening with his relatives at the home of Mrs. Henry T. Botts (his wife's cousin, Elizabeth Hull Herndon) on Monterey Square. Plans for the following day included a private reception for his party. But soon after he had reached his stateroom, he was seized by a chill, summoned the ship's doctor, and, for the rest of the night, was in great distress. He spent practically all the next day in bed, the reception and other festivities being put off, so that in spite of great secrecy, news of his illness leaked out. On April 21, he started back for Washington by special train, still sick and weak, anxious to be in his own rooms and with his own doctor.

By the time he reached the city, on the following evening, he was somewhat better. He mustered up the strength to walk from the train to his carriage in the presence of Frelinghuysen, Brewster, Alan Arthur, and many others who had been alarmed by the reports. His tanned face, his assurance that he was quite well, and the insistence of his private secretary that his indisposition had been inordinately exaggerated, served to subdue public anxiety. There had been great concern over the possibility of the country's being deprived by death of both its Vice President and its President. Public anxiety would certainly have been increased had it been known that from this illness Arthur was never fully to recover; but for the time being, concern was allayed by his presence at a full Cabinet meeting on April 24.

On May 25, 1883, Arthur took part in the notable ceremony at the dedication of Brooklyn Bridge. Many of his old acquaintances observed the change in his appearance, the loss of buoyancy, failing ruddiness, and increasing gray in his carefully groomed hair and whiskers. A lightened program of official work, with rigidly curtailed diet and earlier hours, did not effect the expected recovery. In consequence, a trip to the newly developed Yellowstone National Park was organized as a semi-official, semi-recreational expedition, to be made after necessary engagements in the East had been met. It would take him far from the scenes of his worries.

Arthur remained in Washington until July 21. Late that evening he boarded the U.S.S. *Despatch* with his daughter and started a leisurely voyage to New York. They anchored off Cape May while he went ashore for the day. At midnight, hundreds of people lined the beach, which was glowing with bonfires and torches, to see him pulled through the surf to his yacht. Smooth water lay between the cape and New York, which they reached at noon next day.[1]

When he left the metropolis on July 29, he went, by way of Washington, to Louisville, Kentucky, to participate in the formal opening of the Southern Exposition there. At his departure, observers commented on "the tall white hat with a narrow brim which rivals in peculiarity the wonderful white hat of Attorney General Brewster and which, because the President is never seen without it, is rapidly becoming historic." [2] He reached Louisville at six o'clock in the evening, two days later. Secretaries Lincoln and Folger, Postmaster General Gresham, and Daniel G. Rollins were with him, while General Sheridan and his family came from Chicago.

Arthur's public addresses were always short, especially those delivered outdoors in some purely formal capacity. At Louisville, his function was that of officially opening the exposition, and when he had spoken less than five minutes, and said nothing of importance, he turned to pull the silken cord dangling above the stand, "thereby . . . putting in operation all the engines in the machinery department." The old Governor, whose seat was under the cord, thought that Arthur's extended hand was held out to him, and reached to clasp it. With swift tact, Arthur gave that hand to him and, at the same time, with the other, pulled the cord. Simultaneously the machinery, a set of chimes, an organ, a band, and a chorus of five hundred voices started up, the latter singing "the well-known air, 'America.' " [3]

Arthur's Yellowstone party left Chicago for Green River, Wyoming, at noon on August 3, planning to be gone about one month. The expe-

[1] S. D. Greene to Chandler, July 30, 1883, Chandler Papers.
[2] N. Y. *Tribune*, July 30, 1883.
[3] N. Y. *Herald*, Cincinnati *Commercial-Tribune*, Aug. 2, 1883.

dition consisted of: Rollins, Lincoln, Senator Vest of Missouri, General Sheridan, Colonel Michael Sheridan, General Anson Stager, J. Schuyler Crosby, a New Yorker serving as Territorial Governor of Wyoming, Surgeon W. H. Forwood, two other officers, one reporter, and a group of "guides." They set out from Green River in spring wagons for Fort Washakie in the Shoshone Reservation, expecting there to change to saddle horses. August eighth, they spent at the fort, entertained by the Shoshone and Arapahoe Indians with an Indian dance and a sham battle, and by the garrison's cavalry with maneuvers. In Florida, Arthur had declined the well-meant gift of a large young eagle, but at Fort Washakie he gratefully accepted for his daughter Nell an Indian pony proffered by the reservation Indians. It was sent to Washington in the autumn.

Next day, at seven o'clock, they were in the saddle for the long ride through the park. For three hundred miles on horseback, sleeping in tents, stopping over occasionally for a day of fishing and rest, they moved at a leisurely pace toward Livingston, Montana, where, at the end of the month, they returned to railroad travel. Arthur reached Chicago on the afternoon of September 4, much improved in health, his zest for public life temporarily restored.

The day of his arrival in Chicago marked the summit of his popularity. Fourteen columns of friendly and approving letters from prominent persons all over the country had appeared in the Chicago *News* of the day before. Editorials widely commended his public policy. When he appeared on the floor of the Chicago Chamber of Commerce at noon on September 5, five thousand people jammed in the galleries and packed around the floor gave him an ovation and listened with approval to three short sentences in which he expressed his appreciation. A reception directly afterward at the Union League Club was crowded, and the Loyal Legion's dinner at the Calumet Club again proved his great popularity. That evening, hundreds of people passed through the Grand Pacific Hotel at a speed which gave them a close glimpse of the President but no opportunity to shake his hand; yet, at the time of his departure, throngs were still outside awaiting their turn. When he took the train for Washington shortly afterward, weary as he was, he must have been elated by the numbers and enthusiasm of his Chicago admirers.

While Arthur had been in the West, Mrs. McElroy, with her daughter, Jessie, and Nell Arthur, and their two cousins, Susan and Alice Arthur, cruised quietly off the Rhode Island coast on the *Despatch*. As soon as he could get away from the steaming capital, he joined them. Newport society at once captured him. On September 25, he went to Bristol, R. I., to lay the cornerstone for the Burnside Memorial Hall and make a brief address. A few days later, he was fishing for bass off West Island, where he was reported to have pulled in an eighty-pounder, the largest seen in that neighborhood for years! [1]

On November 26, 1883, the city of New York celebrated the centennial of the withdrawal of British troops from that port at the close of the American Revolution. Arthur came from Washington to participate. Despite a steady, soaking downpour, the program was carried through. Gayly decorated boats paraded up the North River and back around the Battery and then up the East River and back. Soldiers, militia, civic organizations and bands marched past a reviewing stand at Bowling Green. At noon, for five minutes, all the whistles of the city joined in a carnival din, and shortly afterward, on the steps of the Sub-Treasury on Wall Street, a bronze statue of George Washington, of heroic proportions, was unveiled on the site where he first took the President's oath, in the immediate presence of Arthur, Grant, and the Governors of eleven of the original thirteen States. It was publicly presented to the Federal Government by the president of the New York Chamber of Commerce and officially accepted by Arthur, in a terse speech. The principal orator of the day was George William Curtis. At Delmonico's that evening, Arthur sat at the right hand of the toastmaster of the Evacuation Day banquet, and Curtis, Arthur's unremitting critic, at his left.

A week later, the President's third annual message was being read to a newly assembled Congress. It was, in the main, a perfunctory digest of the individual reports from the departments, but specially emphasized three major matters: use of surplus revenues to improve national defense, conservation of forests, and provision for orderly presidential succession in all contingencies.

The new Senate, having a Republican majority of four, organized with Senator George F. Edmunds of Vermont as president *pro tem*. Edmunds occupied the Vice President's room in the Capitol and wrote his correspondence on stationery with the heading, "Office of the Vice

[1] N. Y. *Tribune,* Sept. 29, 1883.

President." He was to be Arthur's successor, should the latter fail to complete his term.

The House of Representatives did not so readily organize. It was entirely controlled by the Democratic majority of seventy-seven, but among them, a warm contest had developed between ex-Speaker Randall and the younger John G. Carlisle for the place of Speaker. Carlisle, representing the active low-tariff sentiment of the party, carried the caucus and secured the prize. In appointing committees, he put his defeated rival at the head of the powerful Committee on Appropriations, then the dominating group in the House, while as chairman of the Committee on Ways and Means, from which any tariff bill would proceed, he named William R. Morrison of Illinois.

Whatever the party divisions might be over tariff matters, they were generally inclined to sustain Randall's views with respect to appropriations. He upheld the traditional party attitude, insisting upon closely restricted governmental functions and strict economy in Federal expenditures in contrast to the more liberal handed centralization fostered by the Republicans. The most prodigal act he permitted in this session was the grant of one million dollars to the directors of the World's Industrial and Cotton Centennial Exposition at New Orleans, in the form of a loan, in addition to the $300,000 appropriated for government exhibits there. For this, as for other objects, Congress appropriated just about one half what Arthur recommended. He had little influence upon its decisions.

Outside the field of appropriations, Congress passed several laws of some importance. After persistent urging, in which Arthur had joined, limited civil government was at last extended to the Territory of Alaska. Bureaus of Labor and of Animal Industry were created. Chinese immigration was still further restricted.[2] Finally, Congress yielded to Arthur's repeated demand for some encouragement to American shipping. Shipbuilding was made more profitable by the remission of all tariff duties on imported shipbuilding materials and supplies, while navigation was encouraged by a large reduction in tonnage dues,[1] the abolition of consular fees, and less restraint on the hiring and payment of seamen. This law, although beneficial, was to prove inadequate.

[1] 23 *Stat.*, pp. 115 ff.
[2] *Ibid.*, 53 ff.

With some slight accomplishment to its credit, the Forty-eighth Congress adjourned its first session on July 7, 1884. Despite considerable debate, the law of presidential succession remained unchanged, and even with a presidential election only a few months away, no act had been passed to establish the mode of making an electoral count in the event of disputed returns. To promote forest conservation, repeal of the preëmption law of 1841 and the Timber Culture Act of 1873 had been discussed, but the two houses could not agree. National defense, as we have seen,[1] was grudgingly allotted a small portion of the sums Arthur urgently advised. His major recommendations had led to no result.

While legislative results were meager, Congress was not idle. Its *Record* filled 6182 pages; its members busied themselves in investigations and debate. Much time was spent in the House in an ineffectual effort to pass the Morrison bill for a horizontal 20 per cent. reduction of tariff duties. In both House and Senate, the perennial Fitz-John Porter relief bills received disproportionate attention.

In connection with the latter, shortly before the end of the session, Arthur sent to Congress the fourth of his veto messages. Fitz-John Porter's case was notorious. On January 21, 1863, after trial before a court-martial for about two months, General Porter had been deprived of rank, cashiered from the army, and prohibited from holding office of honor or trust under the United States. He had thus become the scapegoat for the disastrous defeat of the Union forces at the second battle of Bull Run, the unfortunate outcome of which was attributed to his insubordination. Porter was a West Point graduate with a distinguished connection and an excellent military record prior to this disgrace. For fifteen years, unremittingly, he sought a retrial and an opportunity to demonstrate beyond doubt that the orders he had failed to obey had been based upon misinformation and, if carried out, would have turned defeat into utter rout. Grant refused to reopen the case, but Hayes yielded. On April 12, 1878, he named a commission consisting of Generals Schofield, Terry, and Getty to examine new evidence.

The findings of the commission completely exonerated Fitz-John Porter from wrong-doing. They led to a series of efforts in Congress to pass some law relieving him of his penalty and eventually elicited

[1] See above, p. 238.

the belated support of ex-President Grant in an effort to free him from "An Undeserved Stigma." [1] Grant insisted to President Arthur:

Porter was right in all that he said and did in the campaign under General Pope and I firmly believe that if Porter had been in command . . . the fighting would have ended then and there.

This tribute to Porter's discretion may have helped in persuading Arthur to extend a pardon to the unfortunate man, since, on May 4, 1882, he removed the continuing disability to hold office under the United States. For any further relief, it was unavailing.

The rightness or wrongness of the judgment by which Porter had been convicted had, through the years, become the concern of the two major parties. Regular Republicans had approved his punishment; Democrats had denounced it and had tried to bring it to an end. Arthur had departed from orthodoxy as far as he was willing when he pardoned Porter; he rejected the much greater step involved in the act which he vetoed on July 2, 1884, with general approval from his party.

The veto message, a copy of which in Arthur's handwriting has been preserved,[2] took two lines, one technical and legal; the other, political. Arthur protested that the bill was either an invasion of the Executive's appointing power, inasmuch as it named the one person to be appointed by him to a special, newly created office, or else it was advice to the Executive which was "unnecessary, . . . ineffective," and able to serve "no useful purpose upon the statute books." In addition, he expressed his unwillingness to sanction any legislation which should "practically annul and set at naught the solemn and deliberate conclusions of the tribunal by which he was convicted and of the President by whom its findings were examined and approved," basing his decision upon the original court-martial's better opportunities to use all pertinent evidence and its undeniable legal competence as a judicial tribunal.[3]

The objections which to Arthur had seemed sufficient did not deter Grover Cleveland from accepting a similar enactment two years later. Congress's authorization to him was approved on July 1, 1886, and, in accordance with its terms, Porter was restored to his old rank and

[1] The title of Grant's article in the *North American Review*, Dec., 1882, pp. 536 ff.
[2] Arthur Papers.
[3] Richardson, *Messages*, Vol. VIII, pp. 221–23.

placed upon the retired list. It has been generally believed that the passage of time made available to Hayes's special commission some decisive evidence which was entirely unobtainable by the court-martial, and a capacity for dispassionate judgment which the earlier body was quite unable to exercise in the days of war. But in 1884, Arthur's veto was sustained. Soon afterward, Congress adjourned and the subject of major public interest became the presidential campaign.

PRESIDENT ARTHUR was making his leisurely trip through the Yellowstone region when John Hay, in Denver, wrote of the political situation to a friend in Europe: "Next year is still absolutely in the air. Arthur is gaining; Lincoln is much talked about; Sherman will have Ohio; and there is a new, quiet boom for Blaine. But it is anybody's race as yet and, in view of the uncertainty of the event, the candidates themselves hardly know whether they want the nomination." [1] The political pot was already gently simmering. The warmth of the reception to Arthur in Chicago a fortnight later almost brought it to a boil, and by the end of the year there could be no doubt that the presidential campaign of 1884 was well past its tentative stages. In August, Arthur may, as Hay suspected, have been uncertain of his true desires; but during that autumn he allowed his friends to exert themselves quietly in his behalf, and by spring he would undoubtedly have welcomed a nomination.

The Chicago *Daily News* seized upon Arthur's visit to the West as an excuse for addressing letters to prominent men all over the country asking their opinion of the character of the Administration. The response was extraordinarily cordial. It was to be expected that old-line political leaders would praise the President. But some of the warmest commendation came from independents and liberals. George William Curtis, old-time opponent of Arthur, wrote: "I say that a President whose accession by means of a most tragical event was generally regarded as a serious misfortune, if not calamity, has not only allayed all apprehension, but his pacific and temperate Administration has gained the general approval of the country." Henry Ward Beecher declared: "I can hardly imagine how he could have done better." A similar statement came from President F. A. P. Barnard of Columbia College. "He deserves all honor for the wisdom with which he has conducted our public affairs in circumstances of peculiar difficulty." Mark Twain wrote characteristically: "I am but one in 55,000,000; still, in the opinion of this one-fifty-five-millionth of the country's population, it would be hard to better President Arthur's Administration. But don't decide till you hear from the

[1] Hay to L. P. Morton, Aug. 17, 1883, Morton Papers (New York Public Library).

rest." The *Daily News* was able to fill fifteen columns with like expressions of praise and confidence.

The Republican nomination for President in 1884 would have seemed to Arthur a vindication of his honor, a conclusive proof that, in the eyes of the party which he most esteemed, his Administration had been conducted creditably. Those Vice Presidents who had previously succeeded to the Presidency had each broken with the adherents and with the policies of the men whom they had replaced. Advised by their experience, Arthur deliberately avoided a clash with the Republican groups responsible for Garfield's nomination. On the contrary, his major quarrels were with the Stalwarts, who, objecting to his conciliatory course, branded its moderation as abject weakness and despicable ingratitude. At the same time, he did not seek the nomination only on the negative ground that his Presidency had produced no factional revolution within the party. The public policy of his Administration he likewise considered worthy of ratification.

Arthur and his Cabinet expected to base their major claims to party approval upon the manner in which they had dealt with the embarrassing surplus revenue. With that in mind, his annual message in December, 1883, urged the wisdom of gradually, rather than abruptly, reducing taxation, and of applying the continuing surplus to payment of the public debt and development of the national defense, rather than to other purposes. He did not recommend the modification of the tariff enacted a few months earlier, perhaps hoping that it was a problem upon which the Democratic majority of the new House of Representatives would divide. On the other hand he was, at this time, attempting to enlarge the country's foreign trade through reciprocity treaties, a means which necessarily involved a decrease of the revenue from tariff duties. His Administration took a truly moderate position on the problems of tax reduction and tariff protection.

Arthur's message was deprived of some of its interest by the previous publication, shrewdly timed to come a week earlier, of the views of James G. Blaine.[1] He proposed an alternative method for disposing of the surplus. Declining to approve of a general distribution to the States, as in 1836, Blaine suggested that the Federal Government collect the excise on intoxicants, the returns from which made up a large part of the excess revenue, and divide it among the States according to

[1] Philadelphia *Press*, Nov. 29, 1883.

their population. This idea had the merit of simplicity. But, with the public debt still so great, it seemed to both Arthur and Folger seriously ill advised, even if the proceeds were used by the States, as ex-President Hayes suggested, to aid education. They stood firmly for moderate reductions in taxation and for expenditure of the surplus in the two conservative forms of national armament and debt reduction.

"It is now understood that there is no concealment of Arthur's candidacy," wrote ex-President Grant, after appearing at the Brooklyn New England Society's dinner to Arthur late in December. "At this time no other person looms up, so that unless there is a change within the next sixty days he will be renominated without much opposition. I feel, however, that he will not get the nomination although it is impossible to predict who may. . . ." The wish was, perhaps, father to the thought, for, later in the pre-convention campaign, he wrote: "The President is now openly a candidate for the nomination in June next, and knows well that I am opposed to it." [1]

Other candidates for the Republican nomination were John A. Logan, John Sherman, and George F. Edmunds. Logan dominated Illinois and was popular with the rising Grand Army of the Republic. Sherman, who was far more indifferent to the nomination in 1884 than he had been in 1880, anticipated a deadlock between more vigorous rivals, hoped to profit from such a situation, and arranged to have his name brought prominently before the convention.[2] Soon after Congress opened, he did what he could to identify himself with a revived sectional Republicanism by instigating an investigation of race riots in Virginia and of comparable disorders in Mississippi. Edmunds, whose irreproachable honesty, free from sanctimoniousness, promised a safe, conservative administration, was the preference of the reform element in the party, but not an eager aspirant.

Arthur's real rival for the nomination was Blaine. He is reported to have been more interested in preventing the choice of Arthur than in obtaining the honor for himself, and he may, in fact, as he later said, have been persuaded against his better judgment to enter the election contest. His following was quite as large as in 1880 and, in the passing weeks, grew larger than that of the President.

[1] Grant to Adam Badeau, Dec. 24, 1883, Mar. 3, 1884, in Badeau, *Grant in Peace*, pp. 553, 556-7.
[2] Correspondence between J. B. Foraker and Sherman printed in Foraker, *Notes of a Busy Life*, Vol. I, pp. 151-57.

During Christmas week, and again in January, Arthur was in New York City consulting Republican leaders about his candidacy. The Union League Club gave a large reception in his honor; and Mrs. William Astor, a small dinner, both of which he no doubt enjoyed; but his principal occupation was an effort to make sure of a favorable New York delegation in June. No single New York Republican leader possessed sufficient skill to establish himself in Conkling's position as "boss" of the State; Conkling was out of politics; and Arthur was obliged to engineer, as quietly as possible, the combination of leaders who could advance his cause.

The overwhelming Republican defeat in New York in 1882, although somewhat offset by recoveries in the next year, made New York a "doubtful" State in 1884. Few thought that Blaine could obtain a majority there, while Arthur's ability was almost as dubious because of his identification with a much disliked faction and with machine methods. In Ohio, it was generally understood that Arthur's candidacy would be unpopular because of what Carl Schurz called "the old Garfield feelings," and ex-Governor Foster declared that it would be "suicidal," although he retracted his strictures on Arthur's Administration and said finally that Arthur would be "a very weak candidate in Ohio." [1] It was abundantly clear that whatever Arthur's political superiority to Blaine might be in New York, it would be fully counterbalanced by antagonism in Ohio, where his followers were business men, not the larger rural population.

On March 6, 1884, Miss Susan B. Anthony and about one hundred delegates from a woman's suffrage convention called upon President Arthur. He received them cordially. The formalities over, Miss Anthony launched into a brief speech in the course of which she told him that if he wished to be President for four more years, he would be much surer of success if, on this occasion, he pledged himself to include in his next inaugural address a recommendation for an amendment to the Constitution granting women the vote. Arthur was rather "nonplussed," but responded with the prudent remark that, "as the ladies were earnest and determined, they would secure what they ought to have."

"Ought not women to have full equality and political rights?" Miss Anthony promptly countered.

[1] Cincinnati *Enquirer,* Jan. 28, Feb. 3, 1884.

"We should probably differ on the details of that question," said Arthur.

After some conversation on other topics, the women withdrew, meeting on the stairs another presidential aspirant, Governor Ben Butler of Massachusetts. Smiling broadly, he said, "significantly,"—"Ladies, I hope to see you here again soon." [1]

In the main, Arthur's strength in New York rested upon the support of business men, to whom his conservative and sensible Administration had been pleasing. On May 20, in response to a call by a numerous group of New York men of business, a mass meeting assembled in Cooper Union to demand his nomination and to demonstrate his popularity. Sherman had written to Foraker that the call was "largely signed by my personal friends," that he had had a "very encouraging" conversation with William M. Evarts, and that the New York Arthur movement was intended more as an anti-Blaine maneuver than as an Arthur procession. [2] Nevertheless, on the hot evening when the meeting came to order, the auditorium was packed, the enthusiasm strong, and the speeches ardent in Arthur's praise.

The speakers were selected to represent all wings of the Republican Party in the State. Benjamin H. Bristow, whom the reform element had favored in 1876, praised Arthur's accomplishments in the field of civil service reform, while from the platform a telegram was read from Dorman B. Eaton, civil service commissioner and reform leader, saying:

President Arthur has done everything the commission has asked him to do in aid of civil service reform, which is vastly indebted to his firm and decided stand in its favor for the success it has achieved during the past year.

Regular Republicanism was represented by Edwards Pierrepont; the Independents, by Parke Godwin; and Republicanism supposedly discriminating, but actually purely regular, by Henry Ward Beecher. J. H. Herrick, president of the New York Produce Exchange and William A. Gellatly, another business man, spoke for their type of New York voter, emphasizing that the mass meeting was no assembly of "political hacks" but rather, of men engaged in commerce and manufacturing, to whom Arthur's financial policy and personal integrity

[1] Cincinnati *Enquirer,* Mar. 7, 1884.
[2] Sherman to Foraker, May 16, 1884, in Foraker, *Notes of a Busy Life,* Vol. I, p. 154.

were thoroughly pleasing. The mass meeting was unquestionably a success. Arthur's knowledge of politics had given him no very high estimate of the value of support among the business interests unless that support were paralleled by the more important assistance of the men "in politics." It may be doubted that the movement would have been of great avail under the best of circumstances; but within a few weeks, the brief but sharp panic of 1884 rendered it ineffective. Arthur's Administration could no longer present so appealing a record to business men.

Arthur's relations with Independent Republicans were not so friendly as Bristow's speech in his behalf might seem to indicate. From Philadelphia, Wayne MacVeagh wrote a sharp letter of rebuke to Bristow, a letter cleverly timed to appear in the papers on the day of the meeting and to attract the comment of editors in issues of the following day. MacVeagh suggested a list of Arthur's claims to the support of honest voters. Beginning with the malicious insinuation that "Guiteau was the original Arthur man," he described Arthur as a New York "machine politician," defiantly contemptuous of Hayes's civil service order, forced by Conkling upon the Chicago convention in 1880, brazenly sustaining Dorsey's use of "soap" in the Indiana elections, upholding Conkling and Platt against Garfield in the "Robertson affair," welcoming into his Cabinet William E. Chandler, a notorious spoilsman, allying himself with disreputable Southern politicians like Mahone in Virginia, Chalmers in Mississippi, and Strobach in Alabama, responsible for "the masterly campaign in New York only two years ago and for its brilliant ending," withholding appointments to vacancies in Pennsylvania, Delaware, and other States until trades for Arthur delegates could be completed, and maintaining throughout his Administration his association with New York "henchmen," of whom several were mentioned by name. The letter was vitriolic! Blaine's friends hastened to interpret it as a clear sign that Arthur would require a campaign fully as "defensive" as would Blaine.[1] Among the staff of *Harper's Weekly*, the Independent Republican periodical, there was a division, some favoring Arthur; others, Edmunds. It did not seem likely, therefore, that the New York Independents, in order to prevent the nomination of Blaine, would be willing to swallow their objections to Arthur.

[1] N. Y. *Tribune*, May 20, 21, 1884.

At the same time that Arthur was being attacked as a spoilsman by MacVeagh and George William Curtis, another line of opposition—shrewdly designed to undermine his strength in New York in a way to yield Democratic advantage if he were nominated, but perhaps also calculated to advance the fortunes of Blaine in the pre-convention contest—was that taken by the New York *World*. Its columns first listed the cooks, valet, barber, stablemen, and other domestics ministering to Arthur's personal comfort and allegedly paid for at public expense rather than out of his private purse, or salary. This was the climax of a "cruel misrepresentation" which led "Uncle Joe" Cannon to assert that "Arthur was defeated by his trousers," by his undeserved reputation as a fop. Next, they printed a fac-simile of the coat-of-arms to be found on Arthur's carriages, insignia which, it was insisted, Arthur had taken from Sir Bernard Burke's book, *Landed Gentry,* and which was there attributed to the Arthurs of Glanomera, County Clare, Ireland, with whom he could not possibly have had any connection. They labeled it "a shoddy coat-of-arms."

The same journal scored a further point by turning to the Reverend William Arthur's book on *Family Names* to consult his derivation of the name of Arthur. They found that he attributed it to British origins, thus revealing, according to the reporter, the family's shame of Irish associations. Finally, after pointing out that Arthur's father had been a Baptist clergyman, they quoted George Bancroft's history to the effect that the Baptists were more consistent than Martin Luther in applying "the doctrines of the Reformation to the social positions of life." [1] This last assault was skillfully aimed at Arthur's connections with Irish-Americans, one of his assets as a New York City "boss." Blaine's Roman Catholic mother and his well-known anti-British views, establishing his right to Irish-American support, remained on the other hand to strengthen his "availability."

* * *

As an aftermath of the unit-rule struggle in the Republican convention of 1880, a change in the scheme of representation was adopted by

[1] Albany *Argus,* May 19, 1884, citing N. Y. *World,* n.d.; N. Y. *World,* May 25, 1884.

the Republican national committee in 1883. Definite district, rather than general State representation was arranged for and the basic principle of the unit-rule thus discarded, but the committee would not go further and adopt the proposal that the number of district delegates be proportionate to the number of Republican votes in the last preceding election. Twice, by a small majority, they declined to accept a new arrangement certain to cut down the number of Southern Republican delegates. William E. Chandler was the chairman of the sub-committee who reported one of these plans, and when that had been rejected in January, 1883, he was one of the minority favoring an alternative project again in December. In view of the fact that Arthur's support in 1884 came largely from the Southern States where presidential patronage easily controlled the delegates, it is a matter of interest that Arthur's leading manager should have twice been thwarted in efforts to diminish those Southern contingents.[1]

The Republican national convention of 1884 assembled at Chicago on June 3. For over two weeks, delegates and politicians had been gathering, with rumors and flags flying, signs and banners everywhere, plumed hats, great badges, bands in brilliant uniforms—everything needed to provide that atmosphere of excited festivity with which party conventions perform their serious task. It was understood that sometime during this period William E. Chandler and Frank Hatton, the First Assistant Postmaster General, would arrive to open up headquarters in the Grand Pacific Hotel and to "engineer" the Arthur "boom." Chandler never came. Hatton of Iowa, George H. Sharpe and Elihu Root of New York, Benjamin Butterworth of Ohio, and O. D. Conger of Michigan were the custodians of Arthur's fortunes in the convention. They would have greatly benefited from Chandler's presence, which Arthur himself was probably unwilling to permit.

Arthur's supporters in the convention were the second largest group, about two hundred and eighty in all. Blaine had the greatest number, taken from a more widely scattered area than those of any other man, and about fifty more than Arthur. Although Blaine could rely upon all the small Maine delegation, he had prevented Arthur from obtaining the united support of the seventy-two from New York. There, the Half-Breed faction had been revived under the leadership not only of White-

[1] See correspondence between Chandler, J. M. Forbes, and John A. Martin in Chandler Papers.

law Reid and Collector Robertson but also of Thomas C. Platt, who was working toward the post from which Conkling had virtually been ousted, that of "boss" of the dominant machine, and who, having had small success with the Arthur Administration in his demands for patronage, and believing that Blaine's "turn had come," cast in his lot temporarily with his former opponents. His decision caused no small surprise and regret among Arthur's friends.[1] The bitterness of feeling between factions had made both readier to elect New York's delegates-at-large from an independent group led by Theodore Roosevelt and George William Curtis, than to risk adding strength to the enemy. Thus it came about that at Chicago, the New York delegation had as its chairman, Curtis, an Edmunds delegate, and numbered twelve for Edmunds, twenty-eight for Blaine, and thirty-two for Arthur.

Arthur's name was placed before the convention by one of the New York delegates, Martin I. Townsend of Troy. In the convention four years before, when Arthur's name was brought forward for the vice-presidential nomination, Stewart L. Woodford of New York had made a graceful and appealing speech. Now, when the stake was so much higher, the speech in Arthur's behalf was distinctly inferior, defensive in its general argument, ineffective in its delivery, and unworthy of its objective. Its most powerful claim for Arthur was that, during his Presidency, he had so far dismissed thoughts of factional advantage that Robertson could safely appear at the convention as a Blaine leader, and Platt, of the old machine, be present to argue that Arthur no longer had machine support. Twice the speech was punctured by hisses, and at its conclusion the ovation was brief. Arthur's seconding speeches were stronger. The spectacular "plumed knight" speech of Robert Ingersoll in the Republican convention of 1876 had emphasized the importance of convention oratory, which in 1880 had been dominated by Conkling and Garfield. Although John D. Long and Joseph B. Foraker made able speeches in 1884, the average of 1880 was probably not upheld, and for this decline, Townsend was largely responsible.

Blaine's advantage over Arthur was shown as the convention organized, but at the same time it became apparent that he did not control a majority of the delegates. When, for example, the temporary chairman was chosen, the first roll call revealed a contest between the Blaine and

[1] Gresham, *op. cit.*, Vol. II, p. 501.

anti-Blaine delegates, the one supporting Powell Clayton of Arkansas; the other, the Negro Congressman, John R. Lynch of Alabama, who was nominated from the floor by Lodge. The vote was 424 to 384 in favor of Lynch, showing that the Arthur, Edmunds, Logan, and Sherman groups must combine quickly if Blaine were to be defeated. As Arthur's vote on the first ballot was 278, while Edmunds, next largest, had 93, Arthur obviously offered the safest alternative to the choice of Blaine. But his managers could win no votes from the Independents.

Edmunds was a man of great worth, a constitutional lawyer whose usefulness in the Senate earned him the habitual deference of his colleagues in matters of constitutional interpretation. But he lacked winning personal qualities and possessed a tireless capacity for picking flaws and raising objections. It was said of him that, when approached by one who wished to procure his nomination for the Presidency, he flatly refused until someone slyly suggested that, as President, he would have an opportunity for many vetoes. His face brightened, we are told, and his objections were forgotten for the moment in the joyous prospect of being able, single-handed, to hold a congressional majority at bay.

Edmunds's followers were mostly from New England, led by Massachusetts, whose Republican chieftain was George F. Hoar. In January, 1883, Hoar had come up for reëlection to the Senate and, with the Administration's friends frankly opposed to him, had barely obtained it.[1] Hoar and Arthur had differed on two other matters of moment. The President had appointed Roland Worthington, a comparatively nonpolitical official, to be Collector of the Customs at Boston, thus offending the Senator by what he chose to call a partiality toward General Ben Butler. Arthur also had vetoed the river and harbor bill in 1882, thus causing Hoar to suffer in Massachusetts for his own espousal of it. Hoar's antagonism to Arthur was, therefore, deep rooted. On the other hand, Blaine was even less acceptable to the Senator than Arthur.

Edmunds's delegates who were practical rather than doctrinaire reformers, or who did not have irrevocable grudges, were ready to transfer their votes from him to one who might win. Those from Massachusetts were reported as ready to break for Arthur.[2] A large pro-

---

[1] James W. Clarke to W. E. Chandler, Dec. 1, 1882, Jan. 20, 1883, Chandler Papers.
[2] Edward R. Sinker to W. E. Chandler, June 7, 1884, Chandler Papers.

portion of the Independents, however, were committed to Edmunds's candidacy because he represented an uncompromising opposition to the "spoils system," which Arthur was known to approve within reasonable limits. These Independents were given the unpleasant alternative of renominating one who could not possibly satisfy them or of nominating a man whose record not only revealed him to be no reformer but probably an avaricious recipient of "graft" as well. Faced with this predicament, 41 voted for Edmunds to the end, apparently content to "stand by their principles" at the perfectly obvious cost of any chance to give them effect. In a sense, they were as guilty of the policy of "rule or ruin" as was the "boss" whom they had driven to cover in New York. If they could not have all, they would have nothing. As a matter of fact, they were to repudiate the nomination which they alone could have prevented, and quixotically to base their hopes of thorough civil service reform upon the first Democratic Administration to get control of Executive patronage in twenty-four years.

Next to the Edmunds delegates in number were those of John A. Logan, favorite son from Illinois. It had been rumored, as early as 1882, that Logan and Blaine had agreed to pool their strength at this convention, the weaker to accept second place, which for Logan would be the Vice Presidency; for Blaine, the Secretaryship of State. Logan and Arthur had ceased to be political friends; from Illinois the President could expect no aid unless his victory were otherwise assured or he could proffer a *quid pro quo*.

The Ohio delegation was not a unit for John Sherman on the first ballot, and thereafter many were restive under Foraker's lead, eager to jump to Blaine's column. After the third ballot, since his group had dwindled from 30 to 25, Sherman telegraphed his withdrawal, and cleared their way.

Arthur's vote was largest on the first ballot. From 278, it dropped to 276, and then to 274. When the fourth, and deciding, vote was taken, his supporters had fallen to 207, 150 of them from the South; Edmunds's to 41; and Blaine's had mounted from 375 to 541. It has been frequently stated that the tide ran irresistibly to Blaine, whose popularity was overwhelming; but, whether true or not, some Arthur men felt that the President's cause had been incompetently advanced. "The management of Mr. Arthur's canvass here was a botch from beginning to end," one of them wrote.[1]

Arthur himself seems to have accepted defeat cheerfully at that time, but to have allowed it to rankle later. From the White House, where he received the news with Lincoln, Chandler, Gresham, and Don Cameron, he promptly telegraphed a message to Blaine promising his "hearty support" and received an acknowledgment of this "cordial assurance." [2] A week later he was in New York, at the Fifth Avenue Hotel, and on the fourteenth, visiting at West Point with Secretary Lincoln.

Arthur was in good spirits, but giving no interviews. His friend and political associate, Colonel George C. Bliss, was, on the contrary, ready to talk to all inquiring reporters. New York State was not "a Republican State," he explained to one, and had been carried in 1880 only "by the skill with which the tariff issue was worked." In New York, Blaine's nomination had caused dissatisfaction but no complaints from those "known as the special friends and supporters of General Arthur." By attributing all Arthur's following at Chicago to patronage, the New York *Tribune*, Blaine's only supporter in the New York City press, was, Bliss said, offending all Stalwarts.[3] Every incentive to factionalism must be suppressed in the interests of November success.

The latent bitterness between Republican groups in the crucial State was stirred in September by the death of Secretary Folger. Arthur, cruising off the Rhode Island coast, on September 4 was informed that his colleague had died suddenly in Geneva, N. Y. A special train brought him from New York City to Geneva, where several of his Cabinet, Governor Cleveland and his staff, and scores of other persons high in public life gathered for the obsequies, and quickly scattered.

Folger's adherents in the disastrous election of 1882 had been quietly reviving the talk that had followed it, talk in which Folger's defeat had been ascribed to the Half-Breeds' having followed Blaine's advice to withhold their support from the Administration's nominee. Early in August, 1884, Blaine had written Folger that he "had never intended to say or do anything to divert support from Judge Folger and had never heard it suggested that he had done so until after his

---

[1] Edmund N. Smith to Chandler, June 8, 1884, Chandler Papers.
[2] Blaine to Arthur (telegram), June 6, 1884, Arthur Papers.
[3] N. Y. *Herald*, June 14, 1884.

nomination for the Presidency," to which Folger answered that he had recently heard complaints but had invariably replied with advice to support "the Republican Party and its nominees." [1] Three weeks after Folger's death, Colonel Bliss endeavored to calm the rising anti-Blaine sentiments by publishing these excerpts.

Folger's closest friends were enraged at what they considered a false denial of Blaine's anti-Folger attitude in 1882 and of the Secretary's justifiable antagonism in return. Answers were published and the quarrel went on,[2] with Republican victory in New York dependent upon the votes of those who had so recently been maligned for adherence to Arthur and the Administration.

The vote of New York in 1884 was cast for Grover Cleveland by a small majority of little more than one thousand votes. For a few days the decision was in some doubt, but eventually the Republicans acknowledged defeat. "Cleveland's election fully conceded today. Great Scott!" wrote Chandler in his diary. Blaine and Logan took defeat more philosophically than some of their adherents. They are said to have first met after the election on a street in Washington, Blaine in a carriage, Logan on foot. As their eyes met, Blaine lifted his hat with dignity. "How are you, Burchard," Logan roared. Blaine flushed. Then both smiled cheerfully and shook hands.[3]

Other Republicans, bitter in defeat, began to discuss the reasons for failure, and everything pointed to the canvass in New York. Rev. Mr. Burchard's speech offending the Irish; the Delmonico dinner organized by Cyrus W. Field, with Jay Gould and other millionaires as hosts; and the secession of Republican voters into the Prohibition Party or the Mugwump ranks—all were charged with responsibility. From the closeness of the vote, it was believed that loyal support from the Stalwarts could have won the day, and it was later remarked that, while Roscoe Conkling openly opposed Blaine, and Folger's loyal followers paid back old scores, President Arthur had done nothing to overcome Stalwart "lukewarmness" or hostility when some slight exertion from him could have produced a victory.

[1] See in N. Y. *Tribune*, Sept. 23, 1884, a communication from George C. Bliss dated Sept. 22, and giving dates of these letters as Aug. 4 and 11.
[2] See N. Y. *Times*, Oct. 8, 1884; N. Y. *Tribune*, Oct. 18, 1884; N. Y. *World*, Oct. 18, 1884; George C. Bliss to James B. Butler, Oct. 9, 1884, Butler Papers (New York Public Library).
[3] Cincinnati *Enquirer*, Dec. 23, 1884.

Chapter XXIV   *Reciprocity, Nicaraguan Canal, and*
                                        Conservatism

PRESIDENT ARTHUR'S conservative course in matters of internal policy, especially in fields of Republican factional concern, was thoroughly sensible in view of the political turbulence attending his advance to the Presidency. In the field of foreign relations, however, his Administration departed from traditionalism. Dropping the bold policy of Secretary Blaine in the War of the Pacific, and postponing indefinitely the Congress of American States which he had summoned, Arthur instead undertook innovations in the form of treaties for commercial reciprocity and for securing a Nicaraguan canal.

At the opening of Arthur's Administration, the era of free trade had definitely passed. Tax necessities of the Civil War had caused the erection in the United States of a protective wall which thereafter defied assault; at the same time, in Europe, the Franco-Prussian War had fostered a high-tariff tendency which in the eighties was well established. In fact, European governments were already resorting to special agreements to obtain limited freedom of trade by exchanging commercial favors. Reciprocity treaties were the means most widely approved in Europe during Arthur's Presidency for developing export trade.

Arthur turned to reciprocity treaties both because of the government's over-abundance of revenues and because of a new conception of the country's economic interests. The time had come when, in manufactures as well as in agricultural produce, the country was capable of an output beyond its own desires, a surplus which must be disposed of abroad. He believed that, instead of simply "protecting" our domestic market while letting our surplus production shift for itself abroad, encouragement should be afforded to foreign trade even at some hazard to the existing blanket advantage at home. To facilitate our prosperity, the Federal government must, he thought, follow the example of European countries and exchange favors with potential neighboring markets.

Reciprocity had previously been attempted by the United States. With Canada, an exchange of both agricultural and manufactured products had continued under treaty from 1854 to 1866, when it was terminated for reasons largely political, rather than economic. With

the Hawaiian Islands, a treaty negotiated in 1875 was in force throughout Arthur's term, although continued after 1883 on a somewhat
changed footing, again for reasons primarily political, rather than
economic. The policy which Arthur undertook to foster was derived
from considerations purely of economic advantage and, as such, met
with difficulties which he may not have foreseen. It was applied to our
immediate neighbors at the south, Mexico and the West Indies.

At the time when Congress was debating the tariff bill of 1883, the
United States and Mexico were negotiating a new treaty of commerce.
An appropriation to cover the expenses of negotiation had been passed
in the preceding session, and on January 15, Ulysses S. Grant and
William H. Trescot commenced meetings at the Department of State
with two representatives of the government of Mexico. Five days later,
all four signed an agreement for reciprocal admission, free of duty, of
a considerable variety of each other's produce. By granting free entry
to twenty-eight Mexican articles, upon which less than $90,000 duty
was normally collected, the United States obtained permission to export into Mexico, without either tariff at the border or vexatious transit
taxes within, seventy-three articles, on many of which the average
previous levy had been very high. Of the American articles, manufactures made up most of the list, while of the Mexican, the two most important were tobacco and sugar. The treaty went to the Senate in
February; its terms ceased to be secret after February 19; but more
than a year passed before ratification was voted.[1]

Meanwhile, conversations had been going on for at least a year between the governments of the United States and Spain concerning
improvement of trade relations between the Spanish West Indies and
this country. Immediately after publication of the Mexican treaty,
John W. Foster, former Minister to Mexico and to Russia, was summoned to the White House by Arthur and commissioned to conclude a
similar agreement with Spain. For about a year and a half, Foster
negotiated at Madrid with successive Spanish governments. He first
procured abolition of the extra taxes upon our exports to the Spanish
West Indies. Finally, on November 18, 1884, he obtained signatures
to a general treaty of trade-reciprocity, and hastened with it to Washington. He reached the capital on December 8; two days later the

[1] Mar. 11, 1884; *Exec. Journal of the Senate,* Vol. XXIV, pp. 209–12.

President communicated the agreement to the Senate.[1] But the entire text of the document had already been cabled from Spain—where an enterprising reporter had obtained it by bribing a Spanish official—and had been published by a New York newspaper before the Senate received it. It was one of several inauspicious happenings.

The British government watched closely the development of Arthur's reciprocity program. It was well understood that British sugar planters would be ruined if their competitors obtained a privileged access to the United States market while they did not. At some pain to its free trade scruples, the Gladstone government opened treaty negotiations in Washington in November, 1884, for the defense of British West India sugar interests. Their overtures were welcomed.

It was soon apparent that the Arthur Administration wished to obtain for American manufacturers an opportunity to enter the British West Indies on terms of equality with those from England, and that in return for this privilege, which Earl Granville and his advisers in the Foreign Office were indisposed to grant, the United States would concede to the products of the British West Indies favors greater than they had sought. In addition to this conflict, which might have been reconciled, another arose which was to prove incapable of adjustment. All the Arthur treaties were conceived of as special bargains for the exclusive benefit of the producers and carriers of the two contracting countries. Great Britain was unwilling to violate other, earlier, treaty obligations by which she had guaranteed equal privileges in the carrying trade to non-British vessels. She was unwilling also, to enter an agreement which should cease to be binding whenever any favors granted in it should be extended to a third party. It seemed a basis altogether too unstable on which to support the development, or continuance, of British sugar interests.[2]

Although a reciprocity treaty with the Dominican Republic was concluded on December 4, 1884, the British government moved with great deliberation. While the last months of Arthur's Administration were passing, the new treaties met strong obstacles in Congress, and it seemed possible that, after all, no treaty would be necessary to protect the British planters.

[1] *Exec. Journal of the Senate,* Vol. XXIV, p. 380.
[2] *Parliamentary Papers,* Commercial No. 4 (1884).

During Foster's absence in Spain, debate on the Mexican reciprocity treaty had eventually culminated in its ratification.[1] An amendment had been attached, however, to silence Constitutional objections that it was a tax measure enacted without participation by the House; it was to go into effect only after appropriate legislation by Congress. Such legislation was unlikely in the last session of Arthur's term, for when he had identified himself with reciprocity, his Republican rivals found that enough reason for opposing it, and when he had been repudiated at Chicago and his party defeated before the country, both his rivals and the opposing party lost interest. The Mexican treaty was never proclaimed in force; the Spanish and Dominican treaties were never ratified; no British treaty was ever even signed.

Arthur's policy was an alternative to strictly high or strictly low tariff legislation. Several events showed that during his term the two parties were moving toward clear opposition on the subject, that the Democrats were to adopt a low-tariff stand; the Republicans, to advocate high protection, and that party minorities on this question would be obliged to accept the orthodox view. Arthur's reciprocity program was moderate, partaking of some of the aspects of both free trade and protection. It was not warmly welcomed in Republican circles. Blaine, for example, opposed all the treaties which Arthur's Administration put before the Senate.[2] Those Republicans who, as a limitation on protection, preferred reciprocity to a generally low tariff always found it possible to object to the particular terms of any agreement, usually on the score that they were unfair to the United States. Thus the treaty with Mexico was declared to be entirely different from that with Spain. The former opened up a market of 10,000,000 persons to American production at a cost of approximately $90,000 in remitted duties; the latter required the sacrifice of many millions a year in revenue on sugar and tobacco imports, without benefit to the consumer and simply in order to obtain a market for the wants of not over 2,000,000 Spanish colonists.[3]

Foster's treaty had nevertheless fulfilled the instructions under which he acted, and presumably represented Arthur's idea of an appropriate means to develop American export trade. While it was being negotiated, he sent a "Central and South American Commission" into Latin-

[1] *Exec. Journal of the Senate*, Vol. XXIV, pp. 210–11 (Mar. 11, 1884).
[2] John W. Foster, *Diplomatic Memoirs*, Vol. II, p. 2.
[3] N. Y. *Tribune*, Dec. 26, 1884.

America to ascertain the best mode of improving economic relations with independent countries there. Reciprocity treaties were one of the means they recommended, but they found that the South American products to be admitted free were hides, already so admitted; sugar, which would eventually compete with our own; and wool, which was a highly protected, well established, domestic interest with a powerful lobby. To develop markets for American manufacturers by reciprocity, it appeared, would necessitate the "sacrifice" of certain agricultural interests. The commission's report went to the Senate on February 12, 1885, supplementing another analysis of the foreign trade of Central and South America, prepared by herculean efforts in the Department of State.[1] Neither produced any action.

When President Cleveland came into office, he promptly withdrew from the Senate the pending treaties with Spain and Santo Domingo and did not again submit them. At the same time, and in the same manner, he recalled an unratified treaty on a different subject between the United States and Nicaragua.

When Arthur became President, the Isthmus of Panama was the scene of a new promising effort to construct an interoceanic canal under the guidance of Ferdinand de Lesseps, engineer of the Suez Canal. Political control of the future canal was a subject of vital interest to the United States. The French government disavowed any intention to exercise special influence through the construction company, but the United States was primarily concerned not merely to prevent the special influence of others but to establish her own. The principal obstacle was an "entangling alliance" with Great Britain, the Clayton-Bulwer treaty of 1850, by the terms of which the two countries were pledged to joint action in fostering construction, and in neutralizing political control, of any means of interoceanic transport across Central America.

In 1850, when a canal had seemed desirable but remote, and when the capital for its construction would necessarily have come from Great Britain, whose power, moreover, seemed to be growing in Central America, that treaty had not seemed inequitable. In 1881, however, the United States was determined to obtain sole and exclusive political supervision of De Lesseps's completed project. Blaine and

[1] The report from the Department of State is 48th Cong., 2nd sess., *Senate Exec. Doc. No. 39.* That from the commission is in several parts. See 48th Cong., 2nd sess., *House Exec. Doc. No. 226* and 49th Cong., 1st sess., *House Exec. Doc. No. 50.*

Frelinghuysen took up a rather fruitless correspondence with the British Foreign Office, the object of which was to end the treaty's restraints, to obtain acknowledgment of American freedom to maintain the Monroe Doctrine. The exchange of notes produced stalemate.

While the Panama tidewater canal progressed deliberately, two other projects for isthmian transit were in the stage of promotion, and both were suppliants for Federal aid. One was a "ship-railway" over Tehuantepec, the original scheme of James B. Eads, which would place seagoing vessels on a giant railroad and haul them from coast to coast. The other was an all-American lock canal across Nicaragua, for which a concession was granted in 1880, subject to the condition that a reliable American company start the work within two (later extended to four) years.

The Maritime Canal Company of Nicaragua organized, secured the favor of General Grant, and vainly urged Congress to guarantee financial aid. Next it sought, likewise unsuccessfully, to obtain from the Central American governments a joint guarantee of a three per cent. return upon a capital of $75,000,000. It then looked for private capital abroad, and finally from an American syndicate, but after a two-years' extension, the concession ended late in 1884, all efforts at private capitalization having been nullified by Grant & Ward's collapse.

Arthur had been interested in Grant's venture, and while he had little confidence in the execution of so vast a project by private means, he believed that in Nicaragua lay the answer to the country's need. If the Monroe Doctrine could be upheld only by armed force, if political control of the Panama Canal were otherwise to become international, then the United States government might itself build a canal in Nicaragua, and exercise, as the rights of a private owner, that exclusive control so necessary to her security and prestige. Such action would, of course, be a flat defiance of the Clayton-Bulwer treaty, from the restraints of which Great Britain had been explicitly declining to release the United States. The British government could be expected to protest at a deliberate violation of a binding agreement. On the other hand, a Nicaragua canal would serve the fundamental, national interest of the United States; and Great Britain, confronted by such insistent opposition, might recede from her objections, if otherwise properly induced. In 1884, therefore, Nicaraguan leaders were approached.

Rumors in the United States of the new negotiations were confirmed in June in a strange manner. A special appropriation of $250,000 "to meet expenses attendant upon execution of the Neutrality Act" was debated in secret in the Senate on June 10, and again, in open session of the House of Representatives, on July 5. Various explanations were offered, none of them authentic, but the general understanding seemed to be that the money would be used either to buy up the expiring Nicaragua concession and obtain its renewal, or to procure an independent concession after that should have lapsed, but in any case to promote the Administration's plans for a government-built canal across Nicaragua. The appropriation was refused by the House, but Frelinghuysen persevered in another direction.

Nicaragua was in a position to welcome overtures from the United States for, with vexing foreign and domestic troubles, she could only profit, it was thought, by an arrangement which would enlist American protection. After various preliminaries, in November, 1884, she sent Señor Joachim Zavala to negotiate directly with Secretary Frelinghuysen in Washington. On December 1, they signed a convention whose terms were a startling departure from conservative diplomacy.

A strip of land stretching across Nicaragua from sea to sea was to be ceded to the United States in fee simple as an exclusive right-of-way. In return for this, the United States was to loan her neighbor $4,000,000 for public improvements, to accept her as joint owner of the canal, and to pay over to her one third of the eventual net revenues. A virtual protectorate was anticipated in the obligation to guarantee and protect the integrity of Nicaragua's lawful territory. "A nation that can take so strong a position as this must have a powerful navy, and it must also be in readiness for military emergencies," warned the editor of the New York *Tribune*.[1]

This admonition was entirely warranted. The violation of an earlier agreement with Great Britain, the terms of which were still in force, was thoroughly rash and imprudent. Such a procedure for bringing a treaty to an end was ill-advised, inviting, as it did, charges of bad faith, and encouraging similar treatment by other countries of treaties which became burdensome upon them. Moreover, the United States was scarcely strong enough to defy Great Britain. Cleveland, in the Venezuela affair, was to take as strong an attitude and to succeed in

[1] Dec. 18, 1884.

inducing Great Britain to yield, but the military and moral position of the United States in that dispute was to be distinctly stronger than in these events of a decade earlier, while the concession he demanded of Great Britain was very much less important to her.

The rashness of Arthur's Nicaraguan treaty lay also in its relation to the Central American situation. The guarantee of Nicaraguan territorial sovereignty was certain to involve the United States in troublesome boundary disputes with Nicaragua's neighbors, and an arrangement with Costa Rica would at once become necessary in order to satisfy her claims to a portion of the proposed canal route. But such an undertaking was essential for any American-owned and American-controlled canal, and as a matter of necessity, the first Roosevelt Administration later made the same sort of promise to the infant state of Panama. The United States was at that time, on the other hand, in a well recognized position to enforce its decrees, while in 1885 it may be doubted that its threats alone could have proved sufficiently influential. Arthur's canal project would, therefore, have led us into the Caribbean policy of the next generation without the twentieth-century means of carrying it into effect.

As soon as the treaty had been signed, Arthur had a naval surveying party sent to Nicaragua to locate the route, and meanwhile submitted the agreement to the Senate on December 10.[1] Before the Senate had acted upon it, the treaty was published in full in the New York *Tribune* of December 18. It created a sensation. While debates were kept secret, a canvass of Senators showed a large number prepared to risk the trouble with Great Britain certain to result from ratification. In fact, when the vote on ratification was taken in executive session on January 29, it stood 32 to 23, in favor, showing that the change of five would mean success.[2] This vote was subsequently reconsidered, leaving final disposition pending. Although Nicaragua ratified the treaty, the United States Senate did not again act upon it during Arthur's Administration. Blaine and the incoming President were jointly responsible for its defeat. Cleveland withdrew it with the reciprocity treaties, and in his annual message explained his reasons for not sending it back.

It was, he said, an "entangling alliance" designed to sustain an exclusive control which was unjustifiable. Such a canal should be "a

---

[1] *Executive Journal of the Senate,* Vol. XXIV, pp. 377–80.
[2] *Ibid.,* Vol. XXIV, p. 453.

trust for mankind, to be removed from the chance of domination by any single power, . . . not a prize for warlike ambitions." Accordingly, while Cleveland was President, the two years allowed for ratification expired. By the time Senator Benjamin Harrison, who had favored ratification, succeeded him, it was too late.[1]

During Arthur's Administration, the United States maintained the old policies in diplomacy—political isolation from Europe, hegemony in this hemisphere, closer relationship to the other American countries, the preservation of the rights and responsibilities of neutral states. It made no advance in establishing its conviction, later more vigorously promoted, of the merits of pacifically settling international disputes. It did progress in that growing contact with the Orient which was to involve some political as well as much economic change. Isolation from Europe was transgressed in the innocuous forms of membership in the International Red Cross, recognition of the flag of the Congo, and participation in the Berlin conference of 1884 concerning the International Association of the Congo. The hue and cry raised at even these insignificant connections with European political organizations was out of all proportion to their importance, and showed the undiscriminating fear of some people in the United States that their naïve statesmen would be led beyond their depths by the guileful navigators of European statecraft.

To prevent the European governments from obtaining greater political influence in Central and South American countries, the United States was induced to agree to act as fiscal agent, without responsibility, for Venezuela in her relations with European debtors; it caused a project for arbitration of a dispute between two Central American governments before a European judge to be dropped; and it strove to force its way through the *cul-de-sac* of the Clayton-Bulwer treaty.

With three exceptions, the tone of foreign affairs in Arthur's Presidency was even and conservative. The first was Blaine's aggressiveness in the War of the Pacific and the International American Congress project, which was quickly changed by Frelinghuysen. The second was the venture into the field of reciprocity conventions, likewise unsuccessful. The extraordinary treaty with Nicaragua, in clear violation of our engagements with Great Britain, was the third. The striking

[1] M. W. Williams, *Anglo-American Isthmian Diplomacy*, p. 286; L. M. Keasbey, *The Nicaragua Canal and the Monroe Doctrine*, pp. 384–436; 47th Cong., 1st sess., *Senate Report No. 368;* Richardson, *Messages and Papers,* p. 327.

changes in policy shortly after Frelinghuysen succeeded Blaine suggest that Arthur followed, rather than guided, his Secretaries of State, but he seems to have been responsible for the reciprocity program, and perhaps for the Nicaraguan treaty of 1884, while in other fields, the course pursued was traditional. His Administration won no great diplomatic triumphs like Fish's Treaty of Washington or Roosevelt's victory in respect to Panama. Yet in the next quarter century, his program of commercial reciprocity won increasing favor, although it has not yet received a real test.

Uncle Sam (to Count Ferdinand de Lesseps) "Is that the kind of neutrality you are going to give *us* at Panama?"

THE CANAL SITUATION IN EGYPT

An American Man-of-War Firing a Salute to a Foreign Fleet (with Pea-Shooters).

AMERICAN NAVAL WEAKNESS

IN New York, one election follows another and politics knows no respite. No sooner was the presidential campaign of 1884 a matter of Republican regrets than the choice of a United States Senator by the incoming legislature became a matter of lively concern. Senator Warner Miller, Half-Breed leader, was to have a new colleague; Senator Lapham's term was running out. It was an opportunity to work toward unified strength or to maintain the separated strands of factional controversy, despite the recent defeat. The problem was to select a Republican candidate identified with the old Stalwarts but not distasteful to the old Half-Breeds.

At the time when Arthur had been nominated for the Vice Presidency, he had been ambitious for the Senatorship later taken by Platt. As his Presidency drew to a close, some of his old associates tried to revive his interest in the position from which Conkling had resigned, and, by presenting him as a candidate, to work toward that reorganization of the party which Whitelaw Reid had pictured in 1881, "with our fellows in and a united party, minus Conkling." [1]

Arthur must have been approached on the matter early in the fall, possibly before the end of the presidential campaign; he was reported by his friend, Congressman Henry G. Burleigh of Whitehall, N. Y., to be willing to serve as Senator but not to enter a contest for his party's nomination.[2] A group of party leaders, after a conference on December 3 in New York, went to consult Arthur on the subject at the White House. James D. Warren, chairman of the Republican state committee, George H. Sharpe, Stephen B. French, and others sought to persuade Arthur that he alone could restore a semblance of unity to the party, and that, if he remained steadfastly before the people as a candidate, after a while rivals would drop out.

As President, Arthur could not with dignity conduct a contest for a subordinate place. The object of his friends was therefore to eliminate the opposition of others. The Republican factions in New York realized, after 1884, that they needed new unity and new leadership; and it is

[1] Reid to Hay, n.d., in Cortissoz, *Reid,* Vol. II, p. 51.
[2] N. Y. *Tribune,* Dec. 1, 1884.

probable that a number of the leaders, including Senator Warner Miller, regarded with favor the movement to choose a compromise candidate for the Senatorship. It would be a step toward amalgamation. The selection of Arthur was, on the other hand, not the only solution of the problem.

During the autumn of 1884, Levi P. Morton had been in the United States on leave from his post as Minister to France. He had come giving assurance that he would "take no part in political discussions during the campaign," but he had exerted himself at Blaine's request to raise campaign funds. Before his return to Paris on November 19, "some influential friends" suggested that he would be a desirable compromise candidate, and on the very eve of his departure, in "a hasty and confidential conversation," Senator Miller promised his support.[1] Morton did not wish to oppose either Whitelaw Reid or Arthur but would gladly have been a candidate upon whom the friends of both men could unite. He left his canvass in Platt's care.

Soon after arriving in Paris, Morton received a cablegram from Platt in response to which he wrote: "As you made no reference to the candidacy of either President Arthur or Mr. Depew in your cablegram, I infer that they are both out of the field." By the middle of December, he received another message, which stated that Arthur was earnestly a candidate, but in writing to James D. Warren, he took the position that, "under the circumstances, I do not see how I can, at this late date, change my position, having already given the same discretionary authority to other friends that I gave to you more than a month ago." He delayed, as long as he dared, writing to Andrew S. Draper, but on January 9, 1885, less than a week before the caucus, said:

I have seen within the last few days an interview of December 18, republished in Paris—with Mr. Phillips, President Arthur's Secretary, in which he states, "The President is not a candidate, has not been, and will not be"; and if I felt at liberty, I could give the names of parties from whom I have received not only assurances to this effect, but also assurances to the effect that my withdrawal would not strengthen him if a candidate, which would, I think, not only satisfy you but all my old and valued friends. While I yield to none in respect for the President [I must] . . . leave you and all other

[1] Morton to Burleigh, Dec. 4, 1884 (from Paris), L. P. Morton Papers (N. Y. Public Library).

friends and party associates to act as they may think for the best interests of the party.

On the day before the caucus, he declined to cable to President Arthur, who was feeling "sore," to reassure him of friendship and to state that his own candidacy was the consequence of an understanding that Arthur would not run.[1]

Morton allowed himself to become a shield for the hostility of Arthur's irreconcilable enemies. Had the President's strength been sufficient, some of them would probably have yielded before the meeting of the Republican caucus, but two developments sustained their hopes: William M. Evarts appeared as a third aspirant, one whose candidacy was bound to cut into Arthur's following; moreover, on December 19, an attack was directed at Arthur which promised to reduce his support much further.

Charges of Arthur's indifference toward Blaine's election had been in circulation since the voting day, but on December 18, B. F. Jones of Pittsburgh, a chairman of the Republican national committee during the recent struggle, came to New York City and made the imputation direct and emphatic. In an interview published in the *Tribune* next day, he advocated Evarts for Senator as a man of sound tariff views and great oratorical abilities, surpassing in the latter field any of his rivals. Arthur, on the other hand, he pronounced an unacceptable person for Senator because, beside holding free trade views, he had not given "loyal support" to Blaine. He had been "ill," "engaged," or "not in" on the three occasions when Chairman Jones had tried to consult him; he had made no contribution to the national committee's expenses, nor had any of his Cabinet; and the only Administration speech made in Blaine's behalf was "Secretary Gresham's admirable address at the Wall Street business men's meeting."

This interview produced a sensation. It also brought forth two denials. Platt, ostentatiously saying nothing about Arthur or his Cabinet, denied at some length a minor charge of disloyalty to the party

---

[1] See letters of L. P. Morton as follows: to W. W. Phelps, December 4, 1884; to Henry D. Burleigh, Dec. 4, 1884; to Theodore Roosevelt, Dec. 4, 1884; to T. C. Platt, Dec. 4, 15, 1884, Jan. 9, 13, 15, 1885; to James D. Warren, Dec. 14, 1884; to Andrew S. Draper, Jan. 9, 1885; Robert McElroy, *Levi Parsons Morton*, pp. 159 ff. McElroy's account, p. 162, wrongly attributes Evarts's candidacy to "the Arthur faction" and seems not to recognize the significance of the Republican caucus.

made in the Jones interview. In the same issue of the newspaper, Secretary Chandler had an open letter declaring Jones's complaints "ungenerous and unjust" and Jones's participation in a New York Senatorial canvass "indecent." "I take occasion to assert from my own personal knowledge," he wrote, "that during the recent campaign neither the President nor any member of his Cabinet lacked desire for Republican success or failed to do all that was asked or could have been reasonably expected of him to accomplish." [1]

Arthur's behavior in the Blaine-Cleveland campaign at once became a subject of earnest discussion in political circles. It was stated that from the McElroy family alone, nine votes went to the Democratic candidate because Arthur had made no effort to prevent it.[2] By some, Jones's interview was upheld,[3] but others rushed to Arthur's defense. He had, they maintained, strictly observed the proprieties of his position; he had done as much for Blaine's election as he had for his own nomination, or was doing to promote his candidacy for the Senate; and he had fulfilled his promise to Blaine of "hearty support." [4]

It happened that Arthur's personal assistance in the campaign had consisted only in a consultation with the New York State Republican committee leaders, James D. Warren and Andrew Sloan Draper;[5] while he had not encouraged his own adherents to be disloyal to Blaine's candidacy, he had done nothing to help Blaine to which his friends could refer as a matter of common knowledge. His conception of dignified conduct at this juncture precluded the publication of confidential or unknown participation in the campaign, especially any facts whose appearance after Jones's charges could be described by his enemies as a "defense." It was a cruel situation.

The Jones interview was not spontaneous and unpremeditated. It bore every appearance of a carefully planned maneuver, and was described as such by one of Chandler's correspondents.[6] It did not matter that William A. Wheeler, Thomas Murphy, Stephen B. French, and other friends of President Arthur had been zealous for Republican success.[7] Jones's confirmation of previous rumor rendered Arthur's

[1] N. Y. *Tribune*, Dec. 20, 1884.
[2] *Ibid.*, Dec. 20, 1884, anonymous interview.
[3] See letter signed "Westchester" in N. Y. *Tribune*, Dec. 22, 1884, and another signed "Pennsylvania Republicans," *Ibid.*, Dec. 26, 1884.
[4] Rochester *Morning Herald*, Jan. 3, 1885.
[5] N. Y. *Times*, Nov. 28, 1886.
[6] C. W. Tyson to Chandler, Dec. 20, 26, 1884, Chandler Papers.
[7] S. S. Smoot to Chandler, Dec. 22, 1884, Chandler Papers.

popularity in New York less than ever, especially among the "Half-Breeds."

During the argument over Arthur's fitness for the Senatorship, the high tariff element in the Republican Party was turned against him by assaults against his reciprocity program and his recent appointment of the "free-trader," Hugh McCulloch, to be Secretary of the Treasury for the remainder of his term. The protectionist views of his rivals, Evarts and Morton, were unquestioned. Moreover, the number of newspaper letters praising Evarts attested that gentleman's popularity with the voters and, inasmuch as he fitted into no factional machine, made the politicians readier to support him. In the Albany *Evening Journal,* three days after the appearance of the Jones interview, a letter from Evarts formally announced his desire for the place and asserted his claims to be regarded as a sound and steadfast Republican.

On January 3, 1885, Arthur indicated that he would not permit his name to go before the caucus. The conditions upon which he had consented to help strengthen party unity had not been met. Evarts was as much a compromise candidate as anyone who could have been put forward, and those who had been urging Arthur's election went over in large numbers to his following, although a considerable proportion preferred Levi P. Morton. Minor candidates withdrew before the caucus, and on January 19, Evarts greatly outdistanced Morton, receiving, next day, final election in the Legislature.[1]

The Senatorial election of 1885 showed that the Republicans of New York were still rather hopelessly divided. The factions had fought bitterly among themselves for the prize. Yet the old lines were frequently crossed, demonstrating how completely the Arthur Administration had failed to reëstablish or replace the defunct Conkling machine. Those who, because of hostility to Arthur, put Morton forward to restore party solidarity were Platt, Cornell, and Payn. All were ex-members of the old Conkling-Arthur machine. They were the men whom Arthur had opposed in 1882, when Folger was nominated in spite of them. On the other hand, a leading member of the pro-Blaine faction, Warner Miller, seems not to have taken any strong part in opposition to Arthur, while those who strongly favored him were his

[1] H. E. Ellis, Morton's private secretary, to T. C. Platt, Jan. 21, 1885, Morton Papers, enclosed cheque for nearly $15,000 for "expenses . . . incurred in his behalf." See also, Brainerd Dyer, *The Public Career of William M. Evarts,* pp. 248–50, for an account of this election.

old friend, George H. Sharpe, and the younger men whose advance he had encouraged, James D. Warren, Andrew S. Draper, and the like. As the event proved, Evarts's victory, while satisfying some of the Mugwumps, simply deferred the day of organized Republican strength. During the lean years of Democratic sway, Platt was to prepare himself for the time when, like Conkling, he should manage the party through an efficient and disciplined machine of which he was the "boss."

One may well doubt that Arthur was eager to serve a term in the Senate for other than party reasons, for he was not a well man; but, even had he been indifferent, the manner in which his candidacy was swept aside must have been exasperating to him. The political code of his times, to which he had adhered persistently, enshrined "regularity" among the cardinal virtues. After a life of devotion to his party, to be publicly attacked as disloyal, as responsible for his party's first major disaster in twenty-four years, and to be unable to crush his accusers, brought bitterness indeed. The imputation that he had placed party interests below his own personal pique was a thrust at a vital spot. Following as it did his vain attempt to gain the Republican nomination for President, in which he had been branded as "the candidate of the officeholders and the office seekers," [1] it impressed him with the futility of altruistic striving. As his Administration drew to a close, he revealed more and more that he considered his presidential struggles to be unappreciated by the party which he could so easily have wrecked, and which, with such difficulty, he had held together and strengthened. He had sacrificed friends and health in the effort and, with old age and debility approaching, he found his labors rewarded by enmities and ingratitude. During his last months in office, he grew despondent.

The United States places a cruel burden upon its Presidents, requiring them not merely to lead parties, manage Congresses, and assume responsibility for the appointment of innumerable men to positions of serious trust, but, in addition, to participate formally in an endless series of ceremonial occasions. The appearance of the President in group photographs had not reached its present-day absurd proportions, nor even been thought of, in Arthur's time. But he laid cornerstones, received statues, pulled silk cords, and, something entirely

1 Hay to Morton, Jan. 19, 1884, in McElroy, *Morton,* p. 155.

new in his day, pushed buttons to satisfy the requirement that the President participate in public ceremonies.

In December, 1884, the World's Industrial and Cotton Centennial Exposition at New Orleans, to which the United States government had loaned a million dollars, was obliged to open, despite the fact that the construction of all its units had not been completed. Arthur could not go to New Orleans, but he was "invited in a novel way to open the New Orleans Exposition. The plan [as it was then outlined], is to clear one of the Western Union wires and attach one end to the motive power of the machinery in the exposition. The other end will be connected with the White House, and at a fixed moment, everything being in readiness in New Orleans, the President, surrounded by his Cabinet, will press a button in the Executive Mansion and instantaneously set the vast machinery . . . in motion." [1]

On December 16, 1884, a large crowd of invited guests assembled in the East Room at one o'clock, prepared to observe an unprecedented occurrence. They stood for one hour. At two o'clock, President Arthur came in and, smiling broadly, stood with his companions beside a small table while awaiting word that in New Orleans, at a parallel assembly, all was in readiness. An hour passed, during which the smile departed and the President grew impatient. At last the signal came and he spoke briefly.

. . . In the presence of the assembled representatives of the friendly nations of the world, of the President of the Senate, of the Speaker of the House of Representatives, the Chief Justice and Associate Justices of the Supreme Court, of a Committee from each House of Congress and of the Members of my Cabinet, I again, and in their name, congratulate the promoters of the Exposition upon the auspicious inauguration of an enterprise which promises such far-reaching results. With my best wishes for the fulfillment of all its great purposes, I now declare that the World's Industrial and Cotton Centennial Exposition is open.

The button was pressed. In New Orleans, under a warm and brilliant sun, with the city in gala array, the crowds observed with delight the effect of Arthur's gesture. In the White House, it was witnessed with relief. Few realized the fact that, instead of saving our Presidents much time in travel, this precedent was to lead to even greater demands upon their time for the simple task of button-pushing.

Four days later, Arthur, Chandler, and a small crowd shivered

[1] Cincinnati *Enquirer*, Dec. 11, 1884.

through the exercises at Dupont Circle at the unveiling of the statue of Admiral Dupont, while Senator Thomas F. Bayard of Delaware, gave the principal speech.

Another ceremonial occasion of greater note was the dedication, on February 22, 1885, of the Washington monument. Its cornerstone had been laid on July 4, 1848, at a time when the country was taking up the great struggle between the sections following the Mexican War. After partial construction, funds ran out, and the unfinished shaft stood stark and ugly through the war by which alone the sectional conflict could be settled. In 1876, Congress provided for renewed efforts which pushed the monument slowly upward, so that, on December 6, 1884, the capstone could be put in place. The formal presentation to the United States was deferred until the next Washington's Birthday.

A clear, cold day, with a keen wind, and with snow covering the ground, provided the setting for the dedication events. At the base of the monument, fitting ceremonies had been arranged. After various preliminaries, the engineer in charge of construction, Colonel Thomas L. Casey, delivered the structure to President Arthur, whose speech, short and to the point, was a tribute to Washington. From the monument, a procession marshaled by General Sheridan moved to the Capitol. President Arthur was escorted by the convivial Ancient and Honorable Artillery Company of Massachusetts, chartered in 1638. In the hall of the House of Representatives, Governor John D. Long of Massachusetts read a speech for Robert C. Winthrop, orator on the occasion in 1848 when the cornerstone had been laid; from Washington's own State, Governor John W. Daniel followed with the last speech of the day. That evening, Arthur gave a reception to the appreciative Artillery. In a little over a week, he was to retire from office.

*   *   *

If inauguration day belongs to the incoming President, he who leaves the White House owns the one before it. It was dawn when Arthur retired at the end of his day, having been busily engaged with a long Cabinet meeting until two o'clock, then by many farewell calls, bills to sign, official correspondence to conclude, and the problem of withdrawing his personal effects. He snatched but a brief sleep before rising at eight o'clock for the last details. His own belongings, in great cases, were packed to go to his house at 123 Lexington Avenue. He

Courtesy L. C. Handy Studios, Washington, D. C.

THE INAUGURATION OF PRESIDENT CLEVELAND

ordered a suitable luncheon to be ready immediately after the inaugural ceremonies. Then, with his usual circumspection, he arrayed himself for the last hours of his Administration.

At ten o'clock, the other participants began arriving. Vice President-elect Thomas A. Hendricks was the first, escorted by Senator Hawley, and some time later, accompanied by Senators Sherman and Ransom, came Grover Cleveland. The President-elect was a great, burly man, on whom a tall silk hat looked small, with few claims to beauty of appearance but clear indications of that force of mind and will on which his character was based. Beside him, President Arthur towered in height, his color, whiskers, and carriage in sharp contrast to the bald ruggedness of his visitor. A little later they started for the Capitol, through the great crowds along the avenue. Arthur went to the President's room, signed the last measures, including the bill for the relief of General Grant, and then the ceremonies began. It was considerably after noon when Arthur returned, shook hands with each of the White House staff, and then, through a cheering crowd, drove off with Frelinghuysen to the latter's house. After a few more days, he left Washington never to return.

Most newspapers were friendly to Arthur at the time of his retirement. Taking account of the state of the Union, they observed that the country was free from internal dissensions, at peace with the world, its public debt much reduced, its treasury overflowing. "We can wish . . . Cleveland no better fortune," said one, "than that when he retires from office he will bear with him the respect and esteem of the people as fully and unreservedly as President Arthur does today." In New York, the *Tribune*, nursing its discomfiture over Blaine's defeat, pronounced his Administration "not a success"—first, for having failed to add to prosperity or prevent economic disaster, and again, for having been the cause of the Democratic victory of 1884. "Failure is not always fault," it continued, "but it will be the judgment of the historian that his scanty measure of success was due in part to favoring circumstances, as well as to creditable and patriotic aims, while his ill-success was due to vital differences of opinion between himself and the majority of the party upon which he depended for support." Except for such inconsolables among the Blaine element, most critics were friendly, and historians have reached a higher estimate of Arthur's Administration than the *Tribune* prophesied.

IN New York, Arthur settled down at home and tried to resume the practice of law with his old partners, S. W. Knevals and R. S. Ransom. He had never been entirely well since his Florida trip, and now, relieved of responsibility and the pressure of work, he expected to improve. To his dismay, he began to fail. The recurrent nervous indigestion for which he had been treated by his doctor during the past two years failed to subside, while a general relaxation of strength and energy became chronic. A trip to the Berkshires did no good and at Christmas time his spirits were better than his health. He spent the better part of the day at the home of his nephew, Arthur Masten, then a young New York lawyer, and amused himself by reading with evident enjoyment some Christmas poetry to the family group.

He accepted the presidency of his college fraternity, Psi Upsilon, and of the reorganized New York Arcade Railway, precursor of the subway system. But when nearly a year had passed without the expected improvement, his doctor prescribed a strict retirement. It was too late. In February, 1886, Bright's disease was recognized, and shortly after that, a dangerous heart trouble. He drew his will, naming Charles E. Miller, Daniel G. Rollins, and Seth Barton French as executors.[1] Word of his condition got out; he was reported "at death's door . . . hopelessly ill," [2] yet somehow he survived.

Arthur spent the summer in New London in a vain quest for health, but, despite some improvement, protracted debility made him continually moody and depressed. In a brief period of cheerfulness, he discussed plans for a trip to the Restigouche fishing region for the next summer, believing that the climate and the sport would again build him up. Not long before his death, however, he said despondently to a friend: "After all, life is not worth living for, and I might as well give up the struggle for it now as at any other time, and submit to the inevitable." [3]

From time to time old friends called, and having been forced out

---

[1] Fac-simile in Arthur Papers, dated Mar. 8, 1886.
[2] Albany *Journal,* Mar. 13, 1886.
[3] Cincinnati *Enquirer,* Nov. 19, 1886.

of active public life he experienced the more serene satisfactions of reminiscence. When the next election day came, since he could not go to the polls, it afforded him some consolation to be paired with his old companion, R. G. Dun. On November 13, he was so hopeful of recovery that he designated Augustus St. Gaudens to make a bust for the Senate wing of the Capitol, a decision pending since the preceding May. One of the happiest days of his illness was Tuesday, November 16. He reversed the program of his days for weeks past and, instead of spending most of his time in bed, arose, dressed, and chatted for a long time with two of his sisters about experiences of their childhood. At the end of the day, he retired in excellent spirits. He never awoke to full consciousness, for a cerebral hemorrhage occurred during the night, and in the morning he was partly paralyzed. The end of his life was a matter of hours.

Propped up in bed, as vitality slowly faded, he breathed out his life throughout the day in a quiet diminuendo of sighs. His face was set in a gentle smile of resignation. With the first gray light of the next morning, his breathing ceased.

His children and sisters were near at hand, but William Arthur was then at San Antonio, Texas. The funeral was set for November 22, a Monday, and, by the exercise of great persistence, was kept a private ceremony. Organizations of all sorts might pass resolutions, or, like the Union League Club, hold special memorial meetings; but no delegations were permitted to appear in the cortège or to engage in any other formal participation. The procession of 125 carriages between the Arthur house and the Church of the Heavenly Rest, the presence there of over a thousand people in a church seating many less, and the high position of the mourners at this service—including President Cleveland and members of his Cabinet, Arthur's Cabinet, ex-President Hayes, James G. Blaine, John and General Sherman, and a host of younger men of prominence—testified to Arthur's position. It had been feared by some that Roscoe Conkling would not attend; he was there in the pew immediately behind ex-Governor Cornell, and showed sincere grief. The family and bearers went on to Albany in the special train, and there, after receiving the formal attentions of the Governor and legislature, went to the Rural Cemetery, for services at his grave.

Chester A. Arthur was buried in the family lot in which his eldest son had been the first to lie. His mother, his father, and his wife had been buried there before him, and there, later, were to rest his daughter and three of his sisters. Eventually, a massive black marble sepulcher, over which broods a bronze angel of death, was placed at the grave of the twenty-first President of the United States. The visitor is impressed with its dignity and grace.

*　　*　　*

Time brought Arthur an obscurity in strange contrast to his significant part in American history. "Governments, like clocks, go from the motion that men give them," as William Penn so wisely wrote. Even when a certain momentum may carry them along, direction is given by the guiding minds of such political leaders as Arthur. It is true, of course, that many men, unimaginative or uninformed, attain a measure of political prominence by their reflection, in the political field, of the illuminating ideas of others before them, or of contemporaries dominant in business and professional life. As men of action, of a sort, such persons have their useful place beside the men of thought. If not the ultimate leaders, as political leaders they are the means of directing the government's sovereign power into whatever channels it takes. Arthur's prominence among them he owed to place rather than to great personal force. Had he not become a President he would have remained a minor character on the historical stage, but as President, he played an important rôle.

Arthur's Administration, with respect to party politics, fell in the transition from strictly Reconstruction questions to those brought forward by vast economic expansion. The major parties were making their way, somewhat reluctantly, to a new set of orthodox positions, and in the process, while avoiding internal schisms over "issues," were finding it impossible to escape factional alignments based upon personal groupings. His function was that of closing the breach in his own bitterly divided party and of attempting to create, in place of the anti-national, Democratic "solid South," an influential Republican opposition there. Although he failed at the South, his harmonizing policy preserved his party as a valuable instrument for reconciling conflicting ideas of public policy.

The foremost Unionist, John Marshall, would have approved his conservative attitudes toward property and the function of government. Toward currency, banking, bankruptcy, and taxation questions the President revealed an attitude governed by paramount considerations of "soundness" and justice. In private conversation, he even expressed to certain Supreme Court justices, his doubts that they had decided correctly in sustaining the power to issue greenbacks in time of peace. The old, established idea that the government's first duty is to preserve peace and order induced him to foster particularly a renovation of obsolete and inefficient arms of the national defense. He deserved praise for his sharp message vetoing an obnoxious rivers and harbors bill, and also for attempting, through the first general civil service law and the prosecution of "Star route" swindlers, to promote honesty and punish dishonesty in administration.

Closely identified with Unionist objectives was Arthur's zeal for an American-owned, American-controlled canal in Nicaragua. The other major effort of his diplomacy, his attempt to commit his party to a program of reciprocal trade concessions to other countries, necessarily involving some breaches in the tariff wall, proved to be premature. It was reserved, in part through Blaine's own opposition, for Blaine himself to undertake later.

If, in the drama of Arthur's Presidency the basic elements were badly mixed, the suspense lacking, the climax at the beginning, and all situations sedulously avoided, in his career as a whole, in the broad development of his character and personality, there is no lack of interest to the student of humanity. Arthur's character has been misunderstood. An estimate widely held might be expressed in a paraphrase of Penn's analogy—Arthur, like a clock, went from the motion imparted to him from without, being directed into higher channels only by the influence of friends and by the grave responsibilities of the Presidency. The supposed contrast between his New York and Washington life has even been seriously compared in degree to St. Paul's conversion. Nothing could be further from the truth.

Arthur came of a good family, was well educated, a man of literary and discriminating tastes, of excellent executive capacity, social gifts, and dignity. He was a gentleman. In New York City, he made a place for himself in circles unimpressed simply by political power. But he did have power, also, as the Republican "boss" of the metropolis, and wielded it with great skill for a decade in behalf of his party's fortunes. The seventies formed a period of sordid politics, with its "Tweed ring" and its "Grantism," its sectional hatred, its conversion of the high principle of Unionism into a cloak for the evil shifts of petty grafters. Amid such political life, the gentleman necessarily appeared incongruous.

Arthur could not associate intimately with "machine politics" as a lieutenant of Senator Roscoe Conkling and not be contaminated by its unsavory aspects. An entirely distinct code governed the action of the men "in politics." Arthur adopted it for his own political behavior but subject to three restraints: he remained to everyone a man of his word; he kept scrupulously free from corrupt graft; he maintained a personal dignity, affable and genial though he might be. These restraints and certain aristocratic tastes and interests distinguished him sharply from the stereotype of politician. The product of his compromises was a "gentleman-boss."

The shot which struck down Garfield brought Arthur into the glaring light of a persistent and unsympathetic publicity. A man with his characteristics was unique. The human mind, especially that of its journalistic exponents, thinks in terms of types. Arthur was fitted by the press into the mental frames devised for "pot-house politicians," "minister's sons," "New York swells," "epicures," and sometimes, "gentlemen," but the general opinion seemed to be that a reform was necessary if he were to be an acceptable President. The transformation was neither as great nor as necessary as it has been imagined.

New York machine politics may not have affected Arthur's character so injuriously as has been thought, but they could not have contributed more than a rudimentary intellectual training for a successful President of the United States. He was sufficiently unsure of himself in his first years to seek advice from all quarters and to act with such cautious circumspection that he seemed procrastinating. In the end, he proved satisfactory to all Republicans except several disappointed factional leaders and querulous, sentimental reformers. If he could not carry his party with him to a moderately protective tariff position, if he made other serious mistakes, he did, on the whole, fill a place of power and responsibility far above his aspirations, bravely and adequately, if not with greatness. He met the test of defeat and discouragement with sturdy resignation. Upon his whole career as a political leader and a gentleman, one must place a higher estimate than did Arthur himself.

*   *   *

More than a decade after his death, loyal friends were gratified by the unveiling in Madison Square of a full length bronze statue of Arthur, done for them by George E. Bissell, sculptor of the Washington monument in Wall Street which in 1883 Arthur had accepted for the government. An address was made by Elihu Root, who paid tribute to "the sweetness and gentleness of his disposition, the rich stores of his cultivated mind, the grace and charm of his courtesy, his grave and simple dignity, and his loyal and steadfast friendship"; Mrs. McElroy released the flag; and two hundred invited guests gazed upon the familiar figure. Characteristically, Arthur is shown with a book in his left hand, eyelglasses in his right, his expression that of quiet dignity and as if he were about to speak. With entire appropriateness, the statue looks out upon the site of the old Union League Club, the district most closely identified with New York Republican politics in his lifetime.

A year later, the Vermont legislature authorized the purchase of a shaft of Barre granite to be erected upon the site of Arthur's birthplace in that State. On the drizzling day when the monument was dedicated, all that remained of the place where the twenty-first President was born, seventy and more years before, was a cellar hole and a clump of willows, in a field of hay, on a lonely road, far from any village.

Select Bibliography

No biography of Chester A. Arthur can be founded upon an extensive collection of his personal papers. The Library of Congress holds some sixty-five letters addressed to him during his Presidency. His brother's papers contain a few letters written by him several years before. Autograph collectors share perhaps twenty-five more which have appeared at auctions. All others have disappeared. A biographer must rely upon the papers of political associates and opponents, such as John Sherman, James A. Garfield, Elihu Washburne, John Russell Young, William E. Chandler, and Walter Q. Gresham in the Library of Congress, James B. Butler and Levi P. Morton at the New York Public Library, and Rutherford B. Hayes, at Fremont, Ohio. Unpublished archives in Washington are fruitful in somewhat lesser degree. Among the published materials, the following are most important:

DIARIES, LETTERS, AND PUBLIC ADDRESSES

Arthur, C. A., in *Messages and Papers of the Presidents, 1789–1897*, James D. Richardson, editor, 10 vols. Washington, 1896–99. Vol. VIII, pp. 33–294.

Blaine, Mrs. James G., *The Letters of Mrs. James G. Blaine*, H. S. B. Beale, editor. 2 vols. New York, 1908.

Curtis, George William, *Orations and Addresses of George William Curtis*, Charles Eliot Norton, editor. 3 vols. New York, 1894.

Adams, Henry, *Letters of Henry Adams, 1858–1891*, Worthington C. Ford, editor. Boston, 1930.

Hayes, Rutherford B., *The Diary and Letters of Rutherford Burchard Hayes*, Charles R. Williams, editor. 5 vols. Columbus, Ohio, 1922–26.

Schurz, Carl, *Speeches, Correspondence, and Political Papers of Carl Schurz*, Frederic Bancroft, editor. 6 vols. New York, 1913.

MEMOIRS

Boutwell, George S., *Reminiscences of Sixty Years in Public Affairs*. 2 vols. New York, 1902.

Crook, William H., *Through Five Administrations. Reminiscences of Colonel William H. Crook, Body-guard to President Lincoln*. Compiled and edited by M. S. Gerry. New York, 1910.

——————, *Memories of the White House*. Compiled and edited by Henry

Rood. Boston, 1911.

Depew, Chauncey M., *My Memories of Eighty Years*. New York, 1922.

Foster, John W., *Diplomatic Memoirs*. 2 vols. Boston, 1909.

Hoar, George F., *Autobiography of Seventy Years*. 2 vols. New York, 1903.

Hudson, William C., *Random Recollections of an Old Political Reporter*. New York, 1911.

Johnson, Robert U., *Remembered Yesterdays*. Boston, 1923.

Logan, Mary S., *Reminiscences of a Soldier's Wife; An Autobiography*. New York, 1913.

McClure, Alexander K., *Colonel Alexander K. McClure's Recollections of Half a Century*. Salem, Mass., 1902.

——————, *Our Presidents and How We Make Them*. New York, 1902.

McCulloch, Hugh, *Men and Measures of Half a Century*. New York, 1888.

Pendel, Thomas F., *Thirty-Six Years in the White House*. Washington, 1902.

Platt, Thomas C., *The Autobiography of Thomas Collier Platt*. New York, 1910.

Poore, Benjamin, *Perley's Reminiscences of Sixty Years in the National Metropolis*. 2 vols. Philadelphia, 1886.

Sherman, John, *Recollections of Forty Years in the House, Senate, and Cabinet*. 2 vols. Chicago, 1895.

Stoddard, Henry L., *As I Knew Them: Presidents and Politics from Grant to Coolidge*. New York, 1927.

Wheeler, Everett P., *Sixty Years of American Life*. New York, 1917.

White, Andrew D., *Autobiography of Andrew Dickson White*. 2 vols. New York, 1905.

Wise, John S., *Recollections of Thirteen Presidents*. New York, 1906.

PAMPHLETS

Blaine, James G., *Foreign Policy of the Garfield Administration*. First published as an article in the *Chicago Weekly Magazine* of September 16, 1882.

Brown, Willard, *Civil Service Reform in the New York Custom-House*. New York, 1882.

Garfield and Arthur Campaign Songster. Cincinnati, 1880.

Gorham, George C., *Roscoe Conkling Vindicated. His Controversy with Mr. Blaine, 1866. His Resignation from the Senate*. New York, 1888.

Hurlbert, William H., *Meddling and Muddling, Mr. Blaine's Foreign Policy*. Privately printed in 1884.

Morgan, James, *America's Egypt*. New York, 1884.

Royall, William L., *The President's Relations with Senator Mahone and Repudiation. An Attempt to Subvert the Supreme Court of the United States*. New York, 1882.

Strobel, Edward H., *Mr. Blaine and His Foreign Policy*. Boston, 1884.

BIOGRAPHIES

Barnes, James A., *John G. Carlisle, Financial Statesman*. New York, 1931.

Bigelow, John, *The Life of Samuel J. Tilden*. 2 vols. New York, 1895.

Busbey, L. W., *Uncle Joe Cannon*. New York, 1927.

Conkling, Alfred R., *The Life and Letters of Roscoe Conkling, Orator, Statesman, Advocate*. New York, 1889.

Connelly, William E., *The Life of Preston B. Plumb, 1837–1891*. Chicago, 1913.

Cortissoz, Royal, *The Life of Whitelaw Reid*. 2 vols. New York, 1921.

Fuess, Claude M., *Carl Schurz, Reformer*. New York, 1932.

Godkin, Edwin L., *Life and Letters of Edwin Lawrence Godkin*, Rollo Ogden, editor. 2 vols. New York, 1907.

Gresham, Matilda, *Life of Walter Quintin Gresham, 1832–1895*. 2 vols. Chicago, 1919.

Hamilton, Gail (Mary Abigail Dodge), *Biography of James G. Blaine*. Norwich, Conn., 1895.

McElroy, Robert McNutt, *Grover Cleveland, the Man and the Statesman*. 2 vols. New York, 1923.

——————, *Levi Parsons Morton*. New York, 1930.

Nevins, Allan, *Grover Cleveland, a Study in Courage*. New York, 1932.

Paine, Albert B., *Thomas Nast; His Period and His Pictures*. New York, 1904.

Savidge, Eugene C., *Life of Benjamin Harris Brewster*. Philadelphia, 1891.

Smith, Theodore C., *The Life and Letters of James Abram Garfield*. 2 vols., New Haven, Conn., 1925.

Stanwood, Edward, *James Gillespie Blaine*. Boston, 1905.

Williams, Charles R., *The Life of Rutherford Burchard Hayes*. 2 vols. Boston, 1914.

SPECIAL SECONDARY WORKS

Alexander, DeAlva S., *A Political History of the State of New York*. 4 vols. New York, 1906–1923.

Bowers, Claude G., *The Tragic Era; the Revolution after Lincoln*. New York, 1929.

Colman, Edna M. H., *White House Gossip from Andrew Johnson to Calvin Coolidge*. New York, 1927.

Coolidge, Mary R., *Chinese Immigration*. New York, 1909.

Dallinger, Frederick W., *Nominations for Elective Office in the United States*. Vol. IV of *Harvard Historical Studies*. New York, 1897.

Eaton, Dorman B., *The Independent Movement in New York*. New York, 1880.

Fish, Carl R., *The Civil Service and the Patronage*. Vol. XI of *Harvard Historical Studies*. New York, 1905.

Glasson, William H., *Federal Military Pensions in the United States*. New York, 1918.

Gosnell, Harold F., *Boss Platt and His New York Machine*. Chicago, 1924.

Hepburn, A. Barton, *A History of the Currency in the United States*. Revised edition, New York, 1924.

Hovgaard, William, *Modern History of Warships*. London, 1920.

Keasbey, Lindley M., *The Nicaragua Canal and the Monroe Doctrine*. New York, 1896.

Latané, John H., *A History of American Foreign Policy*. New York, 1927.

Noyes, Alexander D., *Thirty Years of American Finance*. New York, 1898.

Pearson, Charles C., *The Readjuster Movement in Virginia*. New Haven, 1917.

Schlesinger, Arthur M., *The Rise of the City*. Vol. X of *A History of American Life*. New York, 1933.

Scott, William A., *The Repudiation of State Debts*. New York, 1903.

Shores, Venila, "The Hayes-Conkling Controversy" in *Smith College Studies in History*, Vol. IV, No. 4. July, 1919. Northampton, Mass.

Stanwood, Edward, *American Tariff Controversies in the Nineteenth Century*. 2 vols. Boston, 1903.

Stebbins, Homer A., *A Political History of the State of New York, 1865–1869*. No. 135 of *Columbia University Studies in History, Economics, and Public Law*, Vol. LV, No. 1 (1913).

Tarbell, Ida, *The Tariff in Our Times*. New York, 1911.

Taussig, F. W., *The Tariff History of the United States*. 6th ed., New York, 1914.

Thomas, Harrison C., *The Return of the Democratic Party to Power in 1884*. New York, 1919. Also published as No. 203 of *Columbia University Studies in History, Economics, and Public Law*, Vol. LXXXIX, No. 2 (1919–20).

Williams, Mary W., *Anglo-American Isthmian Diplomacy, 1815–1915*. Washington, 1916.

Index